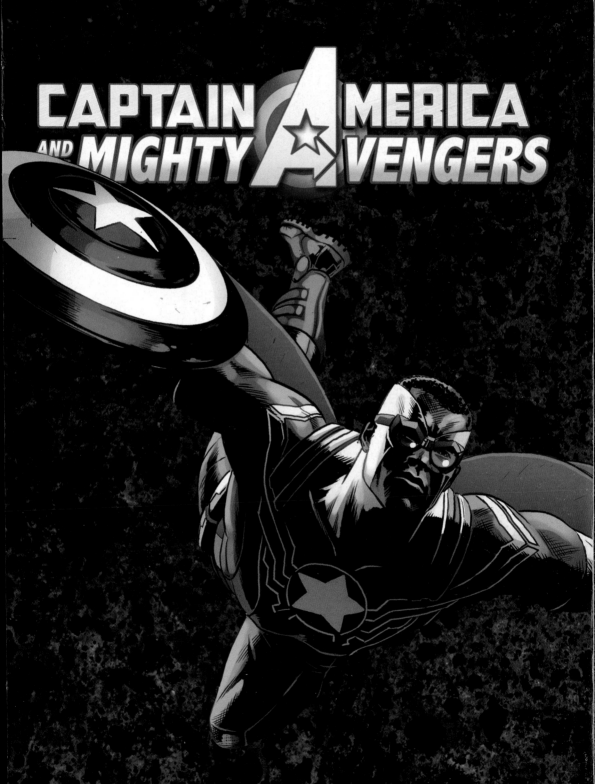

CAPTAIN AMERICA AND MIGHTY AVENGERS

OPEN FOR BUSINESS

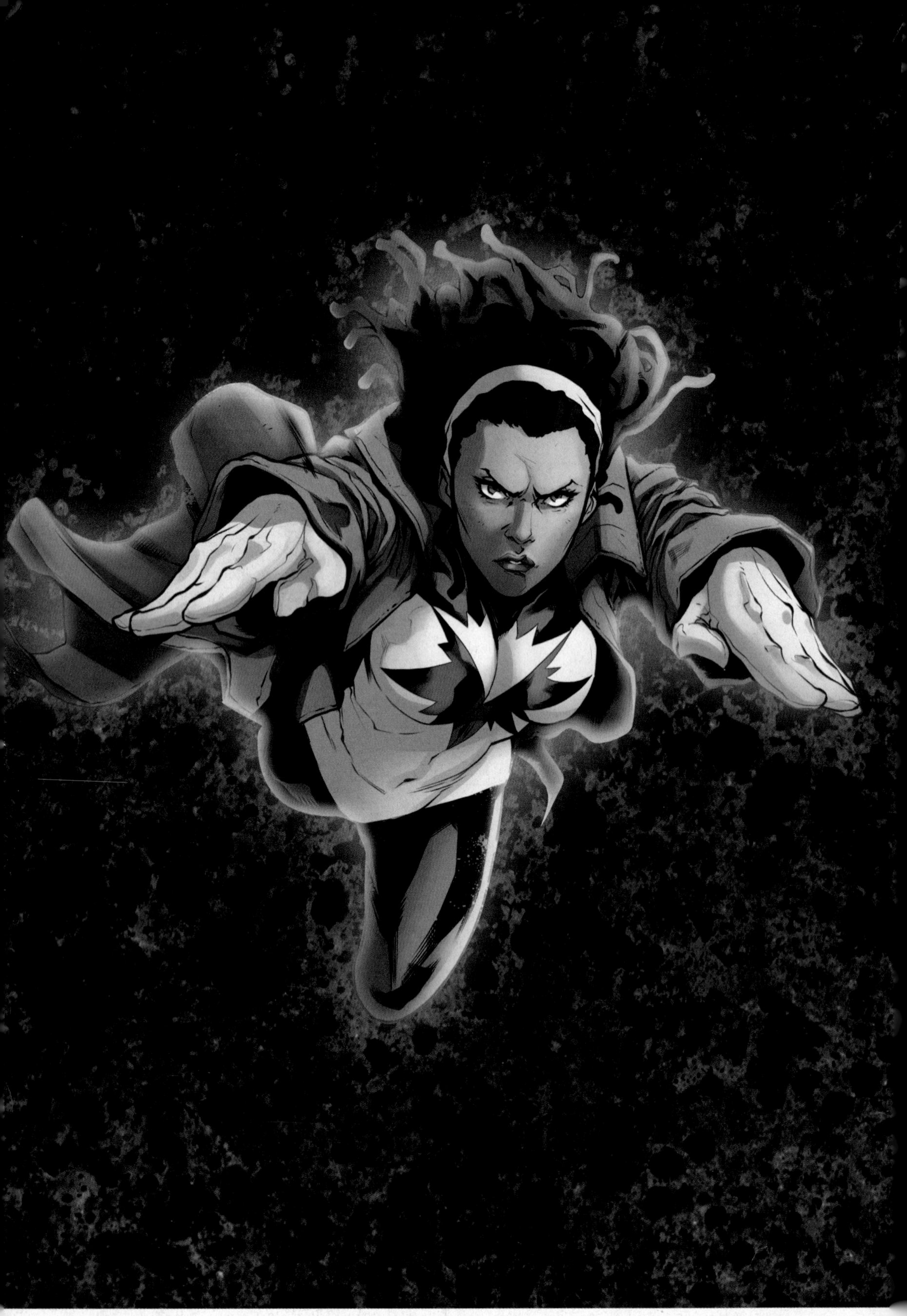

CAPTAIN AMERICA & THE MIGHTY AVENGERS VOL. 1: OPEN FOR BUSINESS. Contains material originally published in magazine form as CAPTAIN AMERICA & THE MIGHTY AVENGERS #1-7. F printing 2015. ISBN# 978-0-7851-9382-1. Published by MARVEL WORLDWIDE, INC., a subsidiary of MARVEL ENTERTAINMENT, LLC. OFFICE OF PUBLICATION: 135 West 50th Street, New York, 10020. **Printed in the U.S.A.** ALAN FINE, President, Marvel Entertainment; DAN BUCKLEY, President, TV, Publishing and Brand Management; JOE QUESA Chief Creative Officer; TOM BREVOORT, SVP of Publishing; DAVID BOGART, SVP of Operations & Procurement, Publishing; C.B. CEBULSKI, VP of International Development & Brand Management; DA GABRIEL, SVP Print, Sales & Marketing; JIM O'KEEFE, VP of Operations & Logistics; DAN CARR, Executive Director of Publishing Technology; SUSAN CRESPI, Editorial Operations Manager; ALEX MORAL Publishing Operations Manager; STAN LEE, Chairman Emeritus. For information regarding advertising in Marvel Comics or on Marvel.com, please contact Jonathan Rheingold, VP of Custom Solutic & Ad Sales, at jrheingold@marvel.com. For Marvel subscription inquiries, please call 800-217-9158. **Manufactured between 4/24/2015 and 6/1/2015 by R.R. DONNELLEY, INC., SALEM, VA, U**

10 9 8 7 6 5 4 3 2 1

CAPTAIN AMERICA AND THE MIGHTY AVENGERS

OPEN FOR BUSINESS

WRITER

AL EWING

ARTISTS

LUKE ROSS (#1-4, #6)
& IBAN COELLO (#2-5, #7)

COLOR ARTIST

RACHELLE ROSENBERG

LETTERERS

VC'S CORY PETIT (#1)
& TRAVIS LANHAM (#2-7)

COVER ART

LUKE ROSS (#1), LUKE ROSS & RICO RENZI (#2-4), SANFORD GREENE (#5-6) AND LEINIL FRANCIS YU & MATT MILLA (#7)

ASSISTANT EDITORS: JAKE THOMAS, JON MOISAN & ALANNA SMITH
EDITORS: TOM BREVOORT WITH WIL MOSS

CAPTAIN AMERICA CREATED BY JOE SIMON & JACK KIRBY

COLLECTION EDITOR: ALEX STARBUCK   ASSISTANT EDITOR: SARAH BRUNSTAD
EDITORS, SPECIAL PROJECTS: JENNIFER GRÜNWALD & MARK D. BEAZLEY
SENIOR EDITOR, SPECIAL PROJECTS: JEFF YOUNGQUIST
SVP PRINT, SALES & MARKETING: DAVID GABRIEL
BOOK DESIGNER: AMANDA SCURTI

EDITOR IN CHIEF: AXEL ALONSO   CHIEF CREATIVE OFFICER: JOE QUESADA
PUBLISHER: DAN BUCKLEY   EXECUTIVE PRODUCER: ALAN FINE

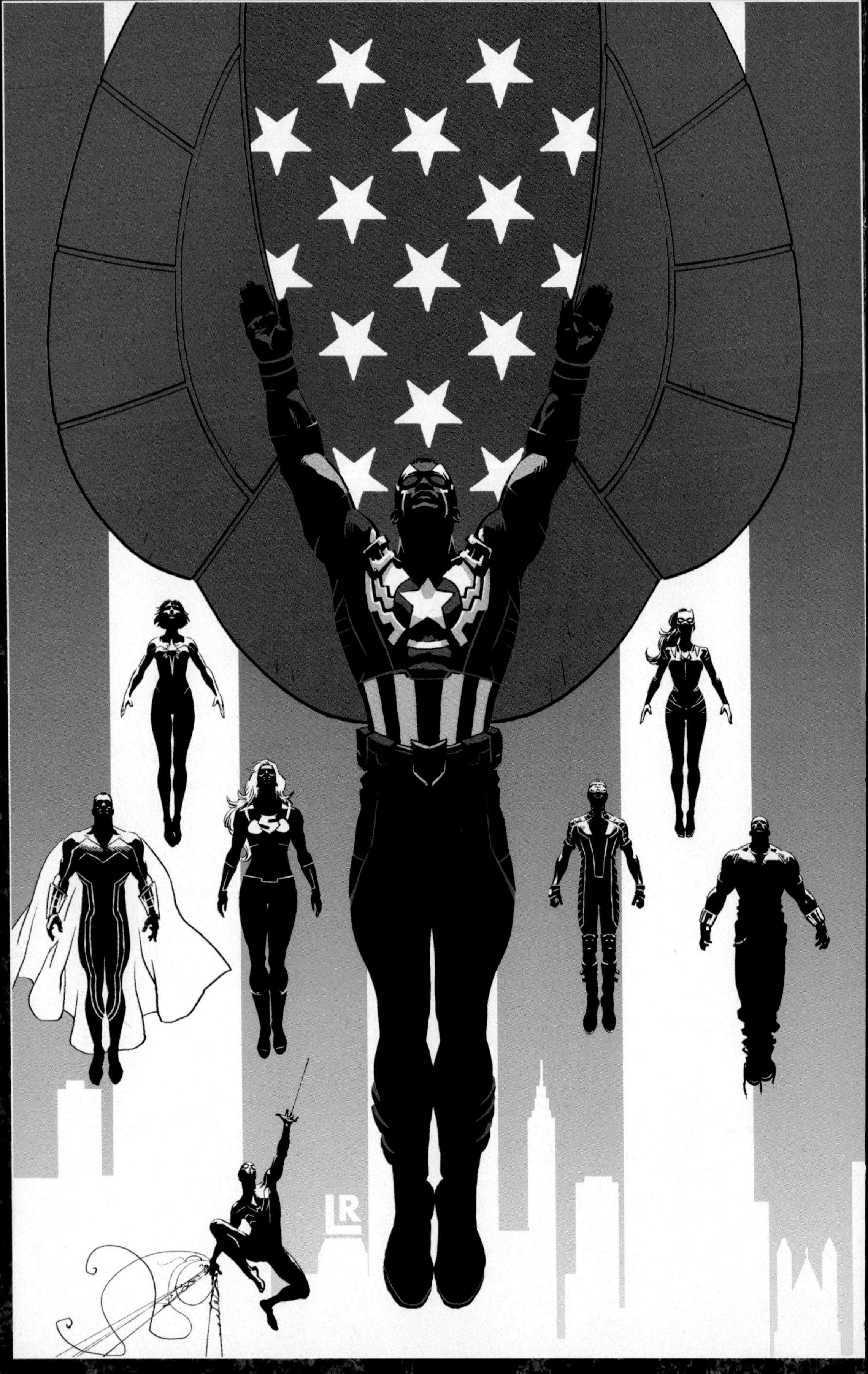

1

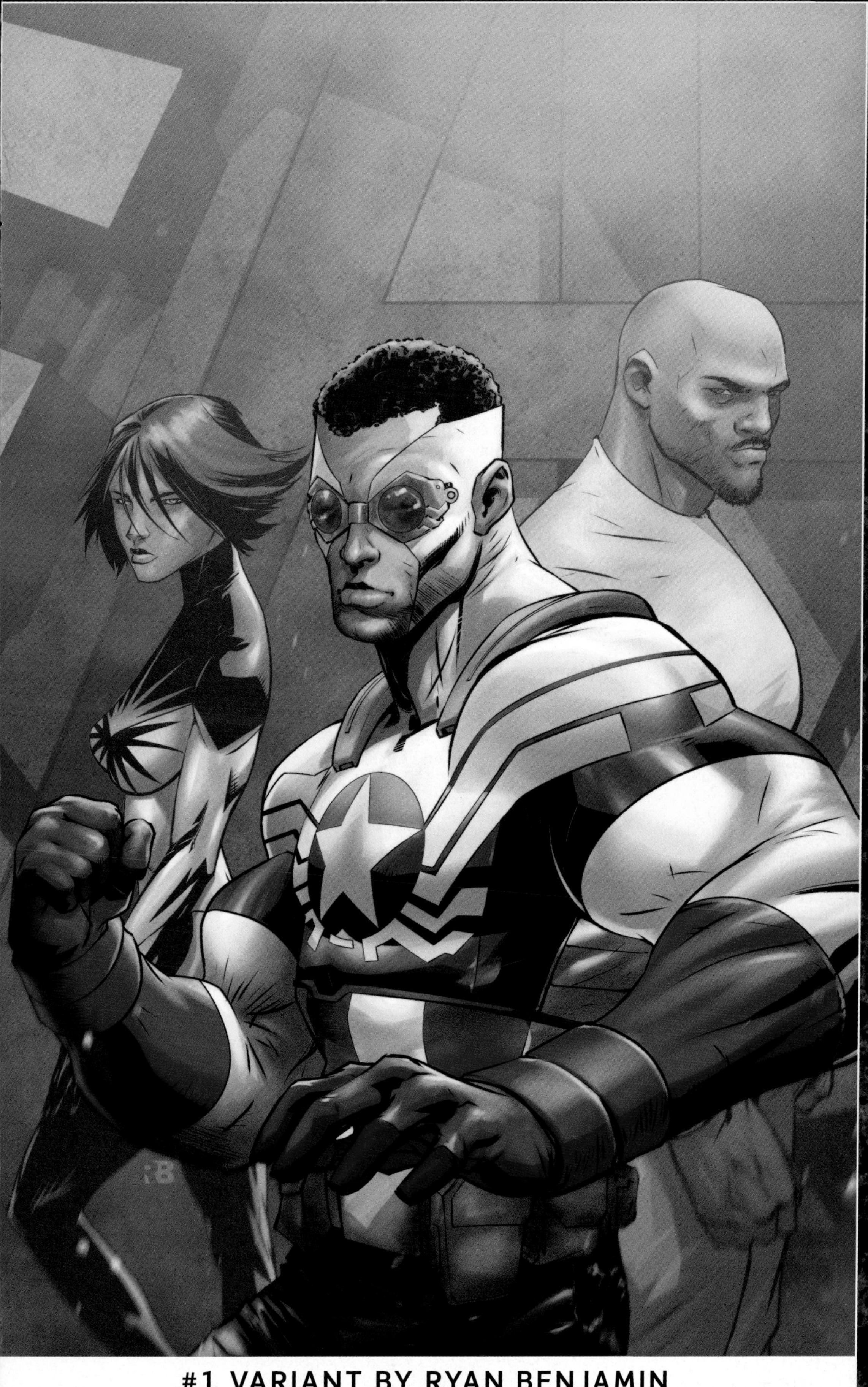

#1 VARIANT BY RYAN BENJAMIN

CAPTAIN AMERICA AND THE MIGHTY AVENGERS

Dear Community,

A while back I, Luke Cage, along with some of my fellow heroes like Falcon (a.k.a. Sam Wilson, who just became the new Captain America. Congrats on the new job, Sam!), Power Man, White Tiger, She-Hulk, Blue Marvel, Spectrum and Spider-Man (until we kicked him out since he was acting like a lunatic thanks to his mind being overtaken by Doctor Octopus--don't ask) reached out to you, the people, to help us all in our quest to help each other. Thus, the new Mighty Avengers were born!

While we are still dedicated to helping our community, recent events-- namely fighting the Red Skull's HATE WAVE-- have caused us to re-examine our mission. We still believe in the power of community action, we just need to recalibrate our approach. Please bear with us as we engage with this change of management and begin this new and exciting approach to our "Mighty" endeavor.

Cordially,

Luke Cage

THAT VOODOO THAT THEY DO SO...WELL?

The Red Skull stole Professor Xavier's brain, using his telepathic powers to create a terrifying HATE WAVE! Scarlet Witch and Doctor Doom worked their magic to attempt to bring the buried consciousness of the heroic Professor X to the fore, while banishing the villainous Red Skull. But ever since the spell, something seems...off. Some of the heroes who were present, like Luke Cage and Sam Wilson, have been acting mighty testy lately, while some of the villains present have been spotted performing good deeds. Has the world been turned upside down on its AXIS, gentle reader?!

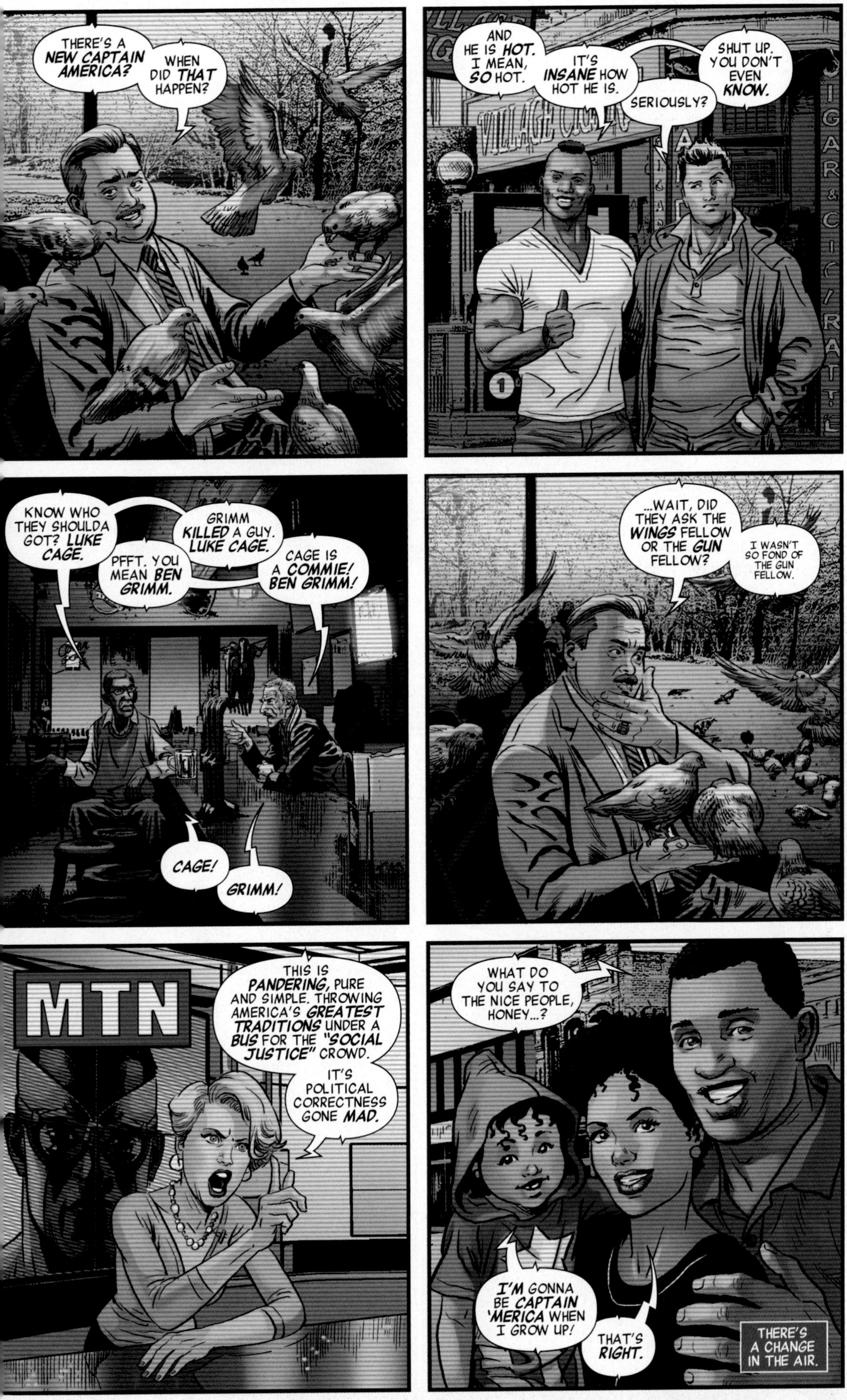
THERE'S A NEW CAPTAIN AMERICA?
WHEN DID THAT HAPPEN?
AND HE IS HOT. I MEAN, SO HOT.
IT'S INSANE HOW HOT HE IS.
SHUT UP. YOU DON'T EVEN KNOW.
SERIOUSLY?
VILLAGE CIGAR
CIGAR & CIGARETTE
KNOW WHO THEY SHOULDA GOT? LUKE CAGE.
GRIMM KILLED A GUY. LUKE CAGE.
PFFT. YOU MEAN BEN GRIMM.
CAGE IS A COMMIE! BEN GRIMM!
CAGE!
GRIMM!
...WAIT, DID THEY ASK THE WINGS FELLOW OR THE GUN FELLOW?
I WASN'T SO FOND OF THE GUN FELLOW.
MTN
THIS IS PANDERING, PURE AND SIMPLE. THROWING AMERICA'S GREATEST TRADITIONS UNDER A BUS FOR THE "SOCIAL JUSTICE" CROWD.
IT'S POLITICAL CORRECTNESS GONE MAD.
WHAT DO YOU SAY TO THE NICE PEOPLE, HONEY...?
I'M GONNA BE CAPTAIN 'MERICA WHEN I GROW UP!
THAT'S RIGHT.
THERE'S A CHANGE IN THE AIR.

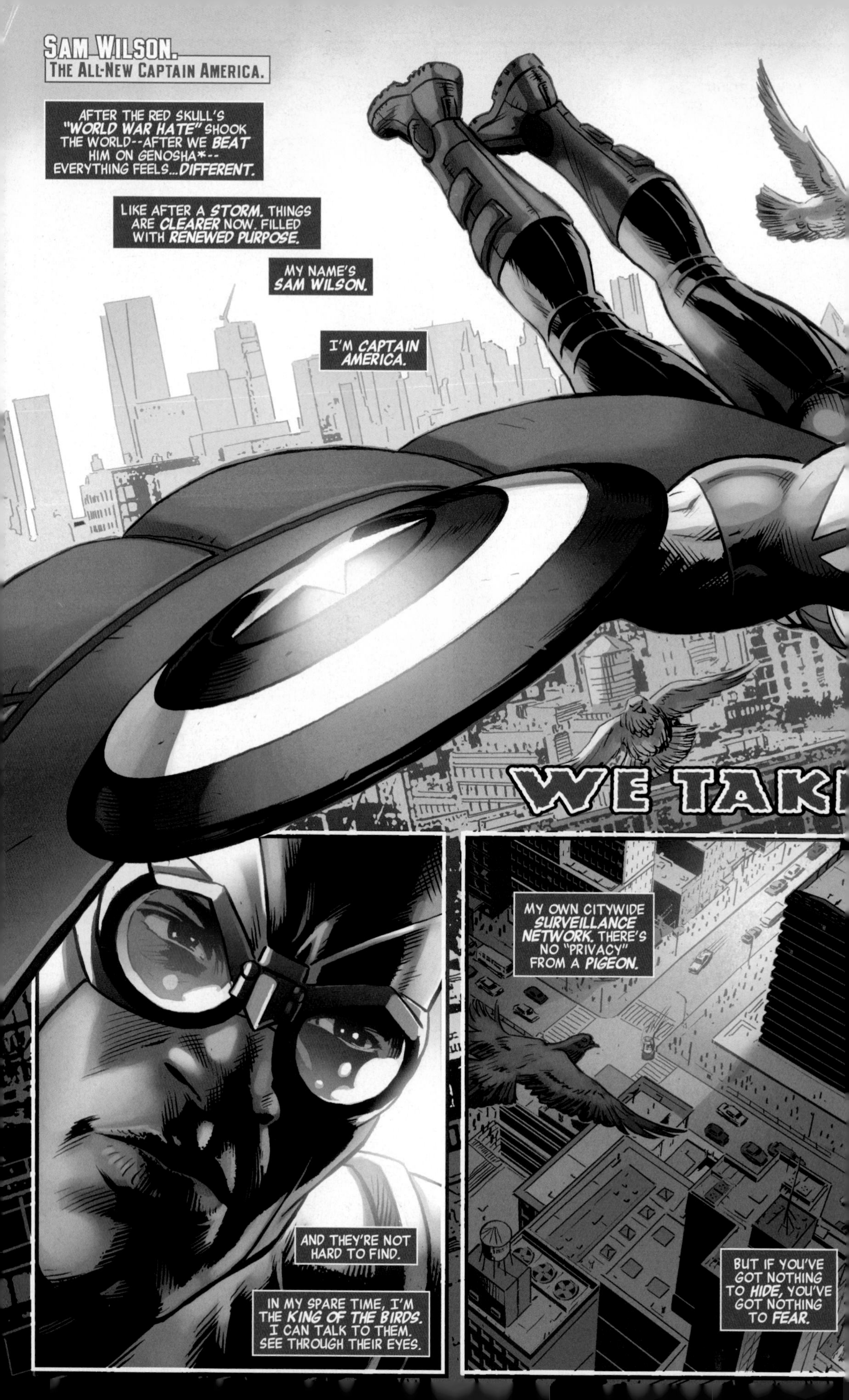
SAM WILSON.
THE ALL-NEW CAPTAIN AMERICA.
AFTER THE RED SKULL'S "WORLD WAR HATE" SHOOK THE WORLD--AFTER WE BEAT HIM ON GENOSHA*-- EVERYTHING FEELS...DIFFERENT.
LIKE AFTER A STORM. THINGS ARE CLEARER NOW. FILLED WITH RENEWED PURPOSE.
MY NAME'S SAM WILSON.
I'M CAPTAIN AMERICA.
WE TAK
AND THEY'RE NOT HARD TO FIND.
IN MY SPARE TIME, I'M THE KING OF THE BIRDS. I CAN TALK TO THEM. SEE THROUGH THEIR EYES.
MY OWN CITYWIDE SURVEILLANCE NETWORK. THERE'S NO "PRIVACY" FROM A PIGEON.
BUT IF YOU'VE GOT NOTHING TO HIDE, YOU'VE GOT NOTHING TO FEAR.

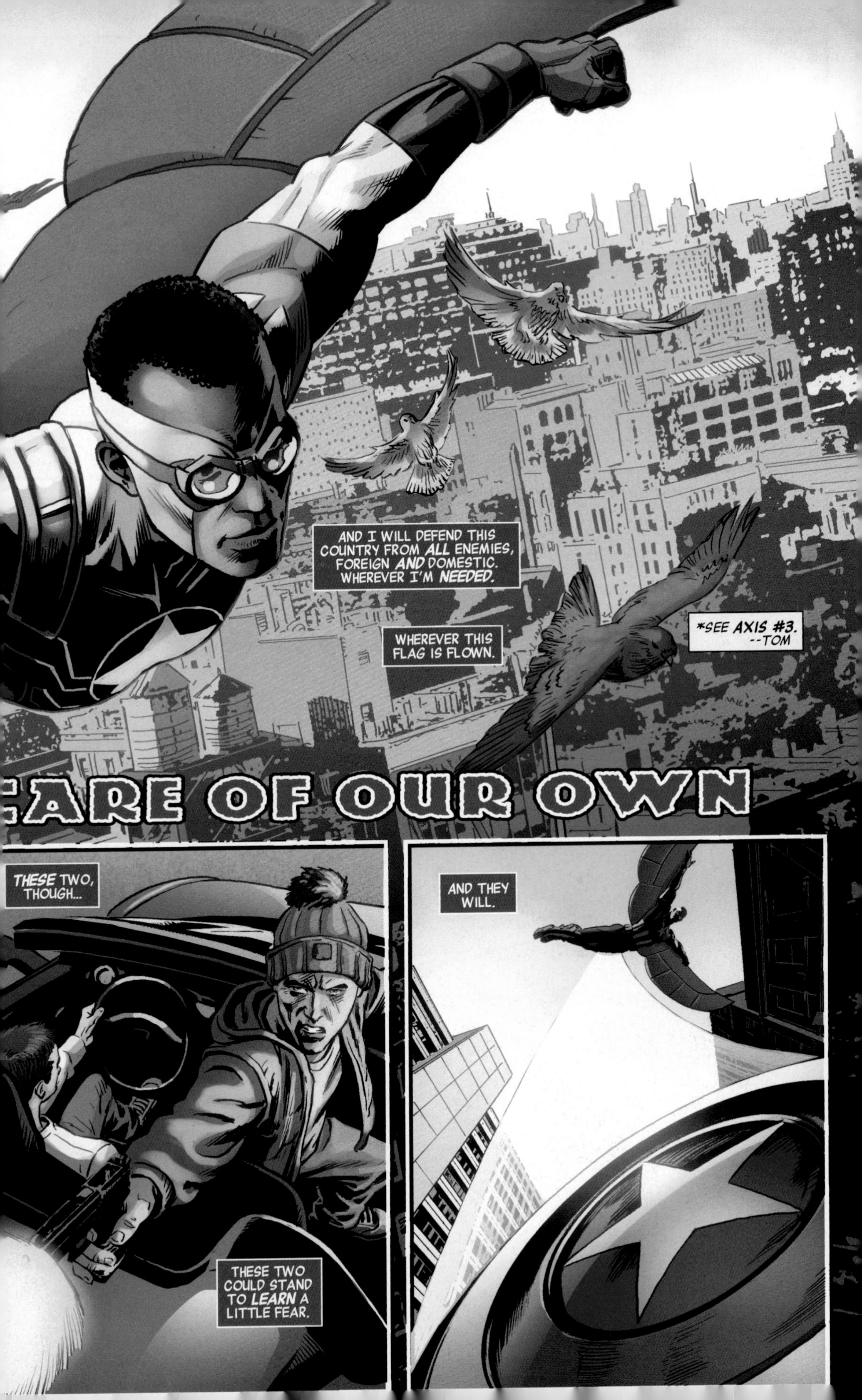
AND I WILL DEFEND THIS COUNTRY FROM ALL ENEMIES, FOREIGN AND DOMESTIC. WHEREVER I'M NEEDED.
WHEREVER THIS FLAG IS FLOWN.
*SEE AXIS #3. --TOM
ARE OF OUR OWN
THESE TWO, THOUGH...
THESE TWO COULD STAND TO LEARN A LITTLE FEAR.
AND THEY WILL.

OBVIOUSLY, I'M NOT QUITE AS GOOD WITH THE SHIELD AS STEVE ROGERS.

WHUH--?

KRAKK

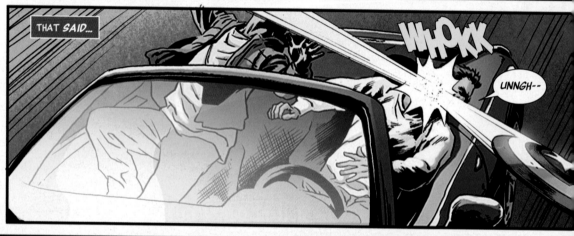

THAT SAID...

WHOKK

UNNGH--

...I DO HAVE MY MOMENTS.

GEEZ--

MOVE--

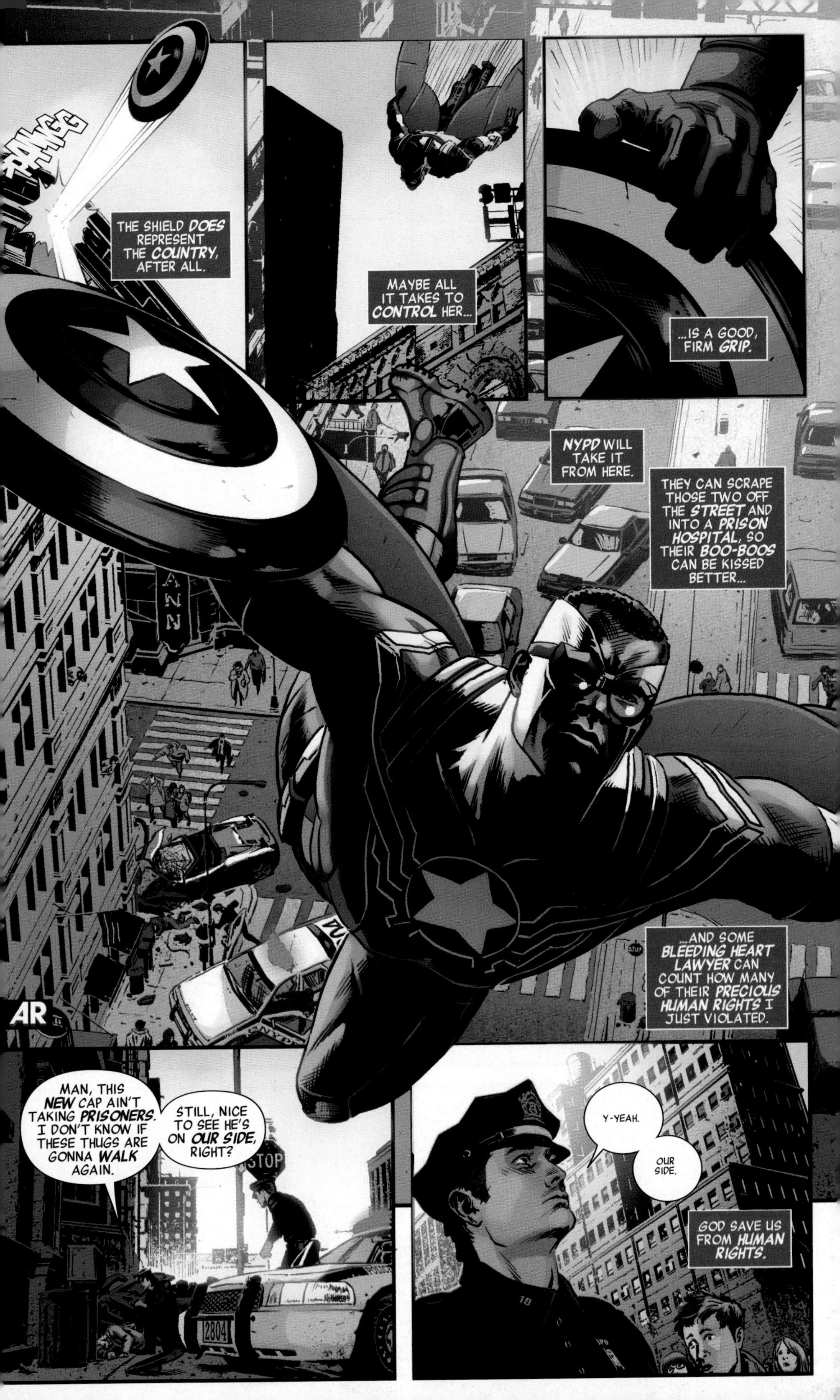

THE SHIELD DOES REPRESENT THE COUNTRY, AFTER ALL.
MAYBE ALL IT TAKES TO CONTROL HER...
...IS A GOOD, FIRM GRIP.
NYPD WILL TAKE IT FROM HERE.
THEY CAN SCRAPE THOSE TWO OFF THE STREET AND INTO A PRISON HOSPITAL, SO THEIR BOO-BOOS CAN BE KISSED BETTER...
...AND SOME BLEEDING HEART LAWYER CAN COUNT HOW MANY OF THEIR PRECIOUS HUMAN RIGHTS I JUST VIOLATED.
MAN, THIS NEW CAP AIN'T TAKING PRISONERS. I DON'T KNOW IF THESE THUGS ARE GONNA WALK AGAIN.
STILL, NICE TO SEE HE'S ON OUR SIDE, RIGHT?
Y-YEAH.
OUR SIDE.
GOD SAVE US FROM HUMAN RIGHTS.
STOP
2804

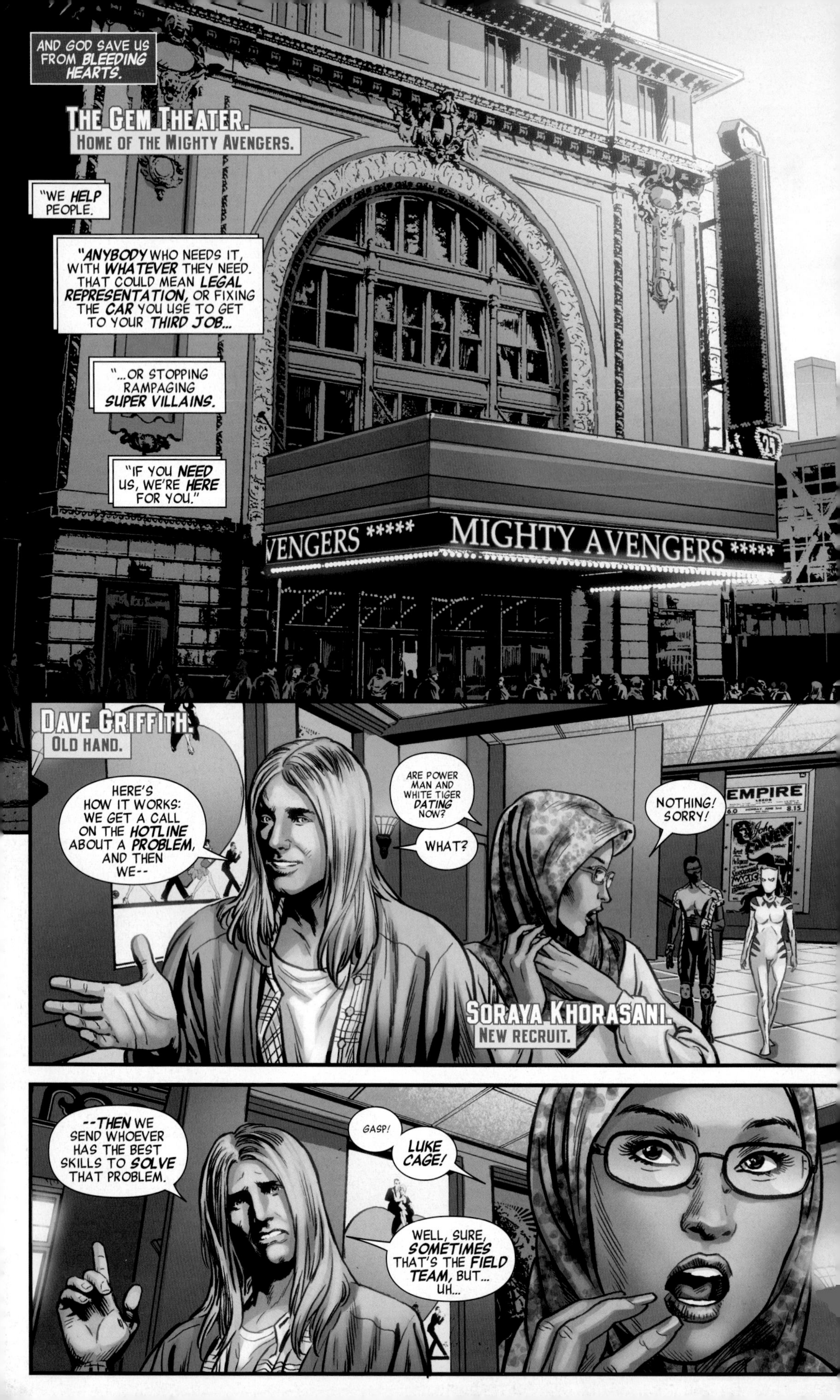
AND GOD SAVE US FROM BLEEDING HEARTS.
THE GEM THEATER.
HOME OF THE MIGHTY AVENGERS.
"WE HELP PEOPLE.
"ANYBODY WHO NEEDS IT, WITH WHATEVER THEY NEED. THAT COULD MEAN LEGAL REPRESENTATION, OR FIXING THE CAR YOU USE TO GET TO YOUR THIRD JOB...
"...OR STOPPING RAMPAGING SUPER VILLAINS.
"IF YOU NEED US, WE'RE HERE FOR YOU."
VENGERS *****
MIGHTY AVENGERS *****
DAVE GRIFFITH.
OLD HAND.
HERE'S HOW IT WORKS: WE GET A CALL ON THE HOTLINE ABOUT A PROBLEM, AND THEN WE--
ARE POWER MAN AND WHITE TIGER DATING NOW?
WHAT?
NOTHING! SORRY!
EMPIRE
SORAYA KHORASANI.
NEW RECRUIT.
--THEN WE SEND WHOEVER HAS THE BEST SKILLS TO SOLVE THAT PROBLEM.
GASP!
LUKE CAGE!
WELL, SURE, SOMETIMES THAT'S THE FIELD TEAM, BUT... UH...

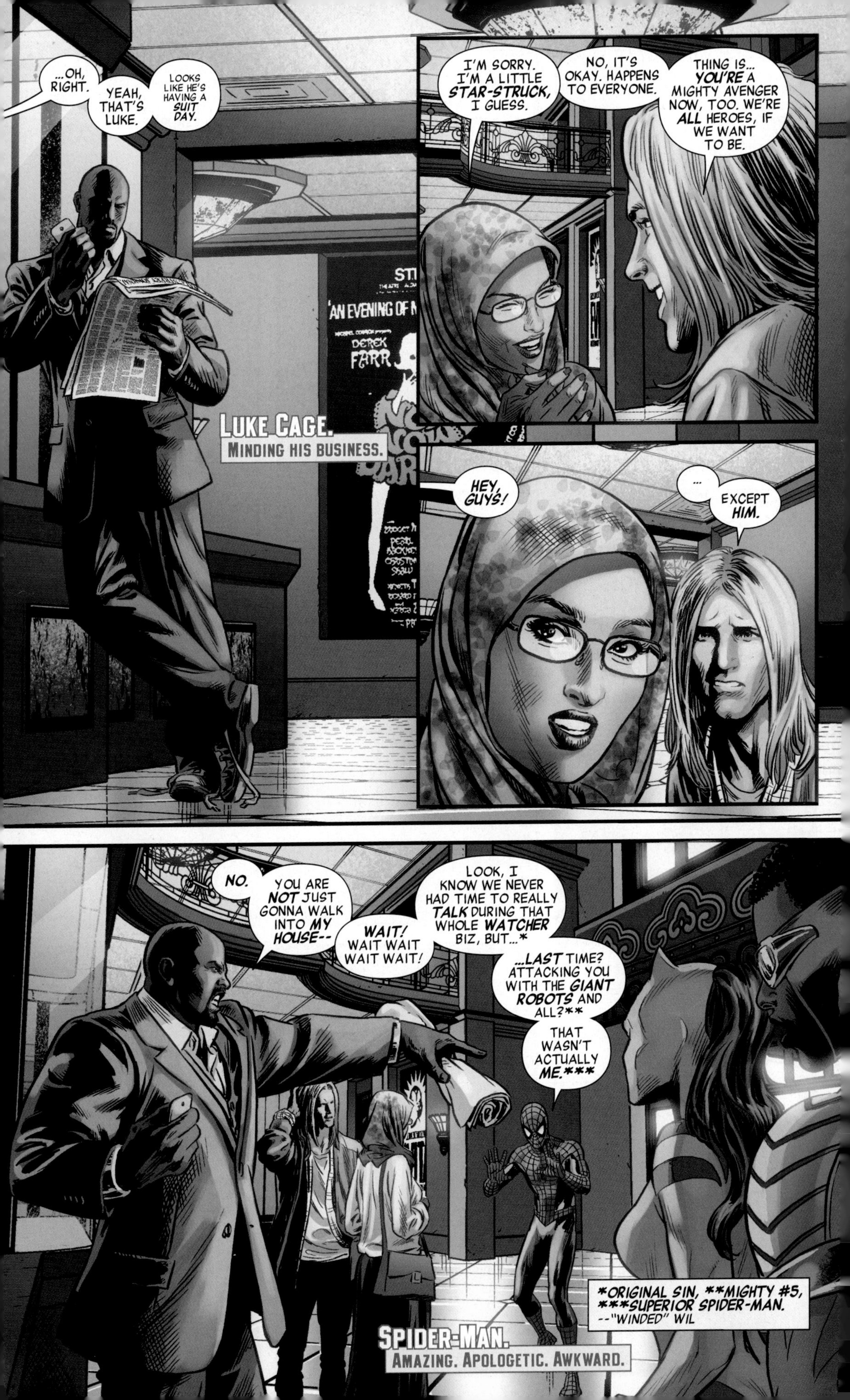
...OH, RIGHT.
YEAH, THAT'S LUKE.
LOOKS LIKE HE'S HAVING A SUIT DAY.
LUKE CAGE.
MINDING HIS BUSINESS.
I'M SORRY. I'M A LITTLE STAR-STRUCK, I GUESS.
NO, IT'S OKAY. HAPPENS TO EVERYONE.
THING IS... YOU'RE A MIGHTY AVENGER NOW, TOO. WE'RE ALL HEROES, IF WE WANT TO BE.
HEY, GUYS!
...
EXCEPT HIM.
NO.
YOU ARE NOT JUST GONNA WALK INTO MY HOUSE--
WAIT! WAIT WAIT WAIT WAIT!
LOOK, I KNOW WE NEVER HAD TIME TO REALLY TALK DURING THAT WHOLE WATCHER BIZ, BUT...*
...LAST TIME? ATTACKING YOU WITH THE GIANT ROBOTS AND ALL?**
THAT WASN'T ACTUALLY ME.***
*ORIGINAL SIN, **MIGHTY #5, ***SUPERIOR SPIDER-MAN. --"WINDED" WIL
SPIDER-MAN.
AMAZING. APOLOGETIC. AWKWARD.

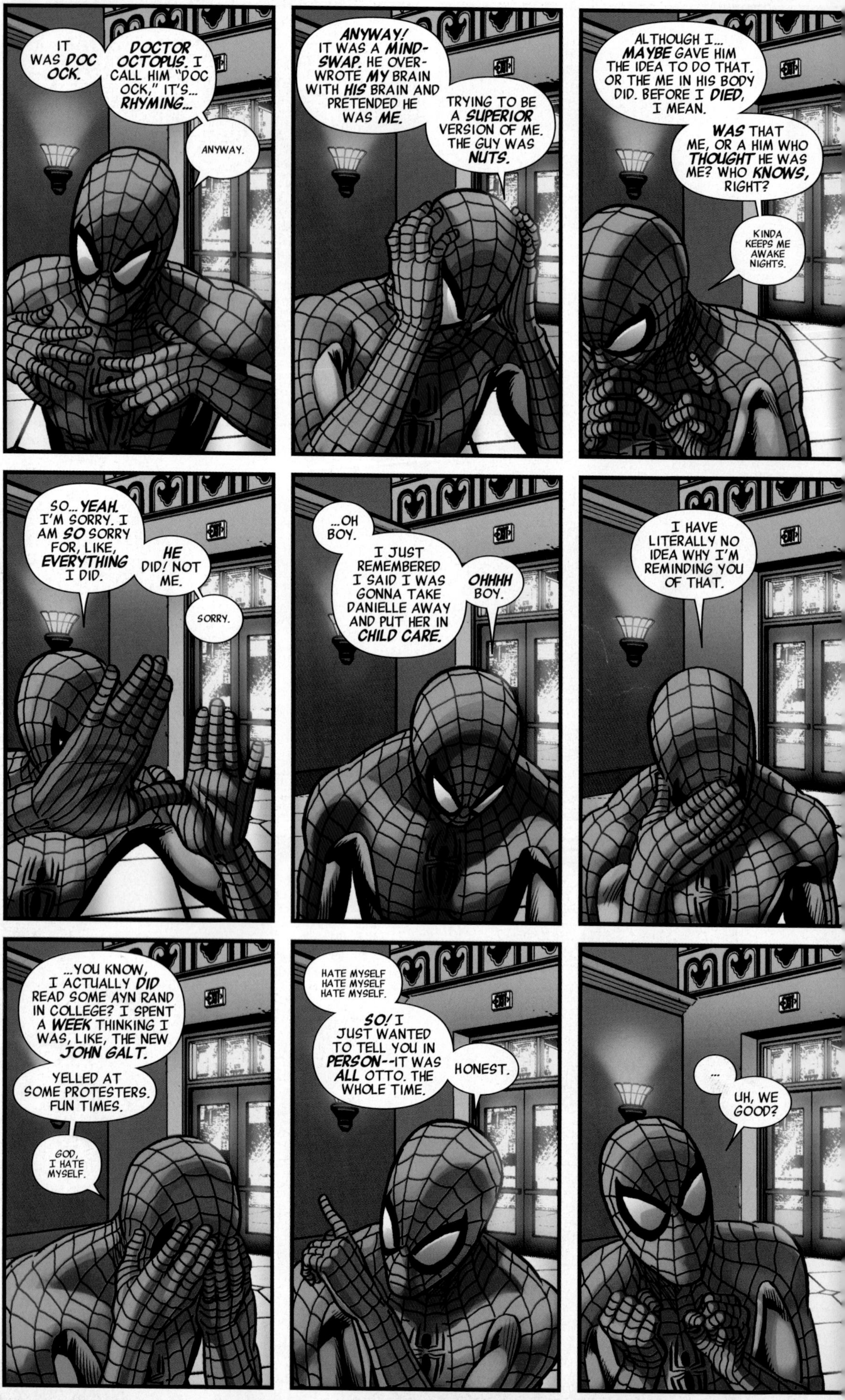
IT WAS DOC OCK.
DOCTOR OCTOPUS. I CALL HIM "DOC OCK," IT'S... RHYMING...
ANYWAY.
ANYWAY! IT WAS A MIND-SWAP. HE OVER-WROTE MY BRAIN WITH HIS BRAIN AND PRETENDED HE WAS ME.
TRYING TO BE A SUPERIOR VERSION OF ME. THE GUY WAS NUTS.
ALTHOUGH I... MAYBE GAVE HIM THE IDEA TO DO THAT. OR THE ME IN HIS BODY DID. BEFORE I DIED, I MEAN.
WAS THAT ME, OR A HIM WHO THOUGHT HE WAS ME? WHO KNOWS, RIGHT?
KINDA KEEPS ME AWAKE NIGHTS.
SO... YEAH. I'M SORRY. I AM SO SORRY FOR, LIKE, EVERYTHING I DID.
HE DID! NOT ME.
SORRY.
...OH BOY.
I JUST REMEMBERED I SAID I WAS GONNA TAKE DANIELLE AWAY AND PUT HER IN CHILD CARE.
OHHHH BOY.
I HAVE LITERALLY NO IDEA WHY I'M REMINDING YOU OF THAT.
...YOU KNOW, I ACTUALLY DID READ SOME AYN RAND IN COLLEGE? I SPENT A WEEK THINKING I WAS, LIKE, THE NEW JOHN GALT.
YELLED AT SOME PROTESTERS. FUN TIMES.
GOD, I HATE MYSELF.
HATE MYSELF HATE MYSELF HATE MYSELF.
SO! I JUST WANTED TO TELL YOU IN PERSON--IT WAS ALL OTTO. THE WHOLE TIME.
HONEST.
...
UH, WE GOOD?

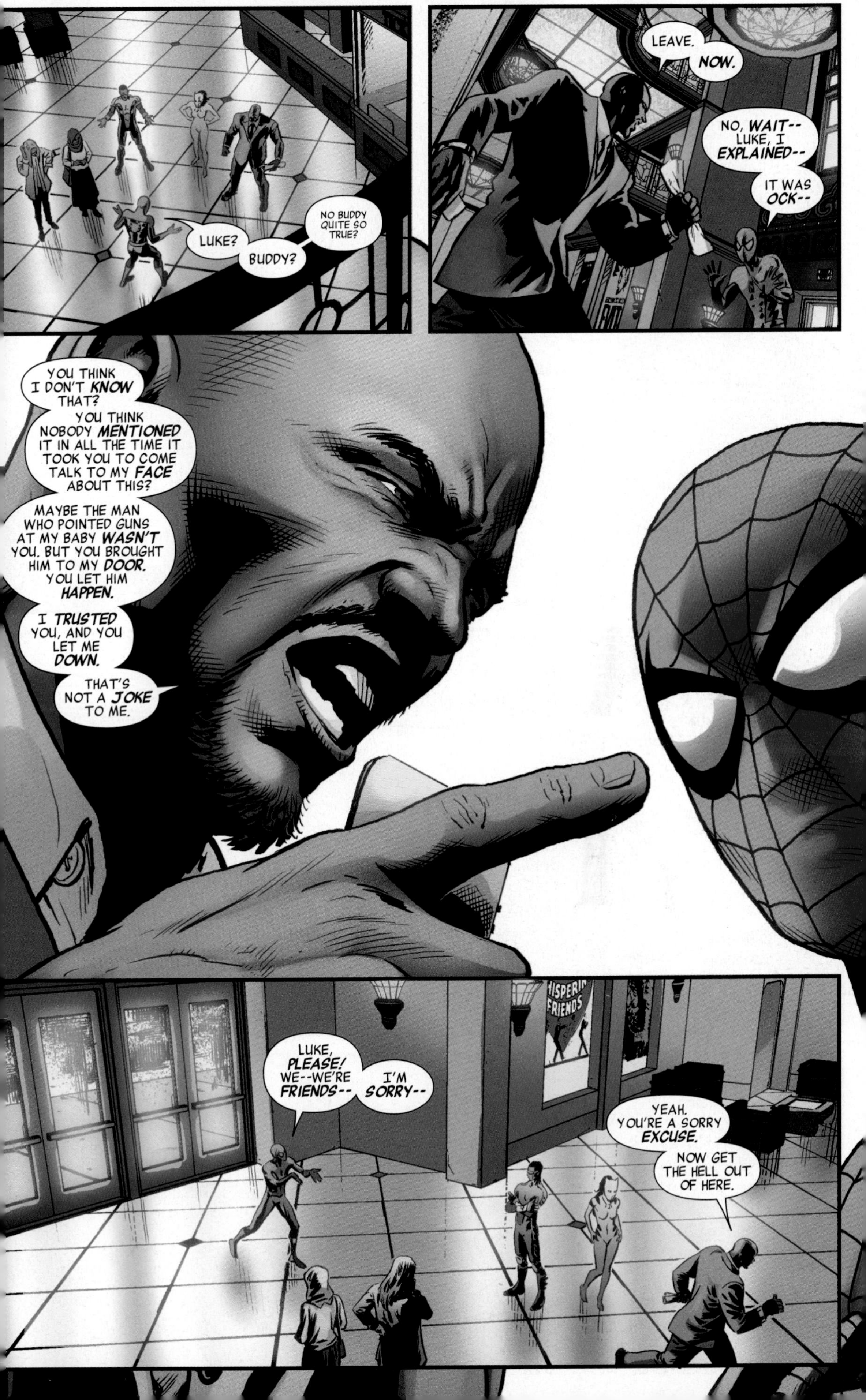

LUKE?
BUDDY?
NO BUDDY QUITE SO TRUE?
LEAVE. NOW.
NO, WAIT-- LUKE, I EXPLAINED--
IT WAS OCK--
YOU THINK I DON'T KNOW THAT?
YOU THINK NOBODY MENTIONED IT IN ALL THE TIME IT TOOK YOU TO COME TALK TO MY FACE ABOUT THIS?
MAYBE THE MAN WHO POINTED GUNS AT MY BABY WASN'T YOU. BUT YOU BROUGHT HIM TO MY DOOR. YOU LET HIM HAPPEN.
I TRUSTED YOU, AND YOU LET ME DOWN.
THAT'S NOT A JOKE TO ME.
LUKE, PLEASE! WE--WE'RE FRIENDS--
I'M SORRY--
YEAH. YOU'RE A SORRY EXCUSE.
NOW GET THE HELL OUT OF HERE.

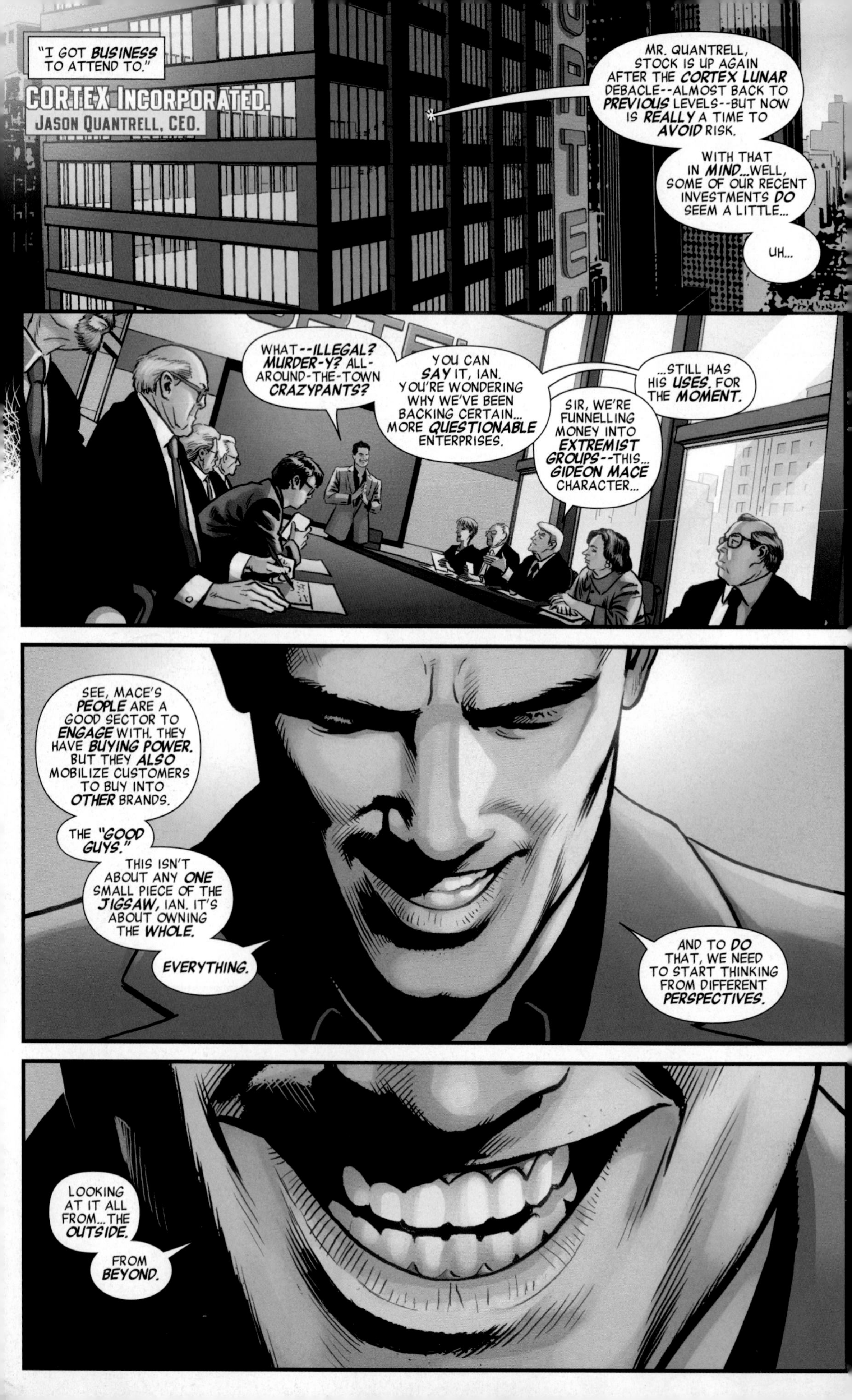
"I GOT BUSINESS TO ATTEND TO."
CORTEX INCORPORATED.
JASON QUANTRELL, CEO.
MR. QUANTRELL, STOCK IS UP AGAIN AFTER THE CORTEX LUNAR DEBACLE--ALMOST BACK TO PREVIOUS LEVELS--BUT NOW IS REALLY A TIME TO AVOID RISK.
WITH THAT IN MIND...WELL, SOME OF OUR RECENT INVESTMENTS DO SEEM A LITTLE...
UH...
WHAT--ILLEGAL? MURDER-Y? ALL-AROUND-THE-TOWN CRAZYPANTS?
YOU CAN SAY IT, IAN. YOU'RE WONDERING WHY WE'VE BEEN BACKING CERTAIN... MORE QUESTIONABLE ENTERPRISES.
SIR, WE'RE FUNNELLING MONEY INTO EXTREMIST GROUPS--THIS... GIDEON MACE CHARACTER...
...STILL HAS HIS USES. FOR THE MOMENT.
SEE, MACE'S PEOPLE ARE A GOOD SECTOR TO ENGAGE WITH. THEY HAVE BUYING POWER. BUT THEY ALSO MOBILIZE CUSTOMERS TO BUY INTO OTHER BRANDS.
THE "GOOD GUYS."
THIS ISN'T ABOUT ANY ONE SMALL PIECE OF THE JIGSAW, IAN. IT'S ABOUT OWNING THE WHOLE.
EVERYTHING.
AND TO DO THAT, WE NEED TO START THINKING FROM DIFFERENT PERSPECTIVES.
LOOKING AT IT ALL FROM... THE OUTSIDE.
FROM BEYOND.

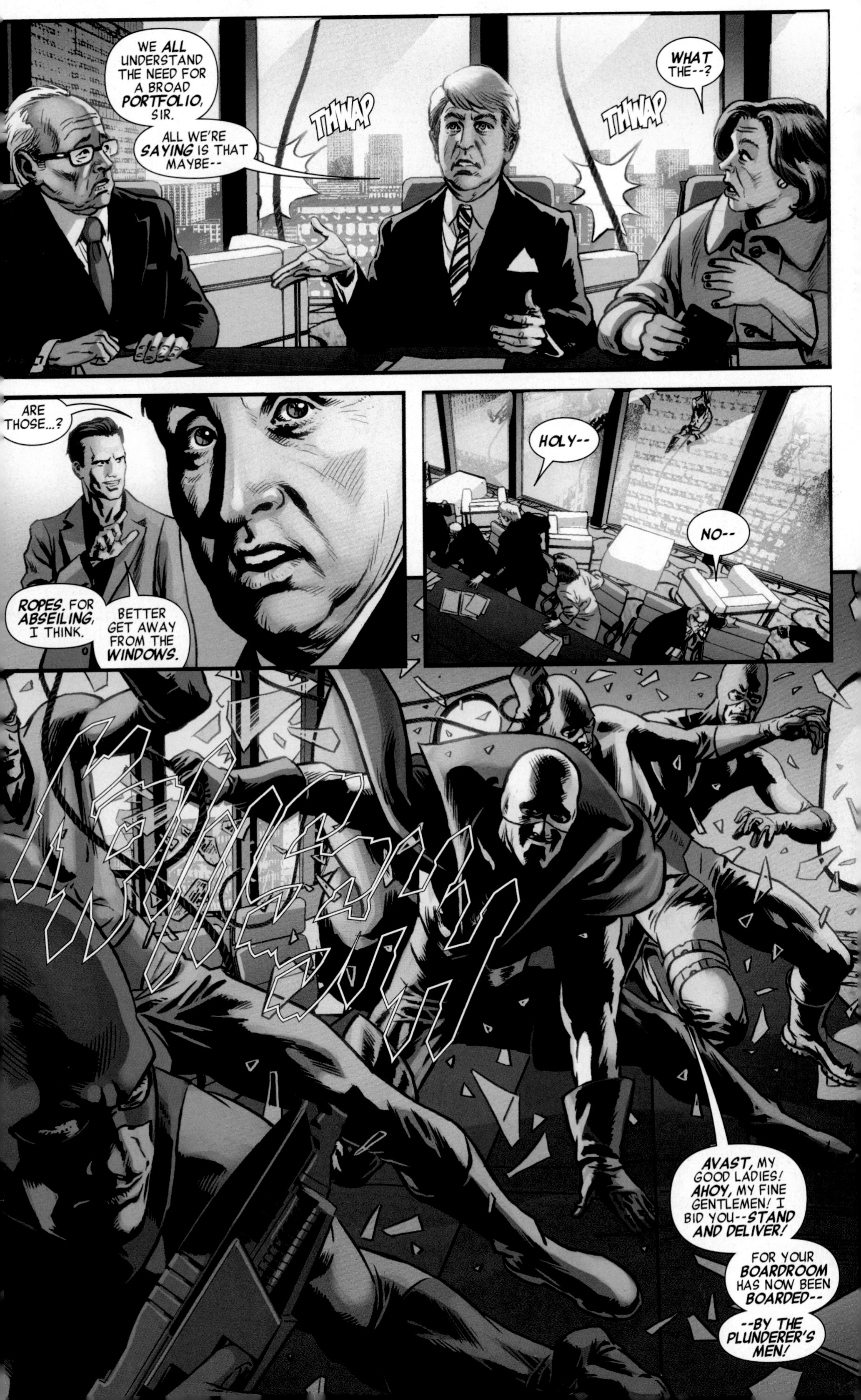

WE ALL UNDERSTAND THE NEED FOR A BROAD PORTFOLIO, SIR.
ALL WE'RE SAYING IS THAT MAYBE--
THWAP
THWAP
WHAT THE--?
ARE THOSE...?
ROPES. FOR ABSEILING, I THINK.
BETTER GET AWAY FROM THE WINDOWS.
HOLY--
NO--
AVAST, MY GOOD LADIES! AHOY, MY FINE GENTLEMEN! I BID YOU--STAND AND DELIVER!
FOR YOUR BOARDROOM HAS NOW BEEN BOARDED--
--BY THE PLUNDERER'S MEN!

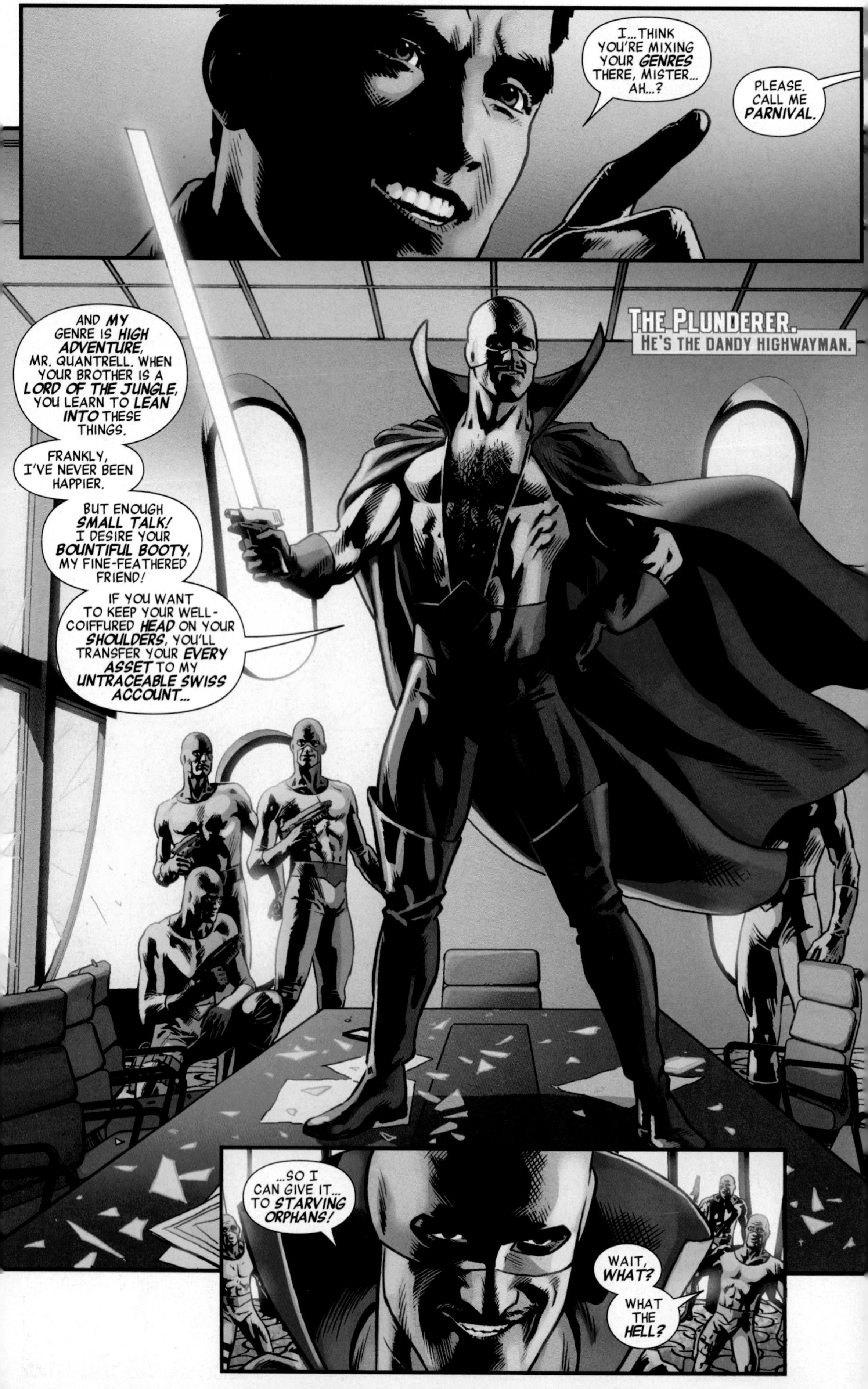

I...THINK YOU'RE MIXING YOUR GENRES THERE, MISTER... AH...?
PLEASE. CALL ME PARNIVAL.
THE PLUNDERER. HE'S THE DANDY HIGHWAYMAN.
AND MY GENRE IS HIGH ADVENTURE, MR. QUANTRELL. WHEN YOUR BROTHER IS A LORD OF THE JUNGLE, YOU LEARN TO LEAN INTO THESE THINGS.
FRANKLY, I'VE NEVER BEEN HAPPIER.
BUT ENOUGH SMALL TALK! I DESIRE YOUR BOUNTIFUL BOOTY, MY FINE-FEATHERED FRIEND!
IF YOU WANT TO KEEP YOUR WELL-COIFFURED HEAD ON YOUR SHOULDERS, YOU'LL TRANSFER YOUR EVERY ASSET TO MY UNTRACEABLE SWISS ACCOUNT...
...SO I CAN GIVE IT... TO STARVING ORPHANS!
WAIT, WHAT?
WHAT THE HELL?

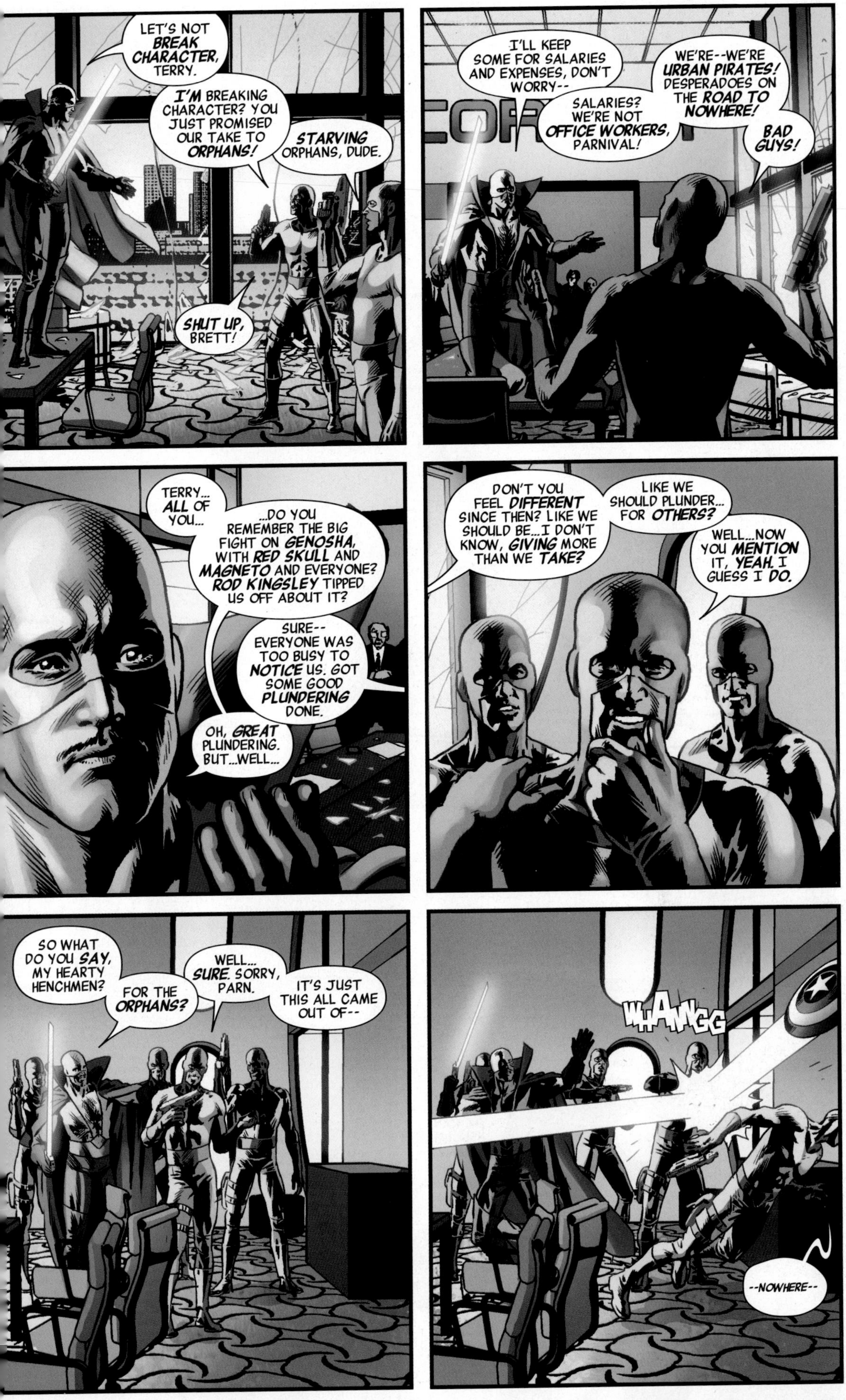

LET'S NOT BREAK CHARACTER, TERRY.
I'M BREAKING CHARACTER? YOU JUST PROMISED OUR TAKE TO ORPHANS!
STARVING ORPHANS, DUDE.
SHUT UP, BRETT!
I'LL KEEP SOME FOR SALARIES AND EXPENSES, DON'T WORRY--
SALARIES? WE'RE NOT OFFICE WORKERS, PARNIVAL!
WE'RE--WE'RE URBAN PIRATES! DESPERADOES ON THE ROAD TO NOWHERE!
BAD GUYS!
TERRY... ALL OF YOU...
...DO YOU REMEMBER THE BIG FIGHT ON GENOSHA, WITH RED SKULL AND MAGNETO AND EVERYONE? ROD KINGSLEY TIPPED US OFF ABOUT IT?
SURE-- EVERYONE WAS TOO BUSY TO NOTICE US. GOT SOME GOOD PLUNDERING DONE.
OH, GREAT PLUNDERING. BUT...WELL...
DON'T YOU FEEL DIFFERENT SINCE THEN? LIKE WE SHOULD BE...I DON'T KNOW, GIVING MORE THAN WE TAKE?
LIKE WE SHOULD PLUNDER... FOR OTHERS?
WELL...NOW YOU MENTION IT, YEAH. I GUESS I DO.
SO WHAT DO YOU SAY, MY HEARTY HENCHMEN?
FOR THE ORPHANS?
WELL... SURE. SORRY, PARN.
IT'S JUST THIS ALL CAME OUT OF--
WHANNGG
--NOWHERE--

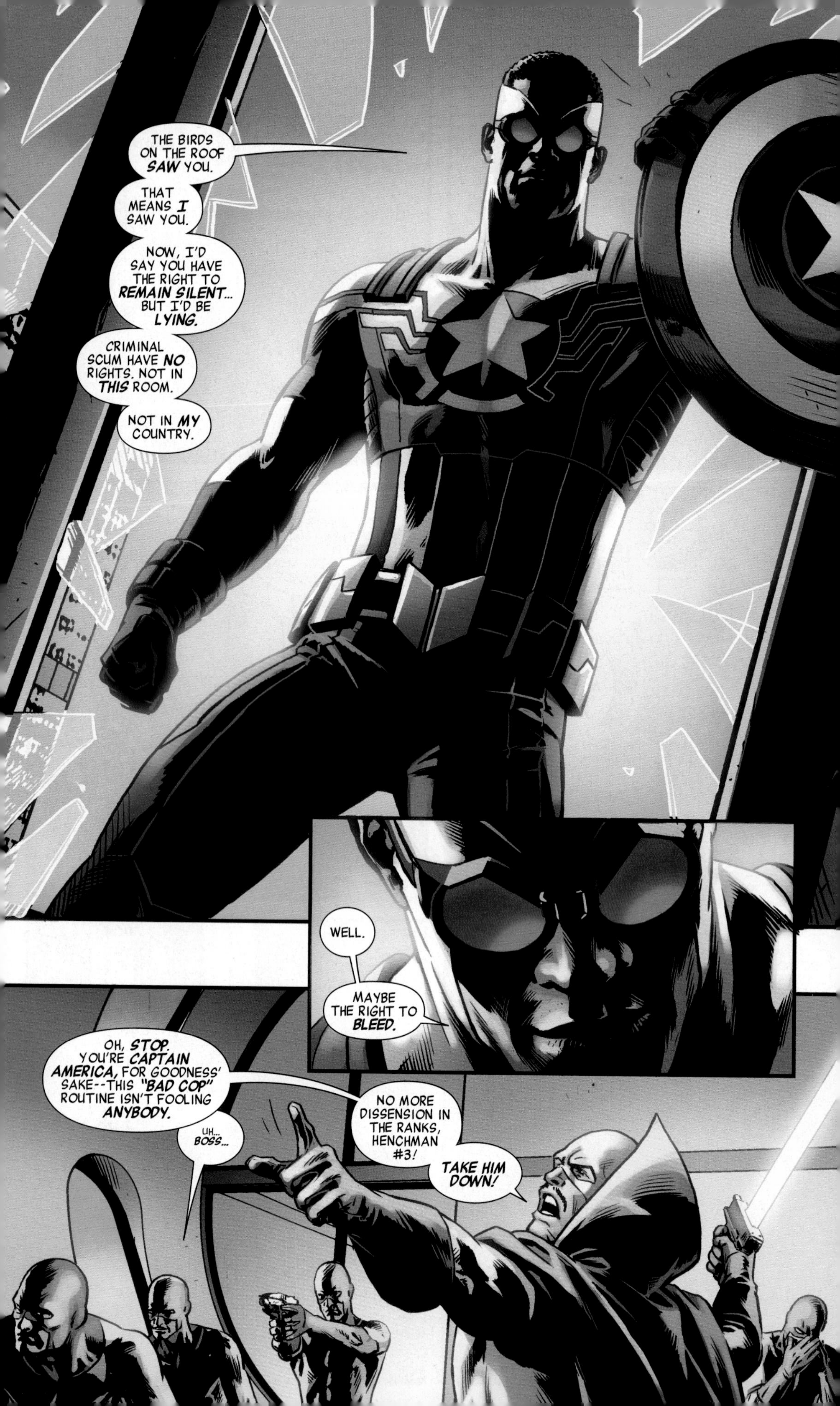

THE BIRDS ON THE ROOF SAW YOU.
THAT MEANS I SAW YOU.
NOW, I'D SAY YOU HAVE THE RIGHT TO REMAIN SILENT... BUT I'D BE LYING.
CRIMINAL SCUM HAVE NO RIGHTS. NOT IN THIS ROOM.
NOT IN MY COUNTRY.
WELL.
MAYBE THE RIGHT TO BLEED.
OH, STOP. YOU'RE CAPTAIN AMERICA, FOR GOODNESS' SAKE--THIS "BAD COP" ROUTINE ISN'T FOOLING ANYBODY.
UH... BOSS...
NO MORE DISSENSION IN THE RANKS, HENCHMAN #3!
TAKE HIM DOWN!

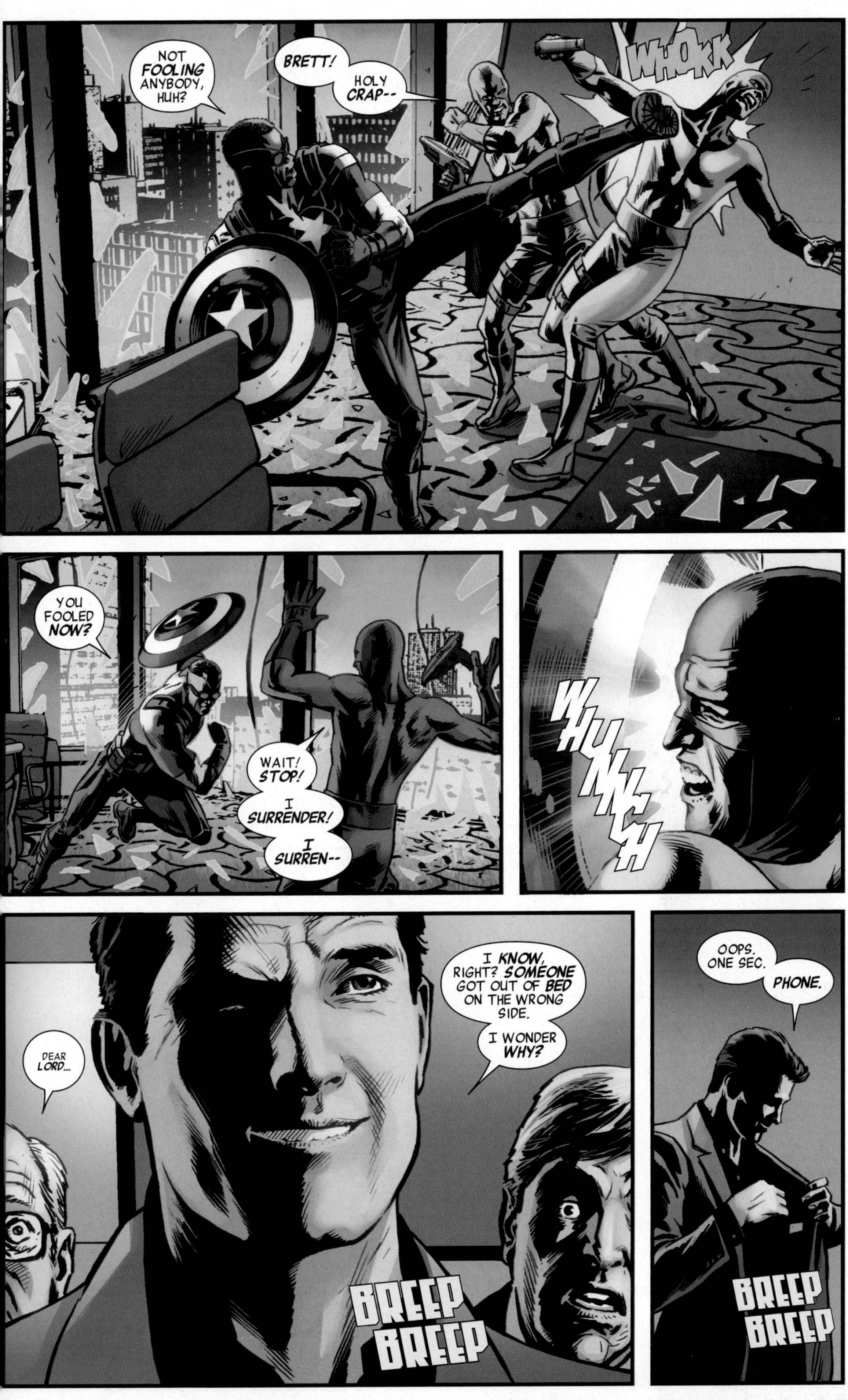
NOT FOOLING ANYBODY, HUH?
BRETT!
HOLY CRAP--
WHOKK
YOU FOOLED NOW?
WAIT! STOP!
I SURRENDER!
I SURREN--
WHUNNCH
DEAR LORD...
I KNOW, RIGHT? SOMEONE GOT OUT OF BED ON THE WRONG SIDE.
I WONDER WHY?
BREEP BREEP
OOPS. ONE SEC.
PHONE.
BREEP BREEP

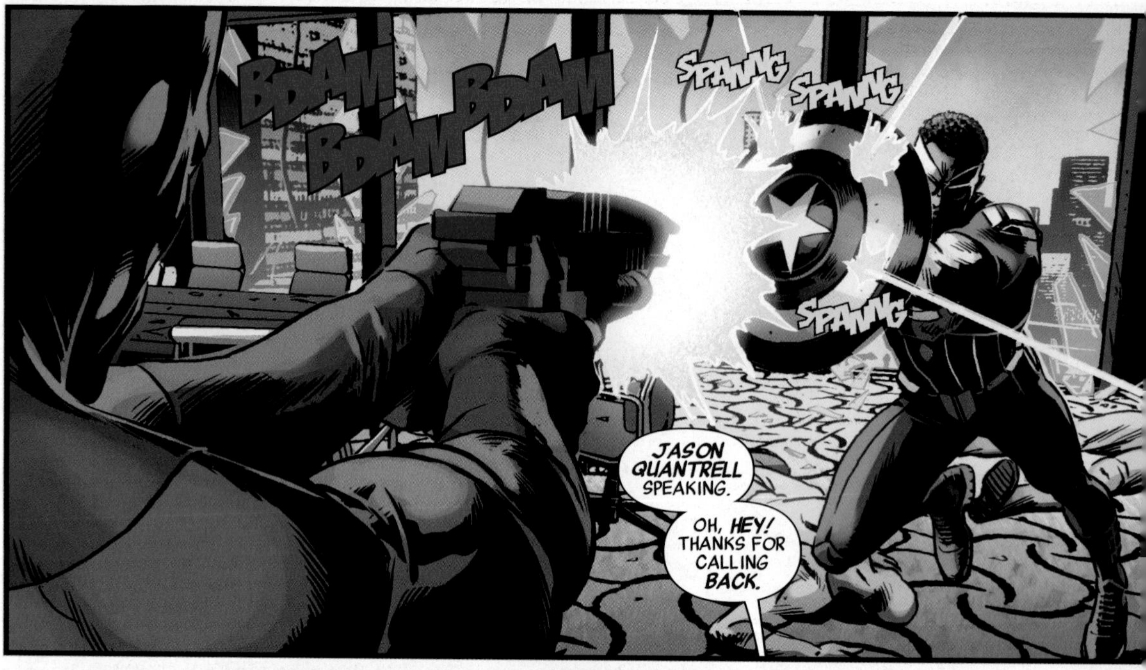
BDAM! BDAM BDAM
SPANNG SPANNG
SPANNG
JASON QUANTRELL SPEAKING.
OH, HEY! THANKS FOR CALLING BACK.

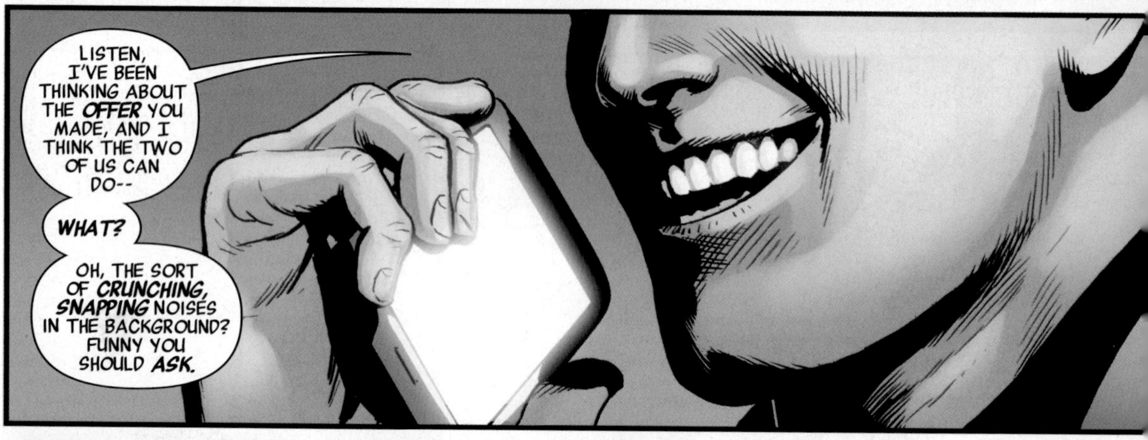
LISTEN, I'VE BEEN THINKING ABOUT THE OFFER YOU MADE, AND I THINK THE TWO OF US CAN DO--
WHAT?
OH, THE SORT OF CRUNCHING, SNAPPING NOISES IN THE BACKGROUND? FUNNY YOU SHOULD ASK.

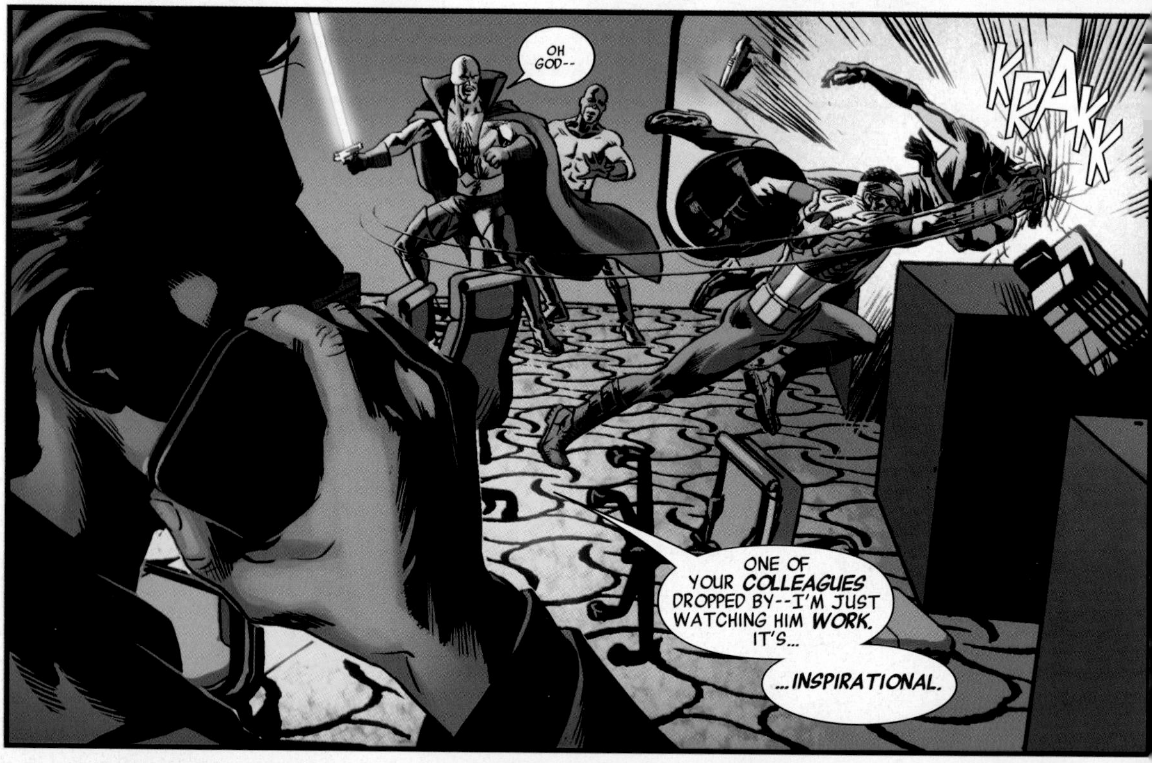
OH GOD--
KRAKK
ONE OF YOUR COLLEAGUES DROPPED BY--I'M JUST WATCHING HIM WORK. IT'S...
...INSPIRATIONAL.

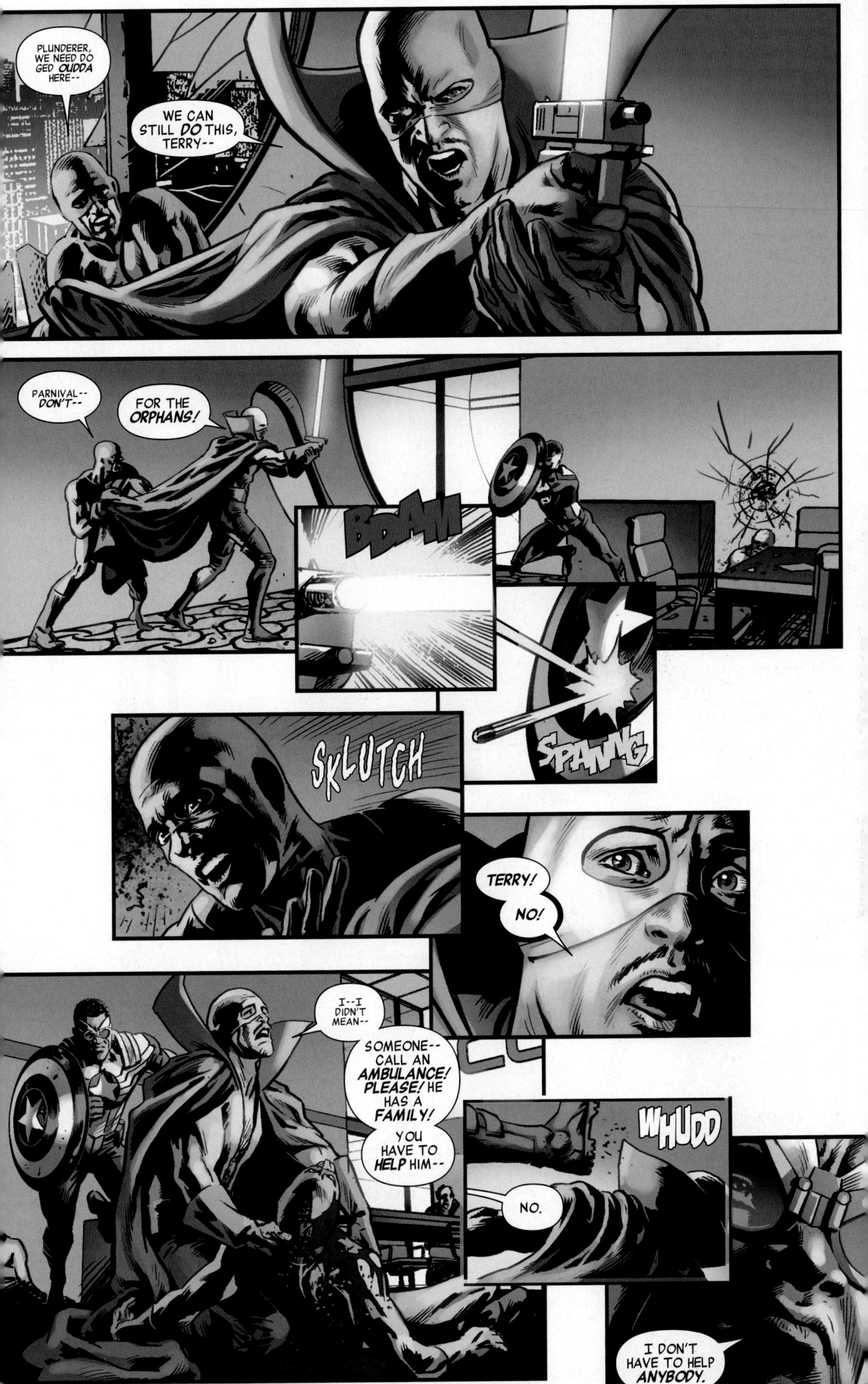
PLUNDERER, WE NEED DO GED OUDDA HERE--
WE CAN STILL DO THIS, TERRY--
PARNIVAL-- DON'T--
FOR THE ORPHANS!
BDAM
SPANNG
SKLUTCH
TERRY!
NO!
I--I DIDN'T MEAN--
SOMEONE-- CALL AN AMBULANCE! PLEASE! HE HAS A FAMILY!
YOU HAVE TO HELP HIM--
WHUDD
NO.
I DON'T HAVE TO HELP ANYBODY.

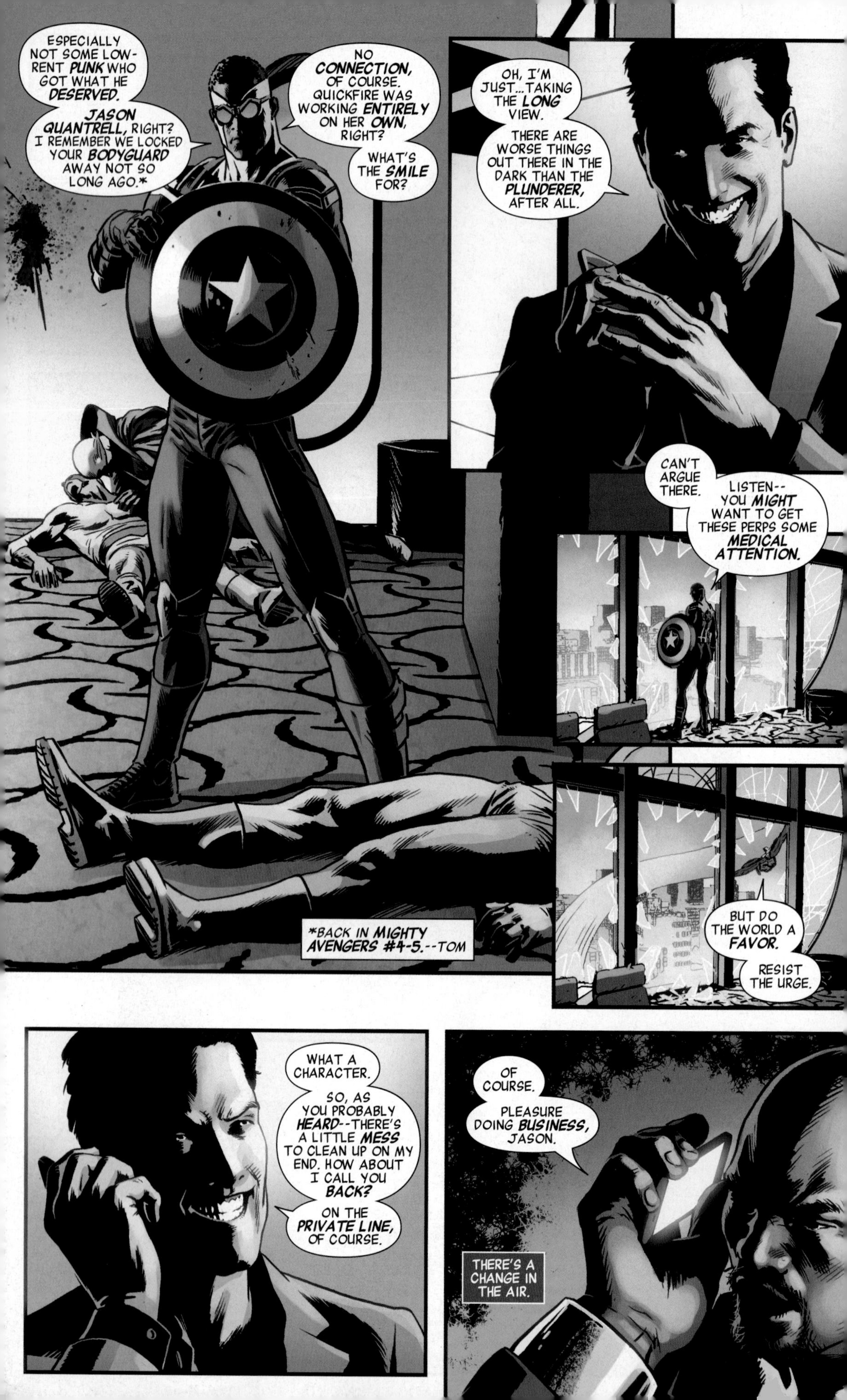
ESPECIALLY NOT SOME LOW-RENT PUNK WHO GOT WHAT HE DESERVED.
JASON QUANTRELL, RIGHT? I REMEMBER WE LOCKED YOUR BODYGUARD AWAY NOT SO LONG AGO.*
NO CONNECTION, OF COURSE. QUICKFIRE WAS WORKING ENTIRELY ON HER OWN, RIGHT?
WHAT'S THE SMILE FOR?
OH, I'M JUST...TAKING THE LONG VIEW.
THERE ARE WORSE THINGS OUT THERE IN THE DARK THAN THE PLUNDERER, AFTER ALL.
*BACK IN MIGHTY AVENGERS #4-5.--TOM
CAN'T ARGUE THERE.
LISTEN-- YOU MIGHT WANT TO GET THESE PERPS SOME MEDICAL ATTENTION.
BUT DO THE WORLD A FAVOR.
RESIST THE URGE.
WHAT A CHARACTER.
SO, AS YOU PROBABLY HEARD--THERE'S A LITTLE MESS TO CLEAN UP ON MY END. HOW ABOUT I CALL YOU BACK?
ON THE PRIVATE LINE, OF COURSE.
OF COURSE.
PLEASURE DOING BUSINESS, JASON.
THERE'S A CHANGE IN THE AIR.

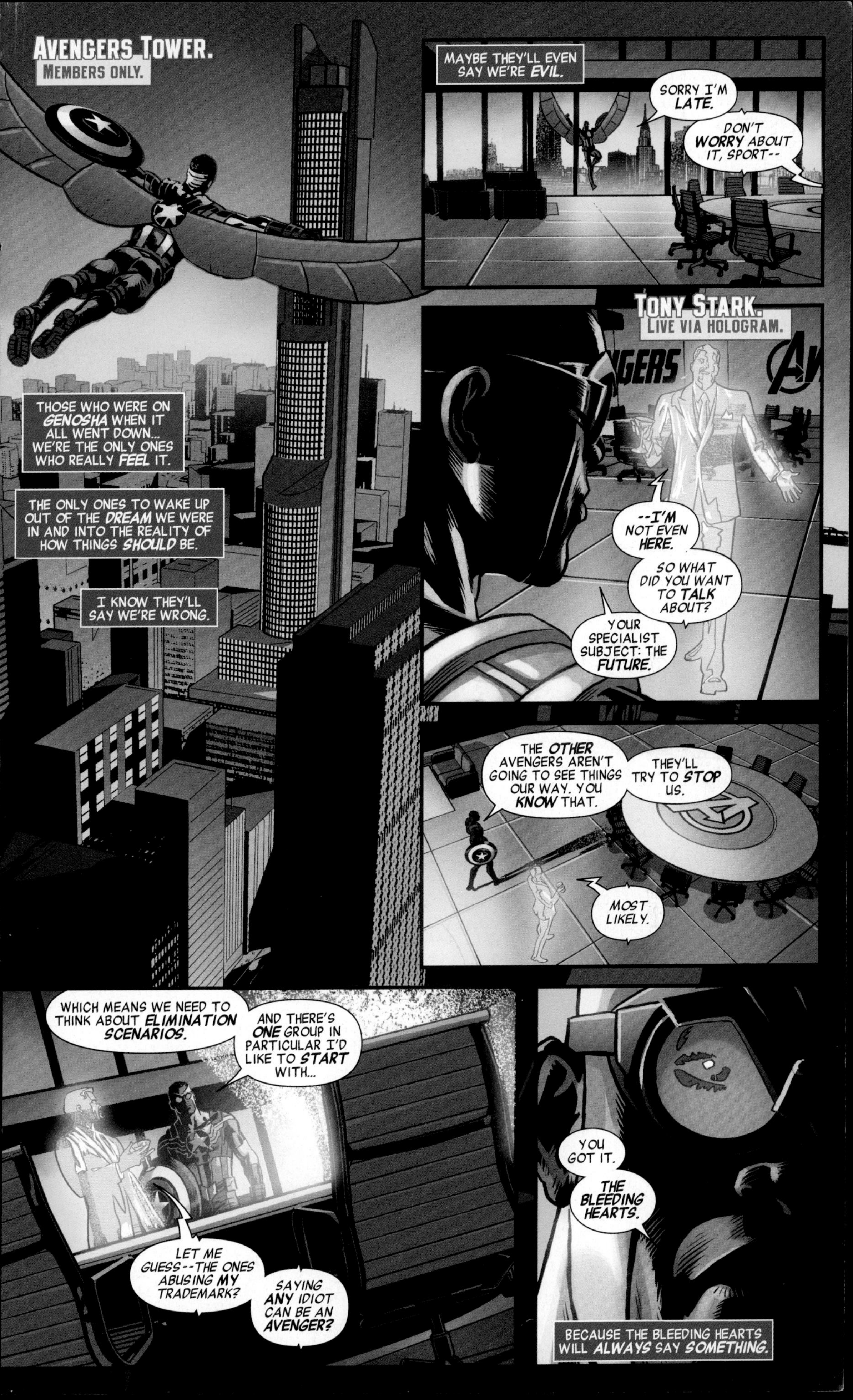
AVENGERS TOWER.
MEMBERS ONLY.
THOSE WHO WERE ON GENOSHA WHEN IT ALL WENT DOWN... WE'RE THE ONLY ONES WHO REALLY FEEL IT.
THE ONLY ONES TO WAKE UP OUT OF THE DREAM WE WERE IN AND INTO THE REALITY OF HOW THINGS SHOULD BE.
I KNOW THEY'LL SAY WE'RE WRONG.
MAYBE THEY'LL EVEN SAY WE'RE EVIL.
SORRY I'M LATE.
DON'T WORRY ABOUT IT, SPORT--
TONY STARK.
LIVE VIA HOLOGRAM.
--I'M NOT EVEN HERE.
SO WHAT DID YOU WANT TO TALK ABOUT?
YOUR SPECIALIST SUBJECT: THE FUTURE.
THE OTHER AVENGERS AREN'T GOING TO SEE THINGS OUR WAY. YOU KNOW THAT.
THEY'LL TRY TO STOP US.
MOST LIKELY.
WHICH MEANS WE NEED TO THINK ABOUT ELIMINATION SCENARIOS.
AND THERE'S ONE GROUP IN PARTICULAR I'D LIKE TO START WITH...
LET ME GUESS--THE ONES ABUSING MY TRADEMARK?
SAYING ANY IDIOT CAN BE AN AVENGER?
YOU GOT IT.
THE BLEEDING HEARTS.
BECAUSE THE BLEEDING HEARTS WILL ALWAYS SAY SOMETHING.

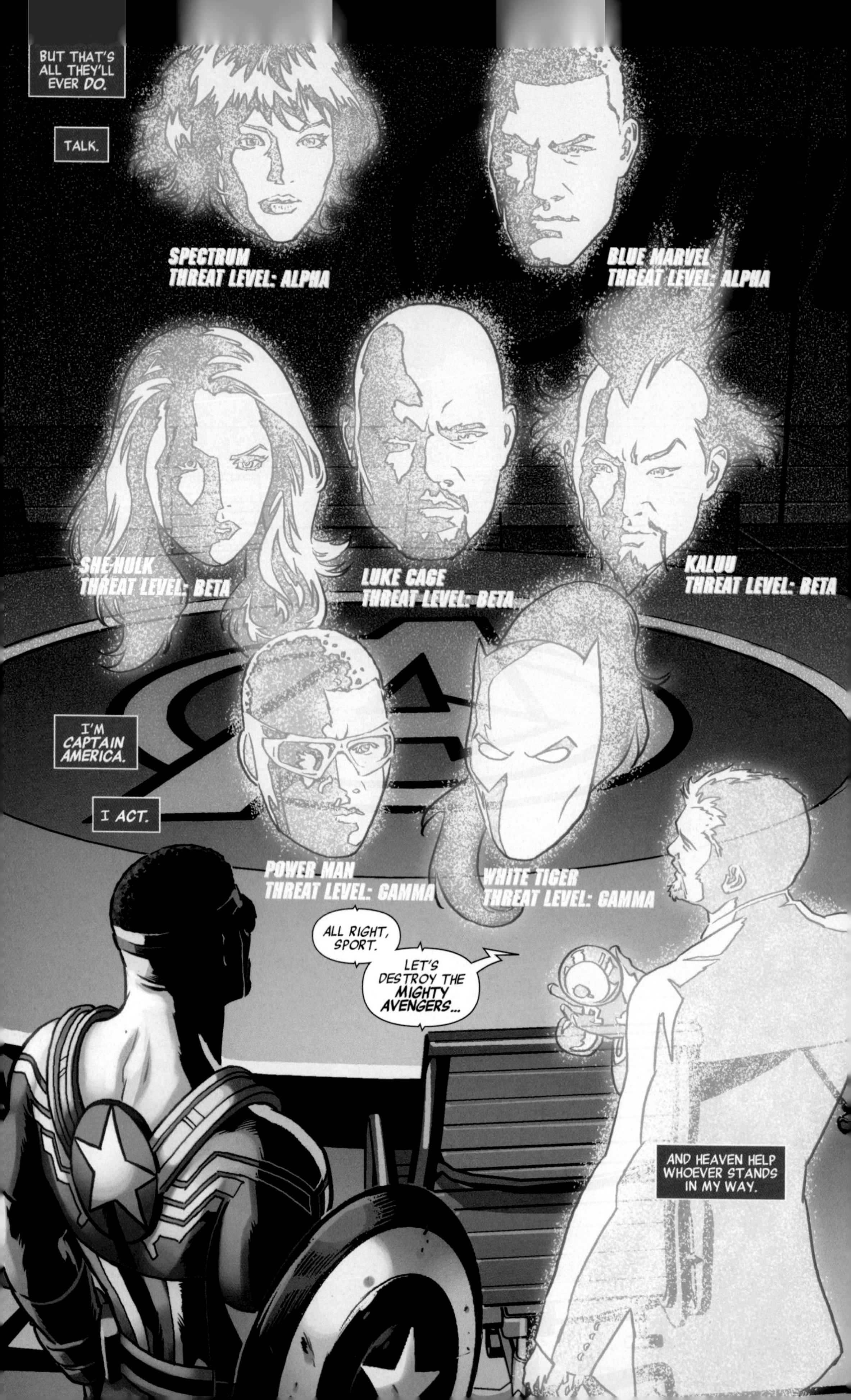
BUT THAT'S ALL THEY'LL EVER DO.
TALK.
SPECTRUM THREAT LEVEL: ALPHA
BLUE MARVEL THREAT LEVEL: ALPHA
SHE-HULK THREAT LEVEL: BETA
LUKE CAGE THREAT LEVEL: BETA
KALUU THREAT LEVEL: BETA
I'M CAPTAIN AMERICA.
I ACT.
POWER MAN THREAT LEVEL: GAMMA
WHITE TIGER THREAT LEVEL: GAMMA
ALL RIGHT, SPORT.
LET'S DESTROY THE MIGHTY AVENGERS...
AND HEAVEN HELP WHOEVER STANDS IN MY WAY.

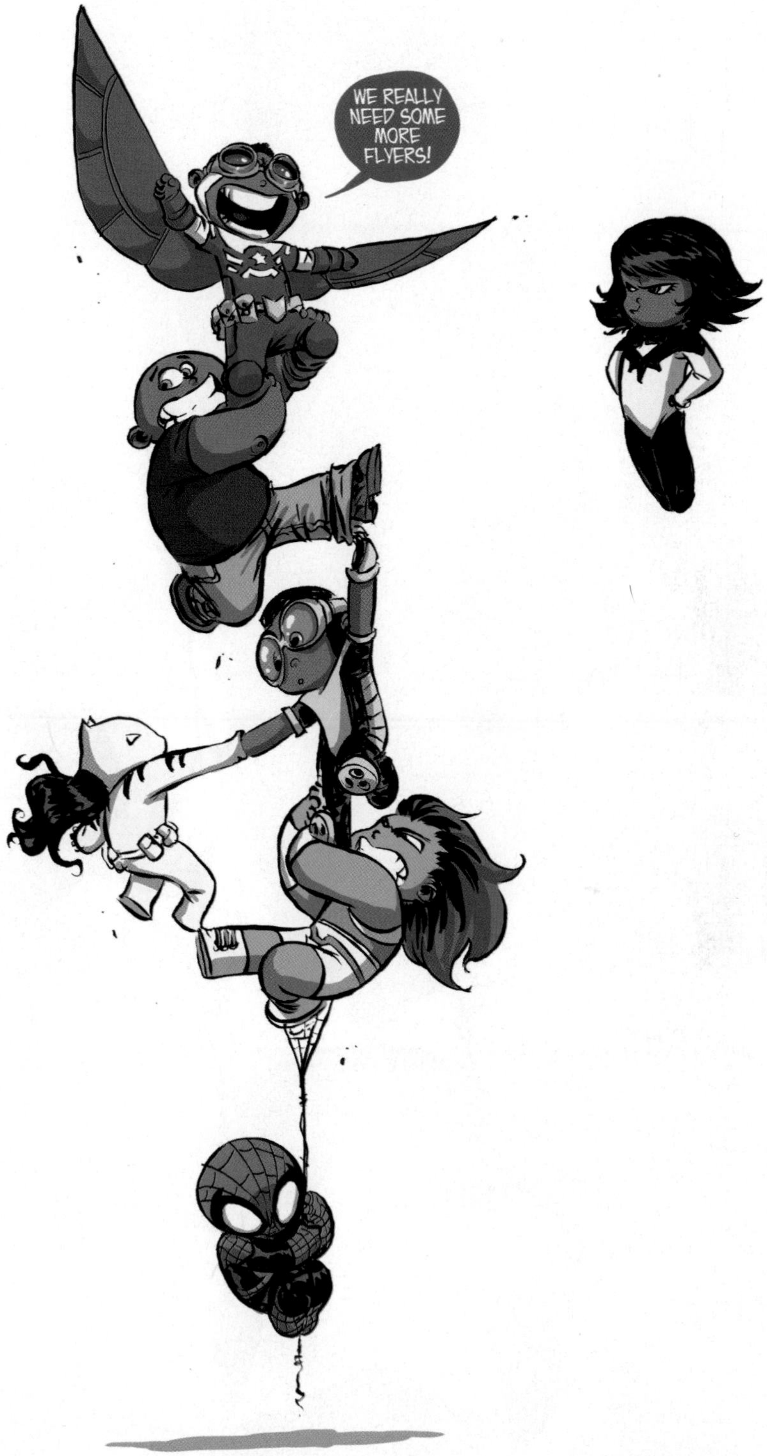
WE REALLY NEED SOME MORE FLYERS!
SY 14

#1 VARIANT BY SKOTTIE YOUNG

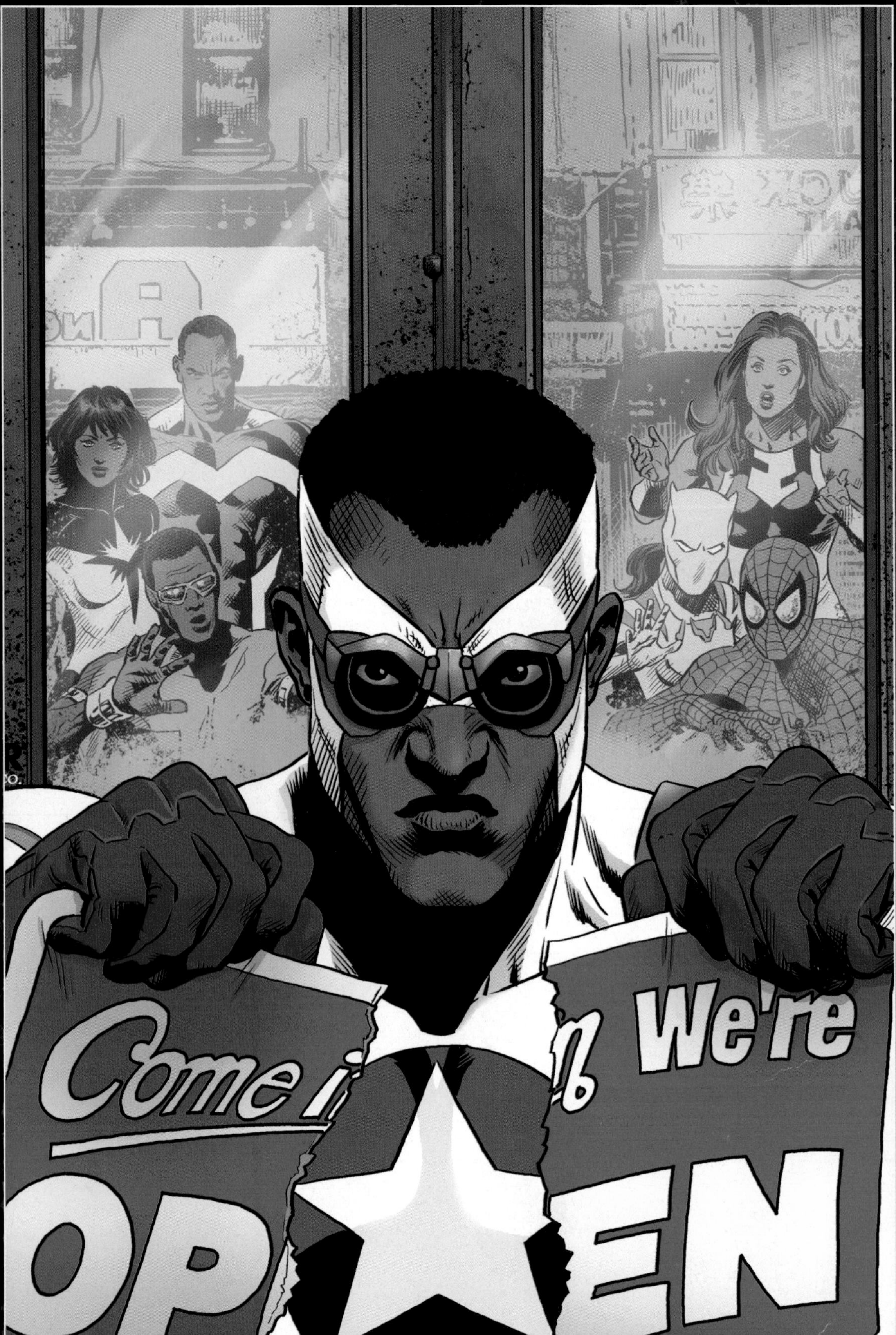
Come i
We're
OP
EN

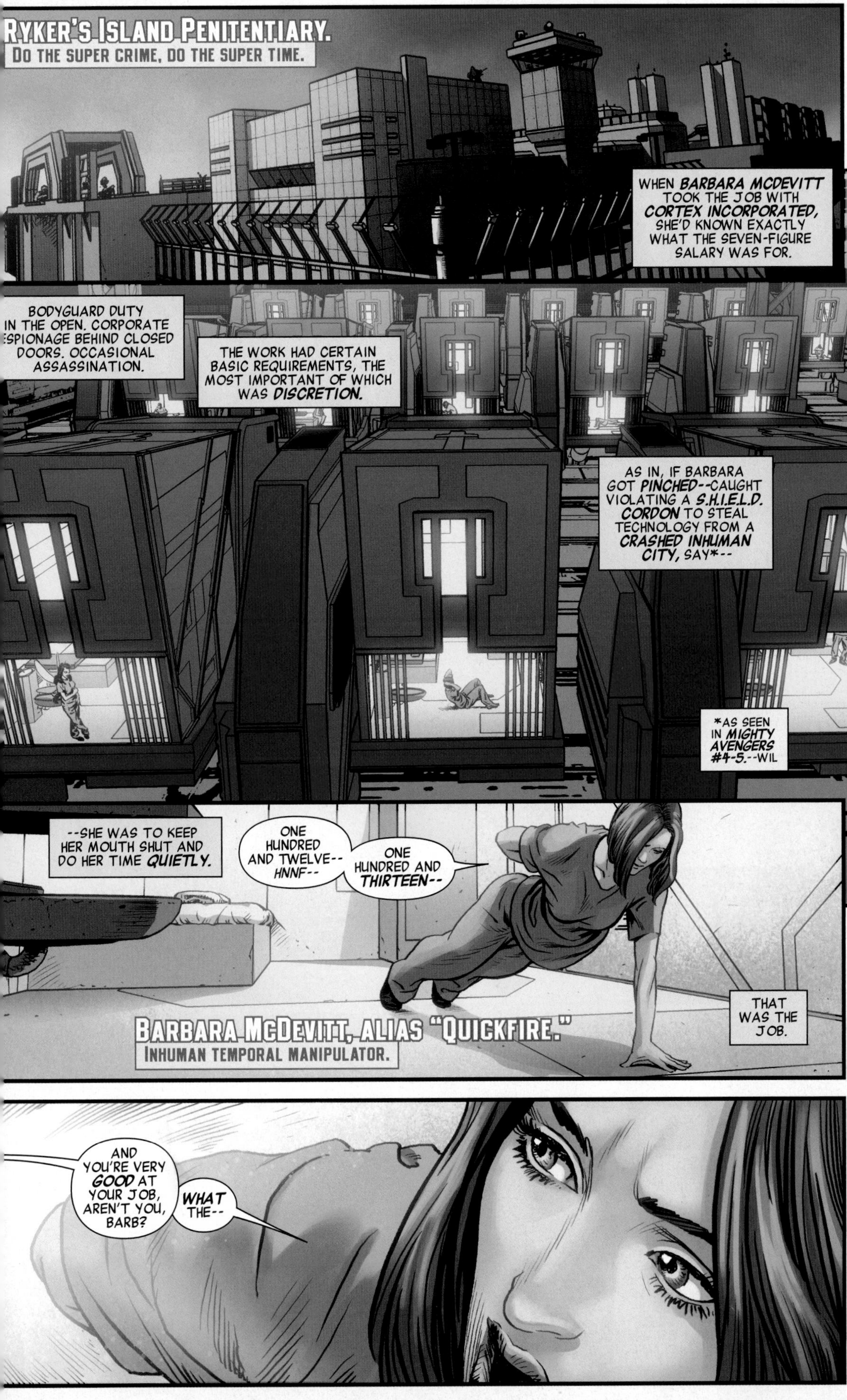
RYKER'S ISLAND PENITENTIARY.
DO THE SUPER CRIME, DO THE SUPER TIME.
WHEN BARBARA MCDEVITT TOOK THE JOB WITH CORTEX INCORPORATED, SHE'D KNOWN EXACTLY WHAT THE SEVEN-FIGURE SALARY WAS FOR.
BODYGUARD DUTY IN THE OPEN. CORPORATE ESPIONAGE BEHIND CLOSED DOORS. OCCASIONAL ASSASSINATION.
THE WORK HAD CERTAIN BASIC REQUIREMENTS, THE MOST IMPORTANT OF WHICH WAS DISCRETION.
AS IN, IF BARBARA GOT PINCHED--CAUGHT VIOLATING A S.H.I.E.L.D. CORDON TO STEAL TECHNOLOGY FROM A CRASHED INHUMAN CITY, SAY*--
*AS SEEN IN MIGHTY AVENGERS #4-5.--WIL
--SHE WAS TO KEEP HER MOUTH SHUT AND DO HER TIME QUIETLY.
ONE HUNDRED AND TWELVE-- HNNF--
ONE HUNDRED AND THIRTEEN--
BARBARA MCDEVITT, ALIAS "QUICKFIRE."
INHUMAN TEMPORAL MANIPULATOR.
THAT WAS THE JOB.
AND YOU'RE VERY GOOD AT YOUR JOB, AREN'T YOU, BARB?
WHAT THE--

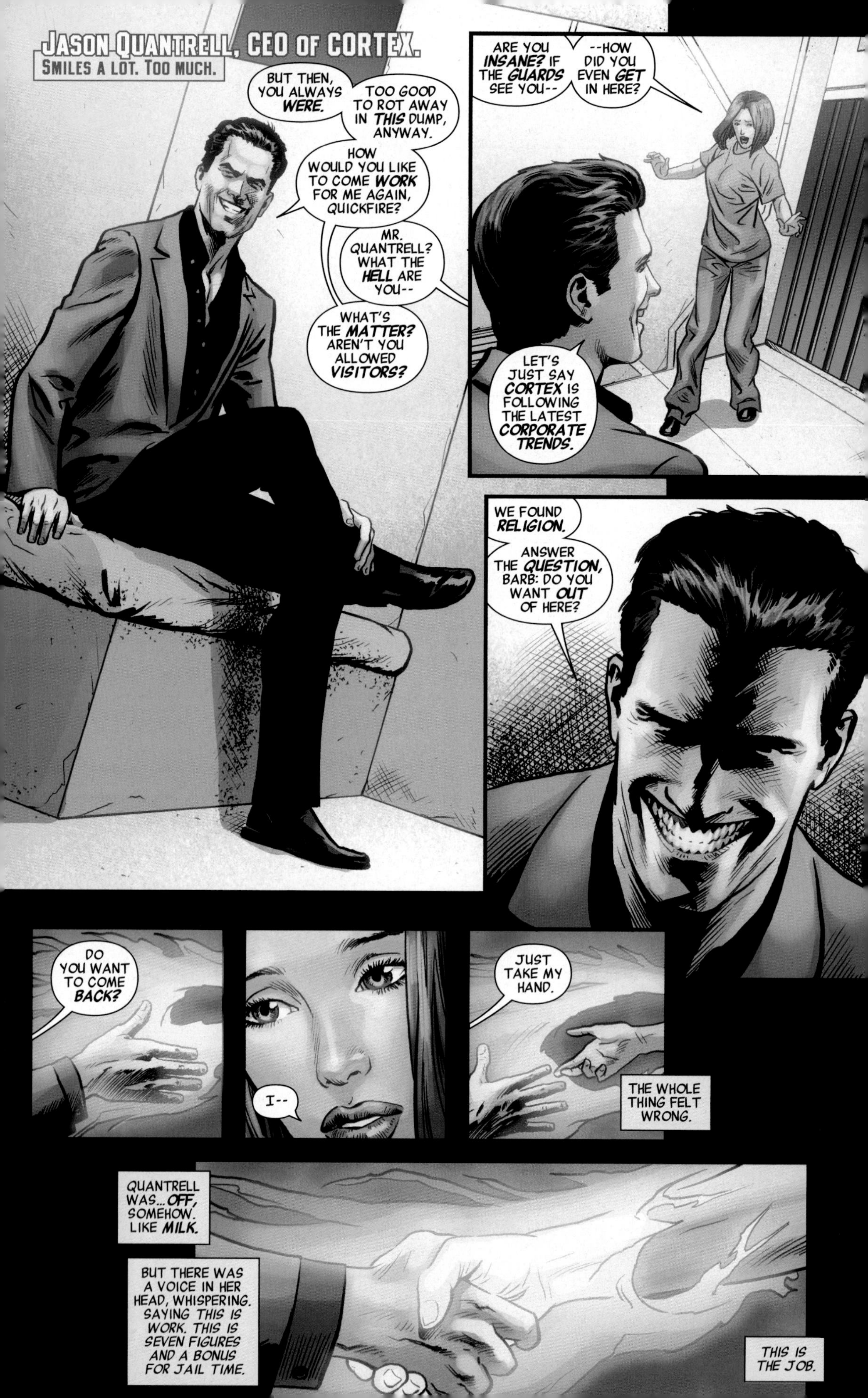
JASON QUANTRELL, CEO OF CORTEX.
SMILES A LOT. TOO MUCH.
BUT THEN, YOU ALWAYS WERE.
TOO GOOD TO ROT AWAY IN THIS DUMP, ANYWAY.
HOW WOULD YOU LIKE TO COME WORK FOR ME AGAIN, QUICKFIRE?
MR. QUANTRELL? WHAT THE HELL ARE YOU--
WHAT'S THE MATTER? AREN'T YOU ALLOWED VISITORS?
ARE YOU INSANE? IF THE GUARDS SEE YOU--
--HOW DID YOU EVEN GET IN HERE?
LET'S JUST SAY CORTEX IS FOLLOWING THE LATEST CORPORATE TRENDS.
WE FOUND RELIGION.
ANSWER THE QUESTION, BARB: DO YOU WANT OUT OF HERE?
DO YOU WANT TO COME BACK?
I--
JUST TAKE MY HAND.
THE WHOLE THING FELT WRONG.
QUANTRELL WAS... OFF, SOMEHOW. LIKE MILK.
BUT THERE WAS A VOICE IN HER HEAD, WHISPERING. SAYING THIS IS WORK. THIS IS SEVEN FIGURES AND A BONUS FOR JAIL TIME.
THIS IS THE JOB.

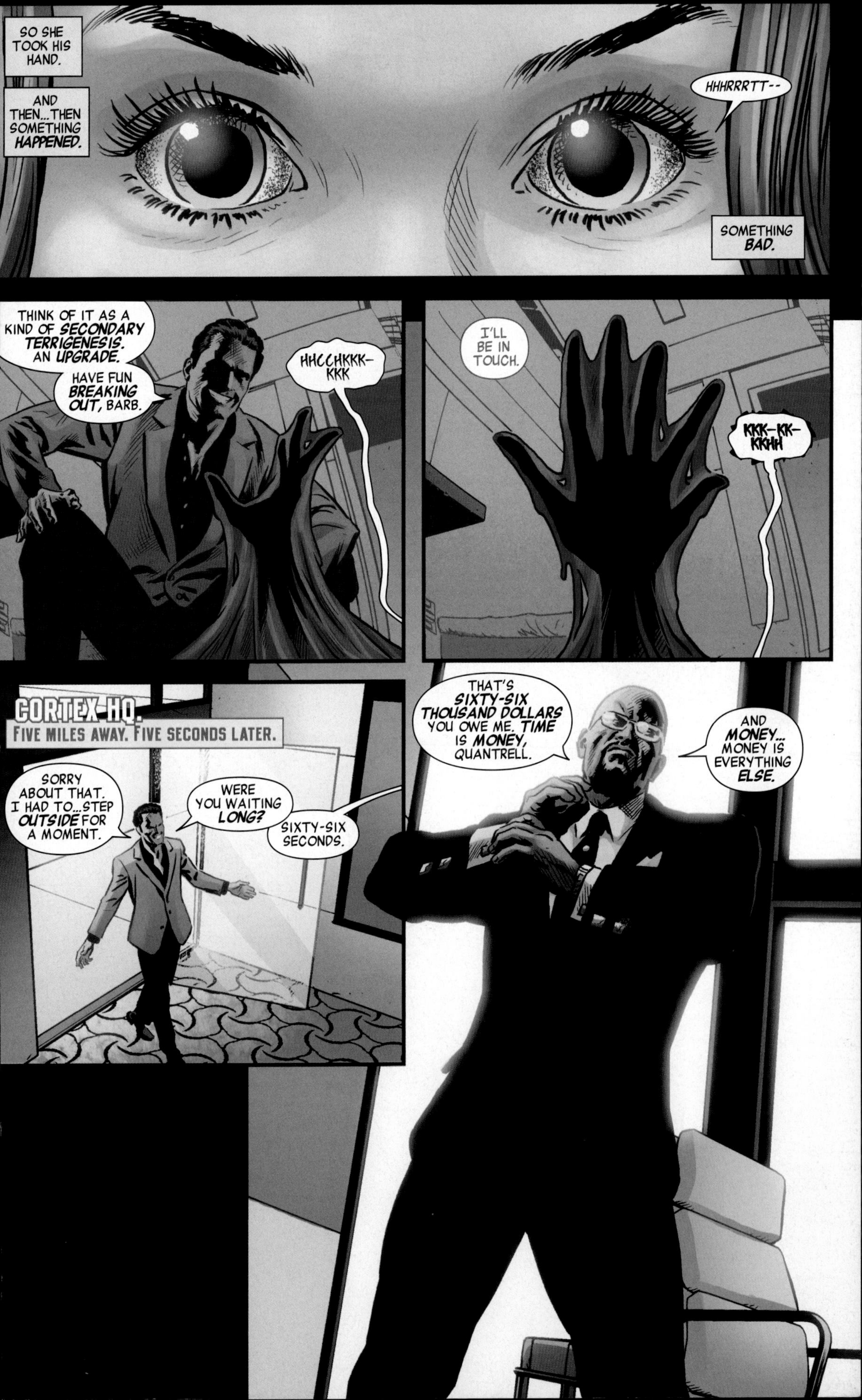
SO SHE TOOK HIS HAND.
AND THEN...THEN SOMETHING HAPPENED.
HHHRRRTT--
SOMETHING BAD.
THINK OF IT AS A KIND OF SECONDARY TERRIGENESIS. AN UPGRADE.
HAVE FUN BREAKING OUT, BARB.
HHCCHKKK-KKK
I'LL BE IN TOUCH.
KKK--KK-KKHH
CORTEX HQ.
FIVE MILES AWAY. FIVE SECONDS LATER.
SORRY ABOUT THAT. I HAD TO...STEP OUTSIDE FOR A MOMENT.
WERE YOU WAITING LONG?
SIXTY-SIX SECONDS.
THAT'S SIXTY-SIX THOUSAND DOLLARS YOU OWE ME. TIME IS MONEY, QUANTRELL.
AND MONEY... MONEY IS EVERYTHING ELSE.

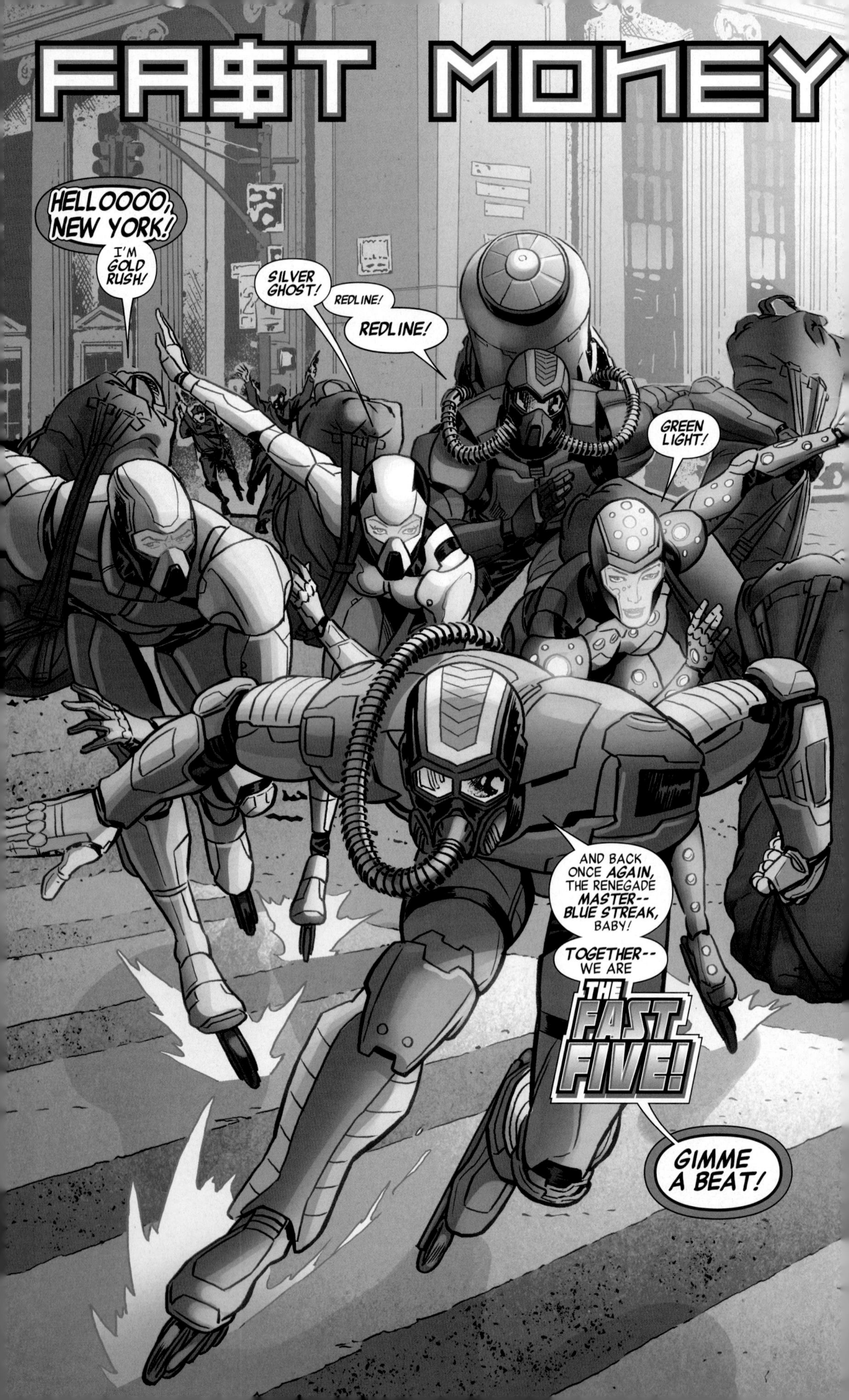
FA$T MONEY
HELLOOOO, NEW YORK!
I'M GOLD RUSH!
SILVER GHOST!
REDLINE!
REDLINE!
GREEN LIGHT!
AND BACK ONCE AGAIN, THE RENEGADE MASTER-- BLUE STREAK, BABY!
TOGETHER-- WE ARE
THE FAST FIVE!
GIMME A BEAT!

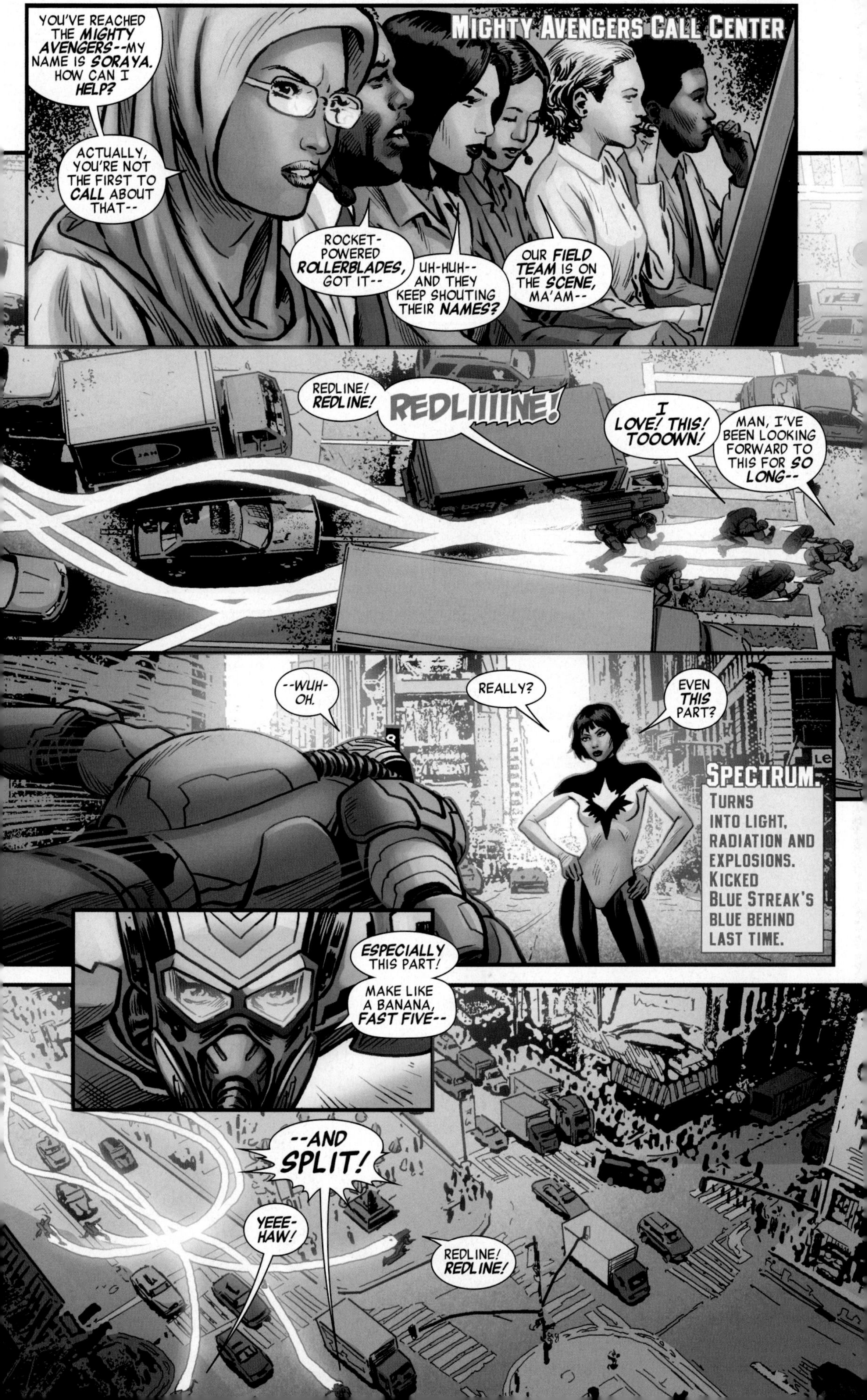
MIGHTY AVENGERS CALL CENTER
YOU'VE REACHED THE MIGHTY AVENGERS--MY NAME IS SORAYA. HOW CAN I HELP?
ACTUALLY, YOU'RE NOT THE FIRST TO CALL ABOUT THAT--
ROCKET-POWERED ROLLERBLADES, GOT IT--
UH-HUH--AND THEY KEEP SHOUTING THEIR NAMES?
OUR FIELD TEAM IS ON THE SCENE, MA'AM--
REDLINE! REDLINE!
REDLIIIIINE!
I LOVE! THIS! TOOOWN!
MAN, I'VE BEEN LOOKING FORWARD TO THIS FOR SO LONG--
--WUH-OH.
REALLY?
EVEN THIS PART?
SPECTRUM.
TURNS INTO LIGHT, RADIATION AND EXPLOSIONS. KICKED BLUE STREAK'S BLUE BEHIND LAST TIME.
ESPECIALLY THIS PART!
MAKE LIKE A BANANA, FAST FIVE--
--AND SPLIT!
YEEE-HAW!
REDLINE! REDLINE!

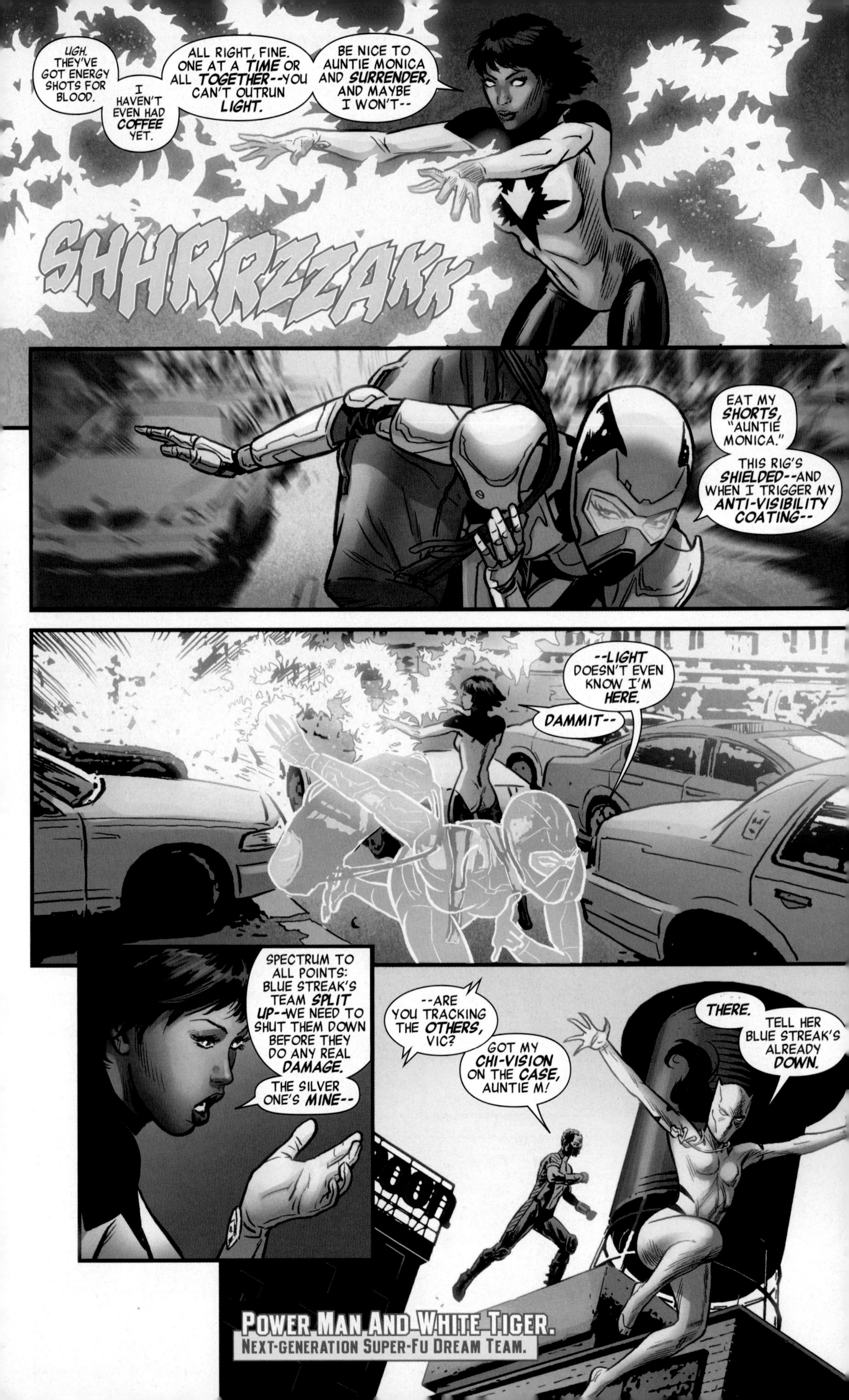
UGH. THEY'VE GOT ENERGY SHOTS FOR BLOOD.
I HAVEN'T EVEN HAD COFFEE YET.
ALL RIGHT, FINE. ONE AT A TIME OR ALL TOGETHER--YOU CAN'T OUTRUN LIGHT.
BE NICE TO AUNTIE MONICA AND SURRENDER, AND MAYBE I WON'T--
SHHRRZZAKK
EAT MY SHORTS, "AUNTIE MONICA."
THIS RIG'S SHIELDED--AND WHEN I TRIGGER MY ANTI-VISIBILITY COATING--
--LIGHT DOESN'T EVEN KNOW I'M HERE.
DAMMIT--
SPECTRUM TO ALL POINTS: BLUE STREAK'S TEAM SPLIT UP--WE NEED TO SHUT THEM DOWN BEFORE THEY DO ANY REAL DAMAGE.
THE SILVER ONE'S MINE--
--ARE YOU TRACKING THE OTHERS, VIC?
GOT MY CHI-VISION ON THE CASE, AUNTIE M!
THERE.
TELL HER BLUE STREAK'S ALREADY DOWN.
POWER MAN AND WHITE TIGER.
NEXT-GENERATION SUPER-FU DREAM TEAM.

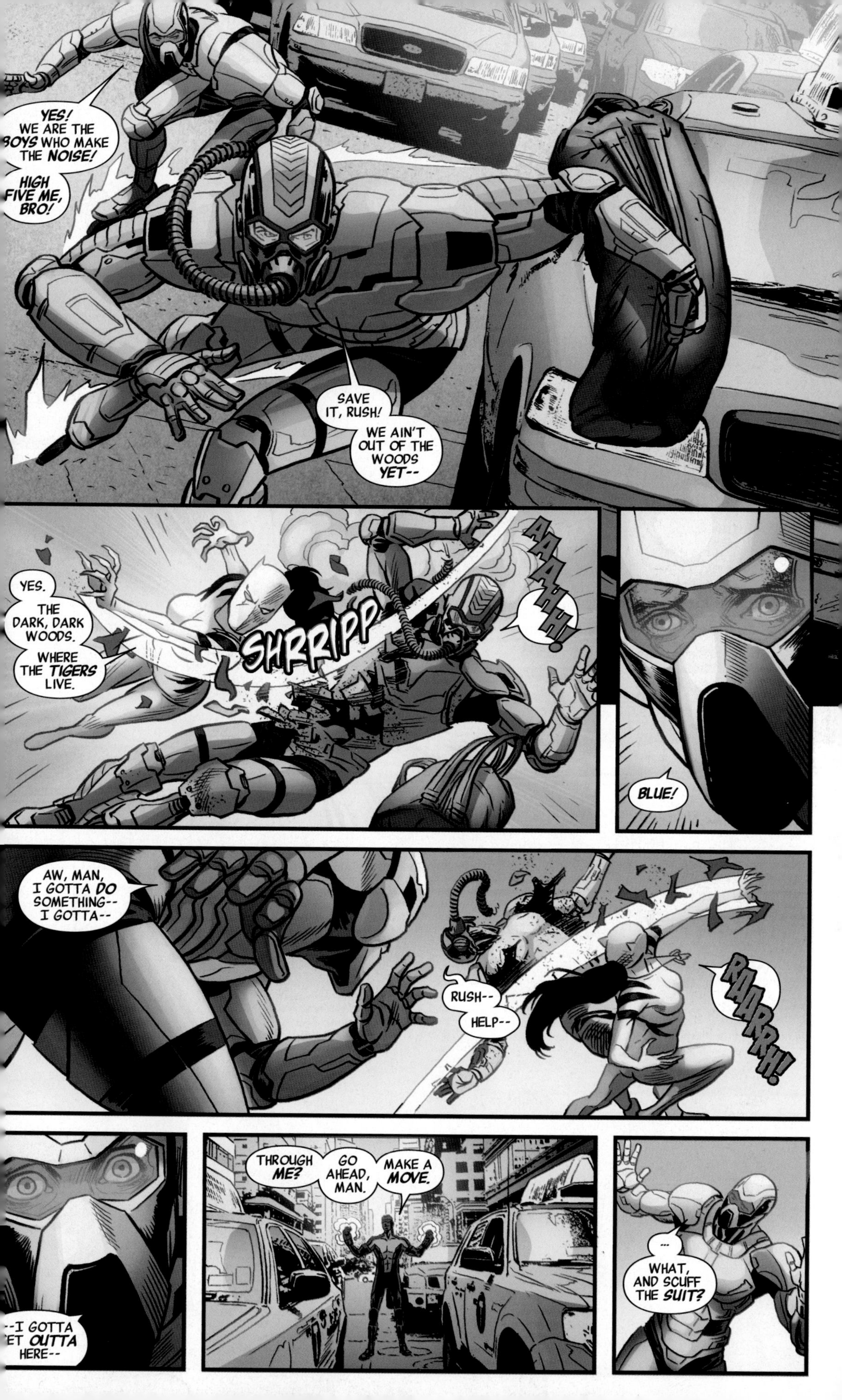

YES! WE ARE THE BOYS WHO MAKE THE NOISE!
HIGH FIVE ME, BRO!
SAVE IT, RUSH!
WE AIN'T OUT OF THE WOODS YET--
YES.
THE DARK, DARK WOODS.
WHERE THE TIGERS LIVE.
SHRRIPP
AAAHH!
BLUE!
AW, MAN, I GOTTA DO SOMETHING-- I GOTTA--
RUSH--
HELP--
RAAARRH!
--I GOTTA ET OUTTA HERE--
THROUGH ME?
GO AHEAD, MAN.
MAKE A MOVE.
...
WHAT, AND SCUFF THE SUIT?

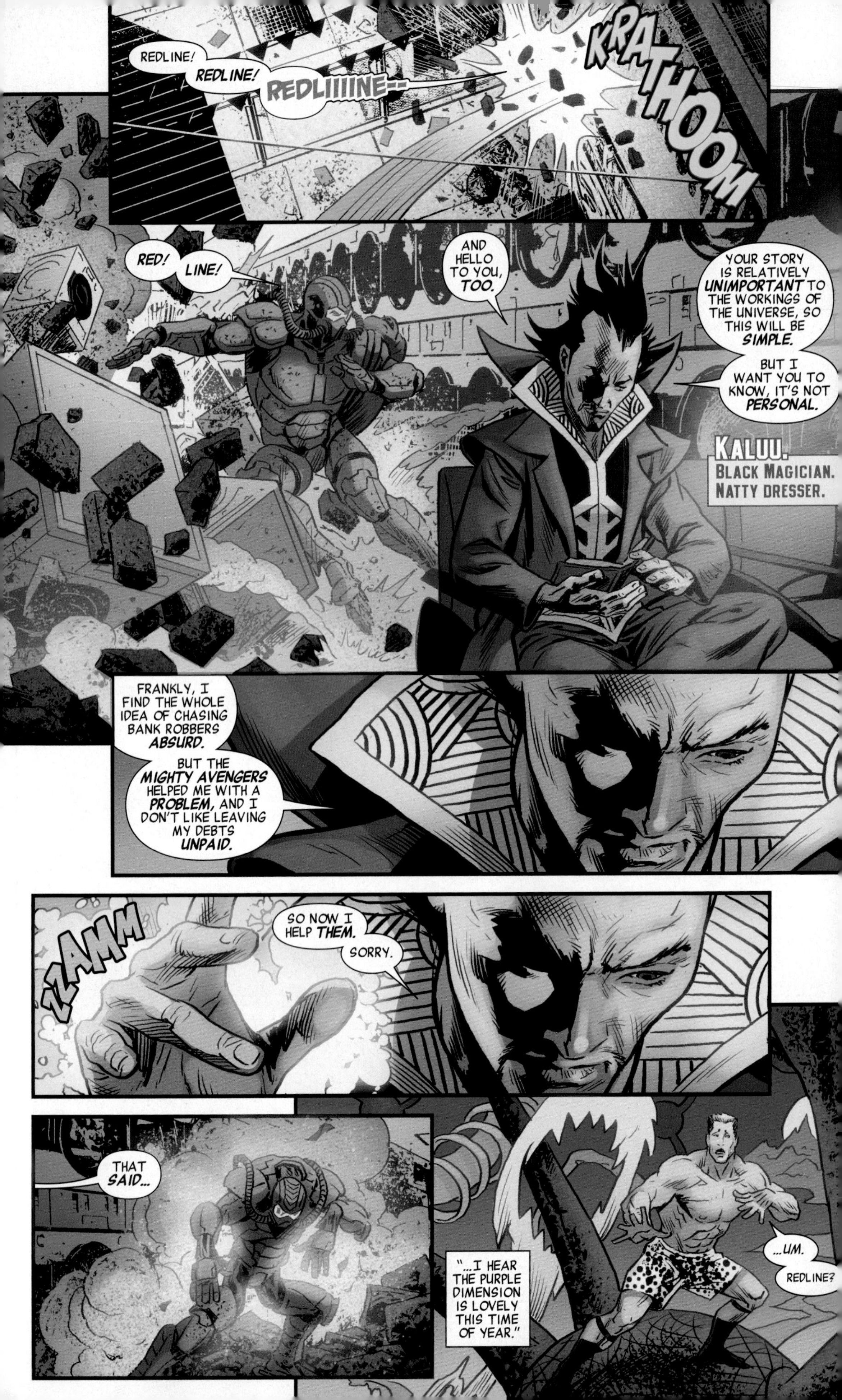

REDLINE!
REDLINE!
REDLIIIIINE--
KRATHOOM
RED!
LINE!
AND HELLO TO YOU, TOO.
YOUR STORY IS RELATIVELY UNIMPORTANT TO THE WORKINGS OF THE UNIVERSE, SO THIS WILL BE SIMPLE.
BUT I WANT YOU TO KNOW, IT'S NOT PERSONAL.
KALUU.
BLACK MAGICIAN.
NATTY DRESSER.
FRANKLY, I FIND THE WHOLE IDEA OF CHASING BANK ROBBERS ABSURD.
BUT THE MIGHTY AVENGERS HELPED ME WITH A PROBLEM, AND I DON'T LIKE LEAVING MY DEBTS UNPAID.
ZZAMM
SO NOW I HELP THEM.
SORRY.
THAT SAID...
"...I HEAR THE PURPLE DIMENSION IS LOVELY THIS TIME OF YEAR."
...UM.
REDLINE?

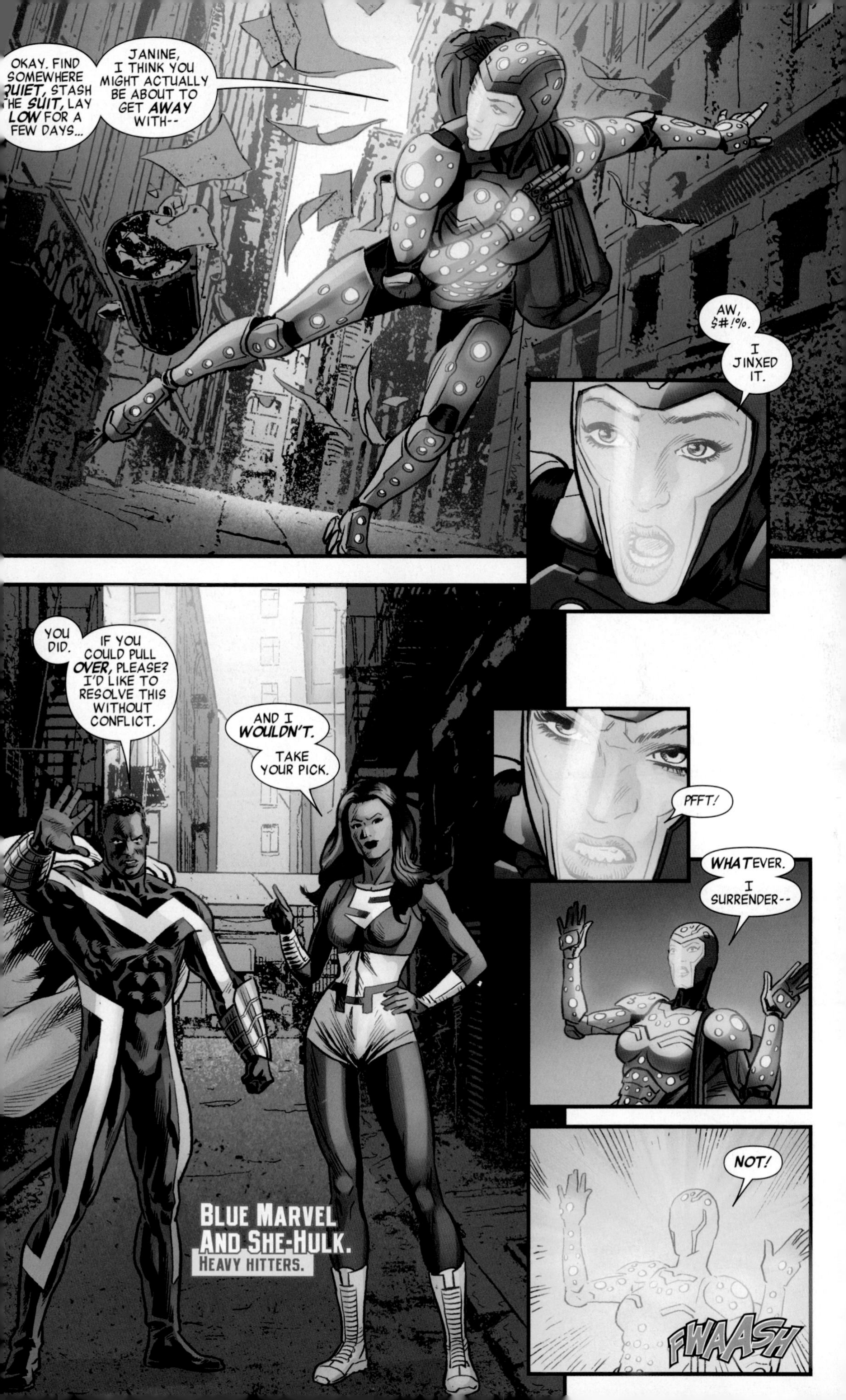
OKAY. FIND SOMEWHERE QUIET, STASH THE SUIT, LAY LOW FOR A FEW DAYS...
JANINE, I THINK YOU MIGHT ACTUALLY BE ABOUT TO GET AWAY WITH--
AW, $#!%.
I JINXED IT.
YOU DID.
IF YOU COULD PULL OVER, PLEASE? I'D LIKE TO RESOLVE THIS WITHOUT CONFLICT.
AND I WOULDN'T.
TAKE YOUR PICK.
BLUE MARVEL AND SHE-HULK.
HEAVY HITTERS.
PFFT!
WHATEVER.
I SURRENDER--
NOT!
FWAASH

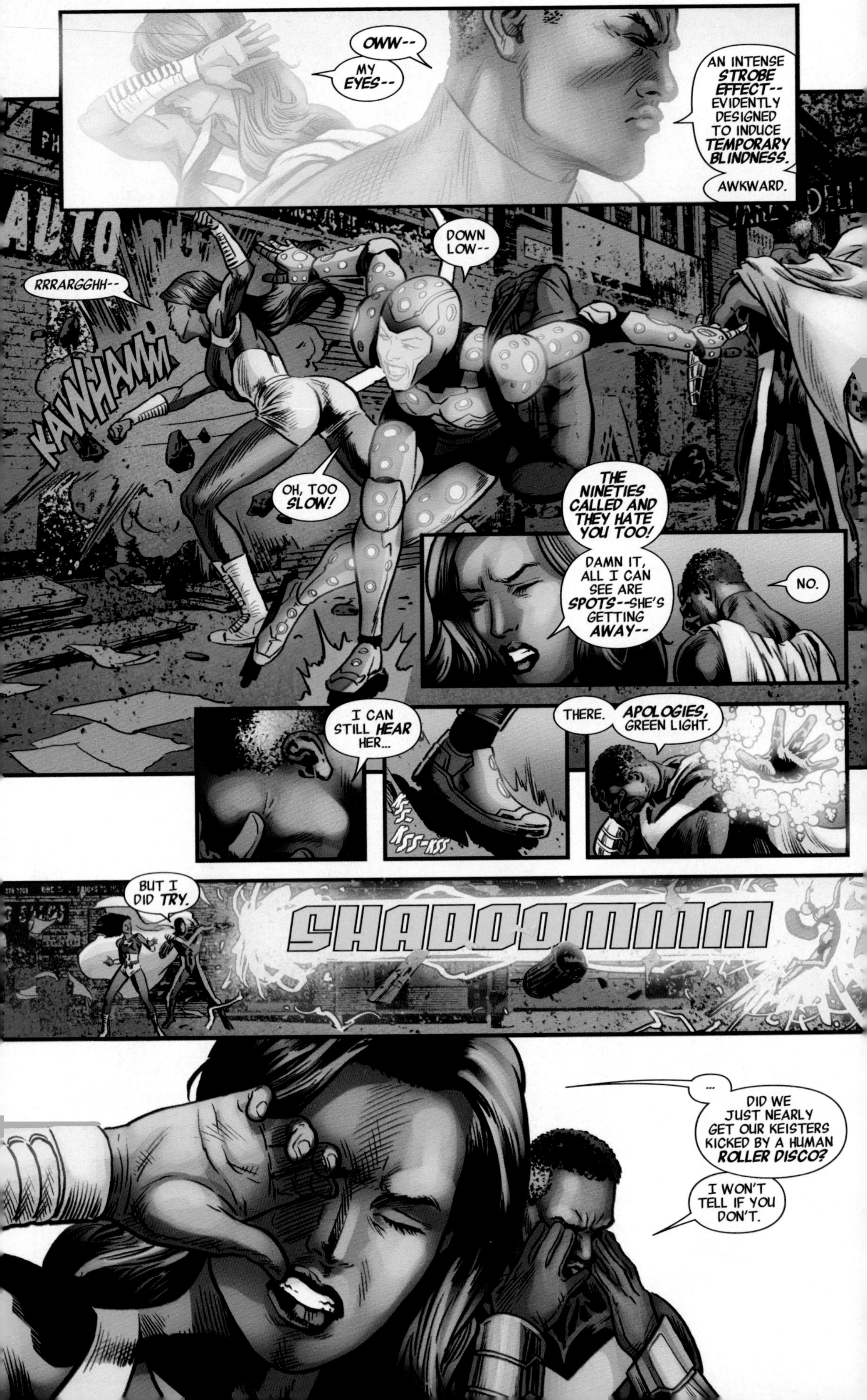
OWW--
MY EYES--
AN INTENSE STROBE EFFECT--EVIDENTLY DESIGNED TO INDUCE TEMPORARY BLINDNESS.
AWKWARD.
RRRARGGHH--
DOWN LOW--
KAWHAMM
OH, TOO SLOW!
THE NINETIES CALLED AND THEY HATE YOU TOO!
DAMN IT, ALL I CAN SEE ARE SPOTS--SHE'S GETTING AWAY--
NO.
I CAN STILL HEAR HER...
THERE.
APOLOGIES, GREEN LIGHT.
BUT I DID TRY.
SHADOOMMM
...
DID WE JUST NEARLY GET OUR KEISTERS KICKED BY A HUMAN ROLLER DISCO?
I WON'T TELL IF YOU DON'T.

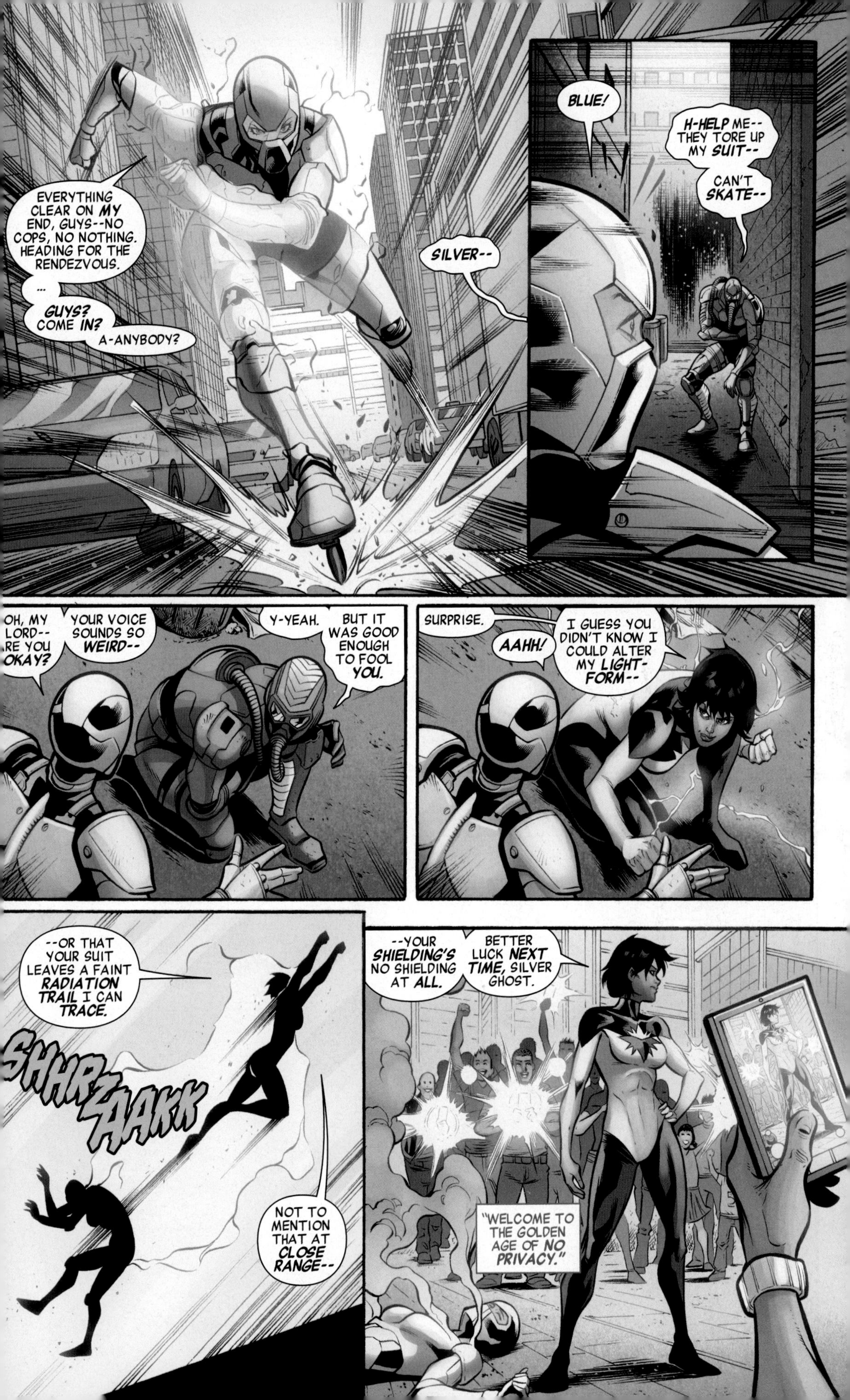
EVERYTHING CLEAR ON MY END, GUYS--NO COPS, NO NOTHING. HEADING FOR THE RENDEZVOUS.
...
GUYS? COME IN?
A-ANYBODY?
SILVER--
BLUE!
H-HELP ME-- THEY TORE UP MY SUIT--
CAN'T SKATE--
OH, MY LORD-- ARE YOU OKAY?
YOUR VOICE SOUNDS SO WEIRD--
Y-YEAH.
BUT IT WAS GOOD ENOUGH TO FOOL YOU.
SURPRISE.
AAHH!
I GUESS YOU DIDN'T KNOW I COULD ALTER MY LIGHT-FORM--
--OR THAT YOUR SUIT LEAVES A FAINT RADIATION TRAIL I CAN TRACE.
SHHRZAAKK
NOT TO MENTION THAT AT CLOSE RANGE--
--YOUR SHIELDING'S NO SHIELDING AT ALL.
BETTER LUCK NEXT TIME, SILVER GHOST.
"WELCOME TO THE GOLDEN AGE OF NO PRIVACY."

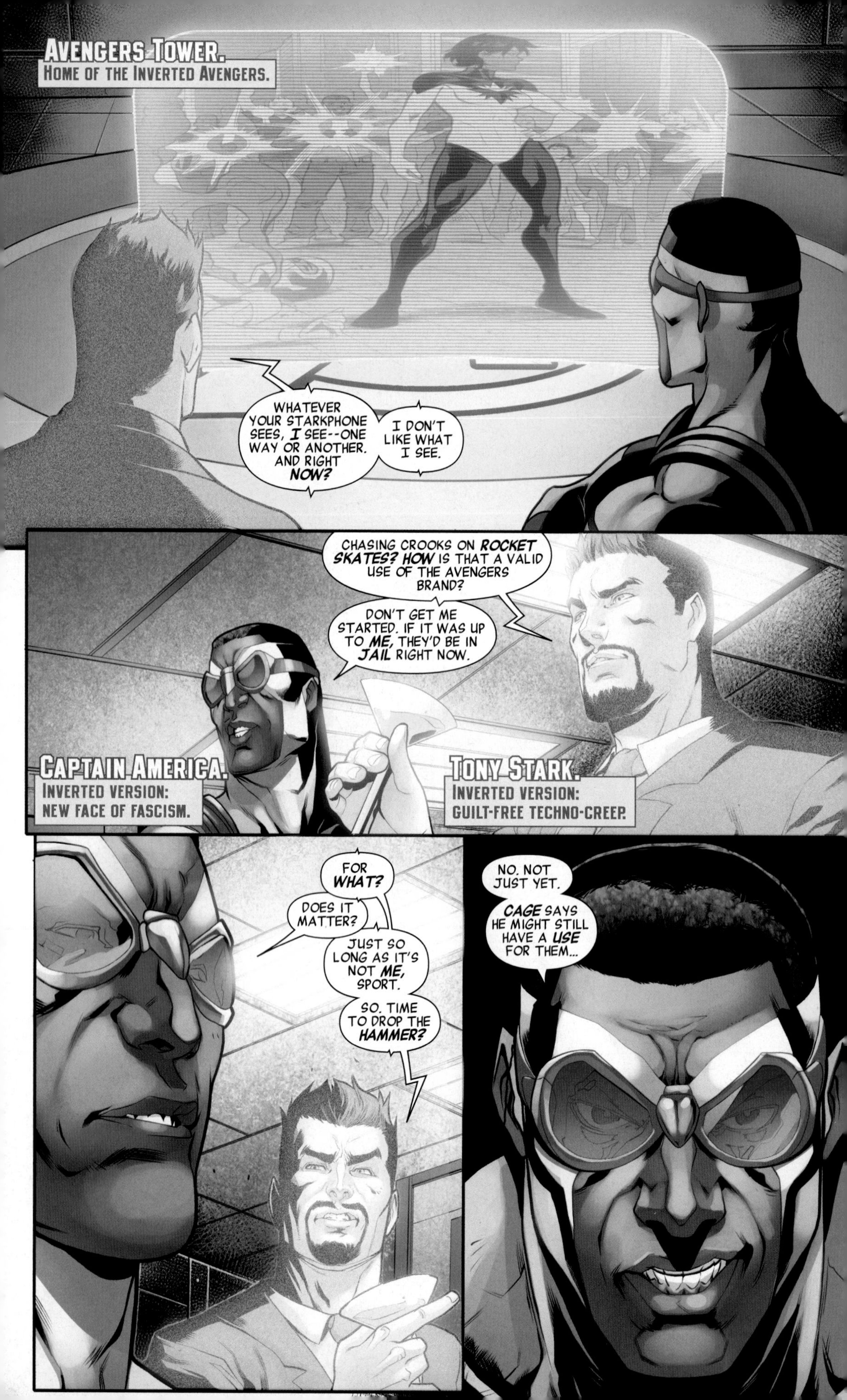

AVENGERS TOWER.
HOME OF THE INVERTED AVENGERS.
WHATEVER YOUR STARKPHONE SEES, I SEE--ONE WAY OR ANOTHER. AND RIGHT NOW?
I DON'T LIKE WHAT I SEE.
CHASING CROOKS ON ROCKET SKATES? HOW IS THAT A VALID USE OF THE AVENGERS BRAND?
DON'T GET ME STARTED. IF IT WAS UP TO ME, THEY'D BE IN JAIL RIGHT NOW.
CAPTAIN AMERICA.
INVERTED VERSION: NEW FACE OF FASCISM.
TONY STARK.
INVERTED VERSION: GUILT-FREE TECHNO-CREEP.
FOR WHAT?
DOES IT MATTER?
JUST SO LONG AS IT'S NOT ME, SPORT.
SO. TIME TO DROP THE HAMMER?
NO. NOT JUST YET.
CAGE SAYS HE MIGHT STILL HAVE A USE FOR THEM...

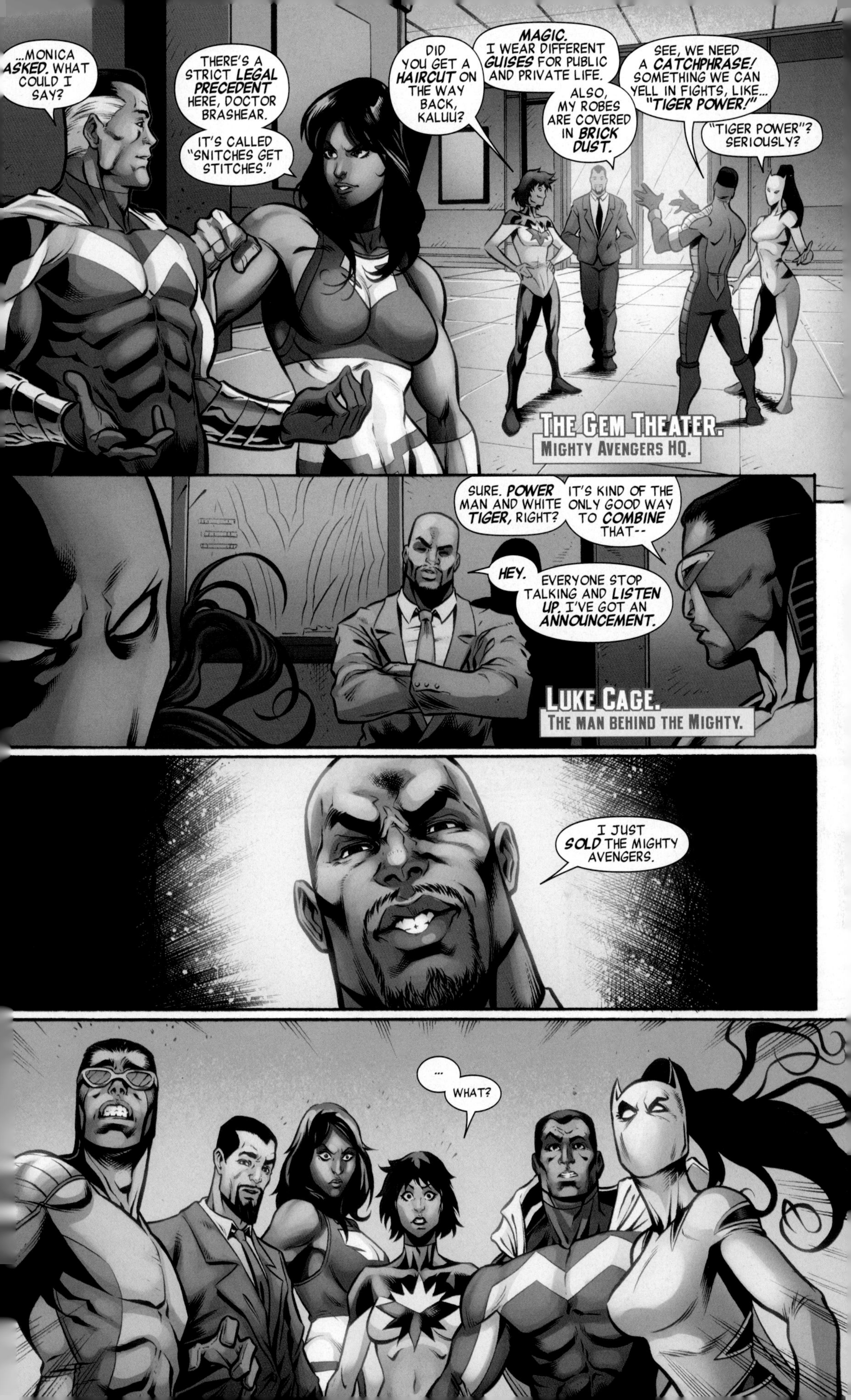

...MONICA ASKED. WHAT COULD I SAY?
THERE'S A STRICT LEGAL PRECEDENT HERE, DOCTOR BRASHEAR.
IT'S CALLED "SNITCHES GET STITCHES."
DID YOU GET A HAIRCUT ON THE WAY BACK, KALUU?
MAGIC. I WEAR DIFFERENT GUISES FOR PUBLIC AND PRIVATE LIFE.
ALSO, MY ROBES ARE COVERED IN BRICK DUST.
SEE, WE NEED A CATCHPHRASE! SOMETHING WE CAN YELL IN FIGHTS, LIKE... "TIGER POWER!"
"TIGER POWER"? SERIOUSLY?
THE GEM THEATER.
MIGHTY AVENGERS HQ.
SURE. POWER MAN AND WHITE TIGER, RIGHT?
IT'S KIND OF THE ONLY GOOD WAY TO COMBINE THAT--
HEY.
EVERYONE STOP TALKING AND LISTEN UP. I'VE GOT AN ANNOUNCEMENT.
LUKE CAGE.
THE MAN BEHIND THE MIGHTY.
I JUST SOLD THE MIGHTY AVENGERS.
... WHAT?

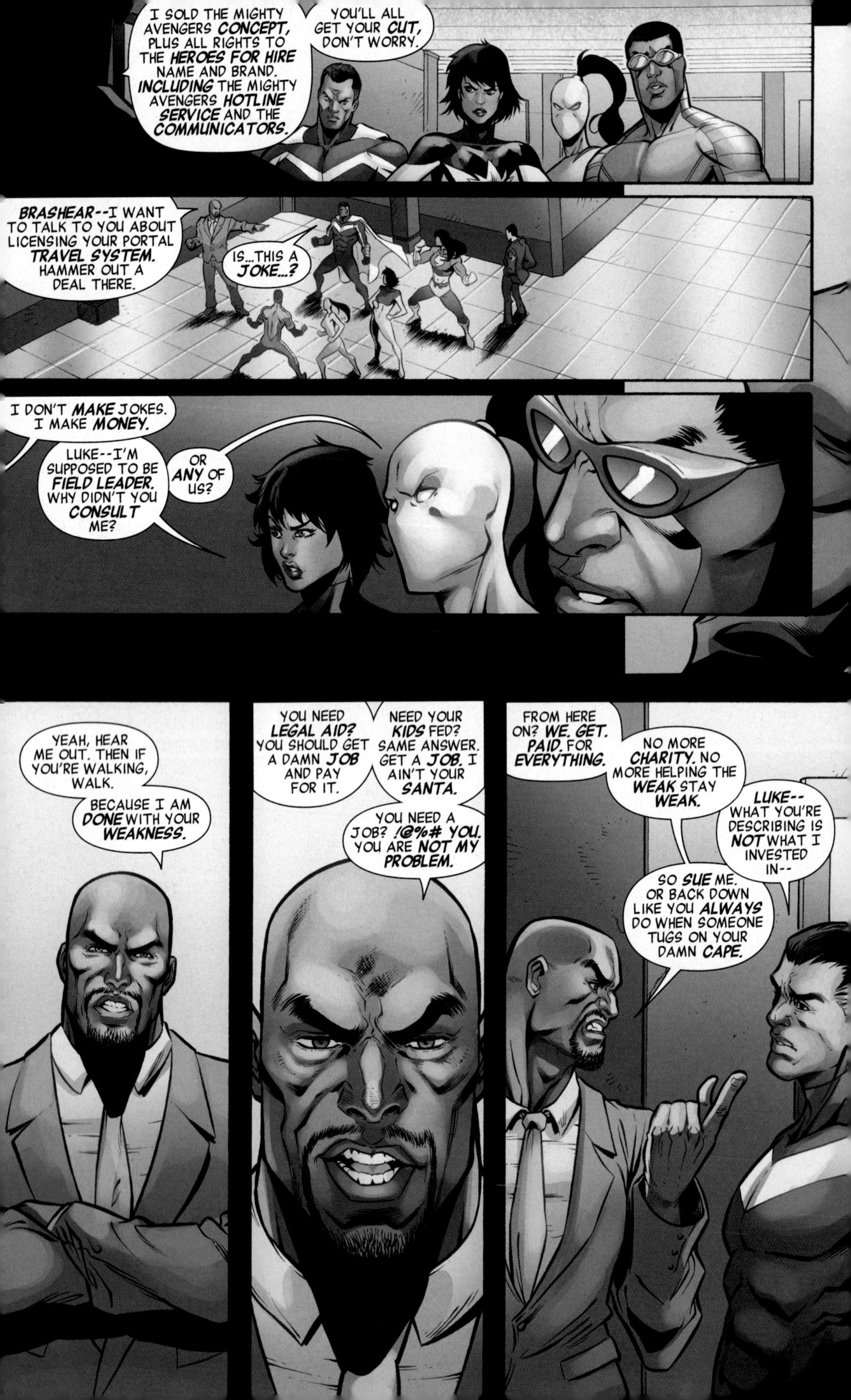
I SOLD THE MIGHTY AVENGERS CONCEPT, PLUS ALL RIGHTS TO THE HEROES FOR HIRE NAME AND BRAND. INCLUDING THE MIGHTY AVENGERS HOTLINE SERVICE AND THE COMMUNICATORS.
YOU'LL ALL GET YOUR CUT, DON'T WORRY.
BRASHEAR--I WANT TO TALK TO YOU ABOUT LICENSING YOUR PORTAL TRAVEL SYSTEM. HAMMER OUT A DEAL THERE.
IS...THIS A JOKE...?
I DON'T MAKE JOKES. I MAKE MONEY.
LUKE--I'M SUPPOSED TO BE FIELD LEADER. WHY DIDN'T YOU CONSULT ME?
OR ANY OF US?
YEAH, HEAR ME OUT. THEN IF YOU'RE WALKING, WALK.
BECAUSE I AM DONE WITH YOUR WEAKNESS.
YOU NEED LEGAL AID? YOU SHOULD GET A DAMN JOB AND PAY FOR IT.
NEED YOUR KIDS FED? SAME ANSWER. GET A JOB. I AIN'T YOUR SANTA.
YOU NEED A JOB? !@%# YOU. YOU ARE NOT MY PROBLEM.
FROM HERE ON? WE. GET. PAID. FOR EVERYTHING.
NO MORE CHARITY. NO MORE HELPING THE WEAK STAY WEAK.
LUKE--WHAT YOU'RE DESCRIBING IS NOT WHAT I INVESTED IN--
SO SUE ME. OR BACK DOWN LIKE YOU ALWAYS DO WHEN SOMEONE TUGS ON YOUR DAMN CAPE.

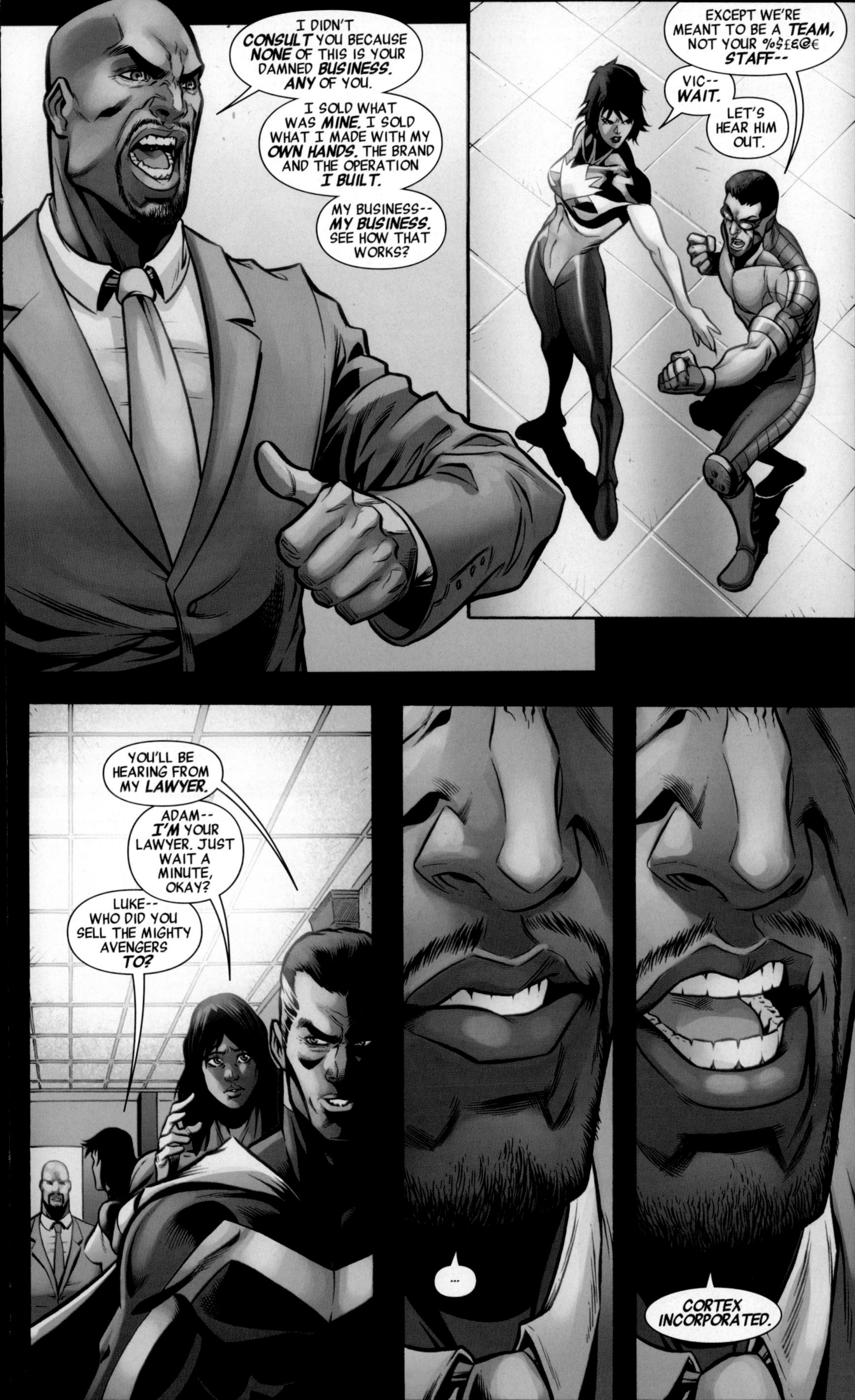
I DIDN'T CONSULT YOU BECAUSE NONE OF THIS IS YOUR DAMNED BUSINESS. ANY OF YOU.
I SOLD WHAT WAS MINE. I SOLD WHAT I MADE WITH MY OWN HANDS. THE BRAND AND THE OPERATION I BUILT.
MY BUSINESS-- MY BUSINESS. SEE HOW THAT WORKS?
EXCEPT WE'RE MEANT TO BE A TEAM, NOT YOUR %$£€@€ STAFF--
VIC-- WAIT.
LET'S HEAR HIM OUT.
YOU'LL BE HEARING FROM MY LAWYER.
ADAM-- I'M YOUR LAWYER. JUST WAIT A MINUTE, OKAY?
LUKE-- WHO DID YOU SELL THE MIGHTY AVENGERS TO?
...
CORTEX INCORPORATED.

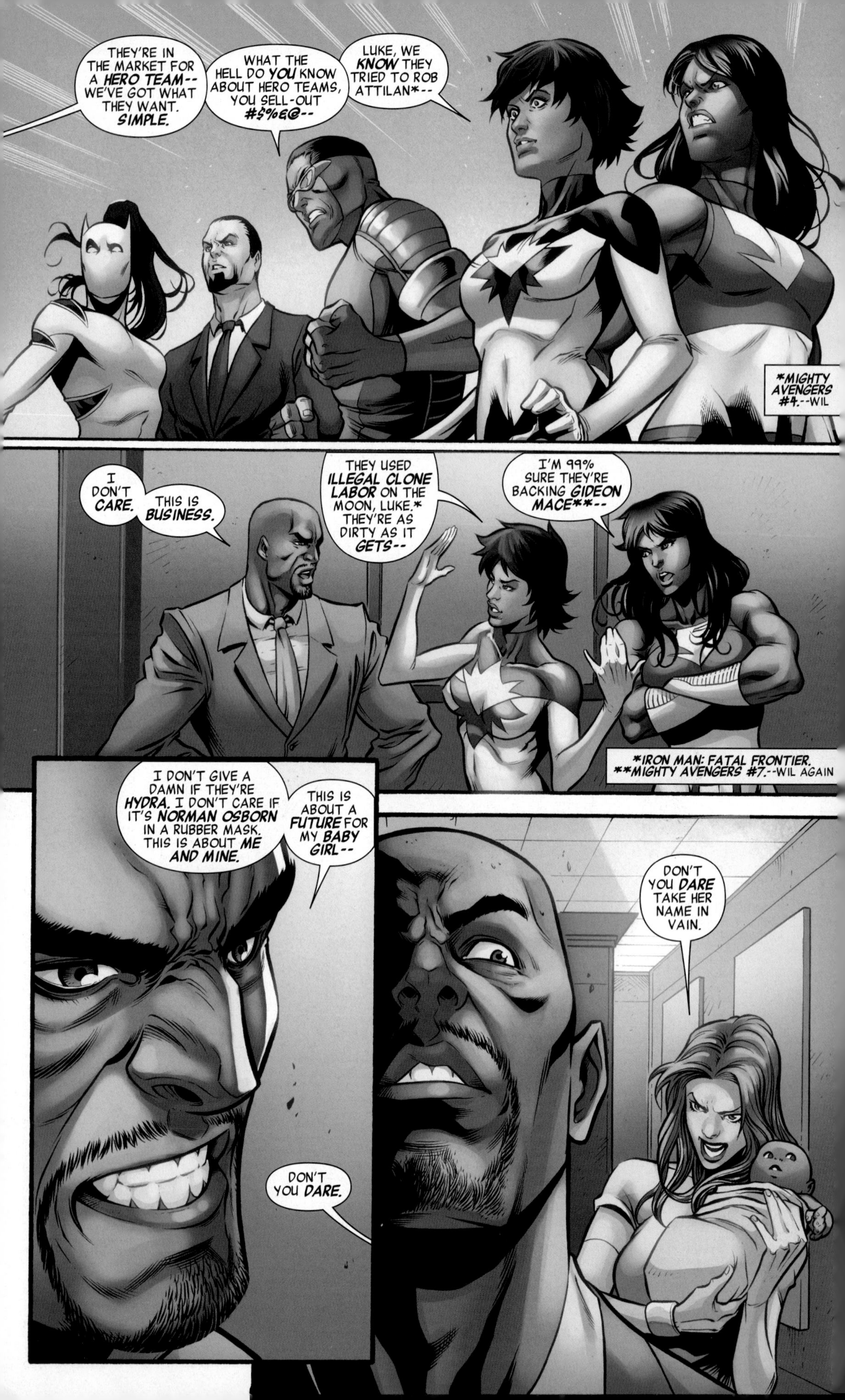
THEY'RE IN THE MARKET FOR A HERO TEAM-- WE'VE GOT WHAT THEY WANT. SIMPLE.
WHAT THE HELL DO YOU KNOW ABOUT HERO TEAMS, YOU SELL-OUT #$%&@--
LUKE, WE KNOW THEY TRIED TO ROB ATTILAN*--
*MIGHTY AVENGERS #4.--WIL
I DON'T CARE.
THIS IS BUSINESS.
THEY USED ILLEGAL CLONE LABOR ON THE MOON, LUKE.* THEY'RE AS DIRTY AS IT GETS--
I'M 99% SURE THEY'RE BACKING GIDEON MACE**--
*IRON MAN: FATAL FRONTIER.
**MIGHTY AVENGERS #7.--WIL AGAIN
I DON'T GIVE A DAMN IF THEY'RE HYDRA. I DON'T CARE IF IT'S NORMAN OSBORN IN A RUBBER MASK. THIS IS ABOUT ME AND MINE.
THIS IS ABOUT A FUTURE FOR MY BABY GIRL--
DON'T YOU DARE TAKE HER NAME IN VAIN.
DON'T YOU DARE.

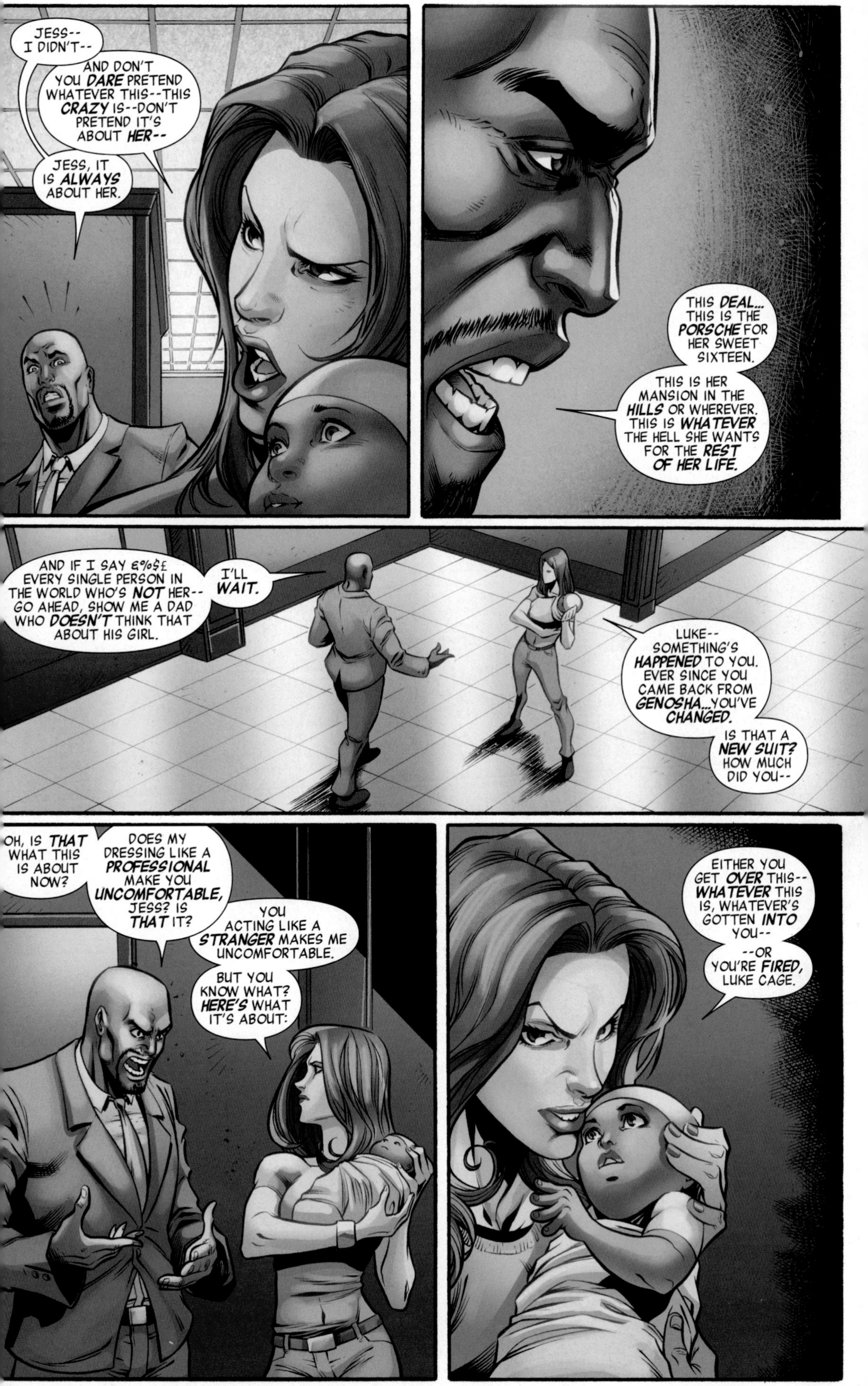
JESS-- I DIDN'T--
AND DON'T YOU DARE PRETEND WHATEVER THIS--THIS CRAZY IS--DON'T PRETEND IT'S ABOUT HER--
JESS, IT IS ALWAYS ABOUT HER.
THIS DEAL... THIS IS THE PORSCHE FOR HER SWEET SIXTEEN.
THIS IS HER MANSION IN THE HILLS OR WHEREVER. THIS IS WHATEVER THE HELL SHE WANTS FOR THE REST OF HER LIFE.
AND IF I SAY &%$£ EVERY SINGLE PERSON IN THE WORLD WHO'S NOT HER--GO AHEAD, SHOW ME A DAD WHO DOESN'T THINK THAT ABOUT HIS GIRL.
I'LL WAIT.
LUKE--SOMETHING'S HAPPENED TO YOU. EVER SINCE YOU CAME BACK FROM GENOSHA...YOU'VE CHANGED.
IS THAT A NEW SUIT? HOW MUCH DID YOU--
OH, IS THAT WHAT THIS IS ABOUT NOW?
DOES MY DRESSING LIKE A PROFESSIONAL MAKE YOU UNCOMFORTABLE, JESS? IS THAT IT?
YOU ACTING LIKE A STRANGER MAKES ME UNCOMFORTABLE.
BUT YOU KNOW WHAT? HERE'S WHAT IT'S ABOUT:
EITHER YOU GET OVER THIS--WHATEVER THIS IS, WHATEVER'S GOTTEN INTO YOU--
--OR YOU'RE FIRED, LUKE CAGE.

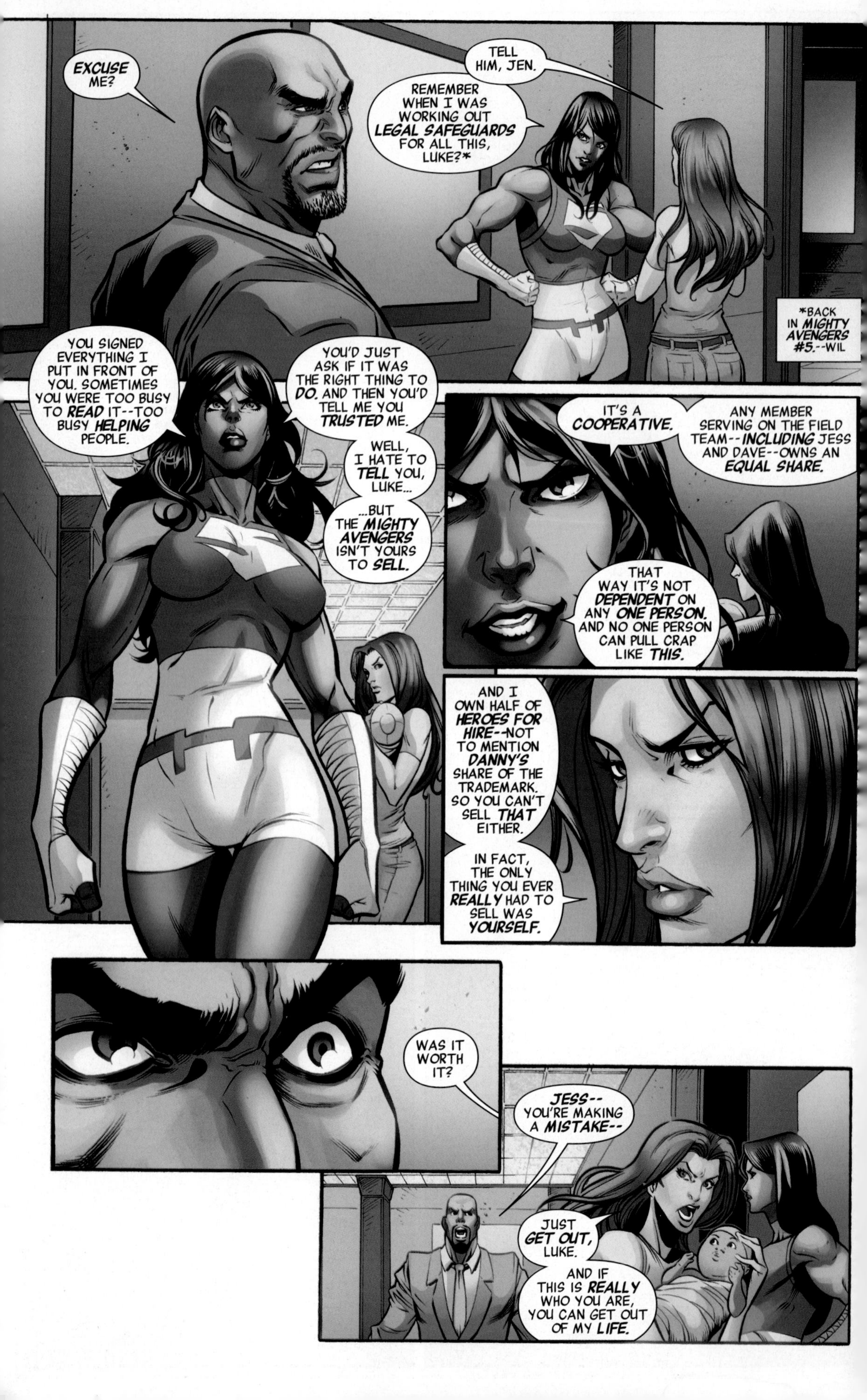
EXCUSE ME?
TELL HIM, JEN.
REMEMBER WHEN I WAS WORKING OUT LEGAL SAFEGUARDS FOR ALL THIS, LUKE?*
*BACK IN MIGHTY AVENGERS #5.--WIL
YOU SIGNED EVERYTHING I PUT IN FRONT OF YOU. SOMETIMES YOU WERE TOO BUSY TO READ IT--TOO BUSY HELPING PEOPLE.
YOU'D JUST ASK IF IT WAS THE RIGHT THING TO DO. AND THEN YOU'D TELL ME YOU TRUSTED ME.
WELL, I HATE TO TELL YOU, LUKE...
...BUT THE MIGHTY AVENGERS ISN'T YOURS TO SELL.
IT'S A COOPERATIVE.
ANY MEMBER SERVING ON THE FIELD TEAM--INCLUDING JESS AND DAVE--OWNS AN EQUAL SHARE.
THAT WAY IT'S NOT DEPENDENT ON ANY ONE PERSON. AND NO ONE PERSON CAN PULL CRAP LIKE THIS.
AND I OWN HALF OF HEROES FOR HIRE--NOT TO MENTION DANNY'S SHARE OF THE TRADEMARK. SO YOU CAN'T SELL THAT EITHER.
IN FACT, THE ONLY THING YOU EVER REALLY HAD TO SELL WAS YOURSELF.
WAS IT WORTH IT?
JESS-- YOU'RE MAKING A MISTAKE--
JUST GET OUT, LUKE.
AND IF THIS IS REALLY WHO YOU ARE, YOU CAN GET OUT OF MY LIFE.

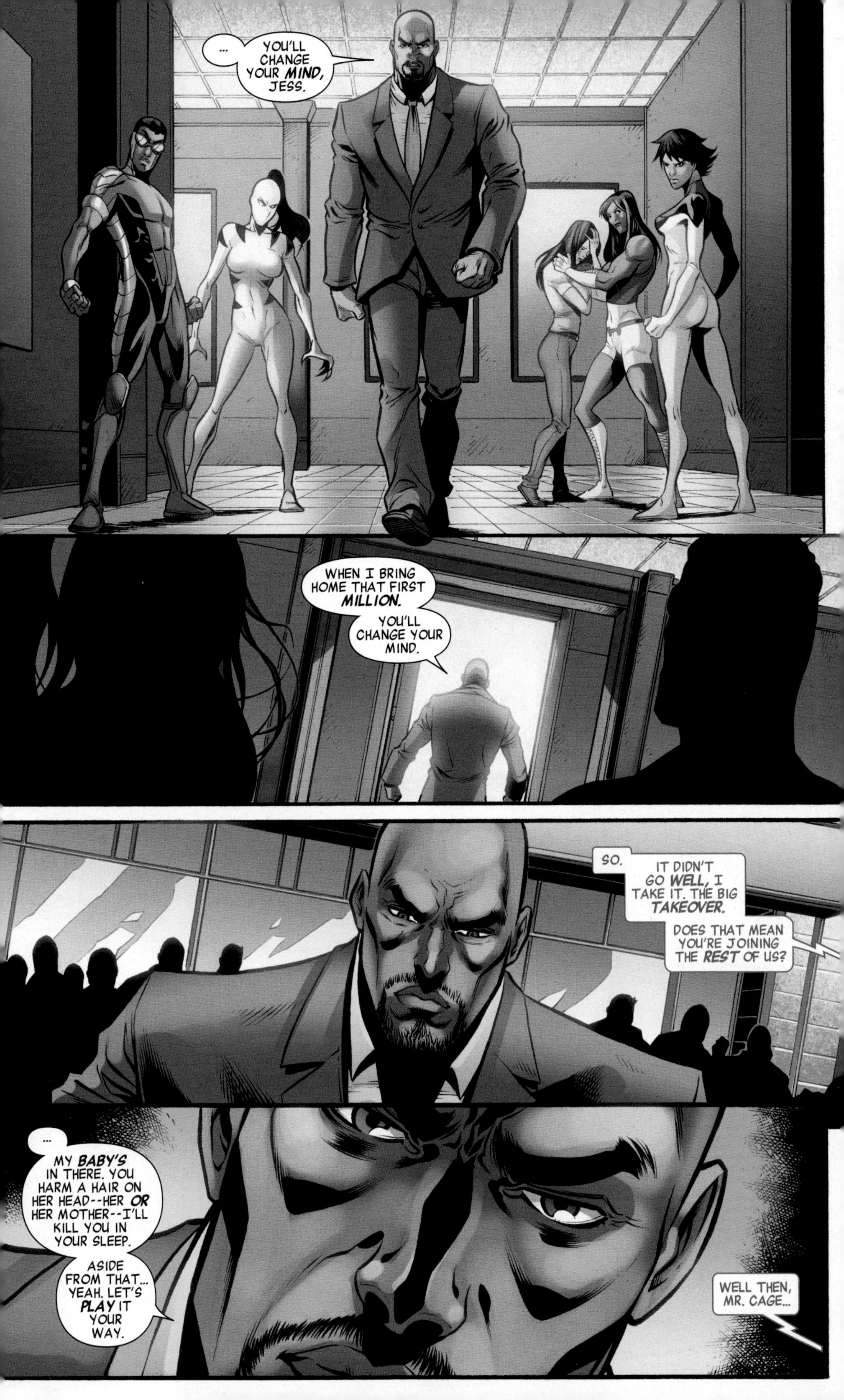
...
YOU'LL CHANGE YOUR MIND, JESS.
WHEN I BRING HOME THAT FIRST MILLION.
YOU'LL CHANGE YOUR MIND.
SO.
IT DIDN'T GO WELL, I TAKE IT. THE BIG TAKEOVER.
DOES THAT MEAN YOU'RE JOINING THE REST OF US?
...
MY BABY'S IN THERE. YOU HARM A HAIR ON HER HEAD--HER OR HER MOTHER--I'LL KILL YOU IN YOUR SLEEP.
ASIDE FROM THAT... YEAH. LET'S PLAY IT YOUR WAY.
WELL THEN, MR. CAGE...

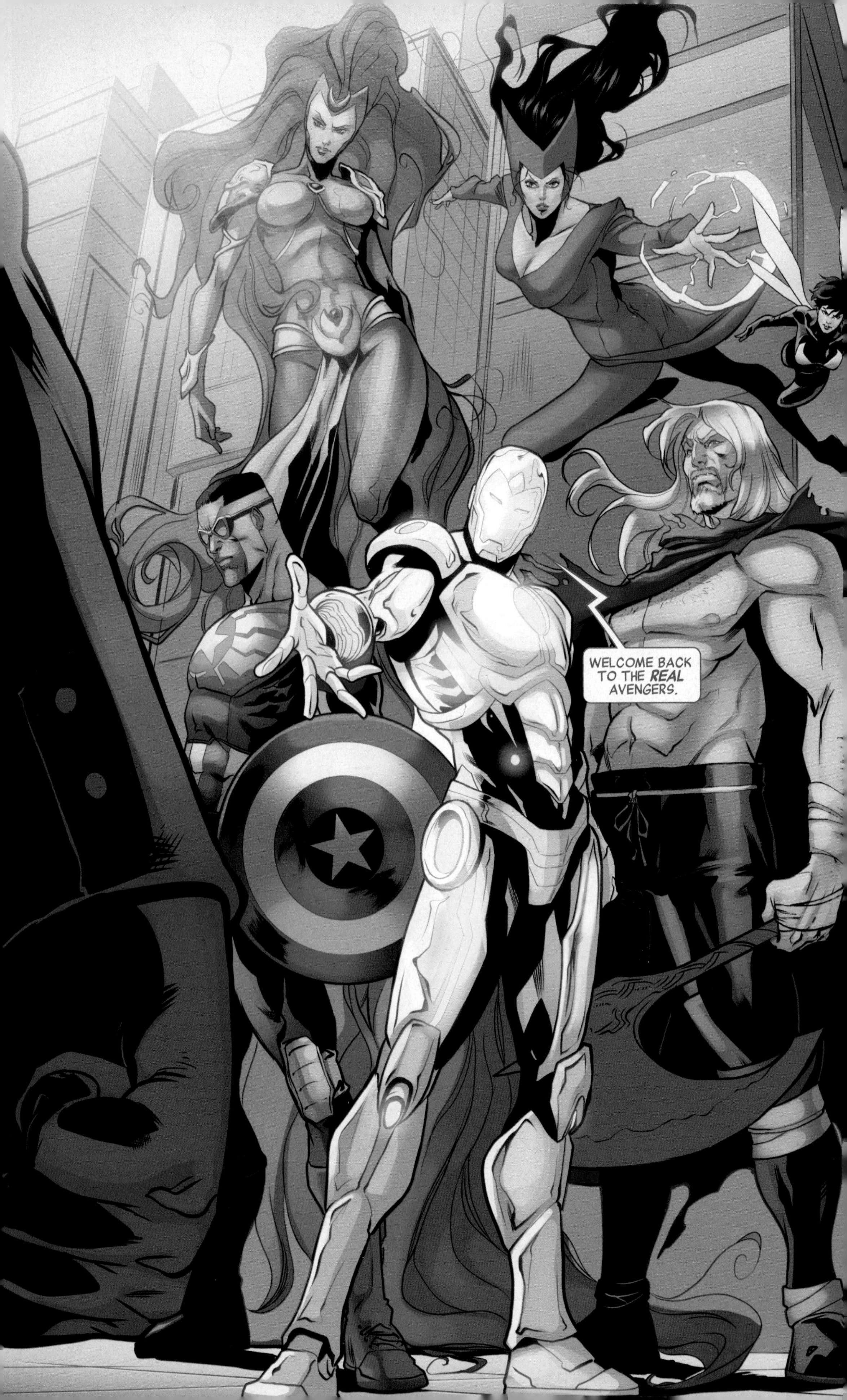
WELCOME BACK TO THE *REAL* AVENGERS.

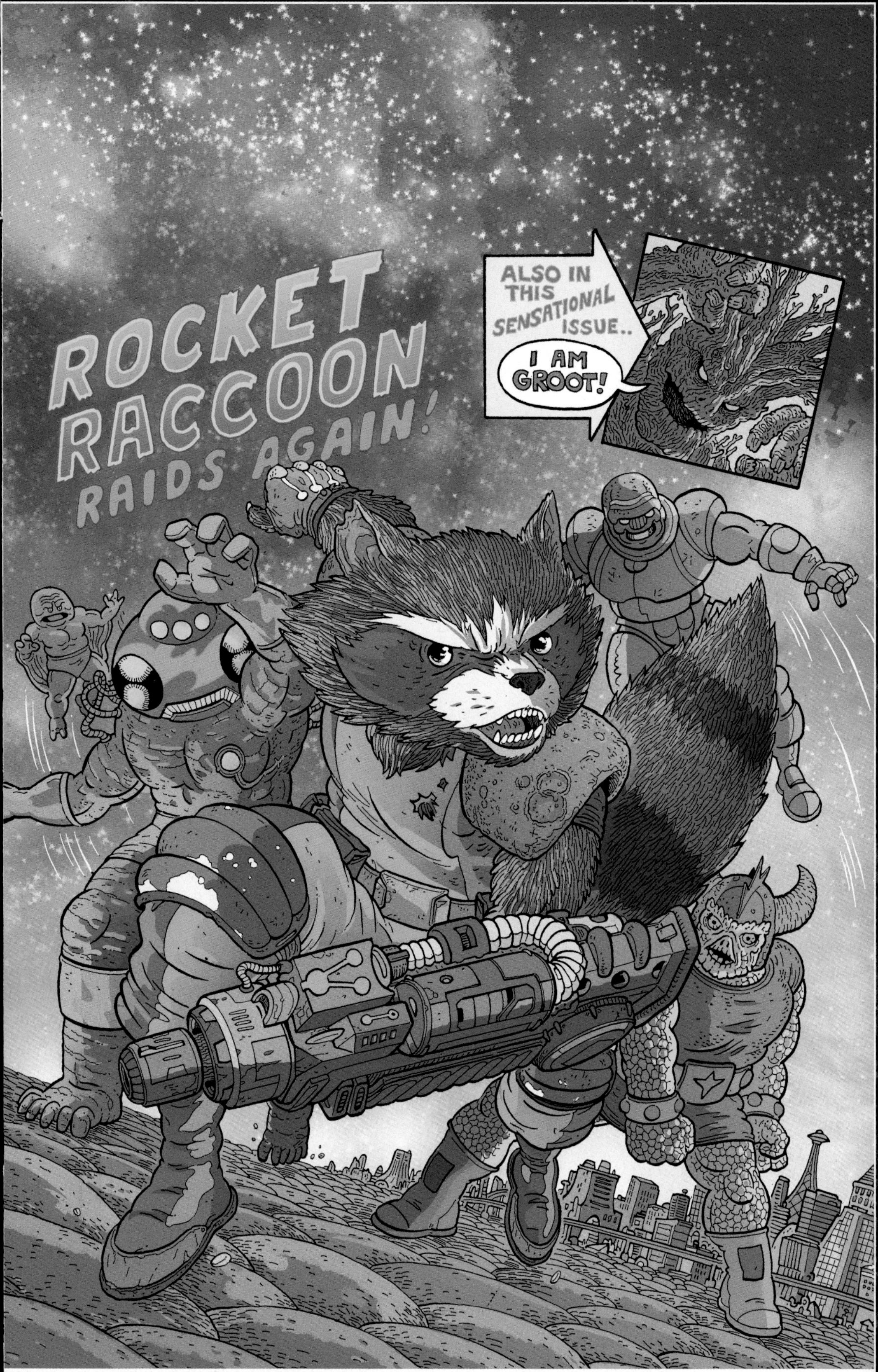
ROCKET RACCOON RAIDS AGAIN!
ALSO IN THIS SENSATIONAL ISSUE..
I AM GROOT!

#1 ROCKET & GROOT VARIANT BY ULISES FARINAS & RYAN HILL

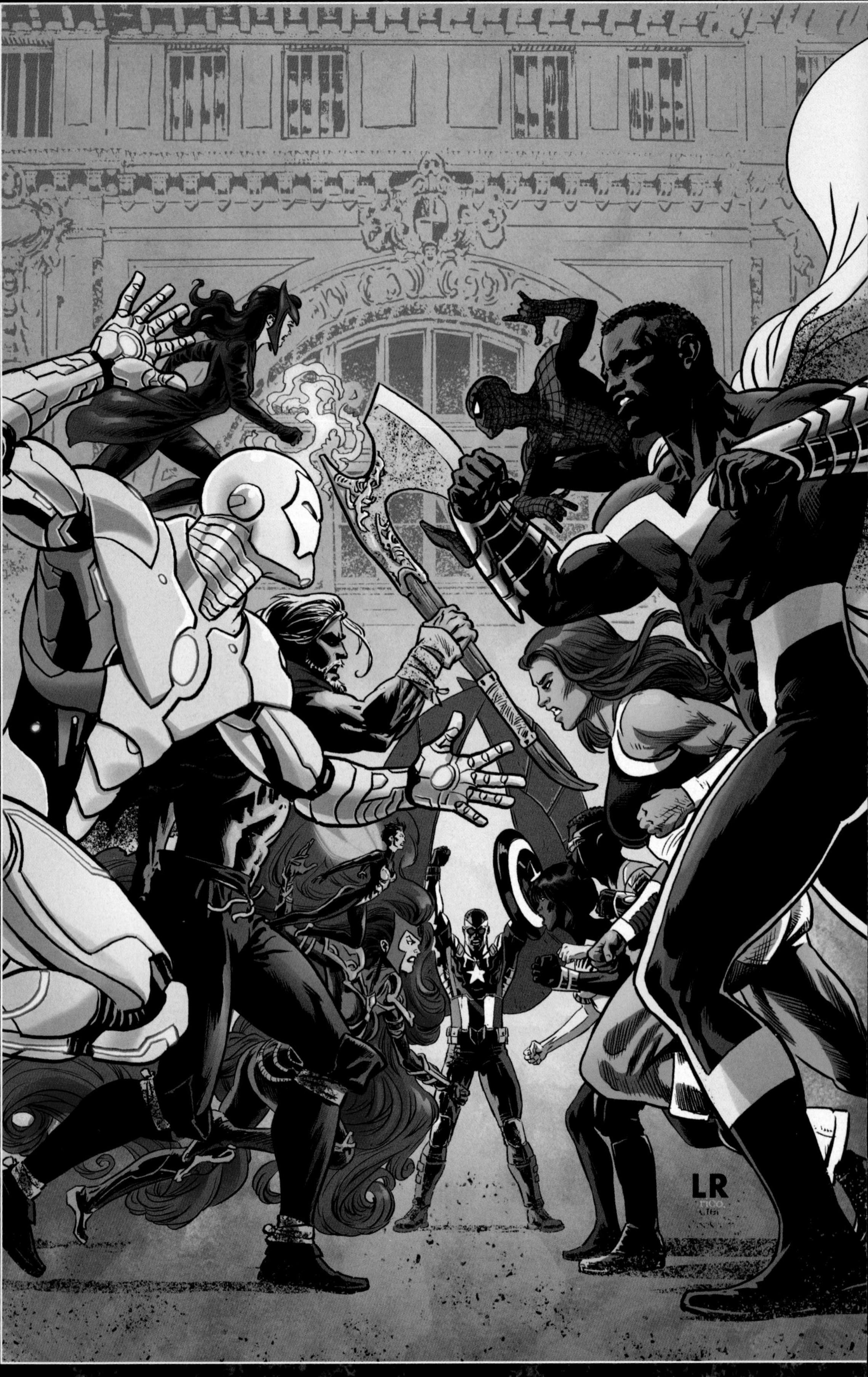
LR

3

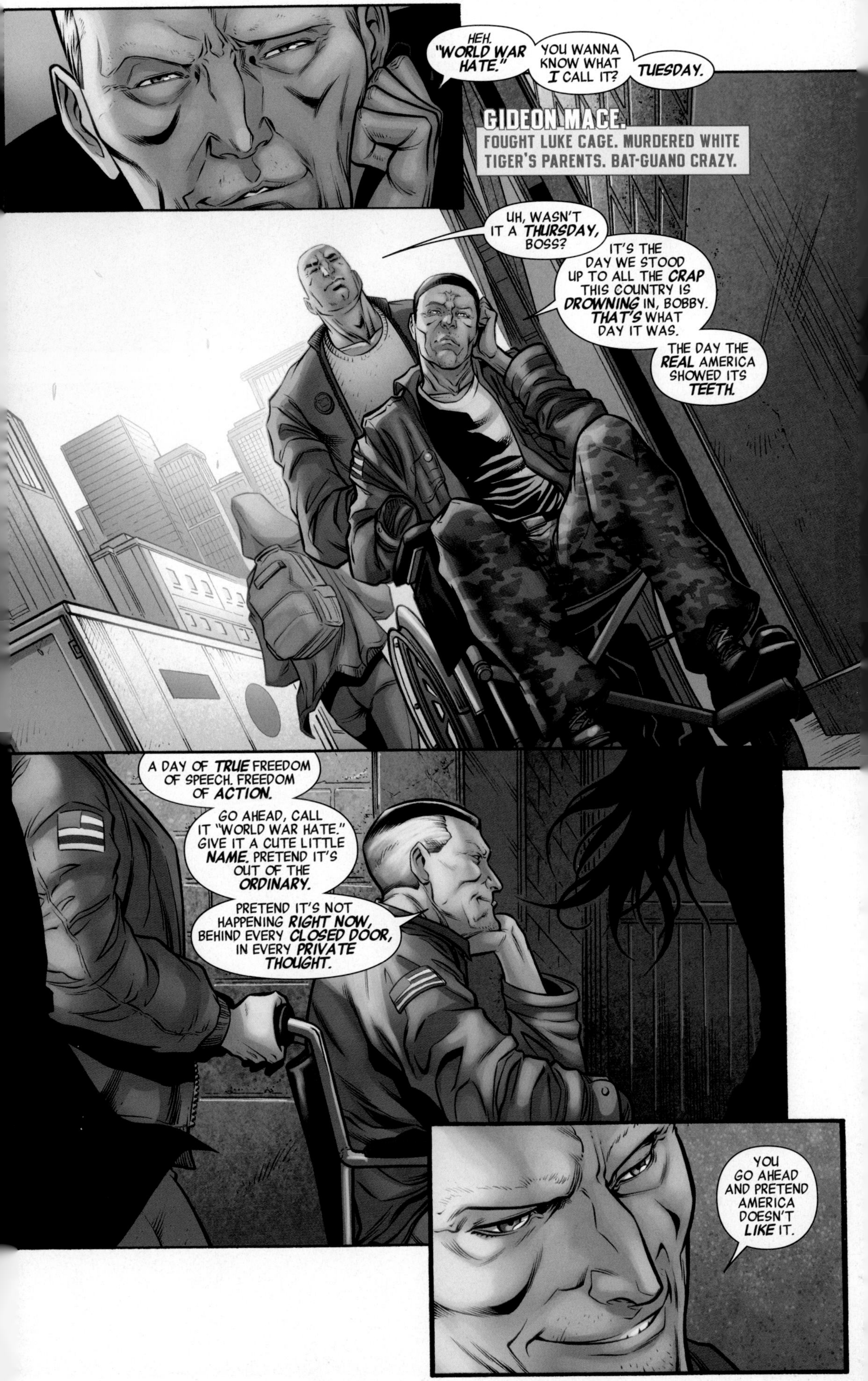
HEH. "WORLD WAR HATE."
YOU WANNA KNOW WHAT I CALL IT?
TUESDAY.
GIDEON MACE.
FOUGHT LUKE CAGE. MURDERED WHITE TIGER'S PARENTS. BAT-GUANO CRAZY.
UH, WASN'T IT A THURSDAY, BOSS?
IT'S THE DAY WE STOOD UP TO ALL THE CRAP THIS COUNTRY IS DROWNING IN, BOBBY. THAT'S WHAT DAY IT WAS.
THE DAY THE REAL AMERICA SHOWED ITS TEETH.
A DAY OF TRUE FREEDOM OF SPEECH. FREEDOM OF ACTION.
GO AHEAD, CALL IT "WORLD WAR HATE." GIVE IT A CUTE LITTLE NAME. PRETEND IT'S OUT OF THE ORDINARY.
PRETEND IT'S NOT HAPPENING RIGHT NOW, BEHIND EVERY CLOSED DOOR, IN EVERY PRIVATE THOUGHT.
YOU GO AHEAD AND PRETEND AMERICA DOESN'T LIKE IT.

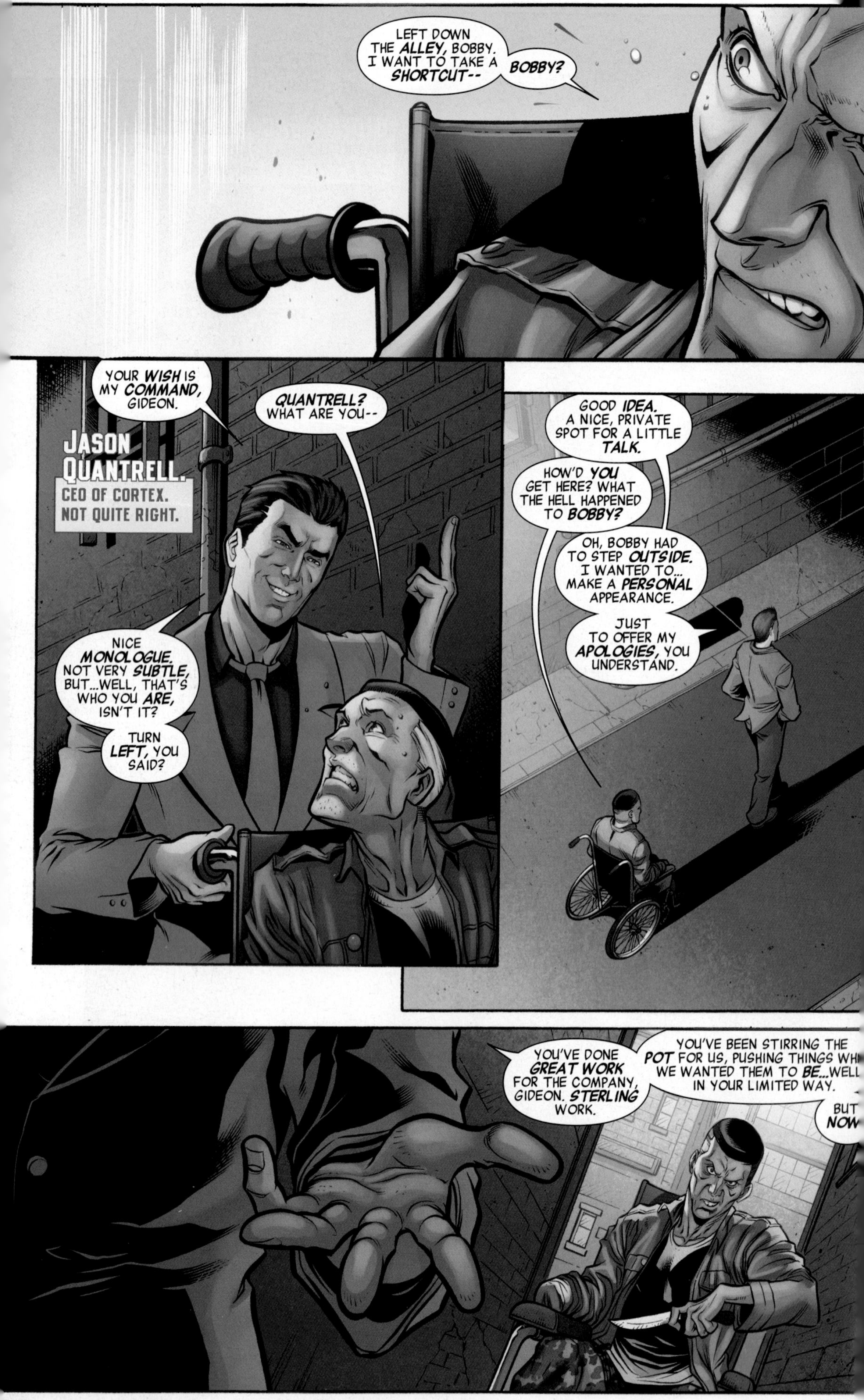

LEFT DOWN THE ALLEY, BOBBY. I WANT TO TAKE A SHORTCUT--
BOBBY?
YOUR WISH IS MY COMMAND, GIDEON.
QUANTRELL? WHAT ARE YOU--
JASON QUANTRELL. CEO OF CORTEX. NOT QUITE RIGHT.
NICE MONOLOGUE. NOT VERY SUBTLE, BUT...WELL, THAT'S WHO YOU ARE, ISN'T IT?
TURN LEFT, YOU SAID?
GOOD IDEA. A NICE, PRIVATE SPOT FOR A LITTLE TALK.
HOW'D YOU GET HERE? WHAT THE HELL HAPPENED TO BOBBY?
OH, BOBBY HAD TO STEP OUTSIDE. I WANTED TO... MAKE A PERSONAL APPEARANCE.
JUST TO OFFER MY APOLOGIES, YOU UNDERSTAND.
YOU'VE DONE GREAT WORK FOR THE COMPANY, GIDEON. STERLING WORK.

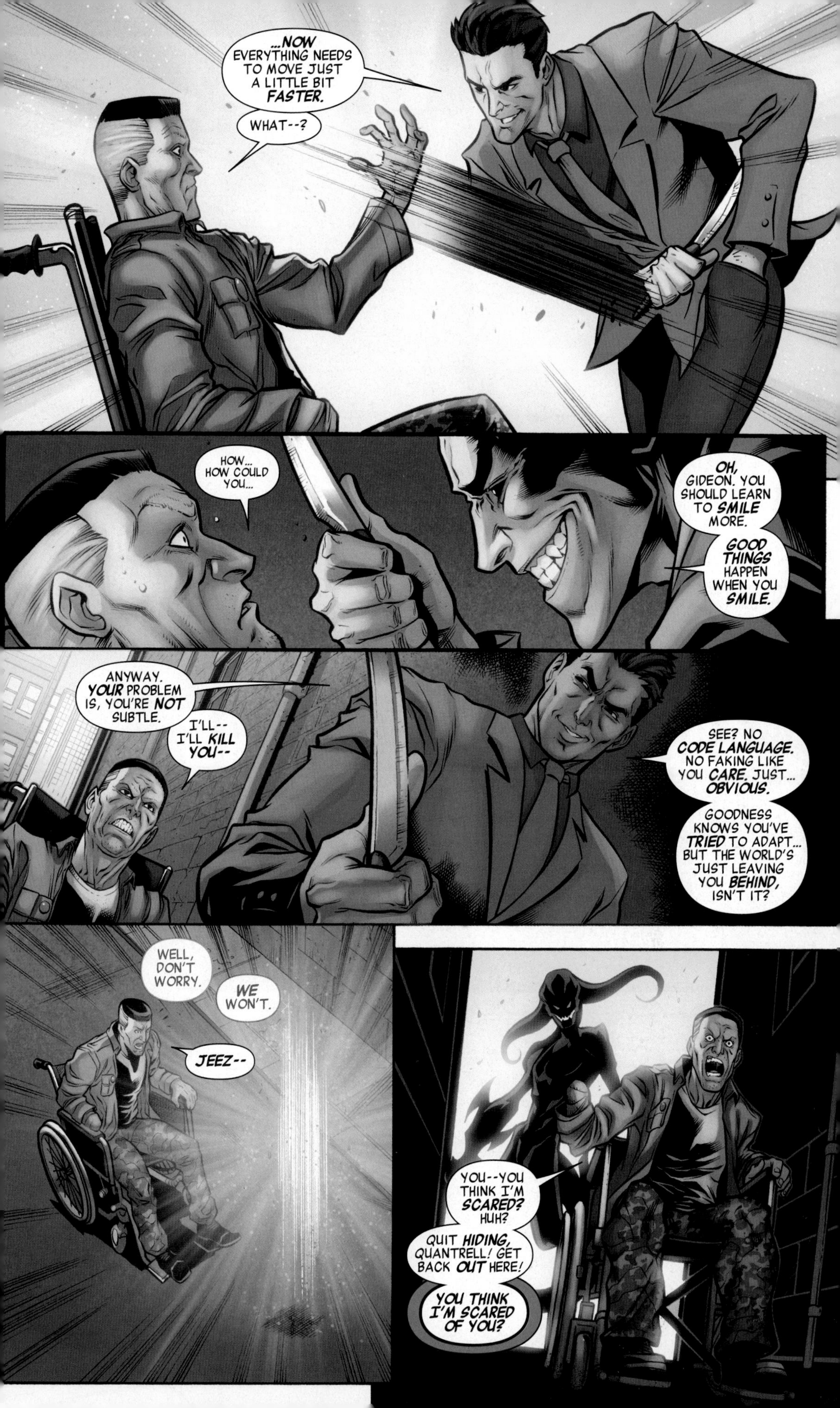

...NOW EVERYTHING NEEDS TO MOVE JUST A LITTLE BIT FASTER.
WHAT--?
HOW... HOW COULD YOU...
OH, GIDEON. YOU SHOULD LEARN TO SMILE MORE.
GOOD THINGS HAPPEN WHEN YOU SMILE.
ANYWAY. YOUR PROBLEM IS, YOU'RE NOT SUBTLE.
I'LL-- I'LL KILL YOU--
SEE? NO CODE LANGUAGE. NO FAKING LIKE YOU CARE. JUST... OBVIOUS.
GOODNESS KNOWS YOU'VE TRIED TO ADAPT... BUT THE WORLD'S JUST LEAVING YOU BEHIND, ISN'T IT?
WELL, DON'T WORRY.
WE WON'T.
JEEZ--
YOU--YOU THINK I'M SCARED? HUH?
QUIT HIDING, QUANTRELL! GET BACK OUT HERE!
YOU THINK I'M SCARED OF YOU?

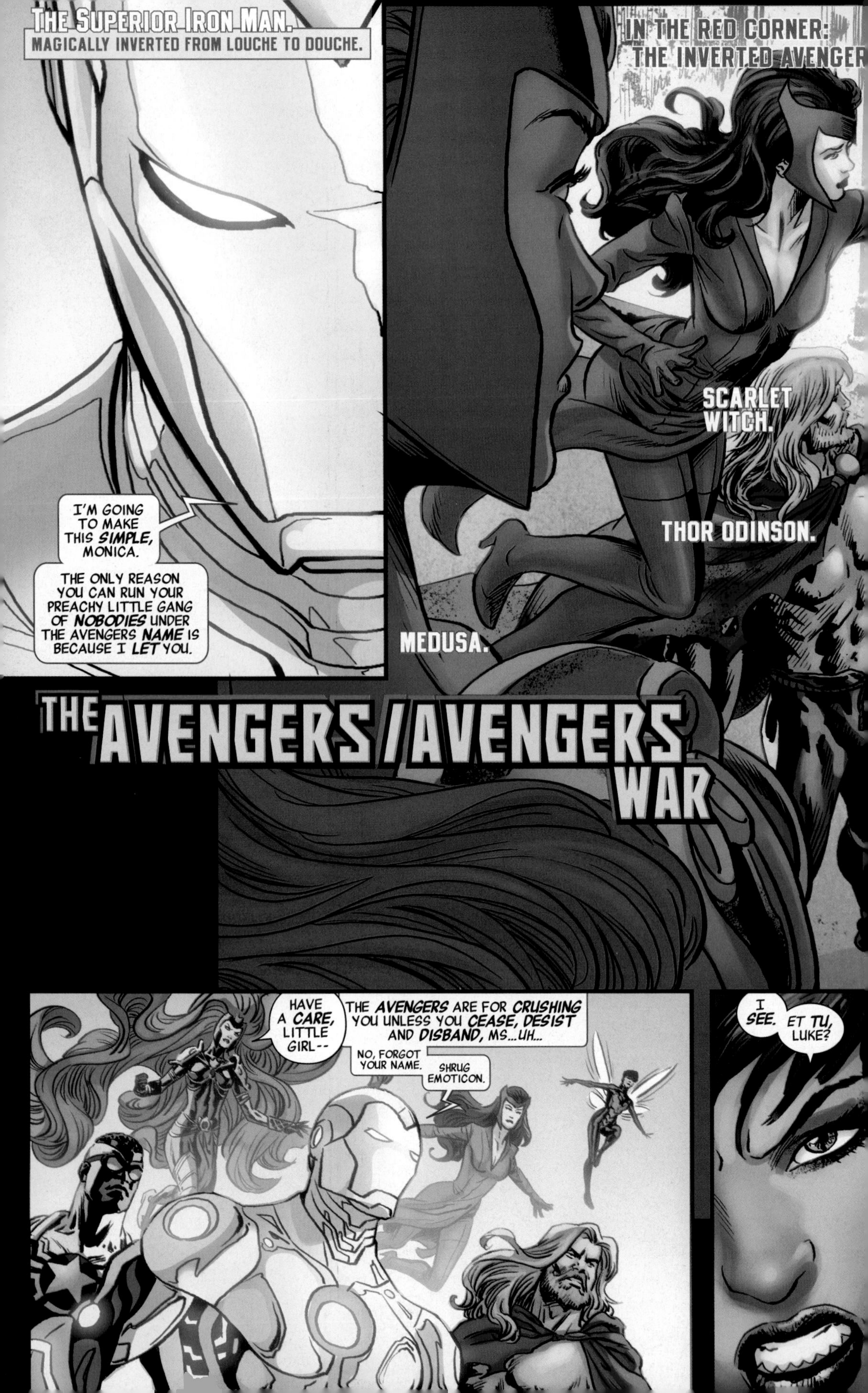
THE SUPERIOR IRON MAN.
MAGICALLY INVERTED FROM LOUCHE TO DOUCHE.
I'M GOING TO MAKE THIS SIMPLE, MONICA.
THE ONLY REASON YOU CAN RUN YOUR PREACHY LITTLE GANG OF NOBODIES UNDER THE AVENGERS NAME IS BECAUSE I LET YOU.
IN THE RED CORNER: THE INVERTED AVENGER
SCARLET WITCH.
THOR ODINSON.
MEDUSA.
THE AVENGERS / AVENGERS WAR
HAVE A CARE, LITTLE GIRL--
THE AVENGERS ARE FOR CRUSHING YOU UNLESS YOU CEASE, DESIST AND DISBAND, MS...UH...
NO, FORGOT YOUR NAME.
SHRUG EMOTICON.
I SEE.
ET TU, LUKE?

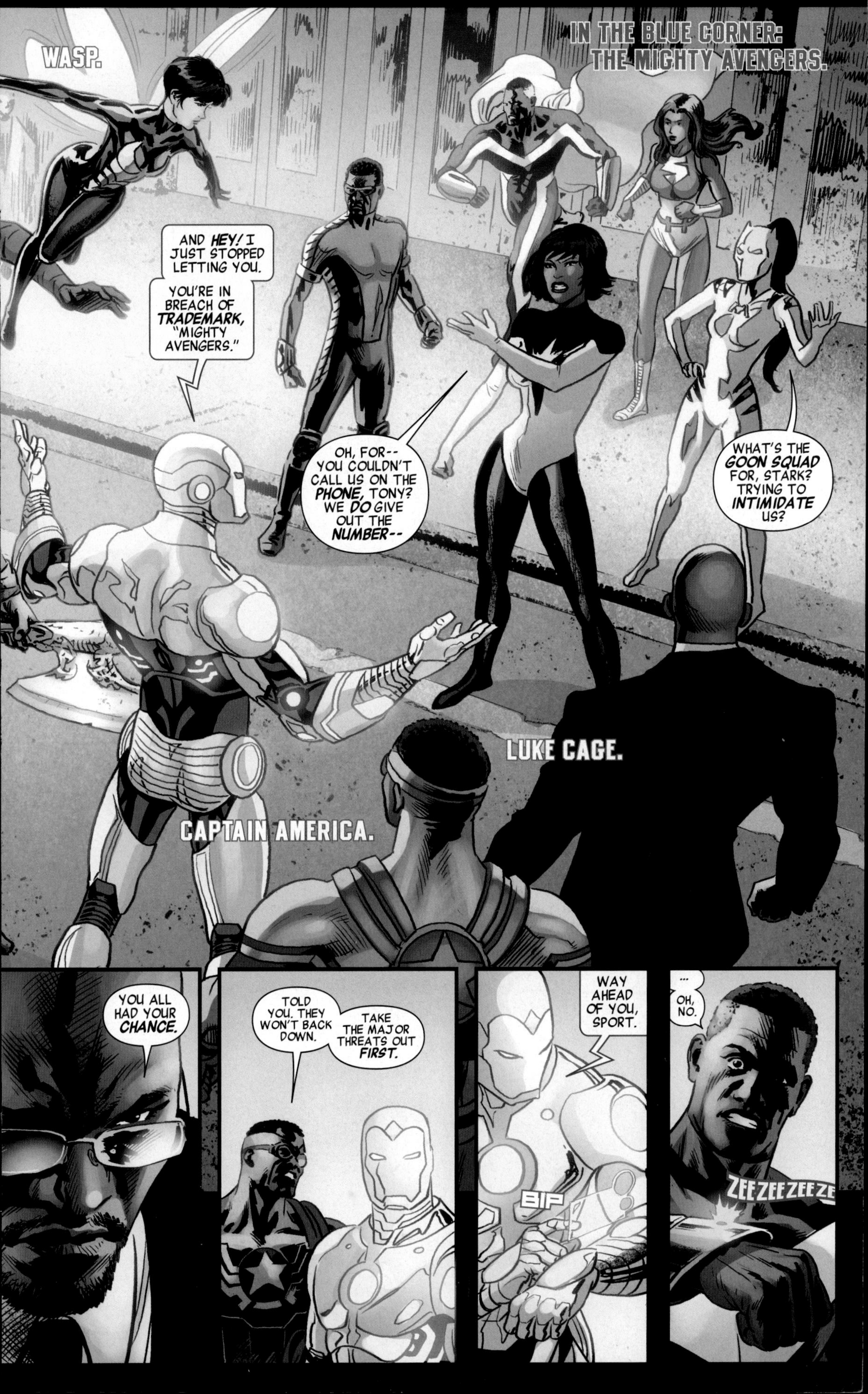
WASP.
IN THE BLUE CORNER: THE MIGHTY AVENGERS.
AND HEY! I JUST STOPPED LETTING YOU.
YOU'RE IN BREACH OF TRADEMARK, "MIGHTY AVENGERS."
OH, FOR-- YOU COULDN'T CALL US ON THE PHONE, TONY? WE DO GIVE OUT THE NUMBER--
WHAT'S THE GOON SQUAD FOR, STARK? TRYING TO INTIMIDATE US?
LUKE CAGE.
CAPTAIN AMERICA.
YOU ALL HAD YOUR CHANCE.
TOLD YOU. THEY WON'T BACK DOWN.
TAKE THE MAJOR THREATS OUT FIRST.
WAY AHEAD OF YOU, SPORT.
BIP
...
OH, NO.
ZEEZEEZEEZE

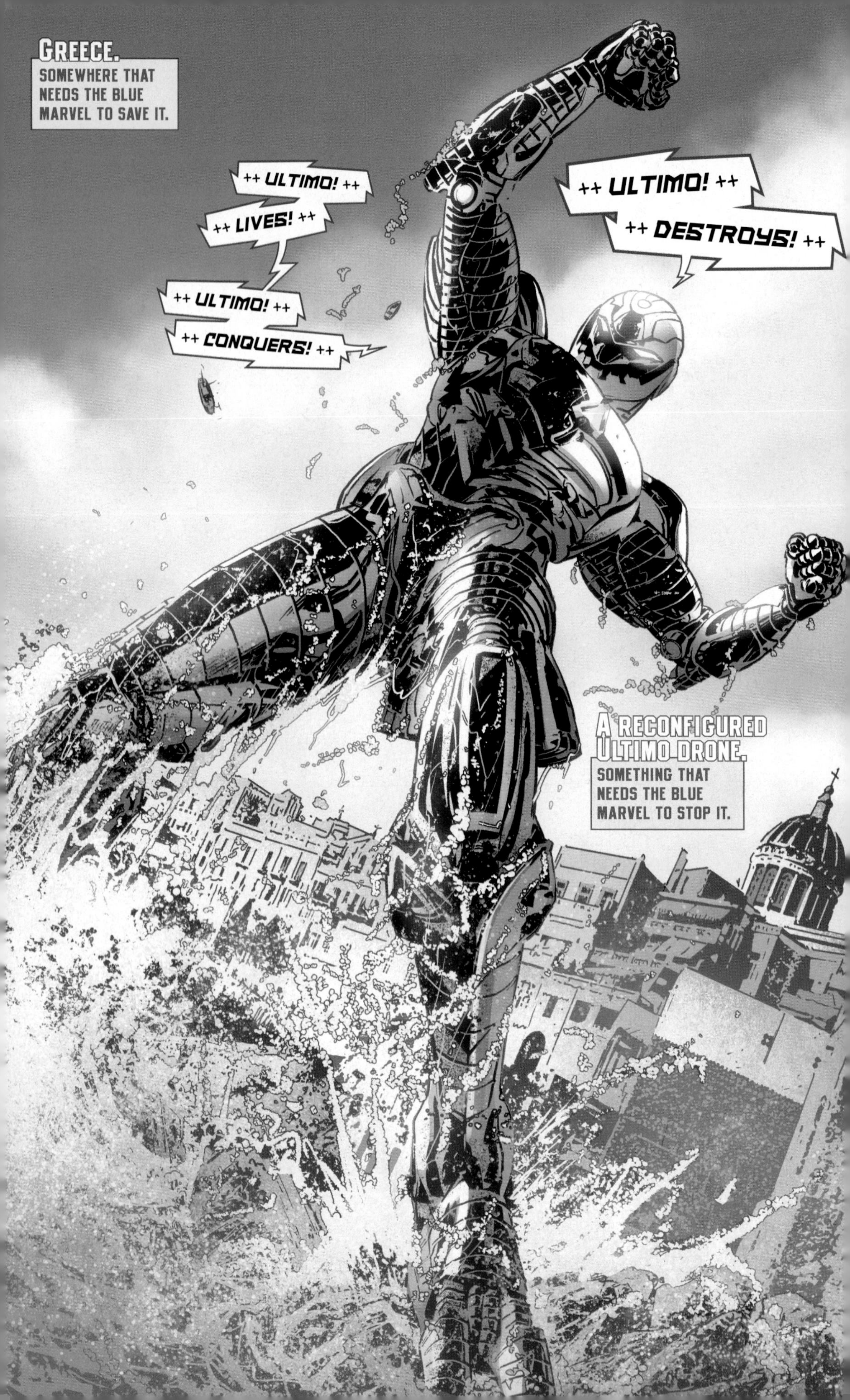
GREECE.
SOMEWHERE THAT NEEDS THE BLUE MARVEL TO SAVE IT.
++ ULTIMO! ++
++ LIVES! ++
++ ULTIMO! ++
++ CONQUERS! ++
++ ULTIMO! ++
++ DESTROYS! ++
A RECONFIGURED ULTIMO DRONE.
SOMETHING THAT NEEDS THE BLUE MARVEL TO STOP IT.

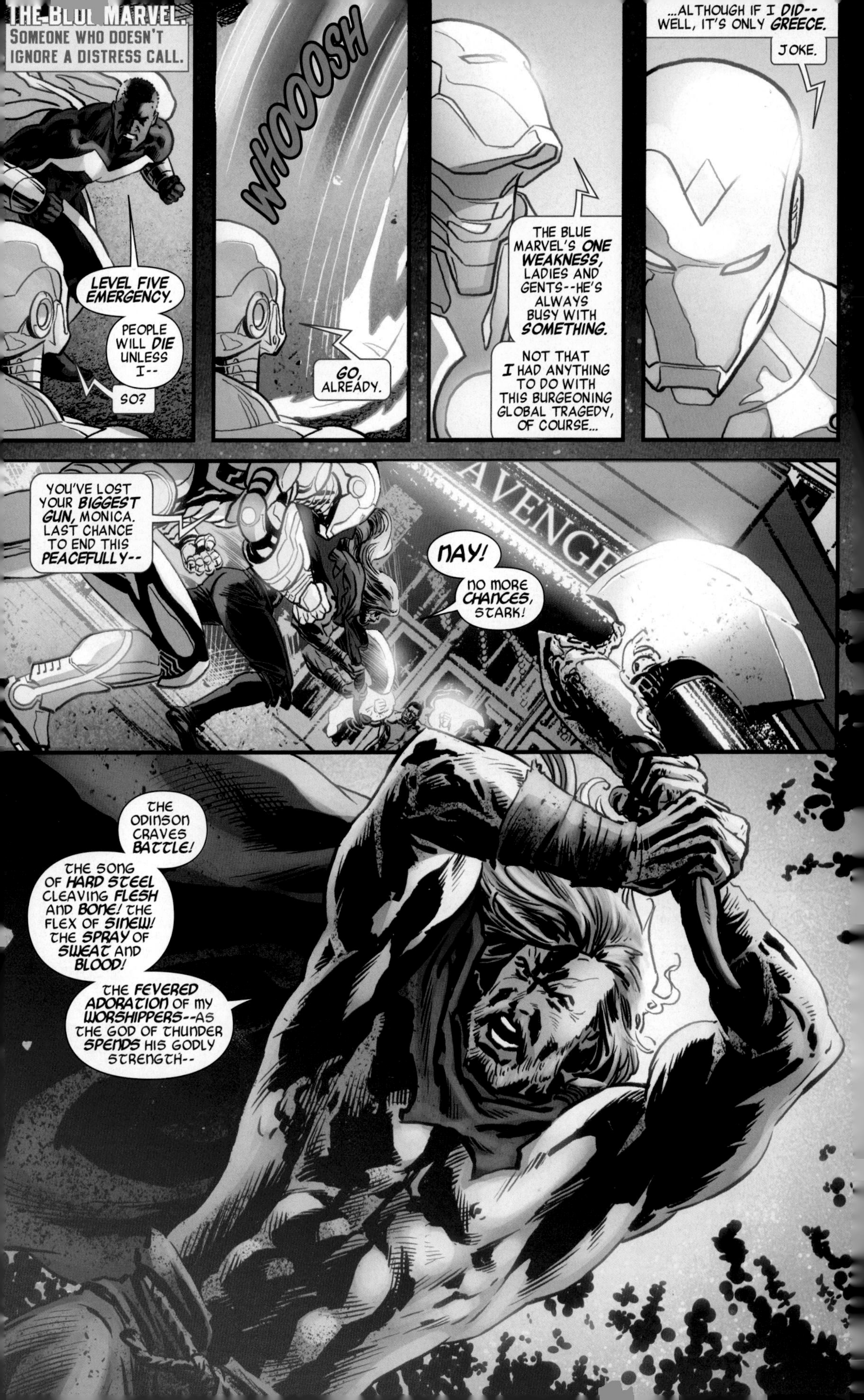

THE BLUE MARVEL.
SOMEONE WHO DOESN'T IGNORE A DISTRESS CALL.
LEVEL FIVE EMERGENCY.
PEOPLE WILL DIE UNLESS I--
SO?
WHOOOSH
GO, ALREADY.
THE BLUE MARVEL'S ONE WEAKNESS, LADIES AND GENTS--HE'S ALWAYS BUSY WITH SOMETHING.
NOT THAT I HAD ANYTHING TO DO WITH THIS BURGEONING GLOBAL TRAGEDY, OF COURSE...
...ALTHOUGH IF I DID--WELL, IT'S ONLY GREECE.
JOKE.
YOU'VE LOST YOUR BIGGEST GUN, MONICA. LAST CHANCE TO END THIS PEACEFULLY--
AVENGE
NAY!
NO MORE CHANCES, STARK!
THE ODINSON CRAVES BATTLE!
THE SONG OF HARD STEEL CLEAVING FLESH AND BONE! THE FLEX OF SINEW! THE SPRAY OF SWEAT AND BLOOD!
THE FEVERED ADORATION OF MY WORSHIPPERS--AS THE GOD OF THUNDER SPENDS HIS GODLY STRENGTH--

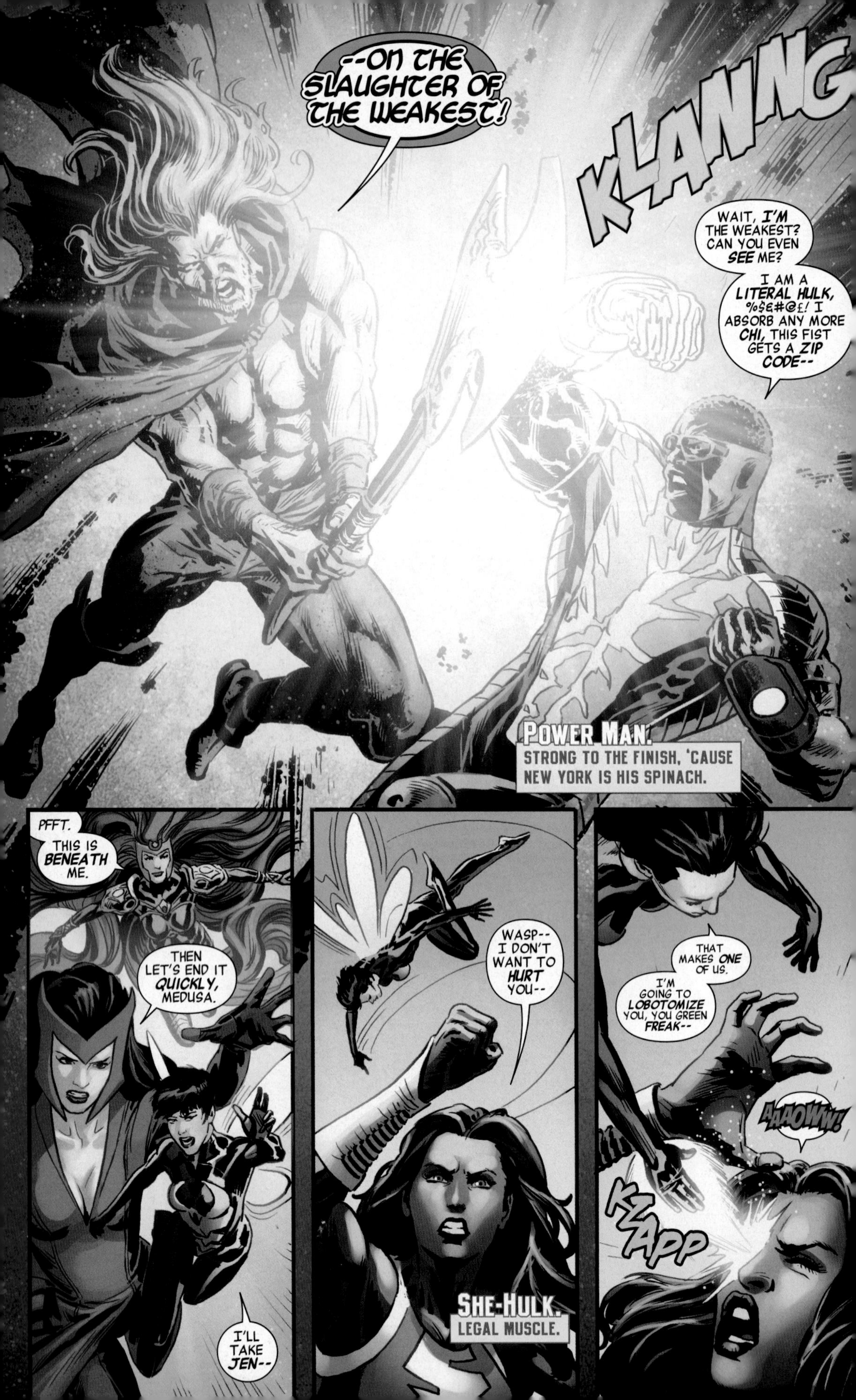
--ON THE SLAUGHTER OF THE WEAKEST!
KLANNG
WAIT, I'M THE WEAKEST? CAN YOU EVEN SEE ME?
I AM A LITERAL HULK, %$&#@£! I ABSORB ANY MORE CHI, THIS FIST GETS A ZIP CODE--
POWER MAN.
STRONG TO THE FINISH, 'CAUSE NEW YORK IS HIS SPINACH.
PFFT.
THIS IS BENEATH ME.
THEN LET'S END IT QUICKLY, MEDUSA.
I'LL TAKE JEN--
WASP-- I DON'T WANT TO HURT YOU--
SHE-HULK.
LEGAL MUSCLE.
THAT MAKES ONE OF US.
I'M GOING TO LOBOTOMIZE YOU, YOU GREEN FREAK--
AAAOWW!
KZAPP

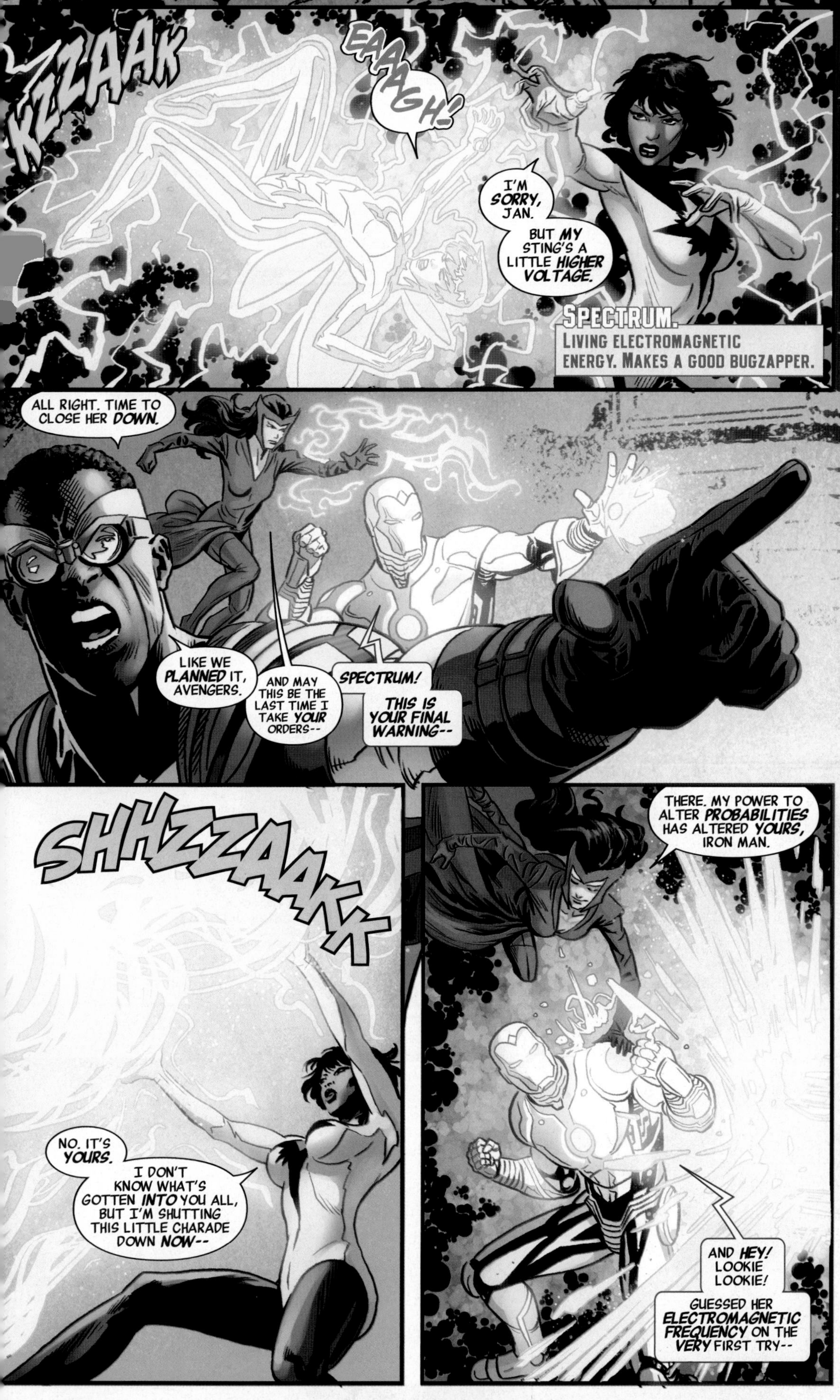

KZZAAK
EAAAAGH!
I'M SORRY, JAN.
BUT MY STING'S A LITTLE HIGHER VOLTAGE.
SPECTRUM.
LIVING ELECTROMAGNETIC ENERGY. MAKES A GOOD BUGZAPPER.
ALL RIGHT. TIME TO CLOSE HER DOWN.
LIKE WE PLANNED IT, AVENGERS.
AND MAY THIS BE THE LAST TIME I TAKE YOUR ORDERS--
SPECTRUM!
THIS IS YOUR FINAL WARNING--
SHHZZAAKK
NO. IT'S YOURS.
I DON'T KNOW WHAT'S GOTTEN INTO YOU ALL, BUT I'M SHUTTING THIS LITTLE CHARADE DOWN NOW--
THERE. MY POWER TO ALTER PROBABILITIES HAS ALTERED YOURS, IRON MAN.
AND HEY! LOOKIE LOOKIE!
GUESSED HER ELECTROMAGNETIC FREQUENCY ON THE VERY FIRST TRY--

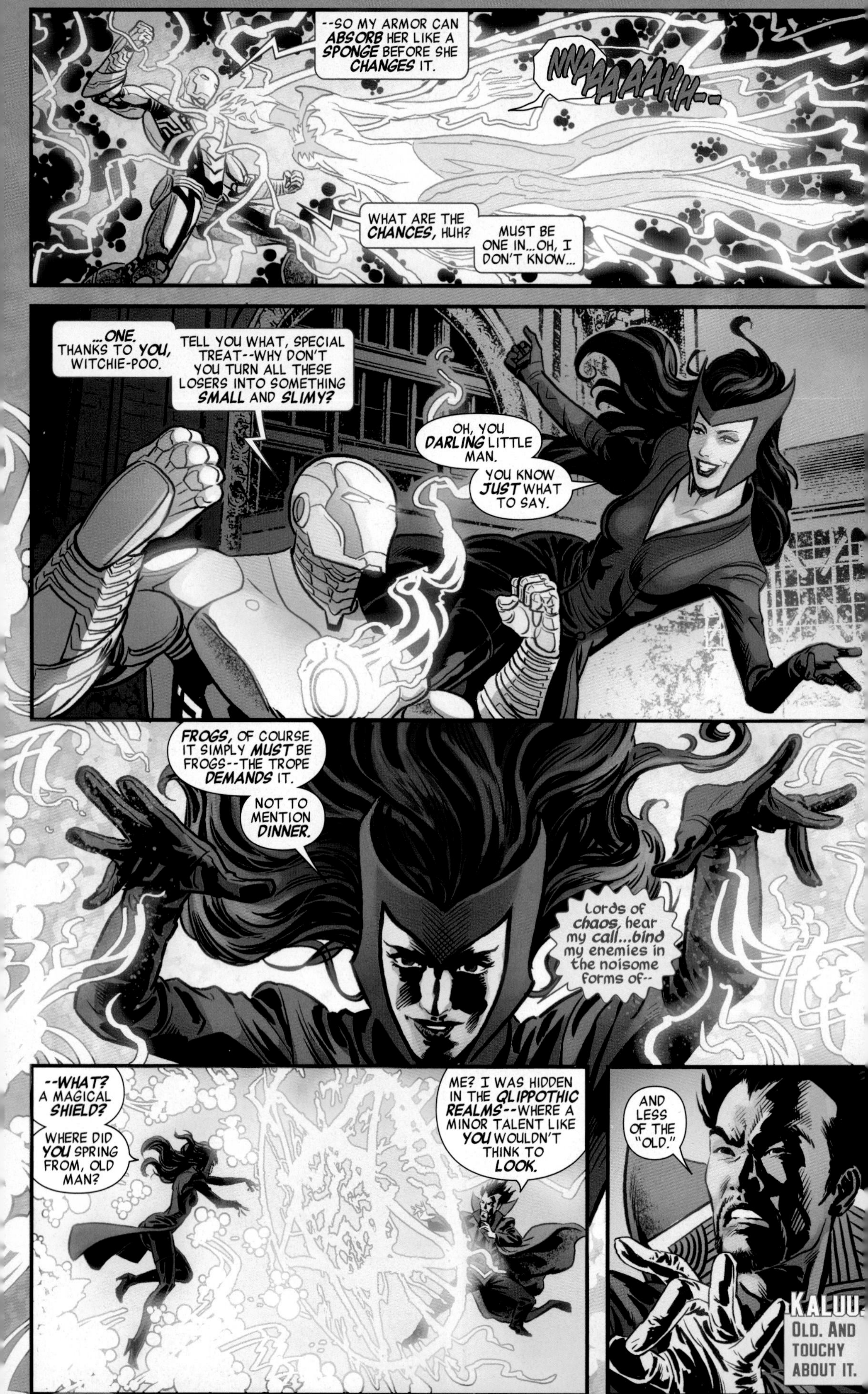

--SO MY ARMOR CAN ABSORB HER LIKE A SPONGE BEFORE SHE CHANGES IT.
NNAAAAAAHH--
WHAT ARE THE CHANCES, HUH?
MUST BE ONE IN...OH, I DON'T KNOW...
...ONE. THANKS TO YOU, WITCHIE-POO.
TELL YOU WHAT, SPECIAL TREAT--WHY DON'T YOU TURN ALL THESE LOSERS INTO SOMETHING SMALL AND SLIMY?
OH, YOU DARLING LITTLE MAN.
YOU KNOW JUST WHAT TO SAY.
FROGS, OF COURSE. IT SIMPLY MUST BE FROGS--THE TROPE DEMANDS IT.
NOT TO MENTION DINNER.
Lords of chaos, hear my call...bind my enemies in the noisome forms of--
--WHAT? A MAGICAL SHIELD?
WHERE DID YOU SPRING FROM, OLD MAN?
ME? I WAS HIDDEN IN THE QLIPPOTHIC REALMS--WHERE A MINOR TALENT LIKE YOU WOULDN'T THINK TO LOOK.
AND LESS OF THE "OLD."
KALUU
OLD. AND TOUCHY ABOUT IT.

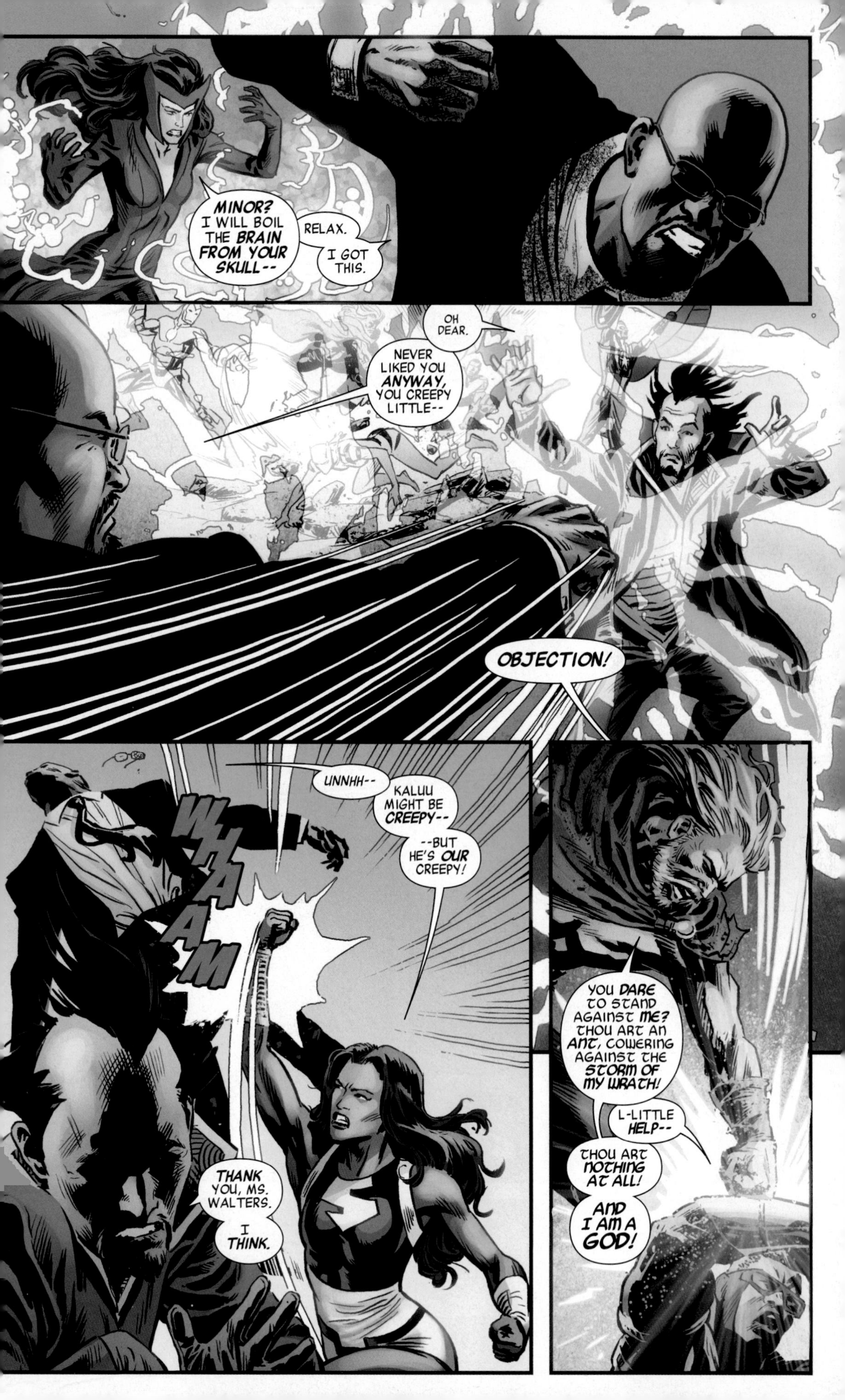
MINOR? I WILL BOIL THE BRAIN FROM YOUR SKULL--
RELAX.
I GOT THIS.
OH DEAR.
NEVER LIKED YOU ANYWAY, YOU CREEPY LITTLE--
OBJECTION!
UNNHH--
KALUU MIGHT BE CREEPY--
--BUT HE'S OUR CREEPY!
WHAAM
THANK YOU, MS. WALTERS.
I THINK.
YOU DARE TO STAND AGAINST ME? THOU ART AN ANT, COWERING AGAINST THE STORM OF MY WRATH!
L-LITTLE HELP--
THOU ART NOTHING AT ALL!
AND I AM A GOD!

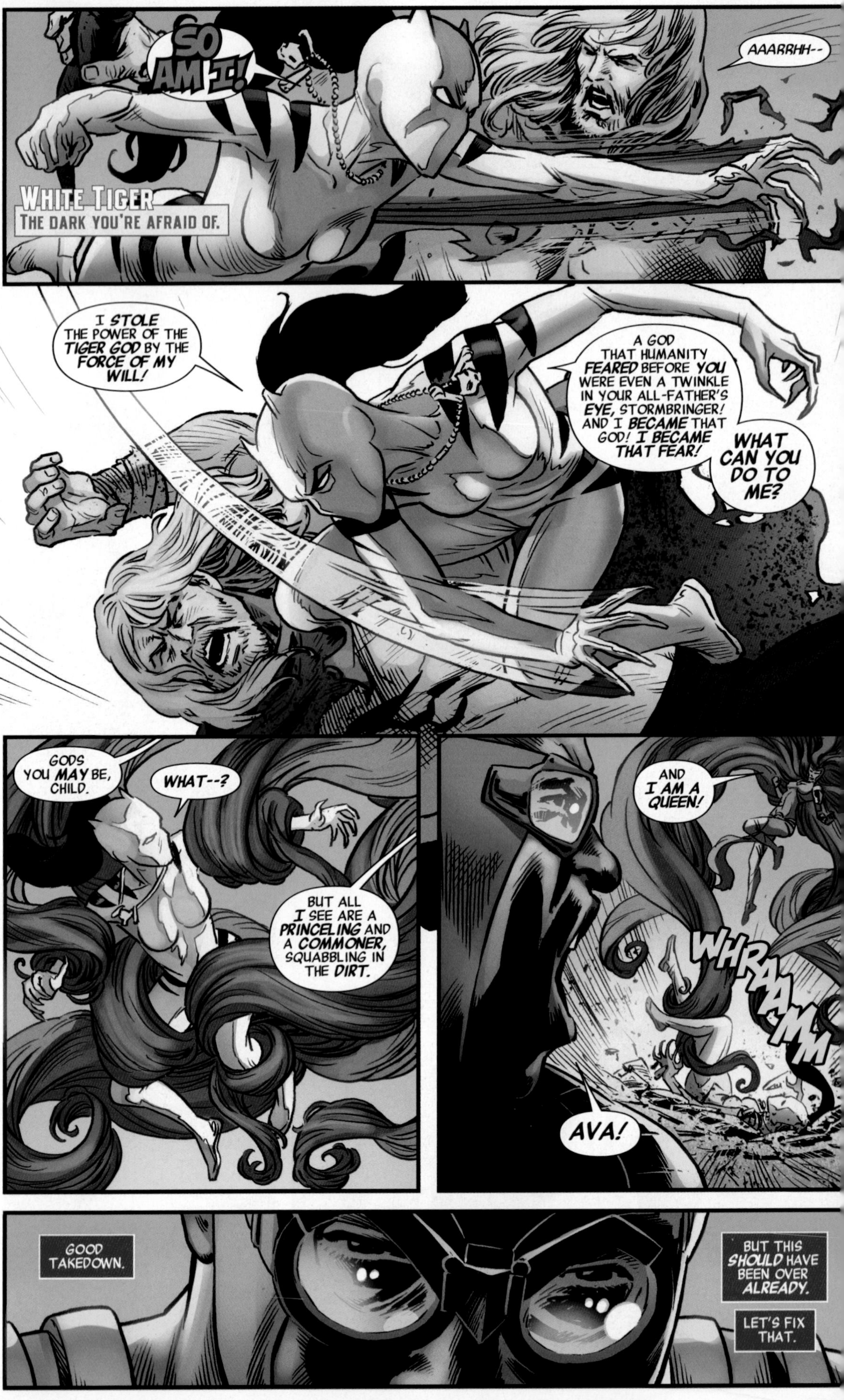
SO AM I!
AAARRHH--
WHITE TIGER
THE DARK YOU'RE AFRAID OF.
I STOLE THE POWER OF THE TIGER GOD BY THE FORCE OF MY WILL!
A GOD THAT HUMANITY FEARED BEFORE YOU WERE EVEN A TWINKLE IN YOUR ALL-FATHER'S EYE, STORMBRINGER! AND I BECAME THAT GOD! I BECAME THAT FEAR!
WHAT CAN YOU DO TO ME?
GODS YOU MAY BE, CHILD.
WHAT--?
BUT ALL I SEE ARE A PRINCELING AND A COMMONER, SQUABBLING IN THE DIRT.
AND I AM A QUEEN!
WHRAAMM
AVA!
GOOD TAKEDOWN.
BUT THIS SHOULD HAVE BEEN OVER ALREADY.
LET'S FIX THAT.

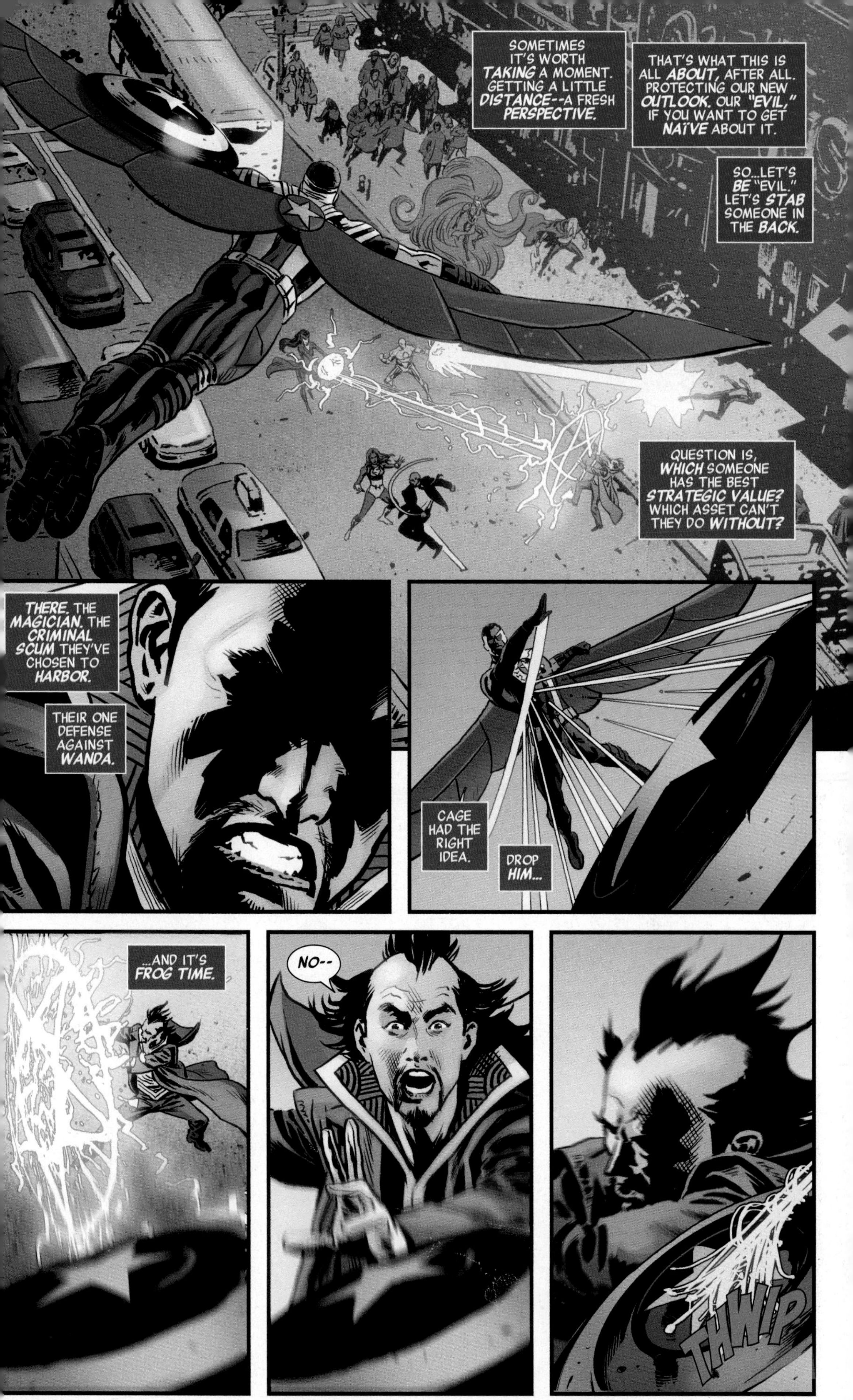

SOMETIMES IT'S WORTH TAKING A MOMENT. GETTING A LITTLE DISTANCE--A FRESH PERSPECTIVE.
THAT'S WHAT THIS IS ALL ABOUT, AFTER ALL. PROTECTING OUR NEW OUTLOOK. OUR "EVIL," IF YOU WANT TO GET NAÏVE ABOUT IT.
SO...LET'S BE "EVIL." LET'S STAB SOMEONE IN THE BACK.
QUESTION IS, WHICH SOMEONE HAS THE BEST STRATEGIC VALUE? WHICH ASSET CAN'T THEY DO WITHOUT?
THERE. THE MAGICIAN. THE CRIMINAL SCUM THEY'VE CHOSEN TO HARBOR.
THEIR ONE DEFENSE AGAINST WANDA.
CAGE HAD THE RIGHT IDEA.
DROP HIM...
...AND IT'S FROG TIME.
NO--
THWIP

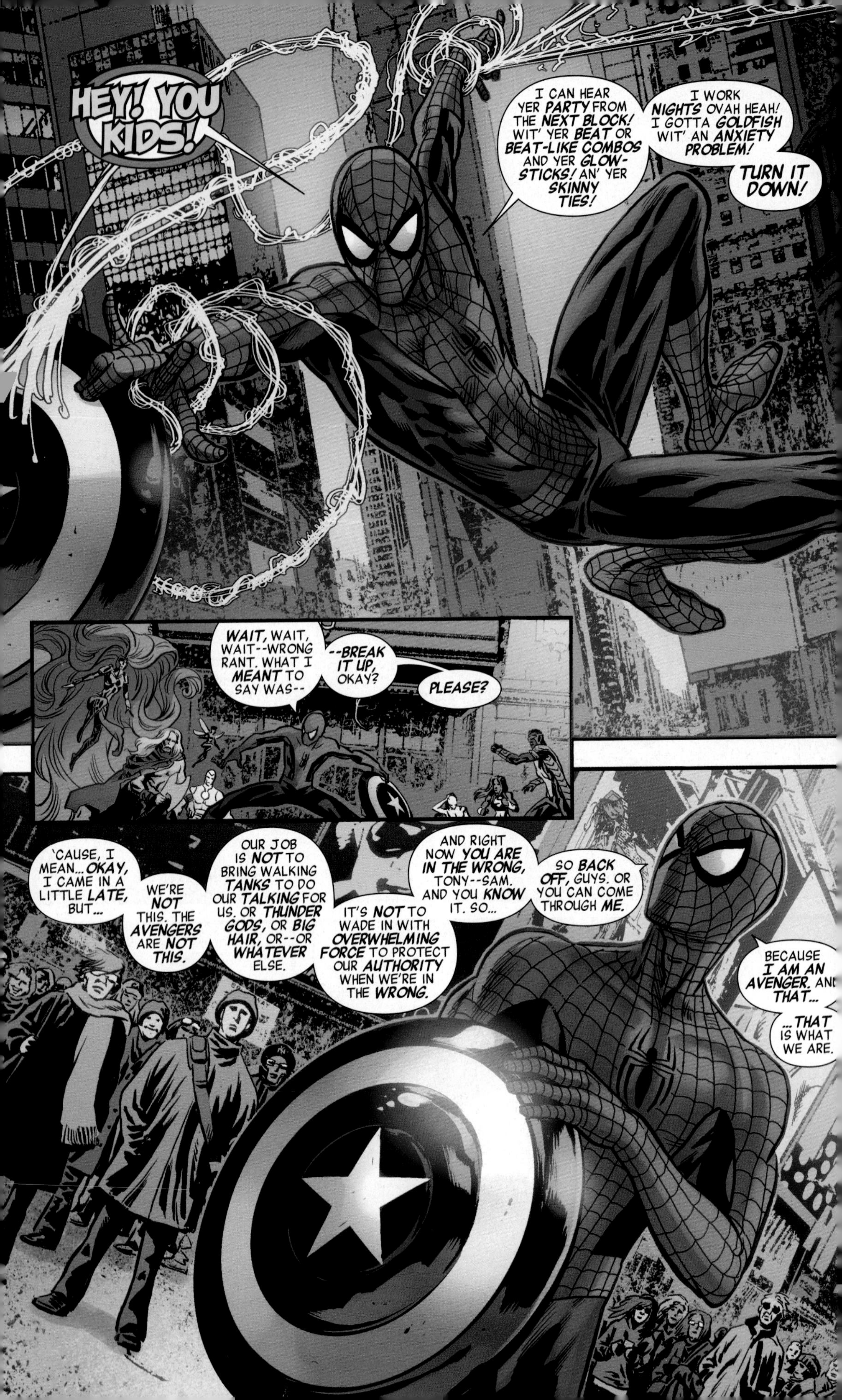
HEY! YOU KIDS!
I CAN HEAR YER PARTY FROM THE NEXT BLOCK! WIT' YER BEAT OR BEAT-LIKE COMBOS AND YER GLOW-STICKS! AN' YER SKINNY TIES!
I WORK NIGHTS OVAH HEAH! I GOTTA GOLDFISH WIT' AN ANXIETY PROBLEM!
TURN IT DOWN!
WAIT, WAIT, WAIT--WRONG RANT. WHAT I MEANT TO SAY WAS--
--BREAK IT UP, OKAY?
PLEASE?
'CAUSE, I MEAN... OKAY, I CAME IN A LITTLE LATE, BUT...
WE'RE NOT THIS. THE AVENGERS ARE NOT THIS.
OUR JOB IS NOT TO BRING WALKING TANKS TO DO OUR TALKING FOR US. OR THUNDER GODS, OR BIG HAIR, OR--OR WHATEVER ELSE.
IT'S NOT TO WADE IN WITH OVERWHELMING FORCE TO PROTECT OUR AUTHORITY WHEN WE'RE IN THE WRONG.
AND RIGHT NOW YOU ARE IN THE WRONG, TONY--SAM. AND YOU KNOW IT. SO...
SO BACK OFF, GUYS. OR YOU CAN COME THROUGH ME.
BECAUSE I AM AN AVENGER. AN
THAT...
...THAT IS WHAT WE ARE.

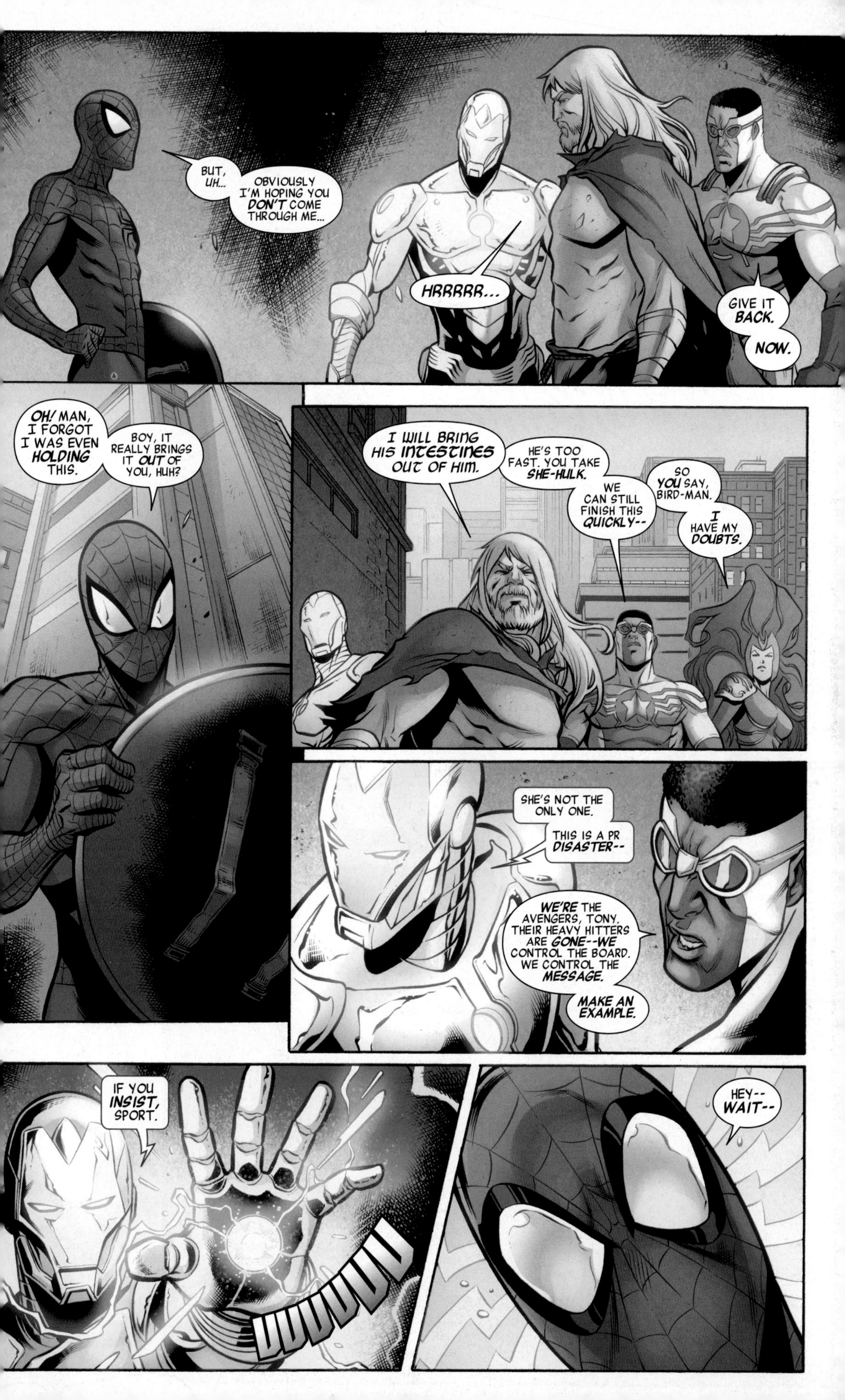
BUT, UH...
OBVIOUSLY I'M HOPING YOU DON'T COME THROUGH ME...
HRRRRR...
GIVE IT BACK.
NOW.
OH! MAN, I FORGOT I WAS EVEN HOLDING THIS.
BOY, IT REALLY BRINGS IT OUT OF YOU, HUH?
I WILL BRING HIS INTESTINES OUT OF HIM.
HE'S TOO FAST. YOU TAKE SHE-HULK.
WE CAN STILL FINISH THIS QUICKLY--
SO YOU SAY, BIRD-MAN.
I HAVE MY DOUBTS.
SHE'S NOT THE ONLY ONE.
THIS IS A PR DISASTER--
WE'RE THE AVENGERS, TONY. THEIR HEAVY HITTERS ARE GONE--WE CONTROL THE BOARD. WE CONTROL THE MESSAGE.
MAKE AN EXAMPLE.
IF YOU INSIST, SPORT.
UUUUUU
HEY-- WAIT--

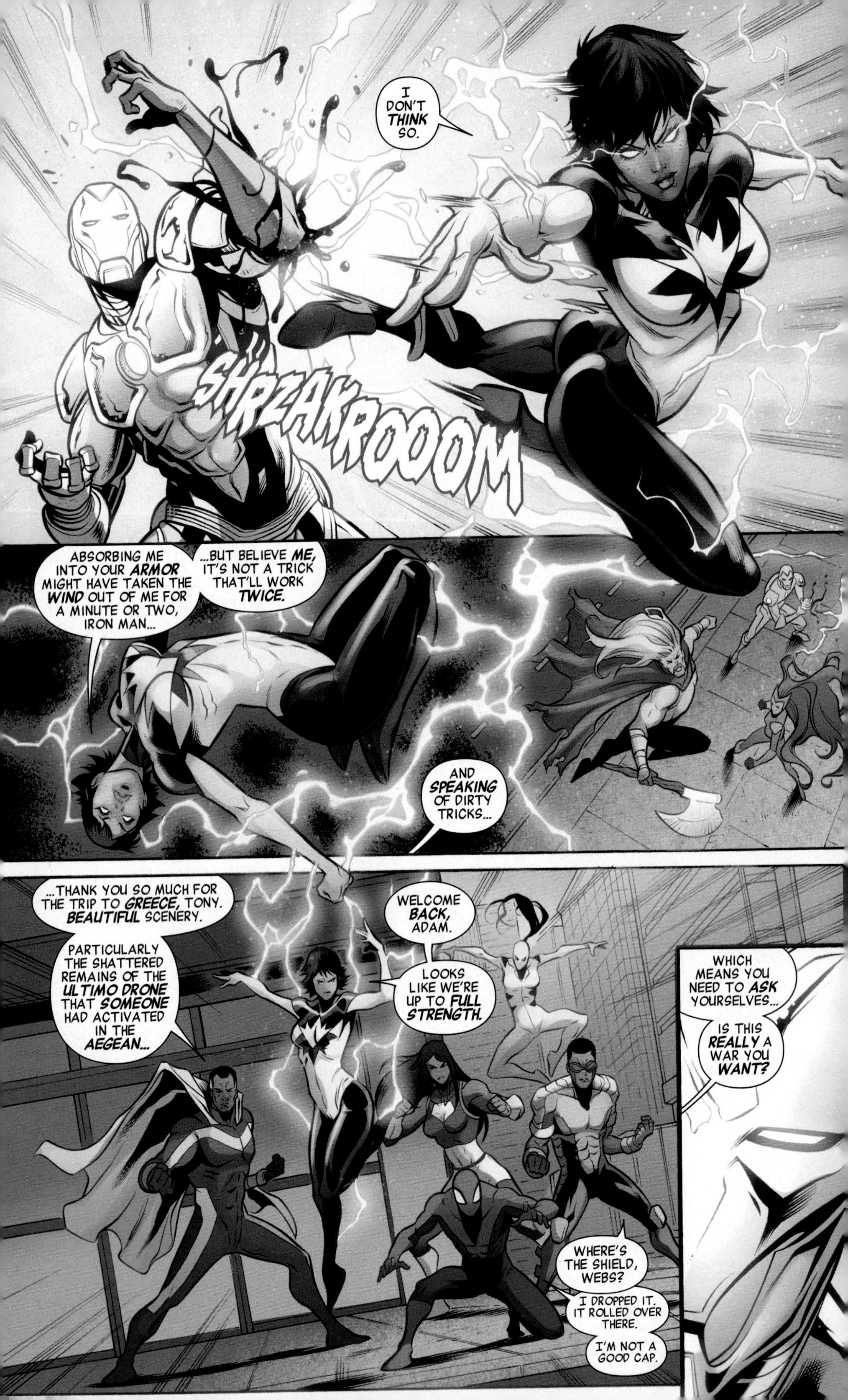
I DON'T THINK SO.
SHRZAKROOOM
ABSORBING ME INTO YOUR ARMOR MIGHT HAVE TAKEN THE WIND OUT OF ME FOR A MINUTE OR TWO, IRON MAN...
...BUT BELIEVE ME, IT'S NOT A TRICK THAT'LL WORK TWICE.
AND SPEAKING OF DIRTY TRICKS...
...THANK YOU SO MUCH FOR THE TRIP TO GREECE, TONY. BEAUTIFUL SCENERY.
PARTICULARLY THE SHATTERED REMAINS OF THE ULTIMO DRONE THAT SOMEONE HAD ACTIVATED IN THE AEGEAN...
WELCOME BACK, ADAM.
LOOKS LIKE WE'RE UP TO FULL STRENGTH.
WHERE'S THE SHIELD, WEBS?
I DROPPED IT. IT ROLLED OVER THERE.
I'M NOT A GOOD CAP.
WHICH MEANS YOU NEED TO ASK YOURSELVES...
IS THIS REALLY A WAR YOU WANT?

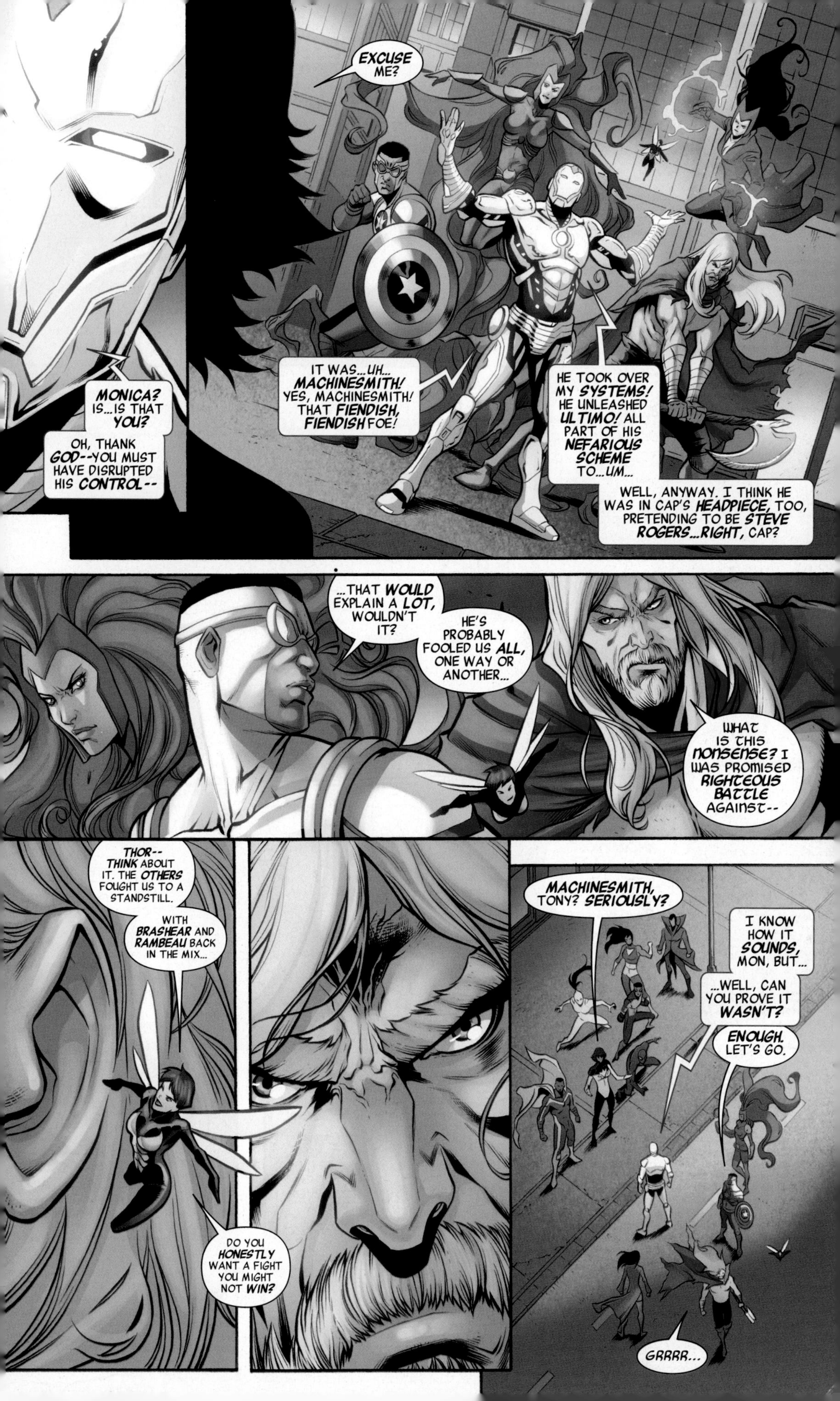
MONICA? IS...IS THAT YOU?
OH, THANK GOD--YOU MUST HAVE DISRUPTED HIS CONTROL--
EXCUSE ME?
IT WAS...UH... MACHINESMITH! YES, MACHINESMITH! THAT FIENDISH, FIENDISH FOE!
HE TOOK OVER MY SYSTEMS! HE UNLEASHED ULTIMO! ALL PART OF HIS NEFARIOUS SCHEME TO...UM...
WELL, ANYWAY. I THINK HE WAS IN CAP'S HEADPIECE, TOO, PRETENDING TO BE STEVE ROGERS...RIGHT, CAP?
...THAT WOULD EXPLAIN A LOT, WOULDN'T IT?
HE'S PROBABLY FOOLED US ALL, ONE WAY OR ANOTHER...
WHAT IS THIS NONSENSE? I WAS PROMISED RIGHTEOUS BATTLE AGAINST--
THOR--THINK ABOUT IT. THE OTHERS FOUGHT US TO A STANDSTILL.
WITH BRASHEAR AND RAMBEAU BACK IN THE MIX...
DO YOU HONESTLY WANT A FIGHT YOU MIGHT NOT WIN?
MACHINESMITH, TONY? SERIOUSLY?
I KNOW HOW IT SOUNDS, MON, BUT...
...WELL, CAN YOU PROVE IT WASN'T?
ENOUGH. LET'S GO.
GRRRR...

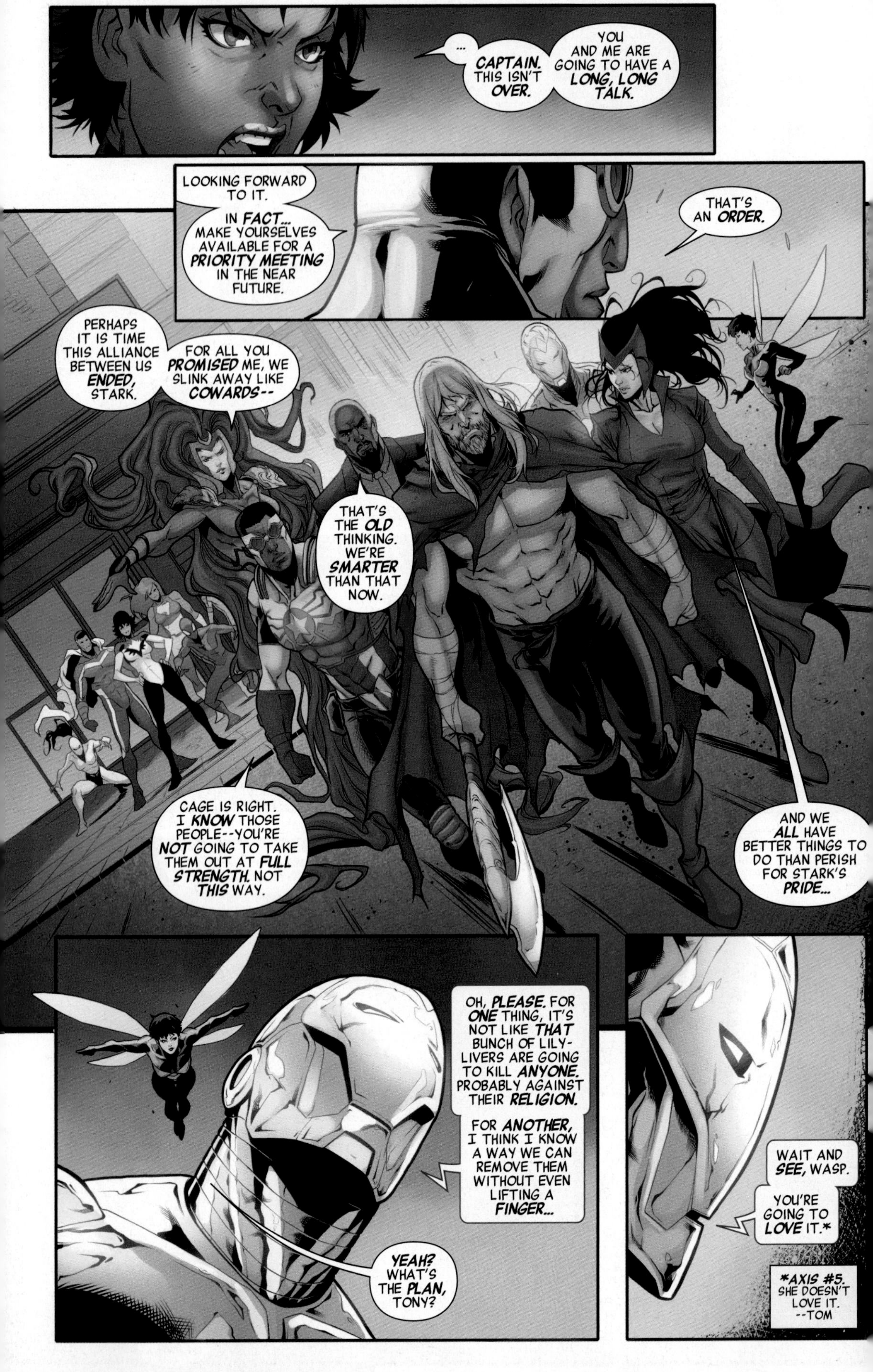

...
CAPTAIN. THIS ISN'T OVER.
YOU AND ME ARE GOING TO HAVE A LONG, LONG TALK.
LOOKING FORWARD TO IT.
IN FACT... MAKE YOURSELVES AVAILABLE FOR A PRIORITY MEETING IN THE NEAR FUTURE.
THAT'S AN ORDER.
PERHAPS IT IS TIME THIS ALLIANCE BETWEEN US ENDED, STARK.
FOR ALL YOU PROMISED ME, WE SLINK AWAY LIKE COWARDS--
THAT'S THE OLD THINKING. WE'RE SMARTER THAN THAT NOW.
CAGE IS RIGHT. I KNOW THOSE PEOPLE--YOU'RE NOT GOING TO TAKE THEM OUT AT FULL STRENGTH. NOT THIS WAY.
AND WE ALL HAVE BETTER THINGS TO DO THAN PERISH FOR STARK'S PRIDE...
OH, PLEASE. FOR ONE THING, IT'S NOT LIKE THAT BUNCH OF LILY-LIVERS ARE GOING TO KILL ANYONE. PROBABLY AGAINST THEIR RELIGION.
FOR ANOTHER, I THINK I KNOW A WAY WE CAN REMOVE THEM WITHOUT EVEN LIFTING A FINGER...
YEAH? WHAT'S THE PLAN, TONY?
WAIT AND SEE, WASP.
YOU'RE GOING TO LOVE IT.*
*AXIS #5. SHE DOESN'T LOVE IT. --TOM

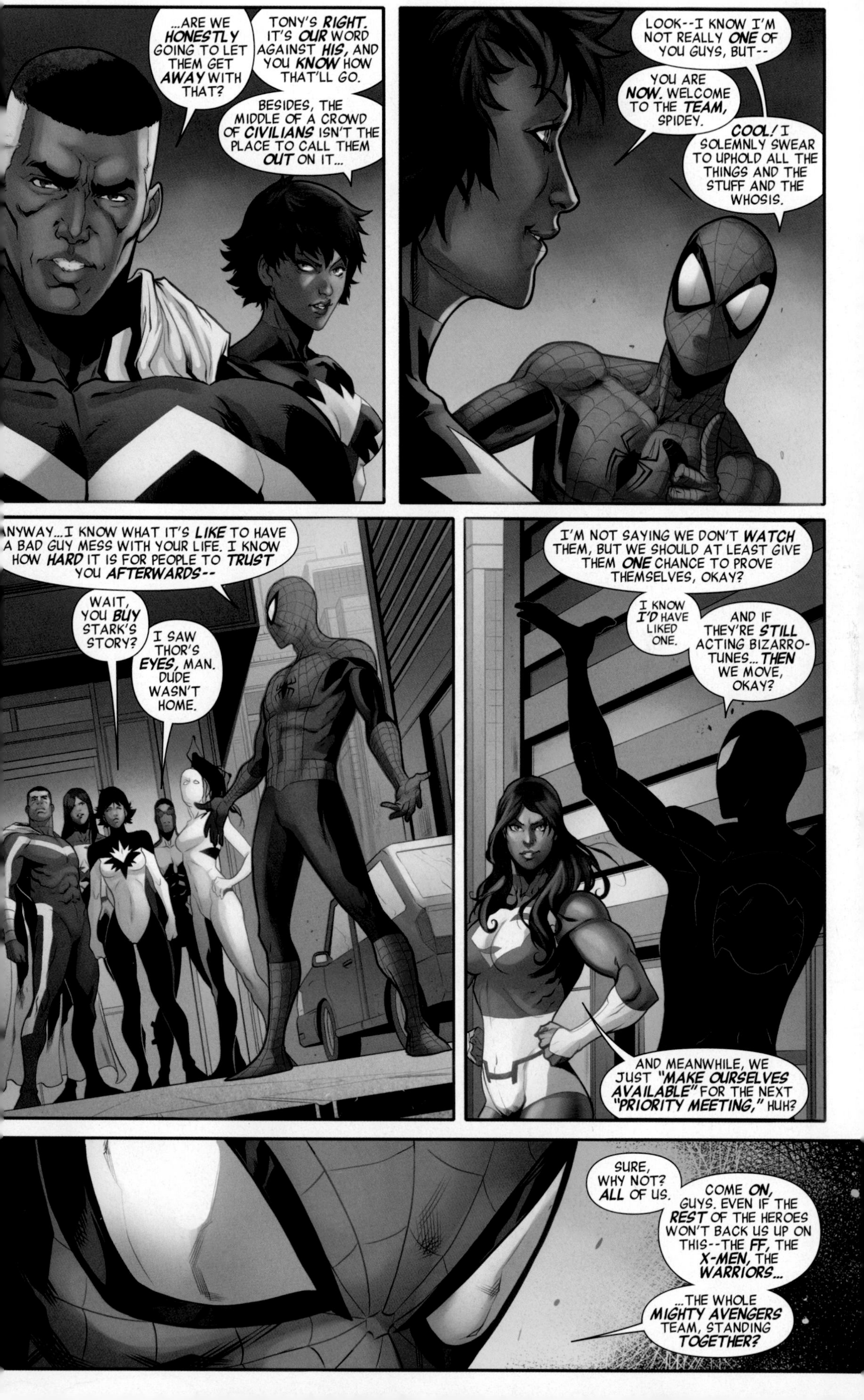
...ARE WE HONESTLY GOING TO LET THEM GET AWAY WITH THAT?
TONY'S RIGHT. IT'S OUR WORD AGAINST HIS, AND YOU KNOW HOW THAT'LL GO.
BESIDES, THE MIDDLE OF A CROWD OF CIVILIANS ISN'T THE PLACE TO CALL THEM OUT ON IT...
LOOK--I KNOW I'M NOT REALLY ONE OF YOU GUYS, BUT--
YOU ARE NOW. WELCOME TO THE TEAM, SPIDEY.
COOL! I SOLEMNLY SWEAR TO UPHOLD ALL THE THINGS AND THE STUFF AND THE WHOSIS.
NYWAY...I KNOW WHAT IT'S LIKE TO HAVE A BAD GUY MESS WITH YOUR LIFE. I KNOW HOW HARD IT IS FOR PEOPLE TO TRUST YOU AFTERWARDS--
WAIT, YOU BUY STARK'S STORY?
I SAW THOR'S EYES, MAN. DUDE WASN'T HOME.
I'M NOT SAYING WE DON'T WATCH THEM, BUT WE SHOULD AT LEAST GIVE THEM ONE CHANCE TO PROVE THEMSELVES, OKAY?
I KNOW I'D HAVE LIKED ONE.
AND IF THEY'RE STILL ACTING BIZARRO-TUNES...THEN WE MOVE, OKAY?
AND MEANWHILE, WE JUST "MAKE OURSELVES AVAILABLE" FOR THE NEXT "PRIORITY MEETING," HUH?
SURE, WHY NOT? ALL OF US.
COME ON, GUYS. EVEN IF THE REST OF THE HEROES WON'T BACK US UP ON THIS--THE FF, THE X-MEN, THE WARRIORS...
...THE WHOLE MIGHTY AVENGERS TEAM, STANDING TOGETHER?

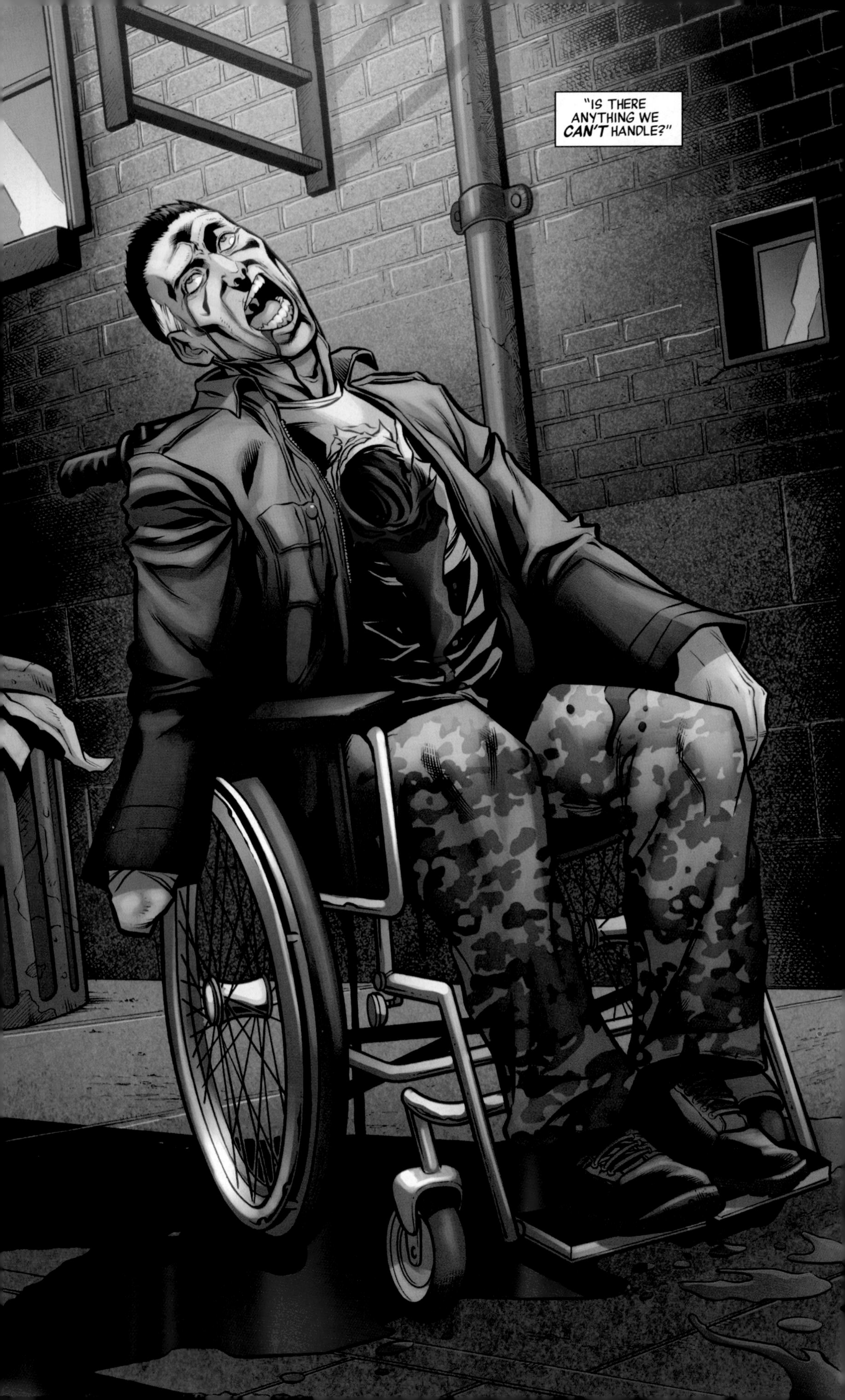
"IS THERE ANYTHING WE CAN'T HANDLE?"

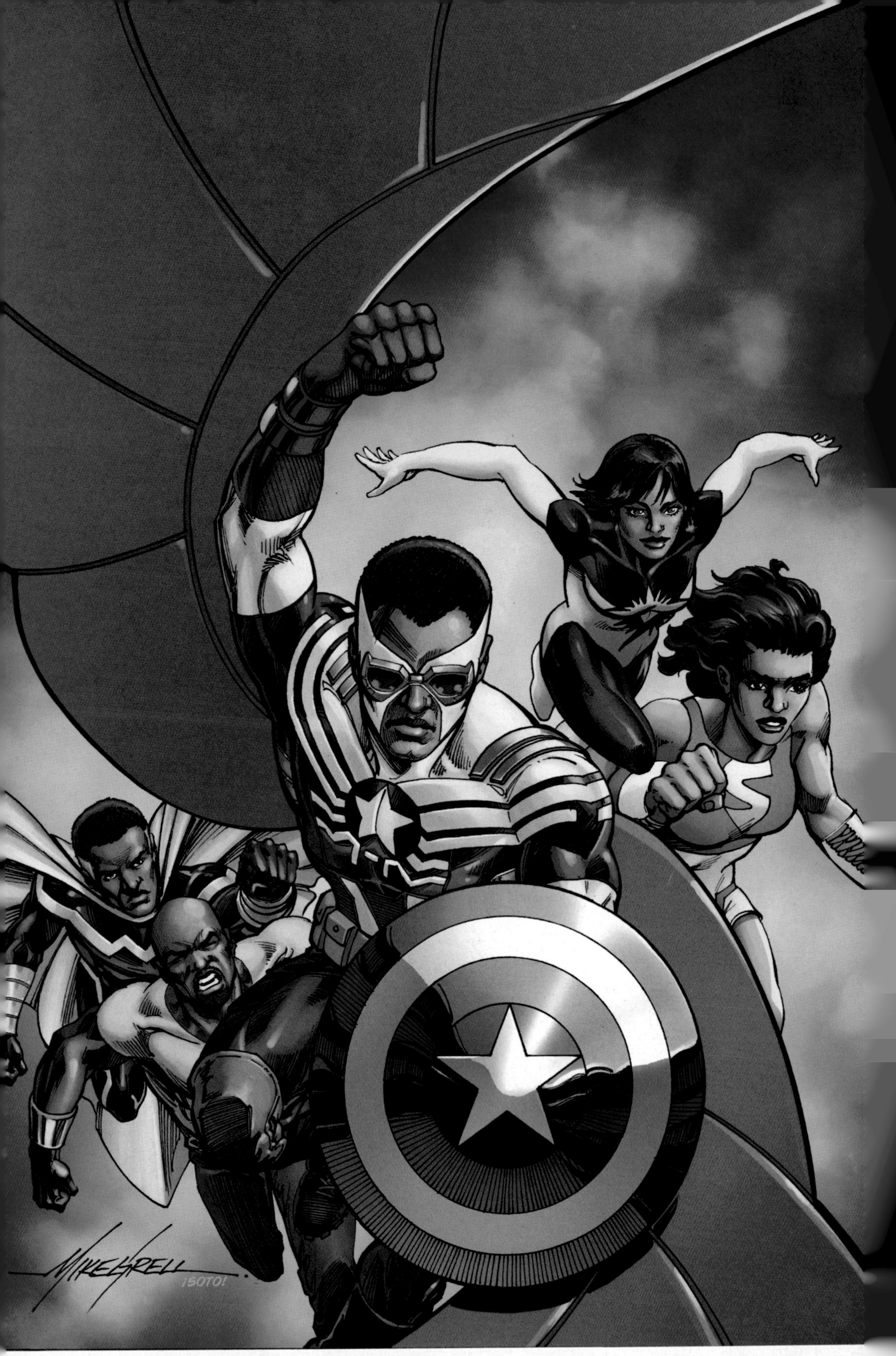
MIKE GRELL
!SOTO!

#1 VARIANT BY MIKE GRELL & CHRIS SOTOMAYOR

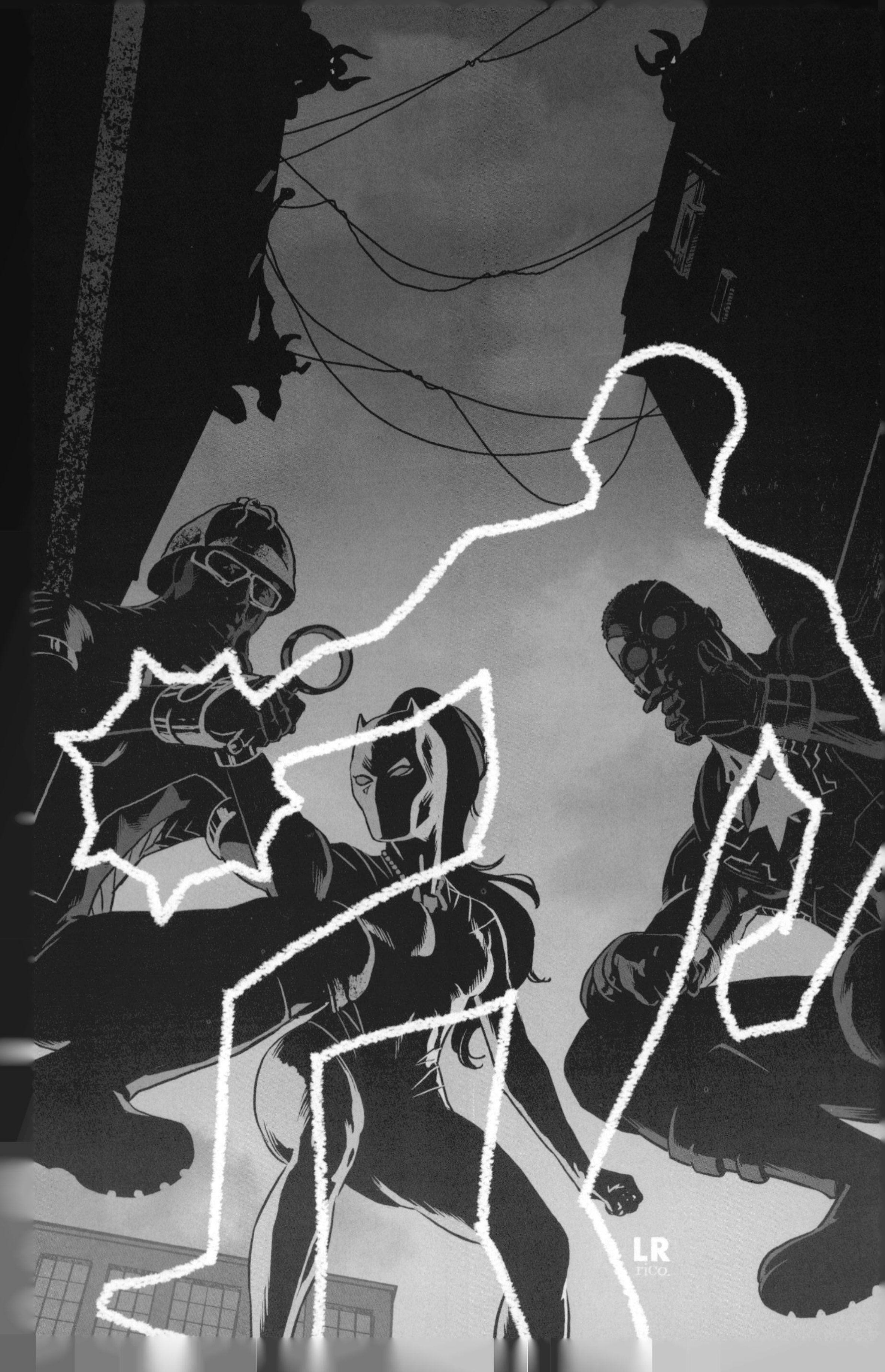
LR
rico.

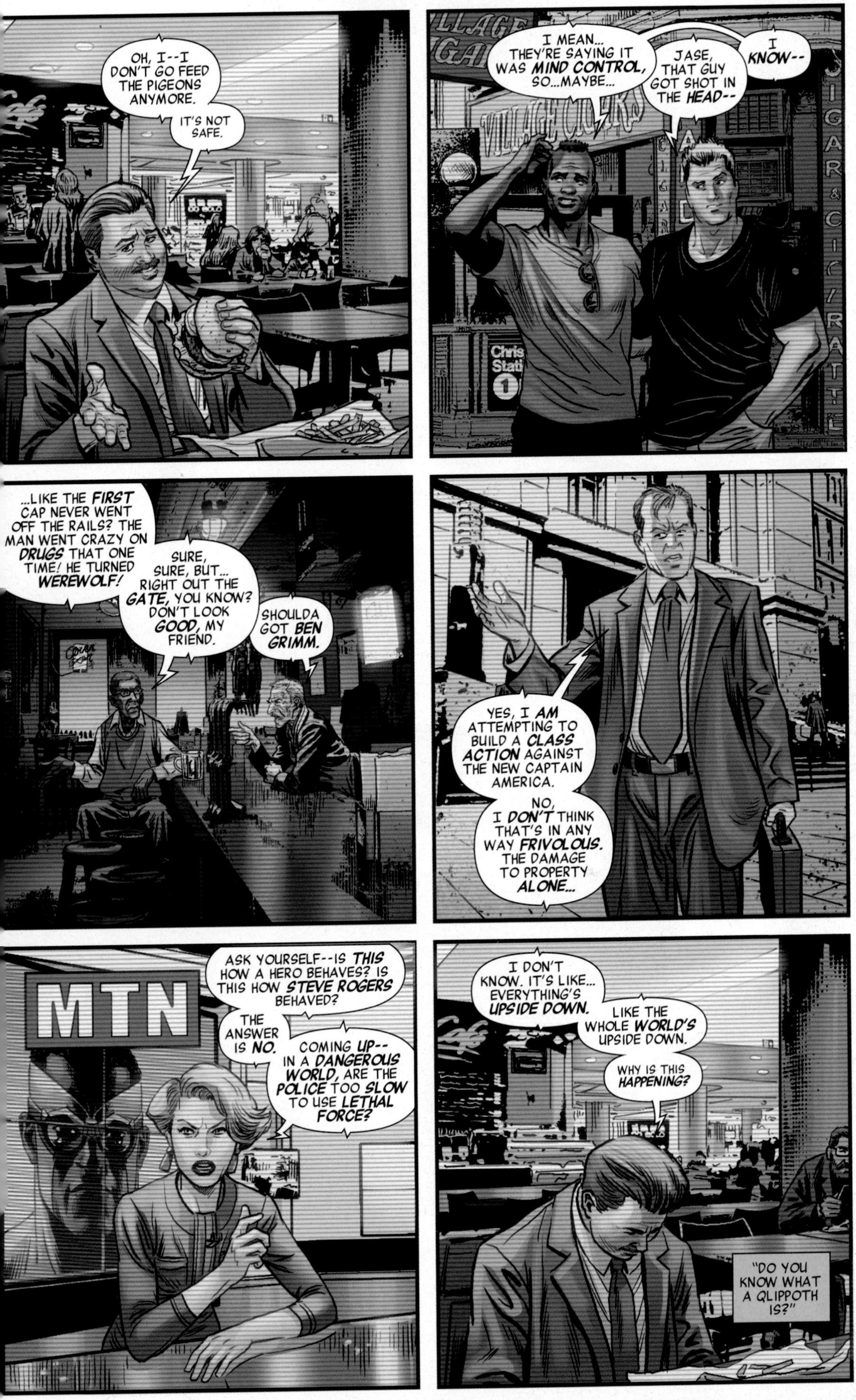
OH, I--I DON'T GO FEED THE PIGEONS ANYMORE.
IT'S NOT SAFE.
I MEAN... THEY'RE SAYING IT WAS MIND CONTROL, SO...MAYBE...
JASE, THAT GUY GOT SHOT IN THE HEAD--
I KNOW--
...LIKE THE FIRST CAP NEVER WENT OFF THE RAILS? THE MAN WENT CRAZY ON DRUGS THAT ONE TIME! HE TURNED WEREWOLF!
SURE, SURE, BUT... RIGHT OUT THE GATE, YOU KNOW? DON'T LOOK GOOD, MY FRIEND.
SHOULDA GOT BEN GRIMM.
YES, I AM ATTEMPTING TO BUILD A CLASS ACTION AGAINST THE NEW CAPTAIN AMERICA.
NO, I DON'T THINK THAT'S IN ANY WAY FRIVOLOUS. THE DAMAGE TO PROPERTY ALONE...
MTN
ASK YOURSELF--IS THIS HOW A HERO BEHAVES? IS THIS HOW STEVE ROGERS BEHAVED?
THE ANSWER IS NO.
COMING UP-- IN A DANGEROUS WORLD, ARE THE POLICE TOO SLOW TO USE LETHAL FORCE?
I DON'T KNOW. IT'S LIKE... EVERYTHING'S UPSIDE DOWN.
LIKE THE WHOLE WORLD'S UPSIDE DOWN.
WHY IS THIS HAPPENING?
"DO YOU KNOW WHAT A QLIPPOTH IS?"

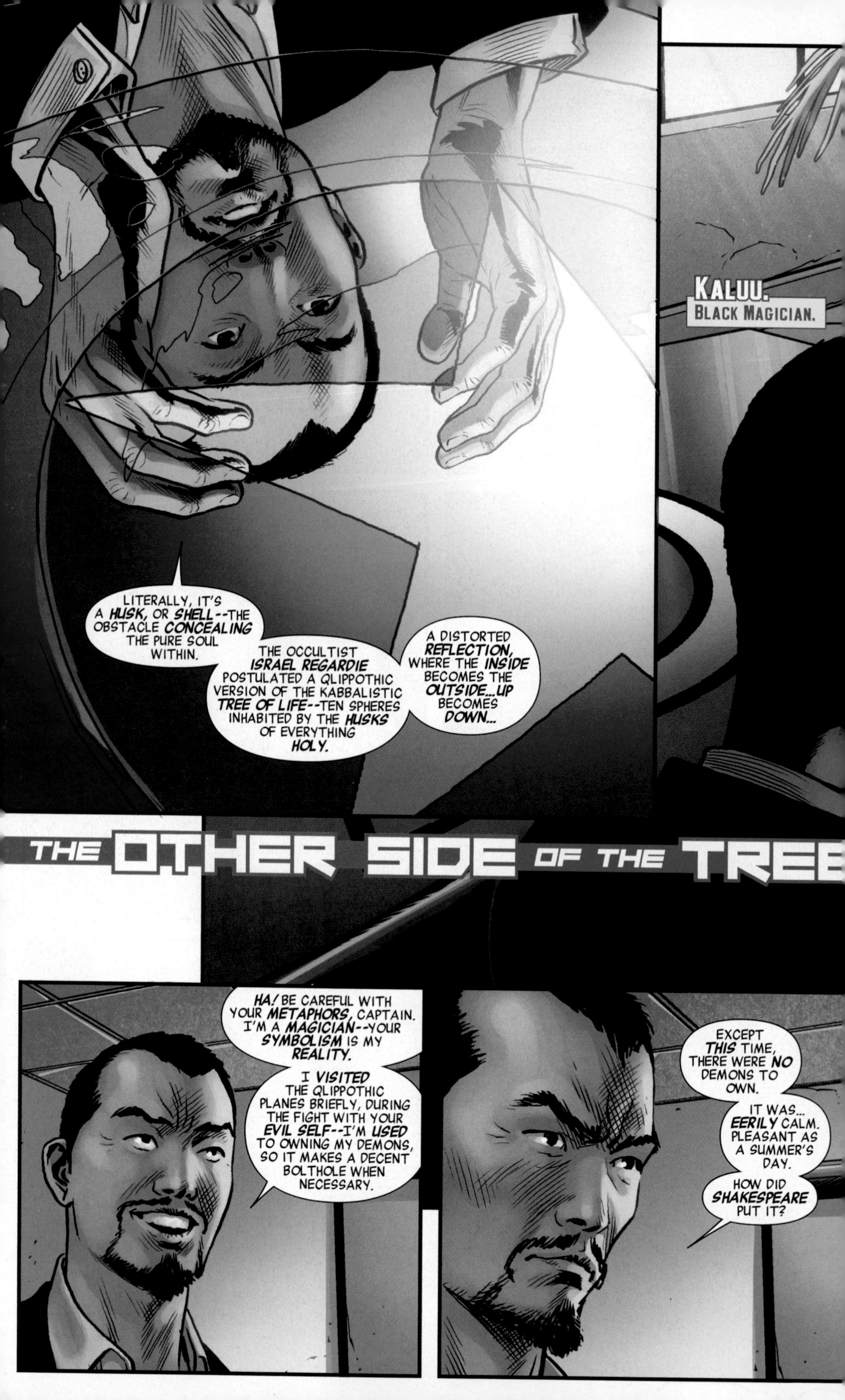
KALUU.
BLACK MAGICIAN.
LITERALLY, IT'S A HUSK, OR SHELL--THE OBSTACLE CONCEALING THE PURE SOUL WITHIN.
THE OCCULTIST ISRAEL REGARDIE POSTULATED A QLIPPOTHIC VERSION OF THE KABBALISTIC TREE OF LIFE--TEN SPHERES INHABITED BY THE HUSKS OF EVERYTHING HOLY.
A DISTORTED REFLECTION, WHERE THE INSIDE BECOMES THE OUTSIDE...UP BECOMES DOWN...
THE OTHER SIDE OF THE TREE
HA! BE CAREFUL WITH YOUR METAPHORS, CAPTAIN. I'M A MAGICIAN--YOUR SYMBOLISM IS MY REALITY.
I VISITED THE QLIPPOTHIC PLANES BRIEFLY, DURING THE FIGHT WITH YOUR EVIL SELF--I'M USED TO OWNING MY DEMONS, SO IT MAKES A DECENT BOLTHOLE WHEN NECESSARY.
EXCEPT THIS TIME, THERE WERE NO DEMONS TO OWN.
IT WAS... EERILY CALM. PLEASANT AS A SUMMER'S DAY.
HOW DID SHAKESPEARE PUT IT?

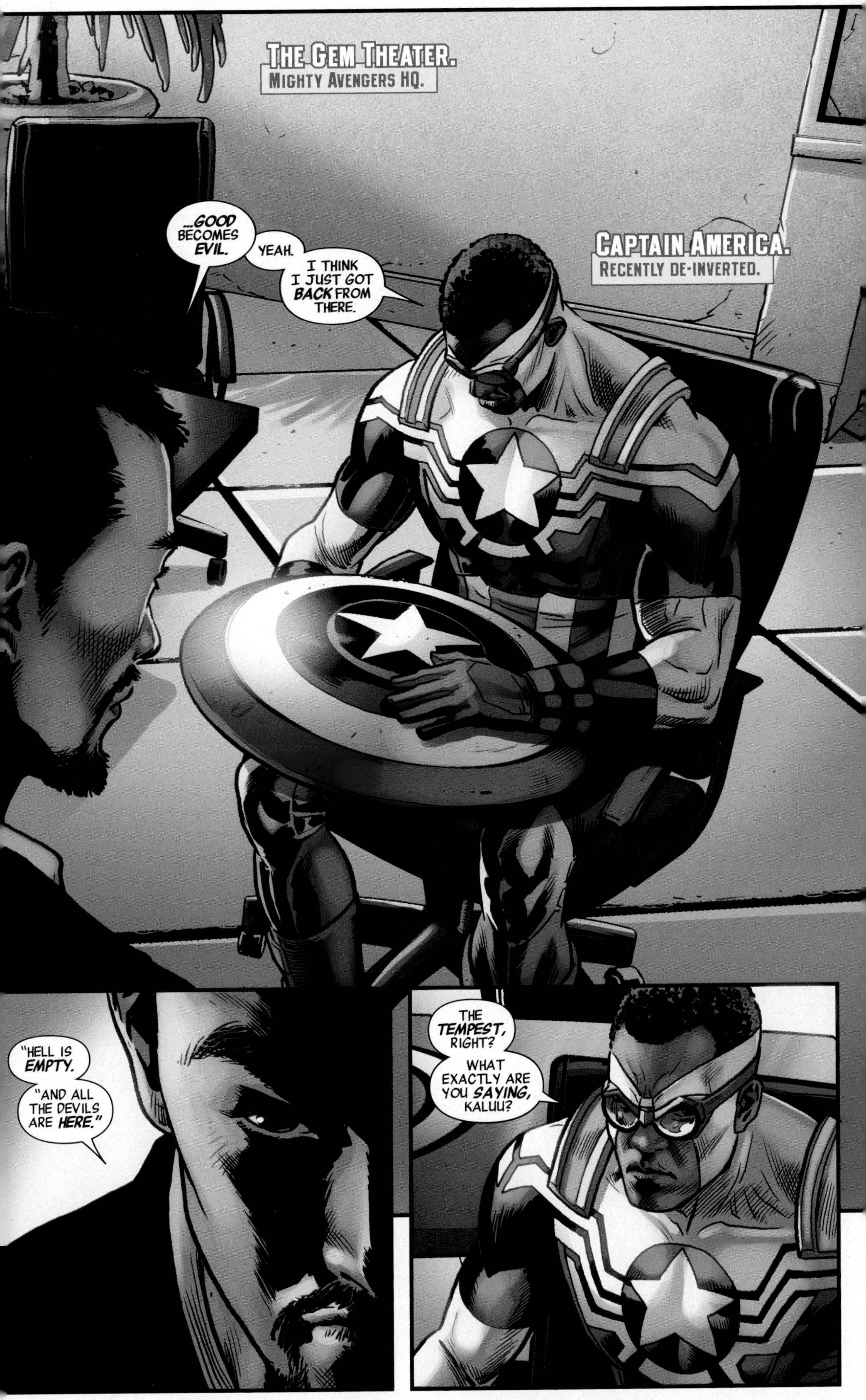

THE GEM THEATER.
MIGHTY AVENGERS HQ.
...GOOD BECOMES EVIL.
YEAH.
I THINK I JUST GOT BACK FROM THERE.
CAPTAIN AMERICA.
RECENTLY DE-INVERTED.
"HELL IS EMPTY.
"AND ALL THE DEVILS ARE HERE."
THE TEMPEST, RIGHT?
WHAT EXACTLY ARE YOU SAYING, KALUU?

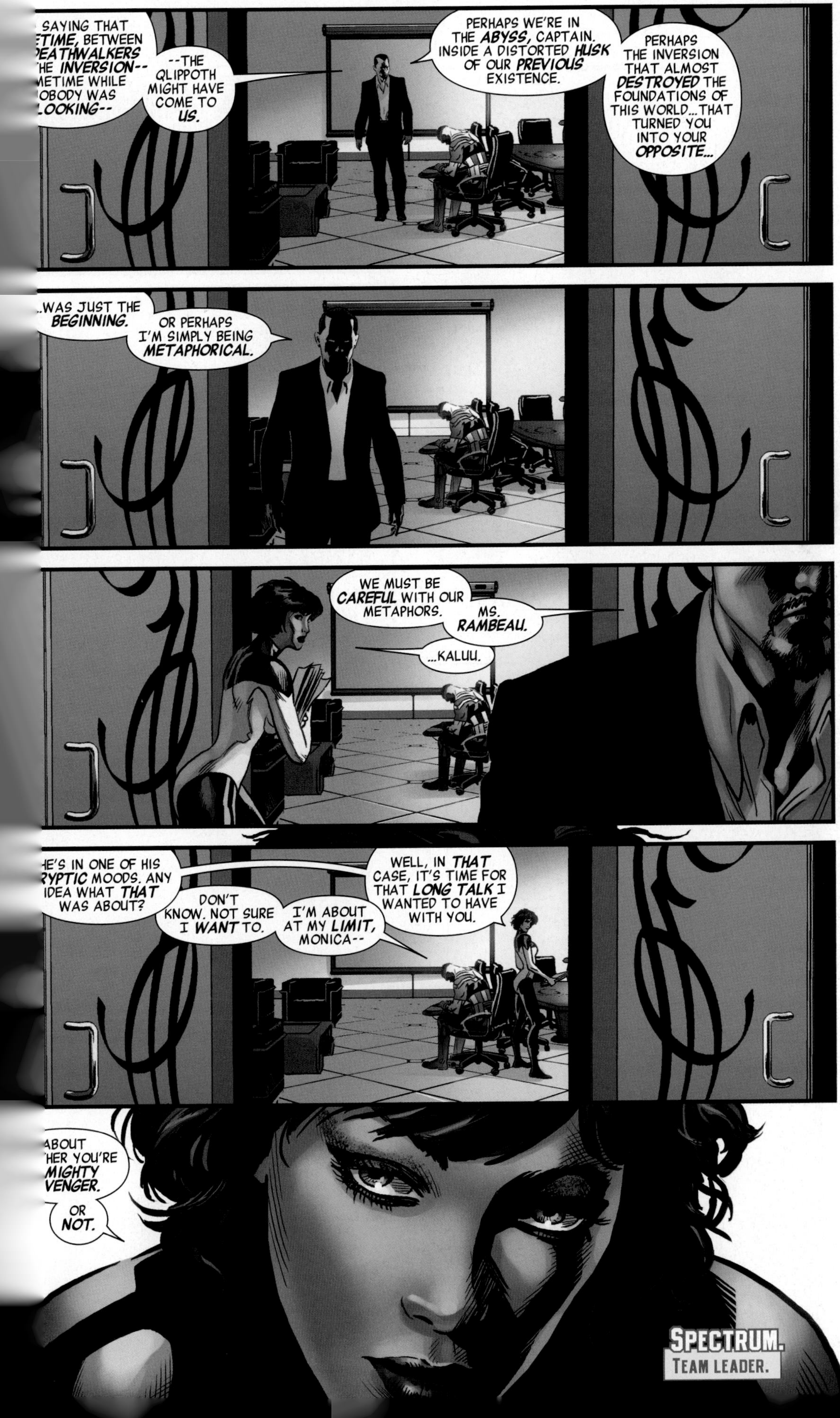
SAYING THAT ETIME, BETWEEN EATHWALKERS THE INVERSION-- METIME WHILE OBODY WAS LOOKING--
--THE QLIPPOTH MIGHT HAVE COME TO US.
PERHAPS WE'RE IN THE ABYSS, CAPTAIN. INSIDE A DISTORTED HUSK OF OUR PREVIOUS EXISTENCE.
PERHAPS THE INVERSION THAT ALMOST DESTROYED THE FOUNDATIONS OF THIS WORLD...THAT TURNED YOU INTO YOUR OPPOSITE...
..WAS JUST THE BEGINNING.
OR PERHAPS I'M SIMPLY BEING METAPHORICAL.
WE MUST BE CAREFUL WITH OUR METAPHORS.
MS. RAMBEAU.
...KALUU.
HE'S IN ONE OF HIS RYPTIC MOODS. ANY IDEA WHAT THAT WAS ABOUT?
DON'T KNOW. NOT SURE I WANT TO.
I'M ABOUT AT MY LIMIT, MONICA--
WELL, IN THAT CASE, IT'S TIME FOR THAT LONG TALK I WANTED TO HAVE WITH YOU.
ABOUT THER YOU'RE MIGHTY VENGER.
OR NOT.
SPECTRUM.
TEAM LEADER.

CORTEX INCORPORATED HQ.
THEY WANT IN. ON EVERYTHING.

THE ANSWER'S *NO*, QUANTRELL. APPARENTLY *LUKE CAGE* AND THE *MIGHTY AVENGERS* ARE NO LONGER *AFFILIATED*.

SO...NO SALE.

JASON QUANTRELL.
CORTEX CEO.

PITY. I'VE BEEN SCOUTING *PROSPECTIVE MEMBERS* FOR THE NEW TEAM-- BE NICE TO HAVE THE *BRAND* IN PLACE...

CAN'T BE HELPED. SOME PEOPLE JUST DON'T KNOW WHAT'S *BEST* FOR THEM.

NOT LIKE *YOU*, EH?

YOU KNOW, THERE'S A *RUMO* THAT YOU WEREN' QUITE *YOURSEL* WHEN WE MADE THAT DEAL.

BUNCH OF GOONS IN *COSTUMES*, SAYING HOW THIS WHOLE THING WAS *THEIR FAULT*? "DON'T BLAME THE NICE AVENGERS"?

SMELLS LIKE *SOME* FOLKS WANT THEIR *ASSES* COVERED...

LUKE CAGE.
WORKING ALONE.

... THAT'S WHY I'M *HERE*.

GOOD.

BUT...DON'T TAKE THIS OPTION *LIGHTLY*, LUKE. I EXPECT *GREAT THINGS* FROM YOU. AND ONCE YOU'RE *IN*...

YOU'RE *IN*.

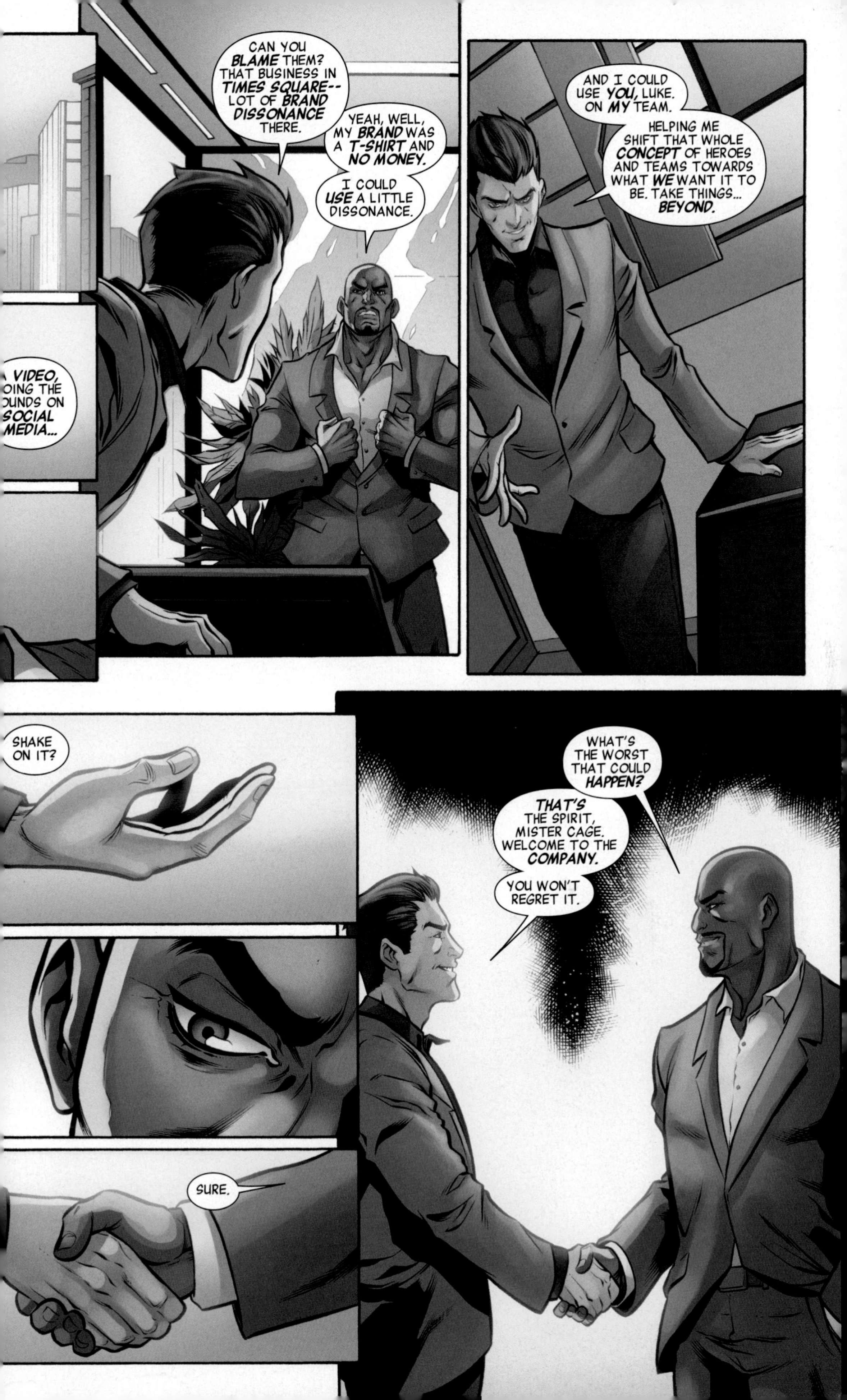
VIDEO, OING THE UNDS ON SOCIAL MEDIA...
CAN YOU BLAME THEM? THAT BUSINESS IN TIMES SQUARE-- LOT OF BRAND DISSONANCE THERE.
YEAH, WELL, MY BRAND WAS A T-SHIRT AND NO MONEY.
I COULD USE A LITTLE DISSONANCE.
AND I COULD USE YOU, LUKE. ON MY TEAM.
HELPING ME SHIFT THAT WHOLE CONCEPT OF HEROES AND TEAMS TOWARDS WHAT WE WANT IT TO BE. TAKE THINGS... BEYOND.
SHAKE ON IT?
SURE.
WHAT'S THE WORST THAT COULD HAPPEN?
THAT'S THE SPIRIT, MISTER CAGE. WELCOME TO THE COMPANY.
YOU WON'T REGRET IT.

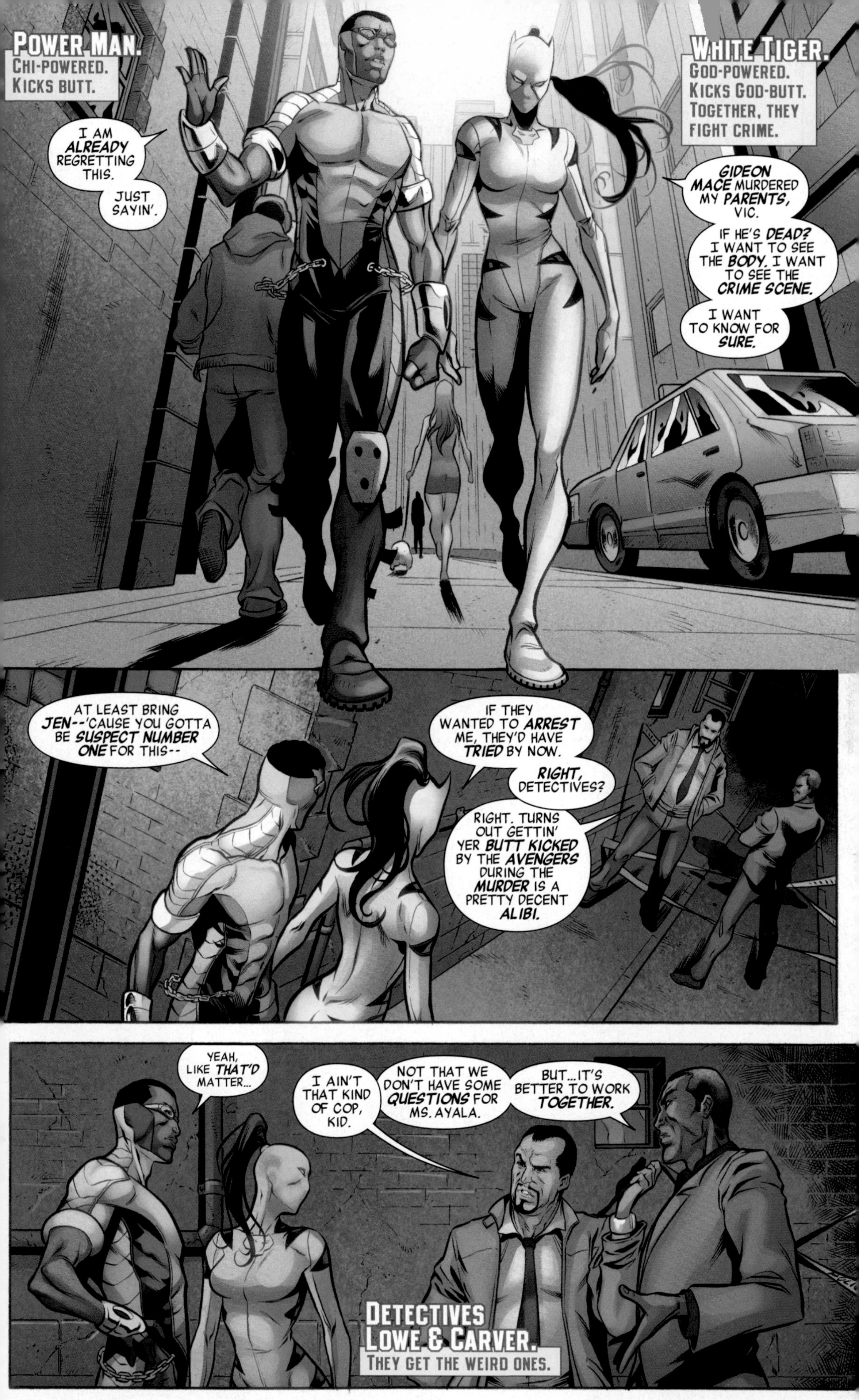

POWER MAN.
CHI-POWERED. KICKS BUTT.
I AM ALREADY REGRETTING THIS.
JUST SAYIN'.
WHITE TIGER.
GOD-POWERED. KICKS GOD-BUTT. TOGETHER, THEY FIGHT CRIME.
GIDEON MACE MURDERED MY PARENTS, VIC.
IF HE'S DEAD? I WANT TO SEE THE BODY. I WANT TO SEE THE CRIME SCENE.
I WANT TO KNOW FOR SURE.
AT LEAST BRING JEN--'CAUSE YOU GOTTA BE SUSPECT NUMBER ONE FOR THIS--
IF THEY WANTED TO ARREST ME, THEY'D HAVE TRIED BY NOW.
RIGHT, DETECTIVES?
RIGHT. TURNS OUT GETTIN' YER BUTT KICKED BY THE AVENGERS DURING THE MURDER IS A PRETTY DECENT ALIBI.
YEAH, LIKE THAT'D MATTER...
I AIN'T THAT KIND OF COP, KID.
NOT THAT WE DON'T HAVE SOME QUESTIONS FOR MS. AYALA.
BUT...IT'S BETTER TO WORK TOGETHER.
DETECTIVES LOWE & CARVER.
THEY GET THE WEIRD ONES.

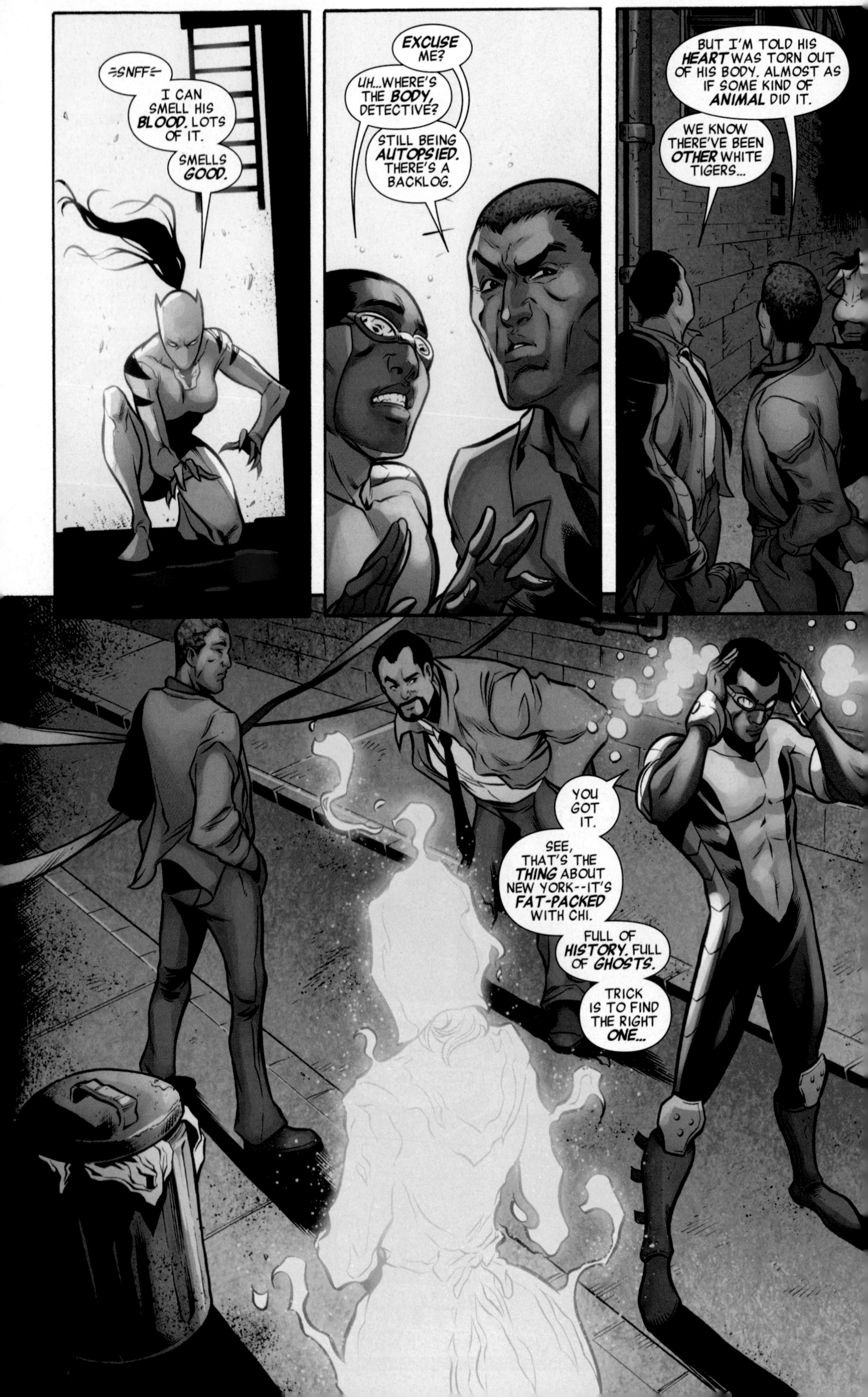
=SNFF=
I CAN SMELL HIS BLOOD. LOTS OF IT.
SMELLS GOOD.
EXCUSE ME?
UH...WHERE'S THE BODY, DETECTIVE?
STILL BEING AUTOPSIED. THERE'S A BACKLOG.
BUT I'M TOLD HIS HEART WAS TORN OUT OF HIS BODY. ALMOST AS IF SOME KIND OF ANIMAL DID IT.
WE KNOW THERE'VE BEEN OTHER WHITE TIGERS...
YOU GOT IT.
SEE, THAT'S THE THING ABOUT NEW YORK--IT'S FAT-PACKED WITH CHI.
FULL OF HISTORY. FULL OF GHOSTS.
TRICK IS TO FIND THE RIGHT ONE...

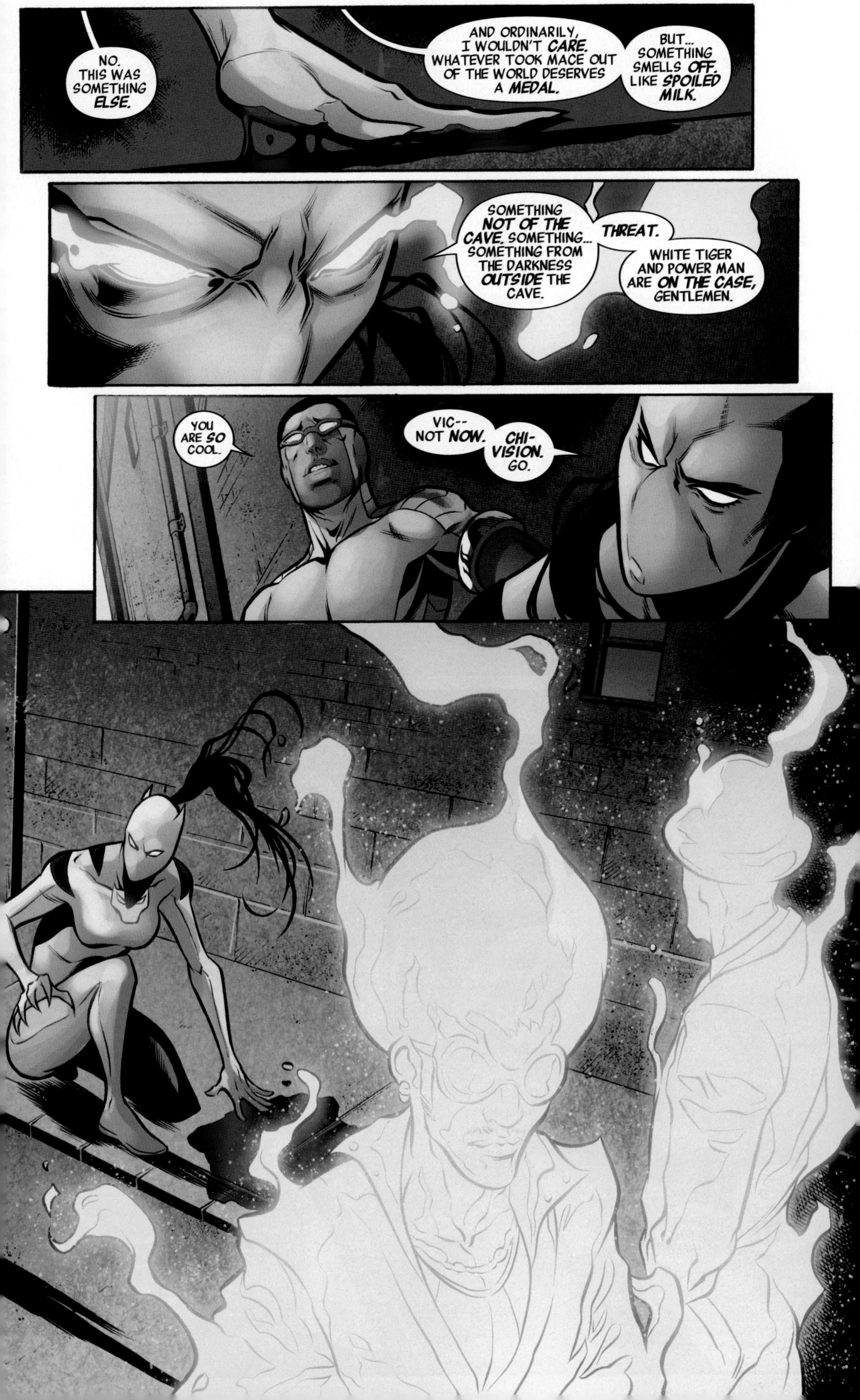
NO. THIS WAS SOMETHING ELSE.
AND ORDINARILY, I WOULDN'T CARE. WHATEVER TOOK MACE OUT OF THE WORLD DESERVES A MEDAL.
BUT... SOMETHING SMELLS OFF. LIKE SPOILED MILK.
SOMETHING NOT OF THE CAVE. SOMETHING... SOMETHING FROM THE DARKNESS OUTSIDE THE CAVE.
THREAT.
WHITE TIGER AND POWER MAN ARE ON THE CASE, GENTLEMEN.
YOU ARE SO COOL.
VIC-- NOT NOW.
CHI-VISION. GO.

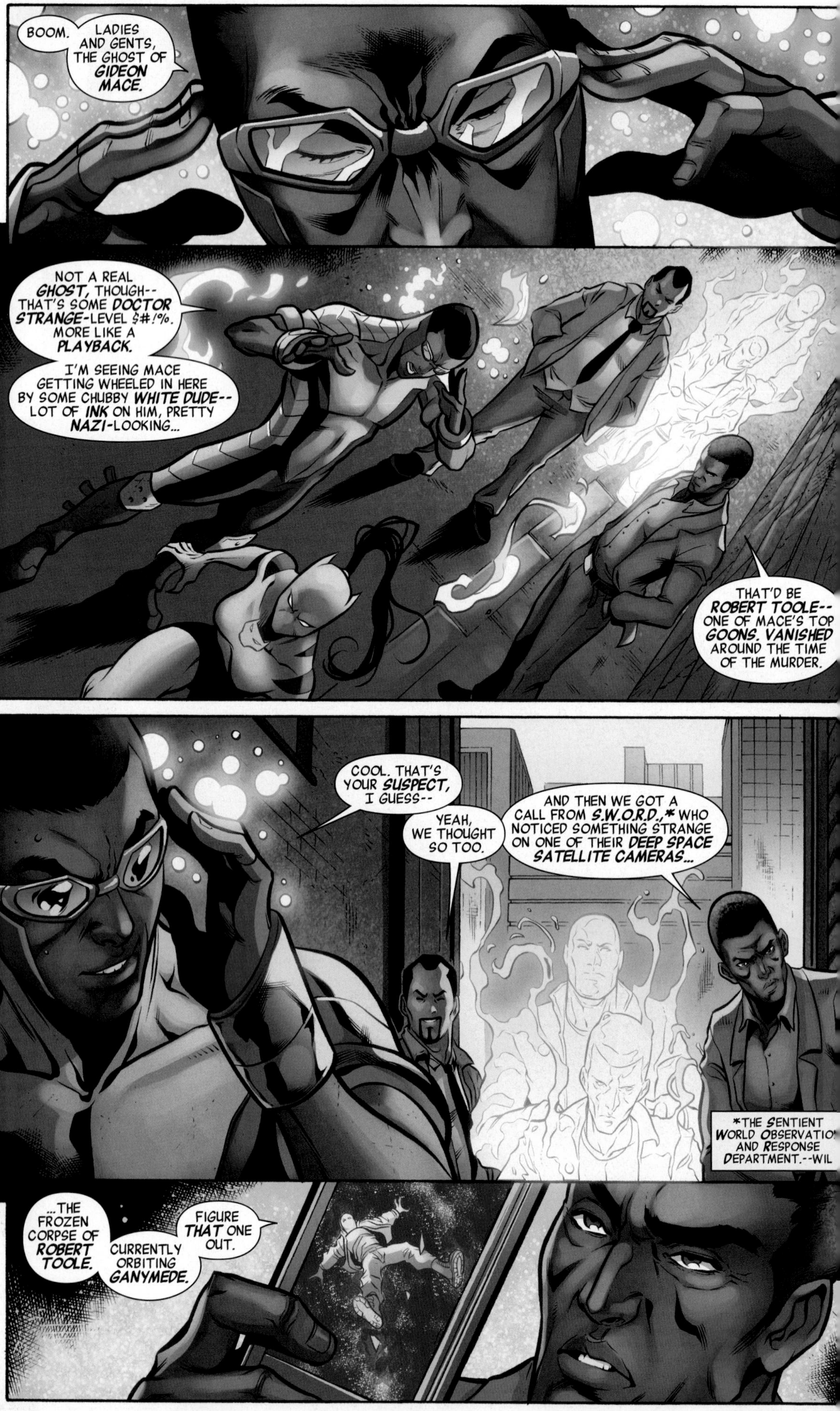

BOOM. LADIES AND GENTS, THE GHOST OF GIDEON MACE.
NOT A REAL GHOST, THOUGH-- THAT'S SOME DOCTOR STRANGE-LEVEL $#!%. MORE LIKE A PLAYBACK.
I'M SEEING MACE GETTING WHEELED IN HERE BY SOME CHUBBY WHITE DUDE-- LOT OF INK ON HIM, PRETTY NAZI-LOOKING...
THAT'D BE ROBERT TOOLE-- ONE OF MACE'S TOP GOONS. VANISHED AROUND THE TIME OF THE MURDER.
COOL. THAT'S YOUR SUSPECT, I GUESS--
YEAH, WE THOUGHT SO TOO.
AND THEN WE GOT A CALL FROM S.W.O.R.D.,* WHO NOTICED SOMETHING STRANGE ON ONE OF THEIR DEEP SPACE SATELLITE CAMERAS...
*THE SENTIENT WORLD OBSERVATIO AND RESPONSE DEPARTMENT.--WIL
...THE FROZEN CORPSE OF ROBERT TOOLE.
CURRENTLY ORBITING GANYMEDE.
FIGURE THAT ONE OUT.

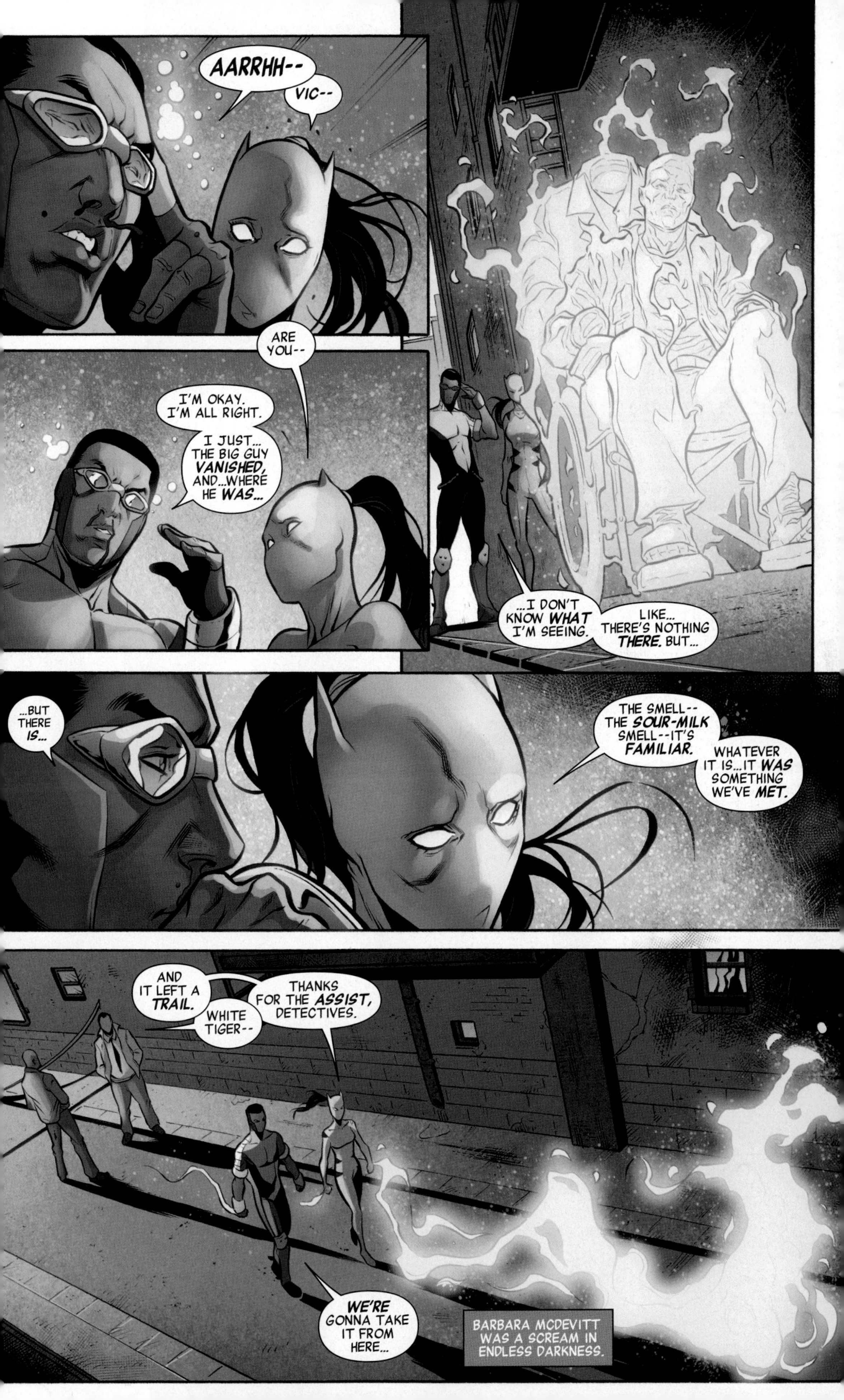
AARRHH--
VIC--
ARE YOU--
I'M OKAY. I'M ALL RIGHT.
I JUST... THE BIG GUY VANISHED, AND...WHERE HE WAS...
...I DON'T KNOW WHAT I'M SEEING.
LIKE... THERE'S NOTHING THERE. BUT...
...BUT THERE IS...
THE SMELL--THE SOUR-MILK SMELL--IT'S FAMILIAR.
WHATEVER IT IS...IT WAS SOMETHING WE'VE MET.
AND IT LEFT A TRAIL.
WHITE TIGER--
THANKS FOR THE ASSIST, DETECTIVES.
WE'RE GONNA TAKE IT FROM HERE...
BARBARA MCDEVITT WAS A SCREAM IN ENDLESS DARKNESS.

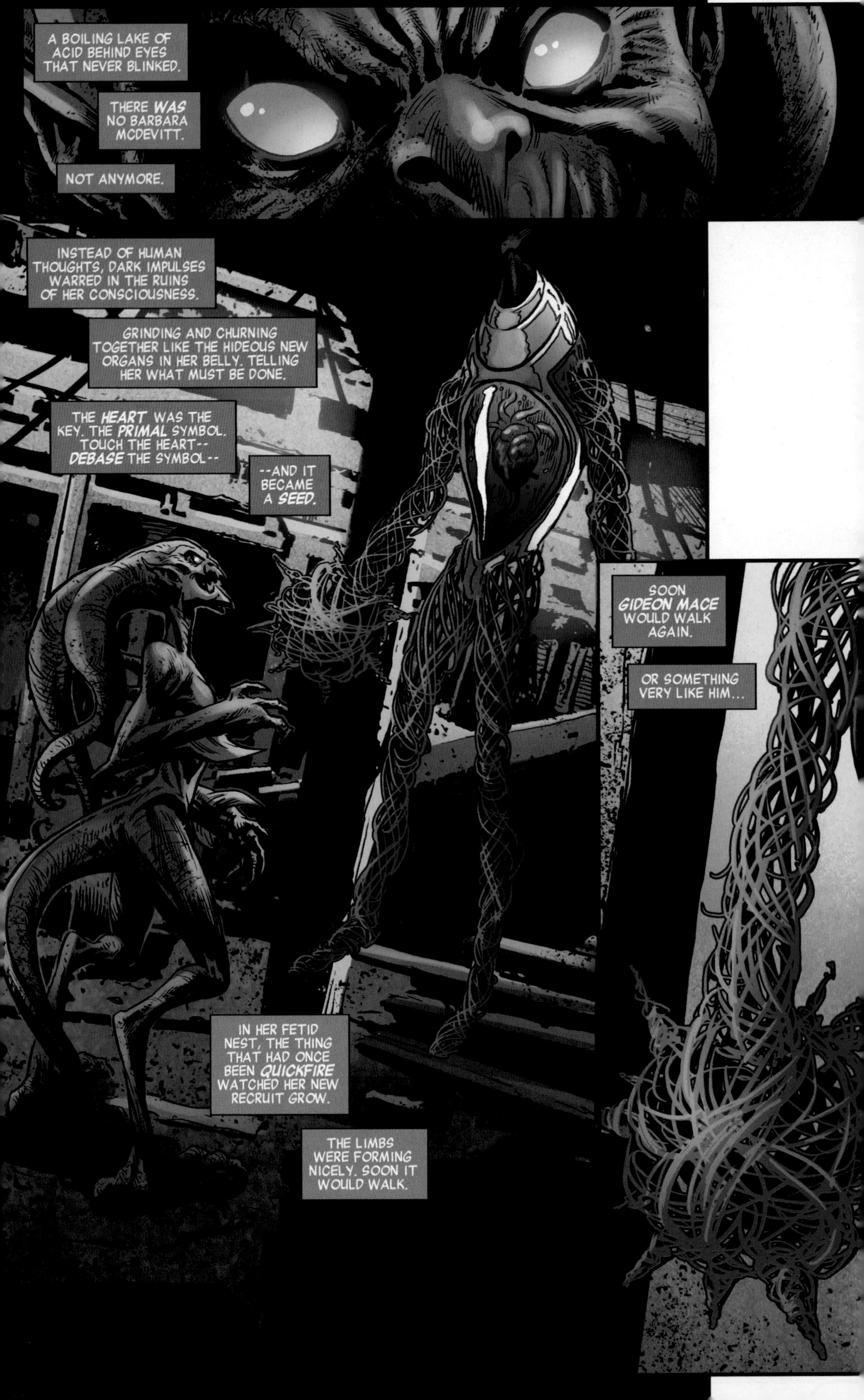
A BOILING LAKE OF ACID BEHIND EYES THAT NEVER BLINKED.
THERE WAS NO BARBARA MCDEVITT.
NOT ANYMORE.
INSTEAD OF HUMAN THOUGHTS, DARK IMPULSES WARRED IN THE RUINS OF HER CONSCIOUSNESS.
GRINDING AND CHURNING TOGETHER LIKE THE HIDEOUS NEW ORGANS IN HER BELLY. TELLING HER WHAT MUST BE DONE.
THE HEART WAS THE KEY. THE PRIMAL SYMBOL. TOUCH THE HEART-- DEBASE THE SYMBOL--
--AND IT BECAME A SEED.
IN HER FETID NEST, THE THING THAT HAD ONCE BEEN QUICKFIRE WATCHED HER NEW RECRUIT GROW.
THE LIMBS WERE FORMING NICELY. SOON IT WOULD WALK.
SOON GIDEON MACE WOULD WALK AGAIN.
OR SOMETHING VERY LIKE HIM...

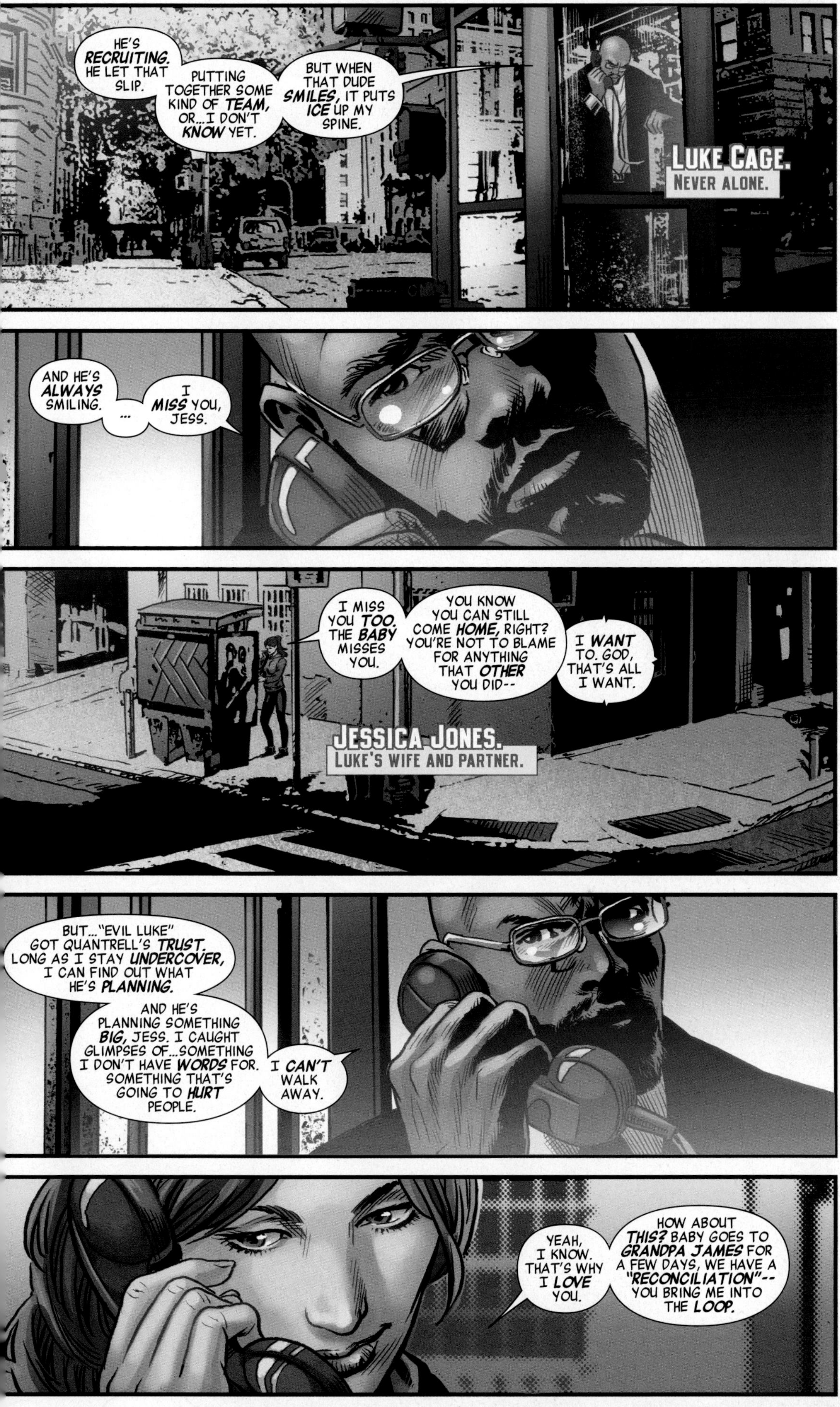

HE'S RECRUITING. HE LET THAT SLIP.
PUTTING TOGETHER SOME KIND OF TEAM, OR...I DON'T KNOW YET.
BUT WHEN THAT DUDE SMILES, IT PUTS ICE UP MY SPINE.
LUKE CAGE.
NEVER ALONE.
AND HE'S ALWAYS SMILING.
...
I MISS YOU, JESS.
I MISS YOU TOO. THE BABY MISSES YOU.
YOU KNOW YOU CAN STILL COME HOME, RIGHT? YOU'RE NOT TO BLAME FOR ANYTHING THAT OTHER YOU DID--
I WANT TO. GOD, THAT'S ALL I WANT.
JESSICA JONES.
LUKE'S WIFE AND PARTNER.
BUT..."EVIL LUKE" GOT QUANTRELL'S TRUST. LONG AS I STAY UNDERCOVER, I CAN FIND OUT WHAT HE'S PLANNING.
AND HE'S PLANNING SOMETHING BIG, JESS. I CAUGHT GLIMPSES OF...SOMETHING I DON'T HAVE WORDS FOR. SOMETHING THAT'S GOING TO HURT PEOPLE.
I CAN'T WALK AWAY.
YEAH, I KNOW. THAT'S WHY I LOVE YOU.
HOW ABOUT THIS? BABY GOES TO GRANDPA JAMES FOR A FEW DAYS, WE HAVE A "RECONCILIATION"-- YOU BRING ME INTO THE LOOP.

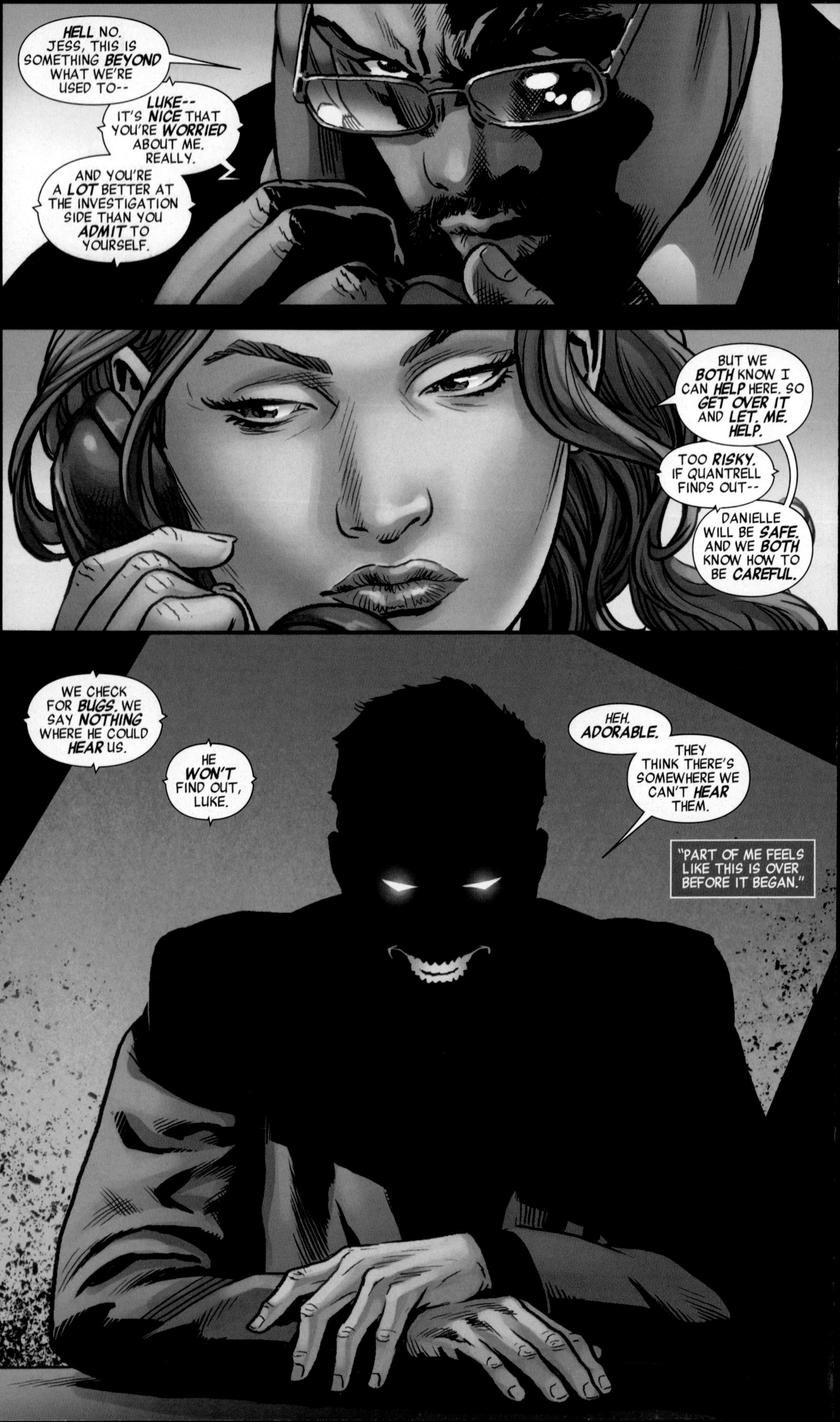
HELL NO. JESS, THIS IS SOMETHING BEYOND WHAT WE'RE USED TO--
LUKE-- IT'S NICE THAT YOU'RE WORRIED ABOUT ME. REALLY.
AND YOU'RE A LOT BETTER AT THE INVESTIGATION SIDE THAN YOU ADMIT TO YOURSELF.
BUT WE BOTH KNOW I CAN HELP HERE. SO GET OVER IT AND LET. ME. HELP.
TOO RISKY. IF QUANTRELL FINDS OUT--
DANIELLE WILL BE SAFE. AND WE BOTH KNOW HOW TO BE CAREFUL.
WE CHECK FOR BUGS. WE SAY NOTHING WHERE HE COULD HEAR US.
HE WON'T FIND OUT, LUKE.
HEH. ADORABLE.
THEY THINK THERE'S SOMEWHERE WE CAN'T HEAR THEM.
"PART OF ME FEELS LIKE THIS IS OVER BEFORE IT BEGAN."

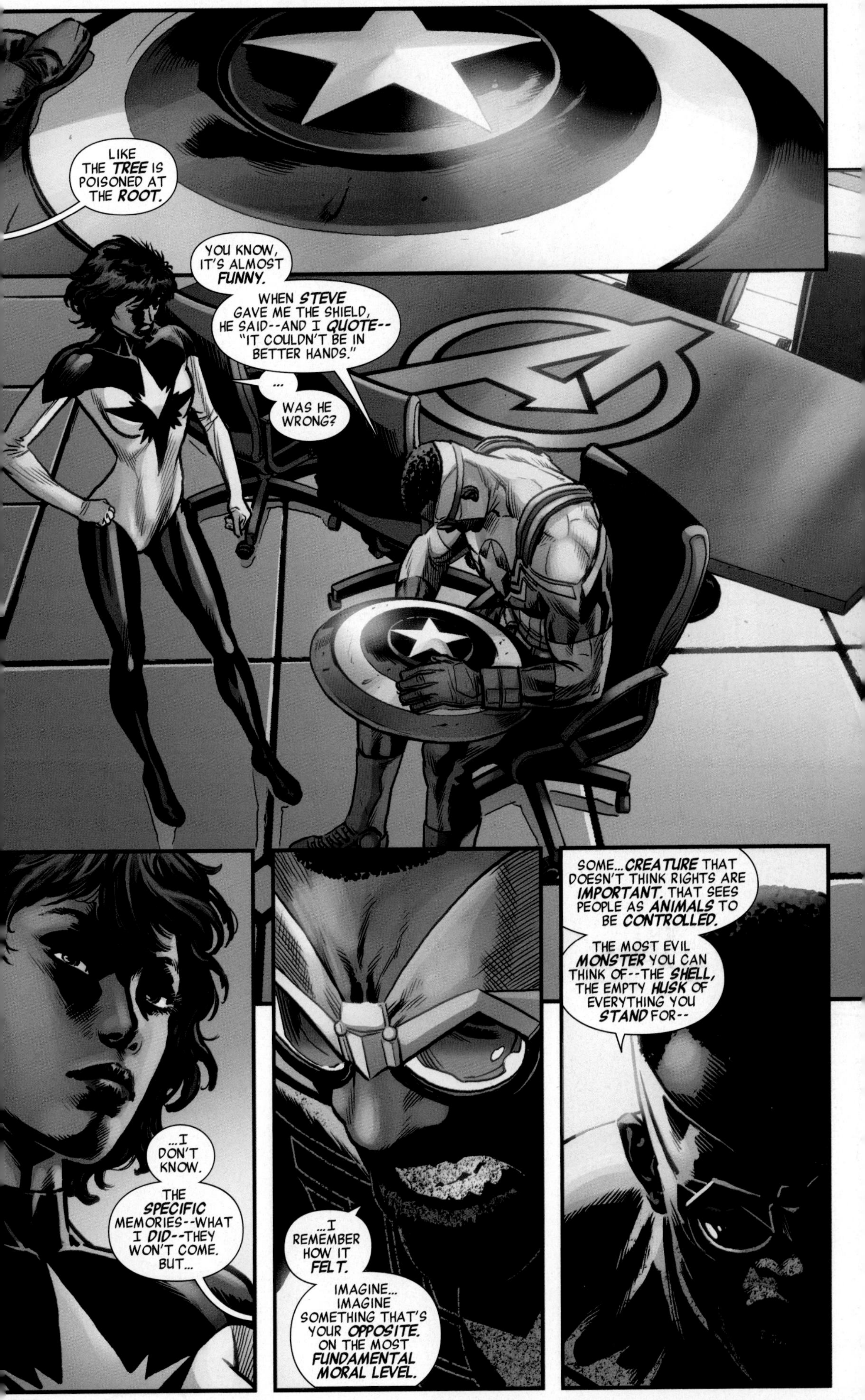

LIKE THE TREE IS POISONED AT THE ROOT.
YOU KNOW, IT'S ALMOST FUNNY.
WHEN STEVE GAVE ME THE SHIELD, HE SAID--AND I QUOTE-- "IT COULDN'T BE IN BETTER HANDS."
...
WAS HE WRONG?
...I DON'T KNOW.
THE SPECIFIC MEMORIES--WHAT I DID--THEY WON'T COME. BUT...
...I REMEMBER HOW IT FELT.
IMAGINE... IMAGINE SOMETHING THAT'S YOUR OPPOSITE. ON THE MOST FUNDAMENTAL MORAL LEVEL.
SOME...CREATURE THAT DOESN'T THINK RIGHTS ARE IMPORTANT. THAT SEES PEOPLE AS ANIMALS TO BE CONTROLLED.
THE MOST EVIL MONSTER YOU CAN THINK OF--THE SHELL, THE EMPTY HUSK OF EVERYTHING YOU STAND FOR--

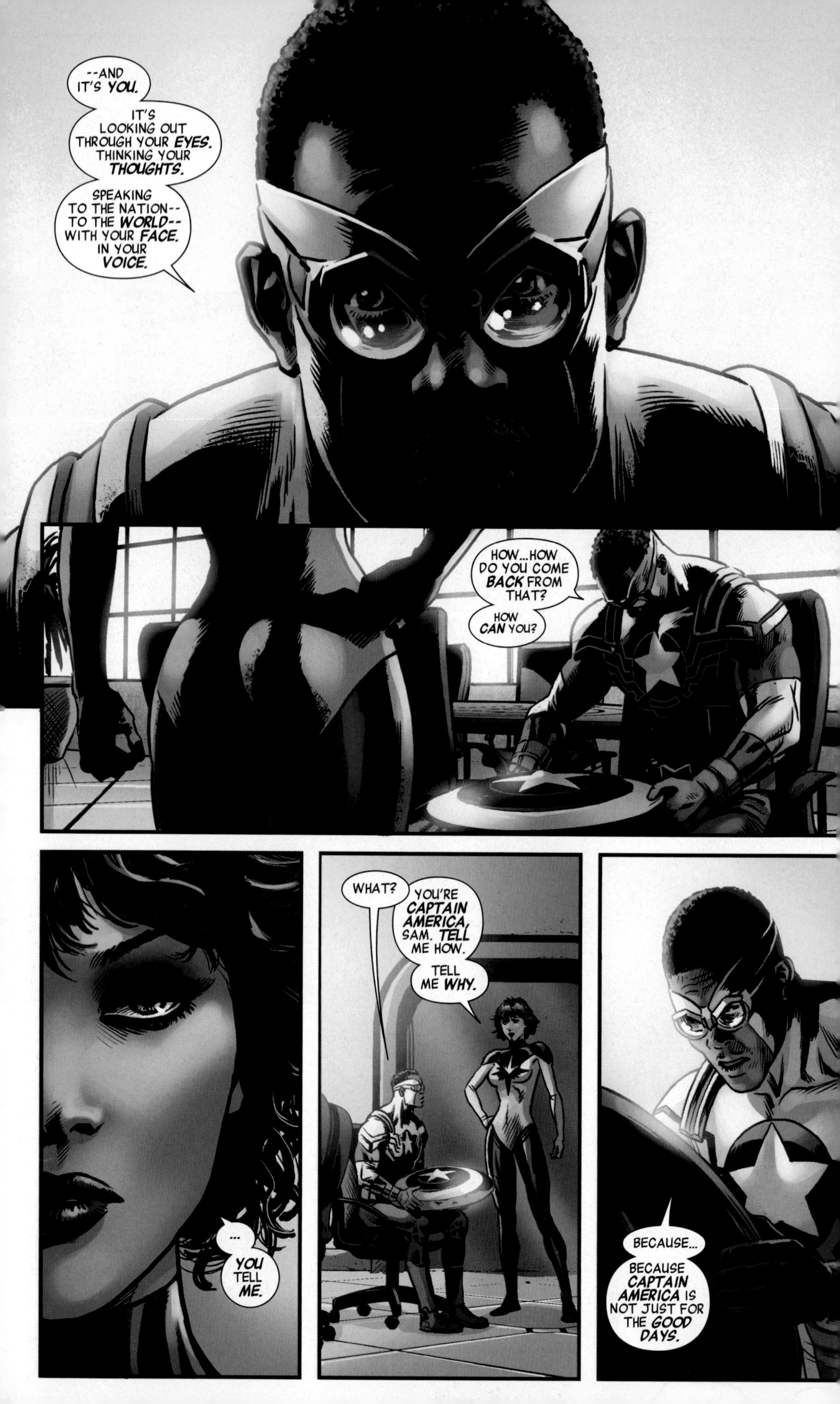
--AND IT'S YOU.
IT'S LOOKING OUT THROUGH YOUR EYES. THINKING YOUR THOUGHTS.
SPEAKING TO THE NATION-- TO THE WORLD-- WITH YOUR FACE. IN YOUR VOICE.
HOW...HOW DO YOU COME BACK FROM THAT?
HOW CAN YOU?
... YOU TELL ME.
WHAT?
YOU'RE CAPTAIN AMERICA, SAM. TELL ME HOW.
TELL ME WHY.
BECAUSE...
BECAUSE CAPTAIN AMERICA IS NOT JUST FOR THE GOOD DAYS.

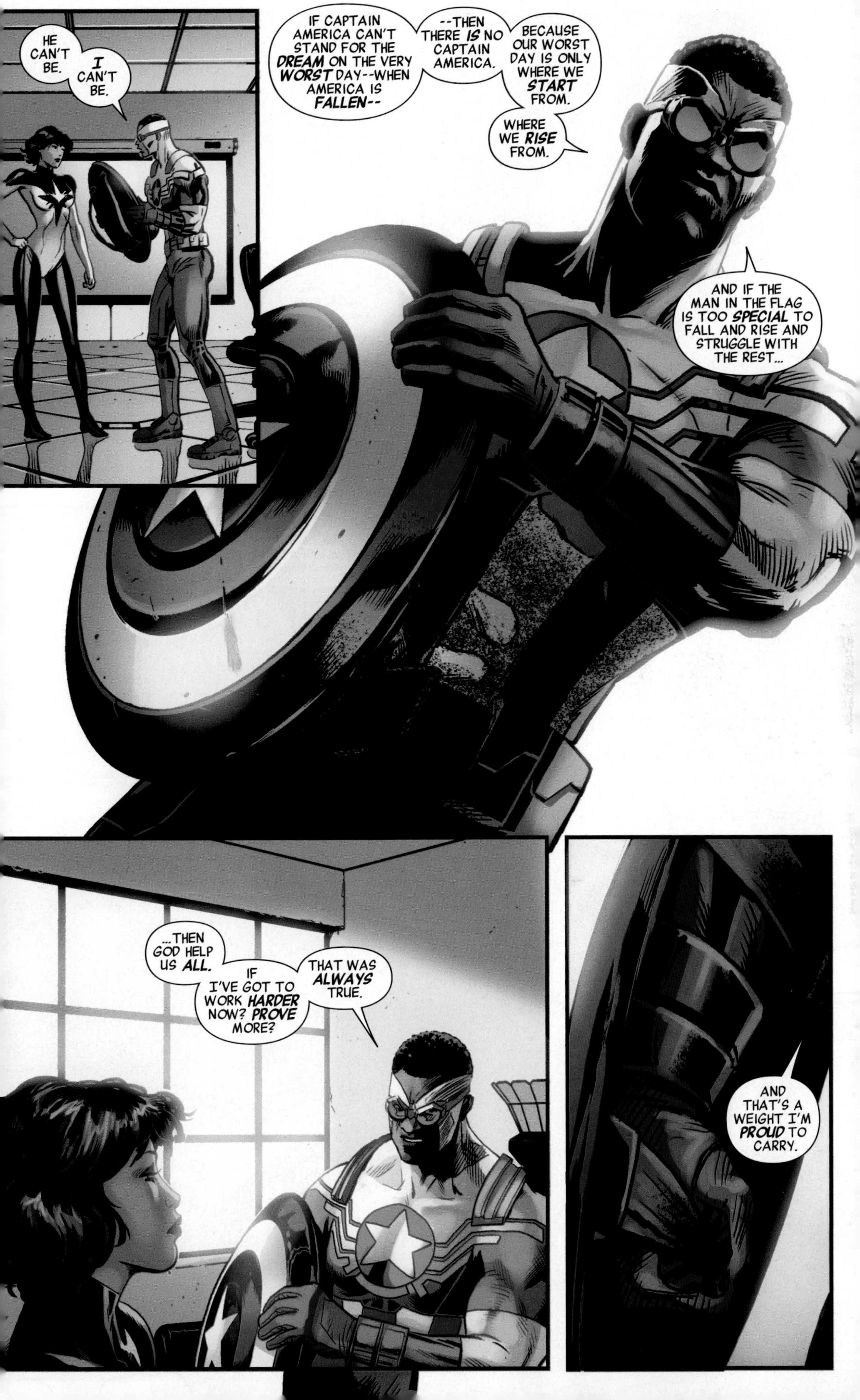
HE CAN'T BE.
I CAN'T BE.
IF CAPTAIN AMERICA CAN'T STAND FOR THE DREAM ON THE VERY WORST DAY--WHEN AMERICA IS FALLEN--
--THEN THERE IS NO CAPTAIN AMERICA.
BECAUSE OUR WORST DAY IS ONLY WHERE WE START FROM.
WHERE WE RISE FROM.
AND IF THE MAN IN THE FLAG IS TOO SPECIAL TO FALL AND RISE AND STRUGGLE WITH THE REST...
...THEN GOD HELP US ALL.
IF I'VE GOT TO WORK HARDER NOW? PROVE MORE?
THAT WAS ALWAYS TRUE.
AND THAT'S A WEIGHT I'M PROUD TO CARRY.

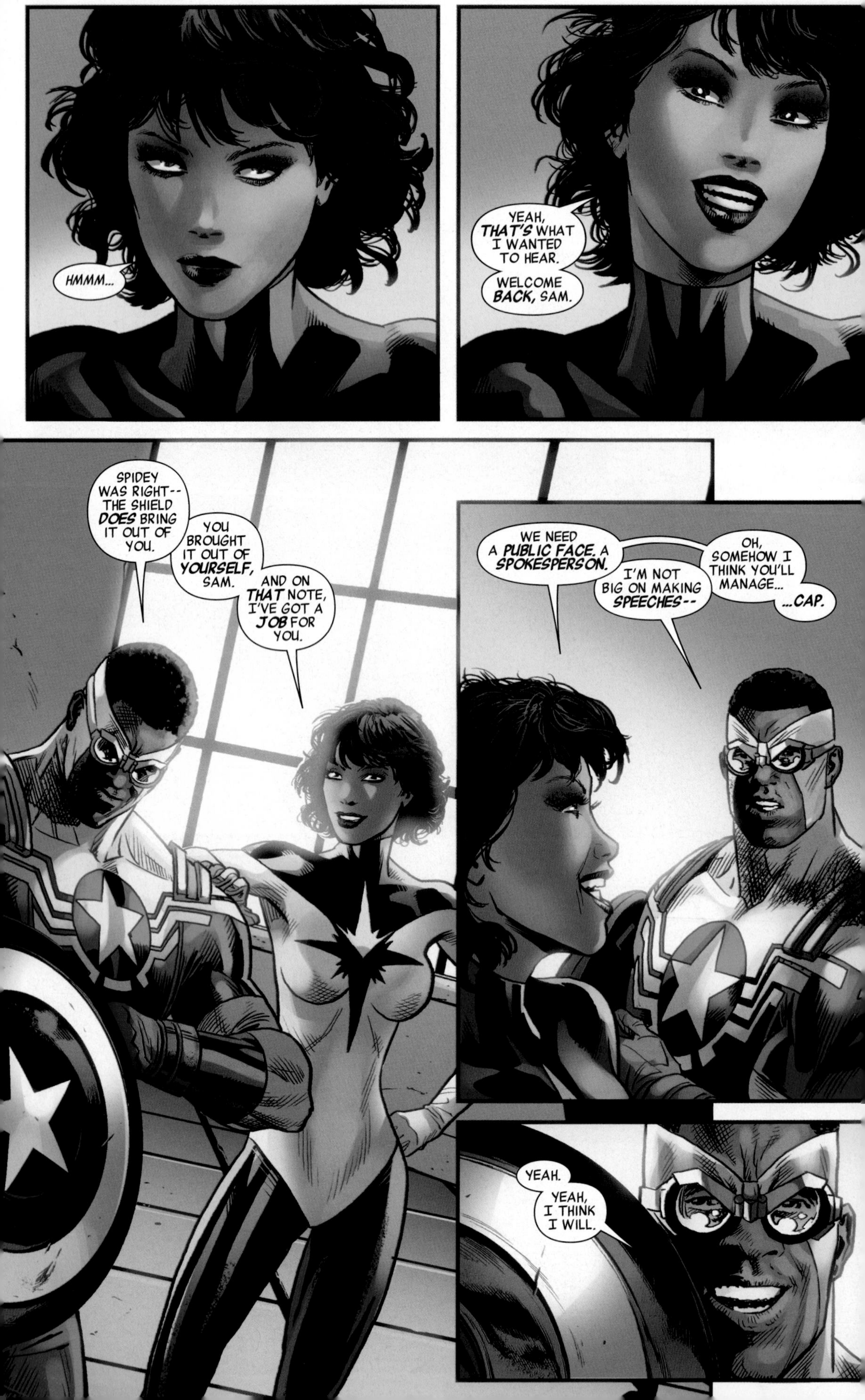
HMMM...
YEAH, THAT'S WHAT I WANTED TO HEAR.
WELCOME BACK, SAM.
SPIDEY WAS RIGHT-- THE SHIELD DOES BRING IT OUT OF YOU.
YOU BROUGHT IT OUT OF YOURSELF, SAM.
AND ON THAT NOTE, I'VE GOT A JOB FOR YOU.
WE NEED A PUBLIC FACE. A SPOKESPERSON.
I'M NOT BIG ON MAKING SPEECHES--
OH, SOMEHOW I THINK YOU'LL MANAGE...
...CAP.
YEAH.
YEAH, I THINK I WILL.

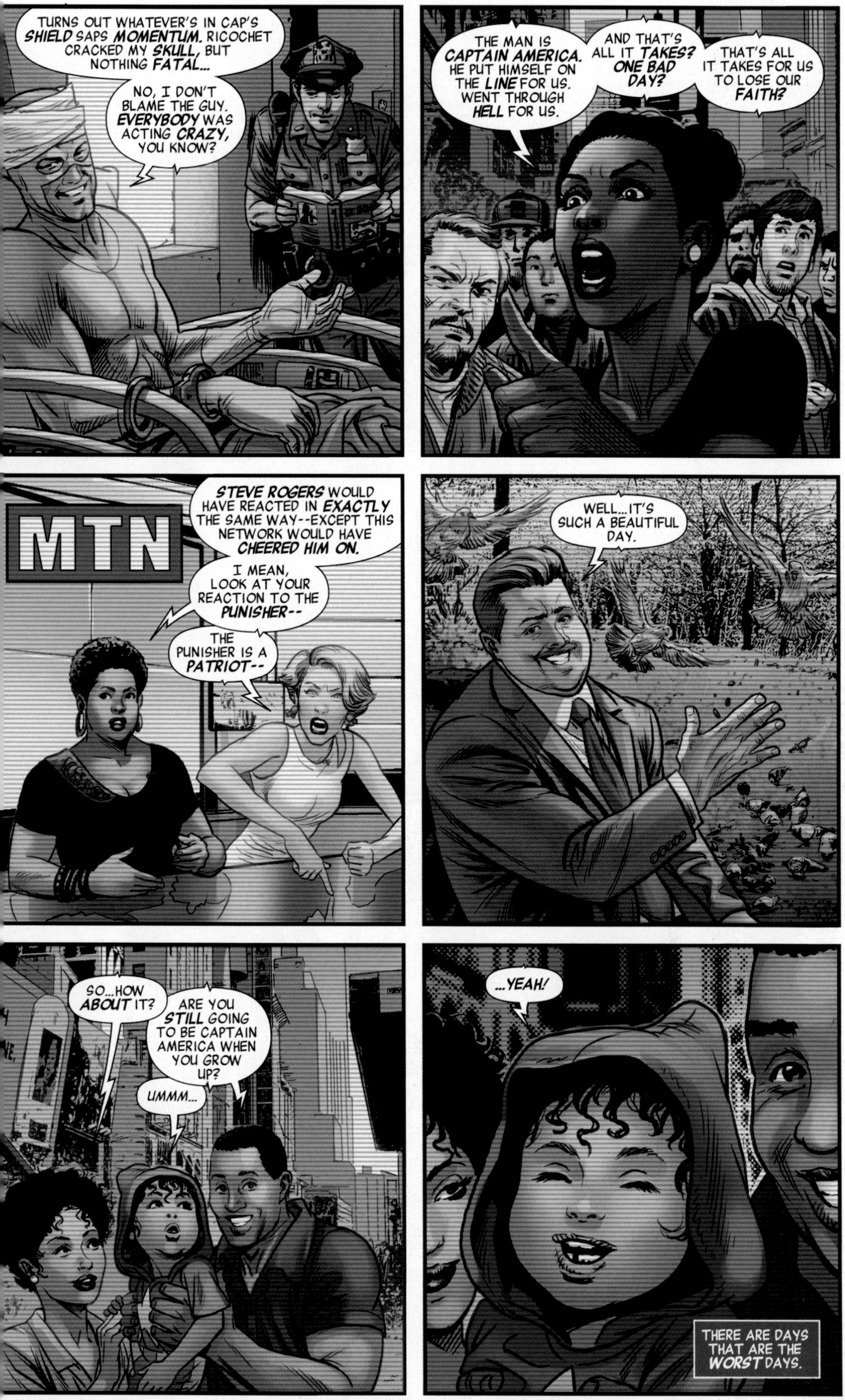
TURNS OUT WHATEVER'S IN CAP'S SHIELD SAPS MOMENTUM. RICOCHET CRACKED MY SKULL, BUT NOTHING FATAL...
NO, I DON'T BLAME THE GUY. EVERYBODY WAS ACTING CRAZY, YOU KNOW?
THE MAN IS CAPTAIN AMERICA. HE PUT HIMSELF ON THE LINE FOR US. WENT THROUGH HELL FOR US.
AND THAT'S ALL IT TAKES? ONE BAD DAY?
THAT'S ALL IT TAKES FOR US TO LOSE OUR FAITH?
MTN
STEVE ROGERS WOULD HAVE REACTED IN EXACTLY THE SAME WAY--EXCEPT THIS NETWORK WOULD HAVE CHEERED HIM ON.
I MEAN, LOOK AT YOUR REACTION TO THE PUNISHER--
THE PUNISHER IS A PATRIOT--
WELL...IT'S SUCH A BEAUTIFUL DAY.
SO...HOW ABOUT IT?
ARE YOU STILL GOING TO BE CAPTAIN AMERICA WHEN YOU GROW UP?
UMMM...
...YEAH!
THERE ARE DAYS THAT ARE THE WORST DAYS.

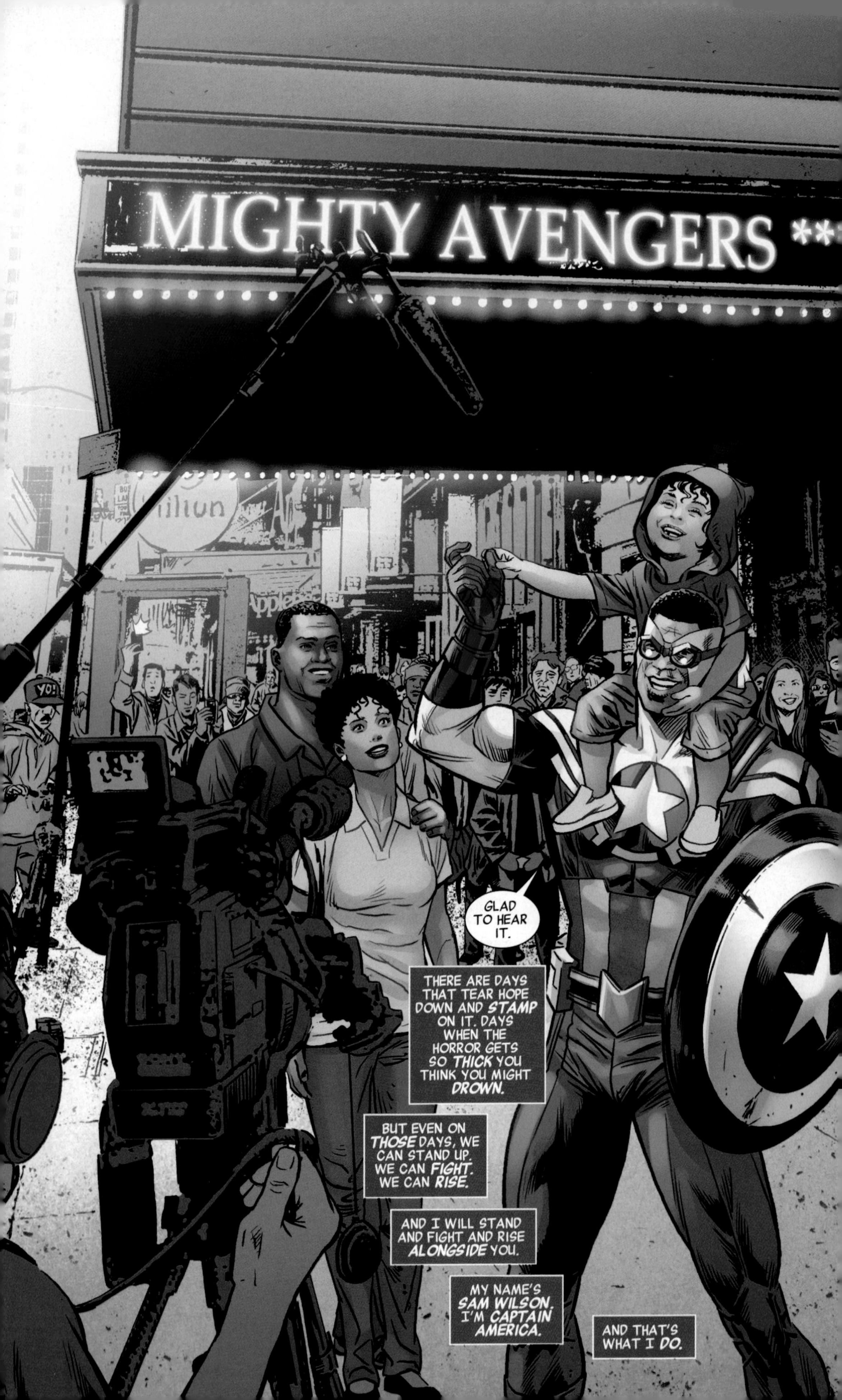

MIGHTY AVENGERS
GLAD TO HEAR IT.
THERE ARE DAYS THAT TEAR HOPE DOWN AND STAMP ON IT. DAYS WHEN THE HORROR GETS SO THICK YOU THINK YOU MIGHT DROWN.
BUT EVEN ON THOSE DAYS, WE CAN STAND UP. WE CAN FIGHT. WE CAN RISE.
AND I WILL STAND AND FIGHT AND RISE ALONGSIDE YOU.
MY NAME'S SAM WILSON. I'M CAPTAIN AMERICA.
AND THAT'S WHAT I DO.

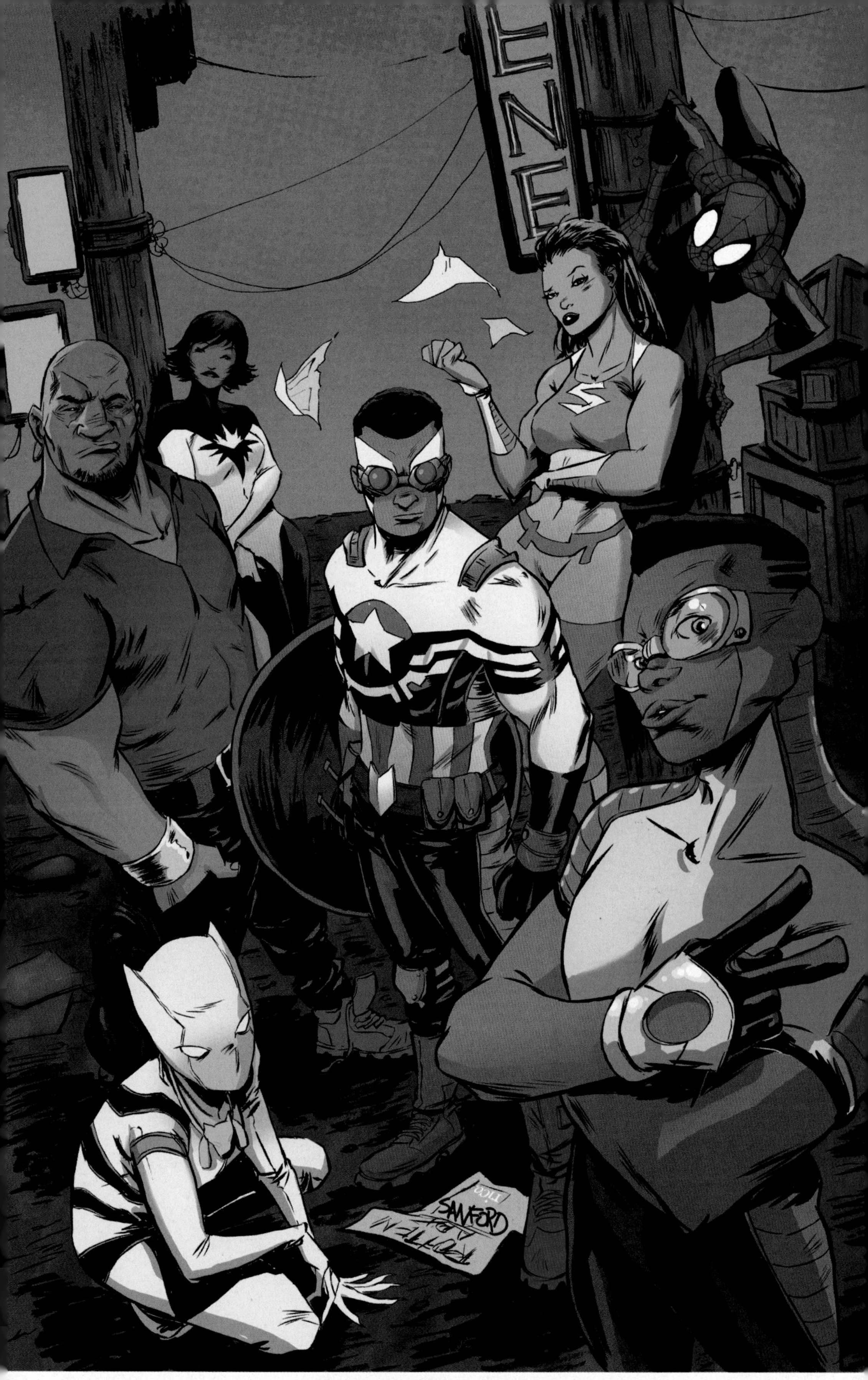
SANFORD
rico

#2 VARIANT BY SANFORD GREENE & RICO RENZI

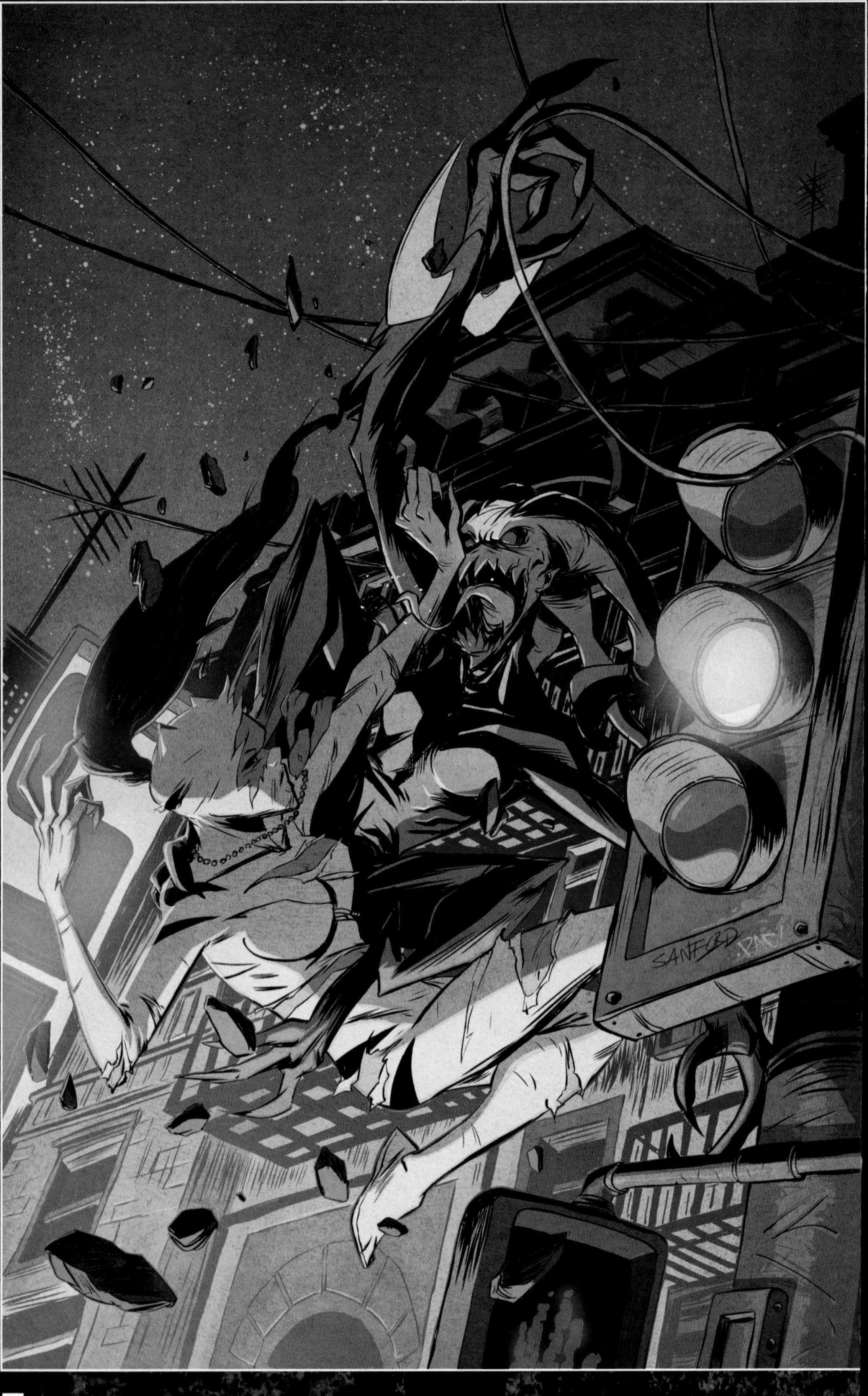
SANFORD

5

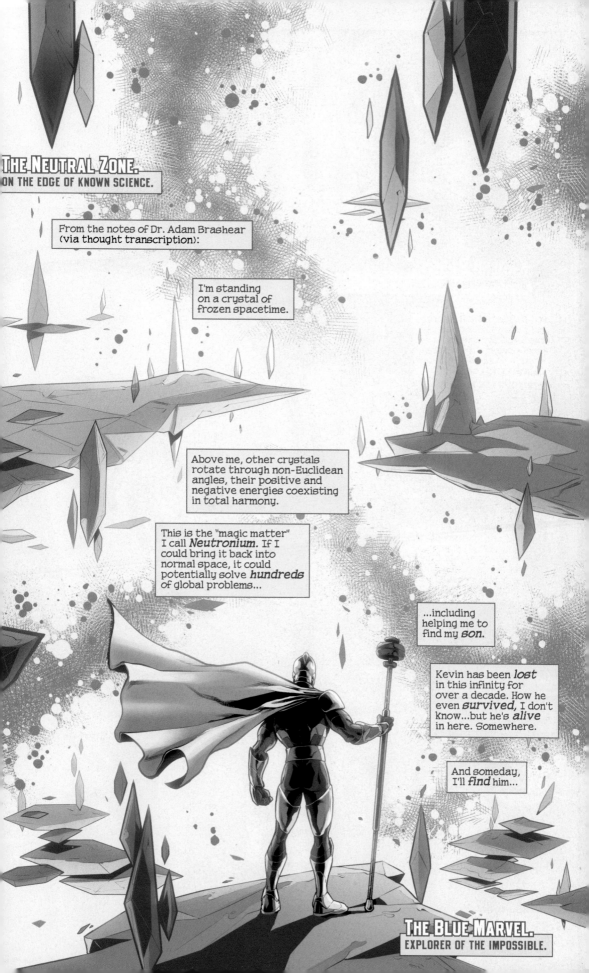

THE NEUTRAL ZONE.
ON THE EDGE OF KNOWN SCIENCE.

From the notes of Dr. Adam Brashear (via thought transcription):

I'm standing on a crystal of frozen spacetime.

Above me, other crystals rotate through non-Euclidean angles, their positive and negative energies coexisting in total harmony.

This is the "magic matter" I call *Neutronium*. If I could bring it back into normal space, it could potentially solve *hundreds* of global problems...

...including helping me to find my *son*.

Kevin has been *lost* in this infinity for over a decade. How he even *survived*, I don't know...but he's *alive* in here. Somewhere.

And someday, I'll *find* him...

THE BLUE MARVEL.
EXPLORER OF THE IMPOSSIBLE.

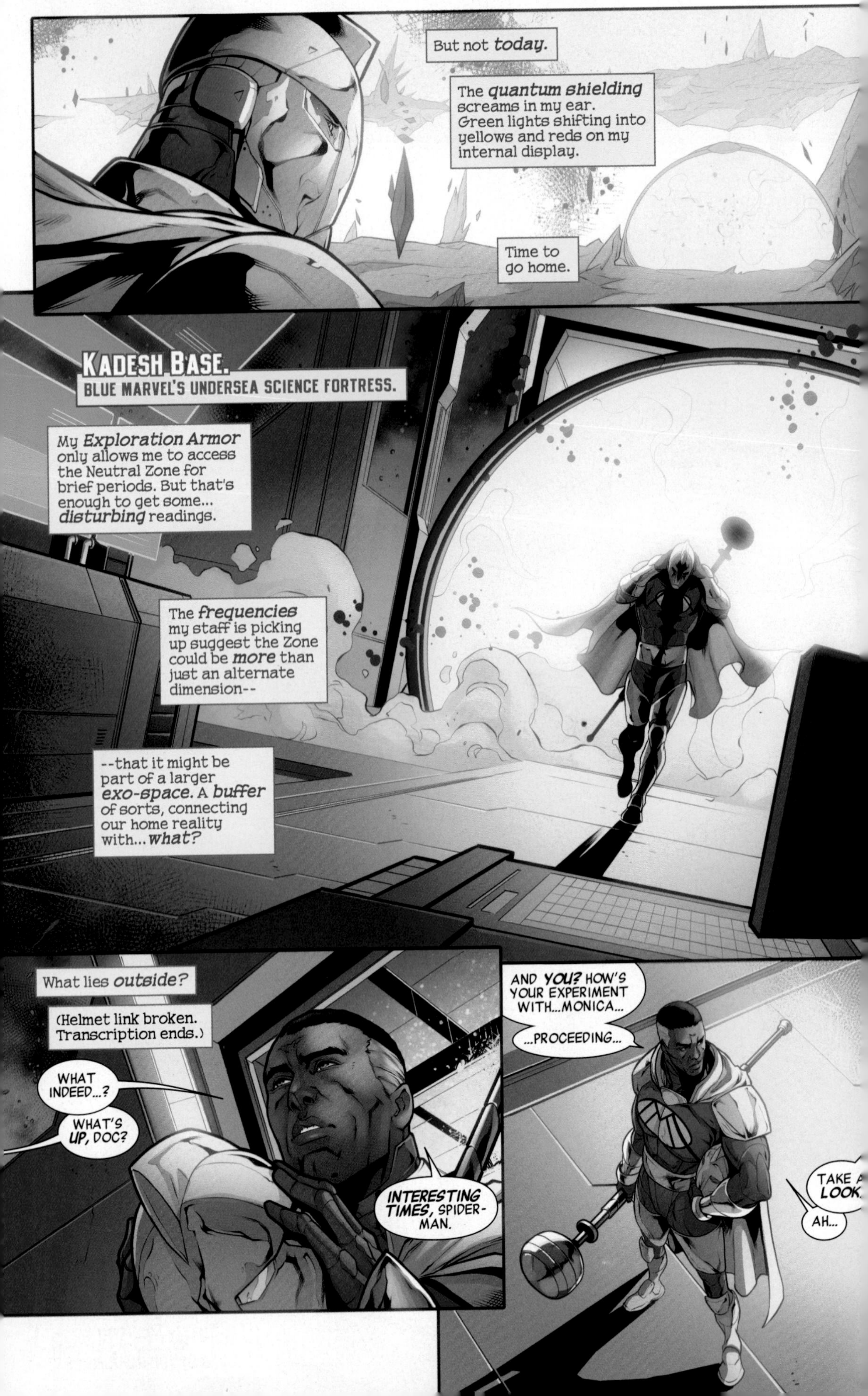
But not today.
The quantum shielding screams in my ear. Green lights shifting into yellows and reds on my internal display.
Time to go home.
KADESH BASE.
BLUE MARVEL'S UNDERSEA SCIENCE FORTRESS.
My Exploration Armor only allows me to access the Neutral Zone for brief periods. But that's enough to get some... disturbing readings.
The frequencies my staff is picking up suggest the Zone could be more than just an alternate dimension--
--that it might be part of a larger exo-space. A buffer of sorts, connecting our home reality with... what?
What lies outside?
(Helmet link broken. Transcription ends.)
WHAT INDEED...?
WHAT'S UP, DOC?
INTERESTING TIMES, SPIDER-MAN.
AND YOU? HOW'S YOUR EXPERIMENT WITH...MONICA...
...PROCEEDING...
TAKE A LOOK.
AH...

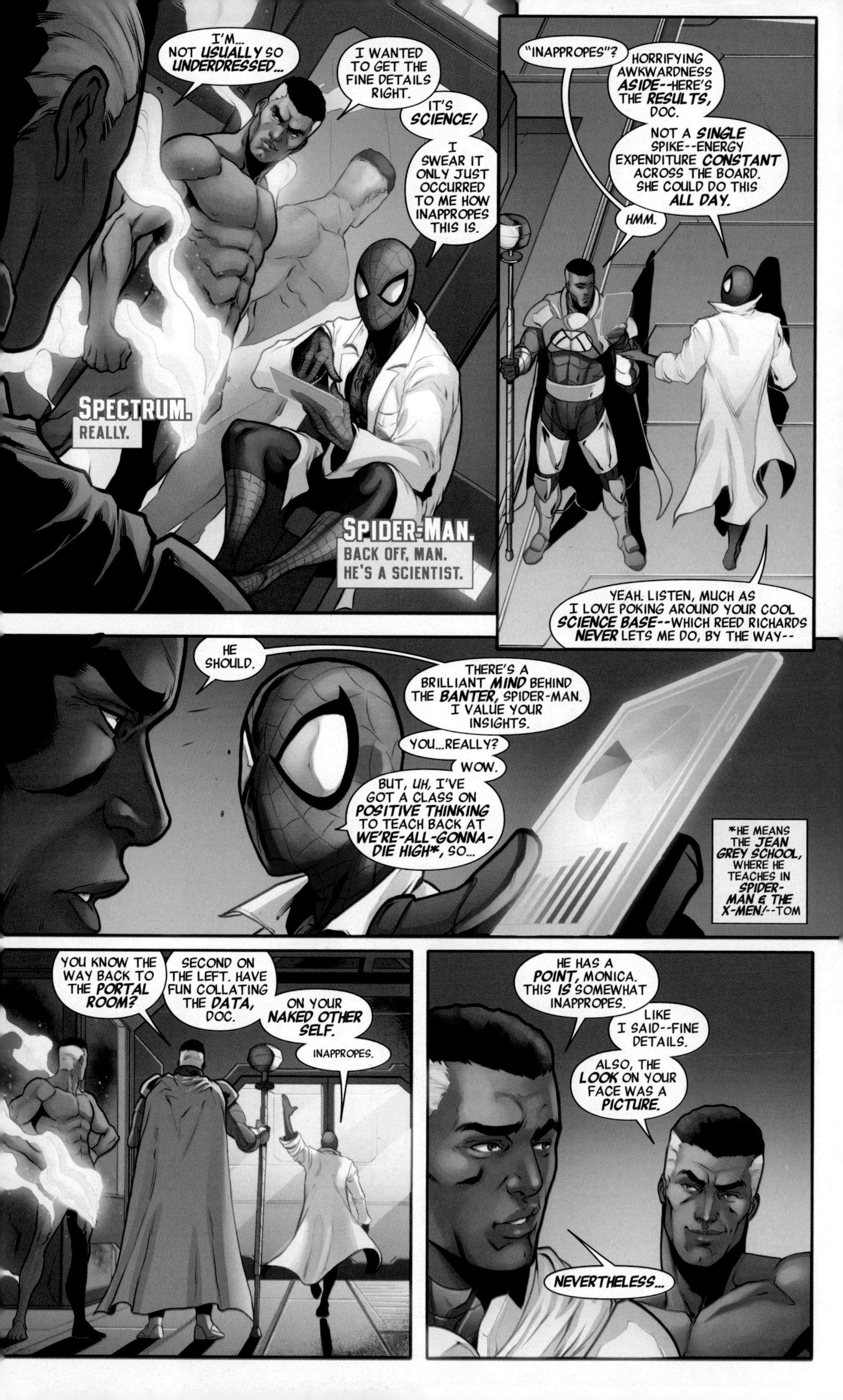

I'M... NOT USUALLY SO UNDERDRESSED...
I WANTED TO GET THE FINE DETAILS RIGHT.
IT'S SCIENCE!
I SWEAR IT ONLY JUST OCCURRED TO ME HOW INAPPROPES THIS IS.
SPECTRUM.
REALLY.
SPIDER-MAN.
BACK OFF, MAN. HE'S A SCIENTIST.
"INAPPROPES"?
HORRIFYING AWKWARDNESS ASIDE--HERE'S THE RESULTS, DOC.
NOT A SINGLE SPIKE--ENERGY EXPENDITURE CONSTANT ACROSS THE BOARD. SHE COULD DO THIS ALL DAY.
HMM.
YEAH. LISTEN, MUCH AS I LOVE POKING AROUND YOUR COOL SCIENCE BASE--WHICH REED RICHARDS NEVER LETS ME DO, BY THE WAY--
HE SHOULD.
THERE'S A BRILLIANT MIND BEHIND THE BANTER, SPIDER-MAN. I VALUE YOUR INSIGHTS.
YOU...REALLY?
WOW.
BUT, UH, I'VE GOT A CLASS ON POSITIVE THINKING TO TEACH BACK AT WE'RE-ALL-GONNA-DIE HIGH*, SO...
*HE MEANS THE JEAN GREY SCHOOL, WHERE HE TEACHES IN SPIDER-MAN & THE X-MEN!--TOM
YOU KNOW THE WAY BACK TO THE PORTAL ROOM?
SECOND ON THE LEFT. HAVE FUN COLLATING THE DATA, DOC.
ON YOUR NAKED OTHER SELF.
INAPPROPES.
HE HAS A POINT, MONICA. THIS IS SOMEWHAT INAPPROPES.
LIKE I SAID--FINE DETAILS.
ALSO, THE LOOK ON YOUR FACE WAS A PICTURE.
NEVERTHELESS...

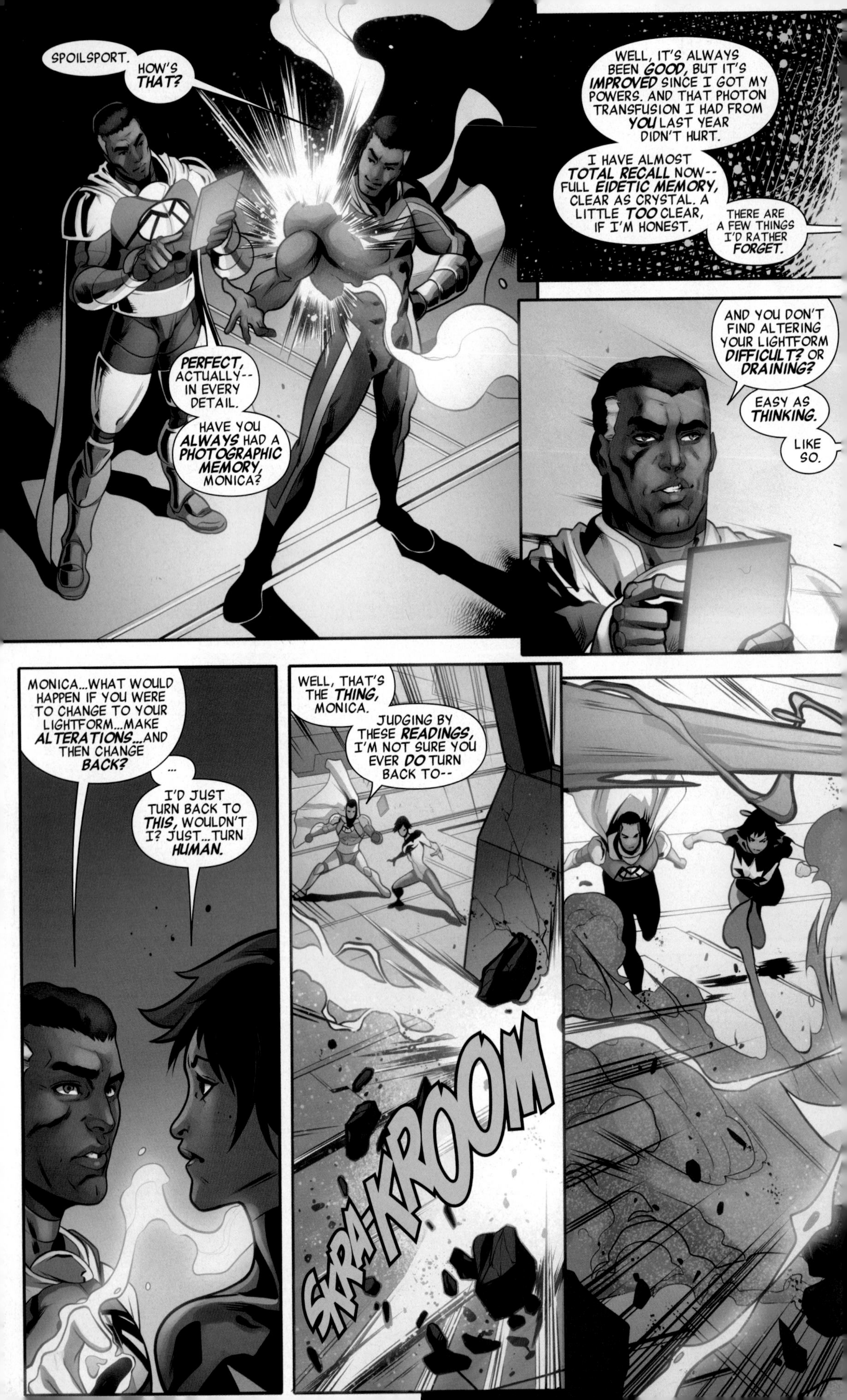
SPOILSPORT.
HOW'S THAT?
PERFECT, ACTUALLY-- IN EVERY DETAIL.
HAVE YOU ALWAYS HAD A PHOTOGRAPHIC MEMORY, MONICA?
WELL, IT'S ALWAYS BEEN GOOD, BUT IT'S IMPROVED SINCE I GOT MY POWERS. AND THAT PHOTON TRANSFUSION I HAD FROM YOU LAST YEAR DIDN'T HURT.
I HAVE ALMOST TOTAL RECALL NOW-- FULL EIDETIC MEMORY, CLEAR AS CRYSTAL. A LITTLE TOO CLEAR, IF I'M HONEST.
THERE ARE A FEW THINGS I'D RATHER FORGET.
AND YOU DON'T FIND ALTERING YOUR LIGHTFORM DIFFICULT? OR DRAINING?
EASY AS THINKING.
LIKE SO.
MONICA...WHAT WOULD HAPPEN IF YOU WERE TO CHANGE TO YOUR LIGHTFORM...MAKE ALTERATIONS...AND THEN CHANGE BACK?
...
I'D JUST TURN BACK TO THIS, WOULDN'T I? JUST...TURN HUMAN.
WELL, THAT'S THE THING, MONICA.
JUDGING BY THESE READINGS, I'M NOT SURE YOU EVER DO TURN BACK TO--
SKRA-KROOM

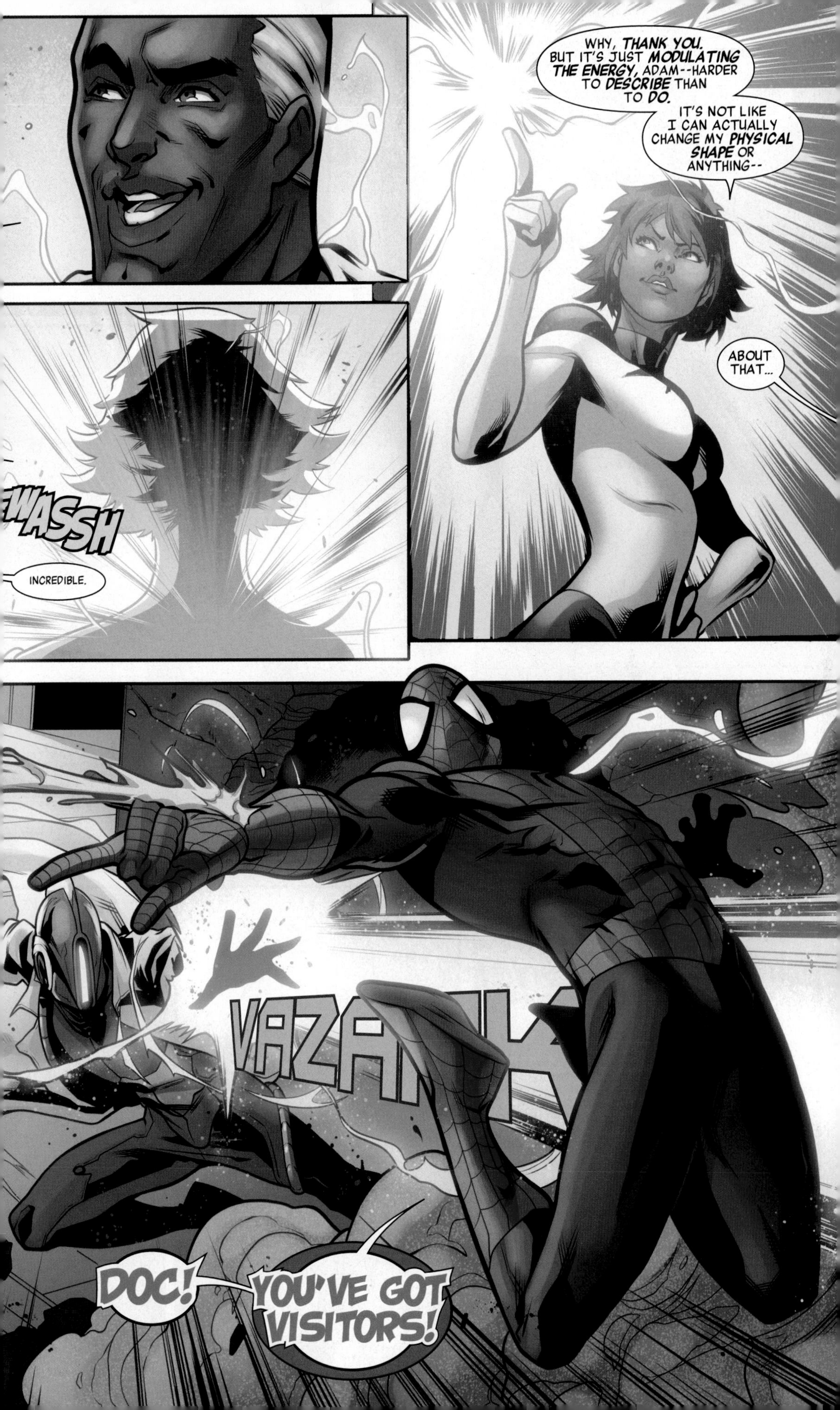
WHY, THANK YOU. BUT IT'S JUST MODULATING THE ENERGY, ADAM--HARDER TO DESCRIBE THAN TO DO.
IT'S NOT LIKE I CAN ACTUALLY CHANGE MY PHYSICAL SHAPE OR ANYTHING--
WASSH
INCREDIBLE.
ABOUT THAT...
VAZA
DOC!
YOU'VE GOT VISITORS!

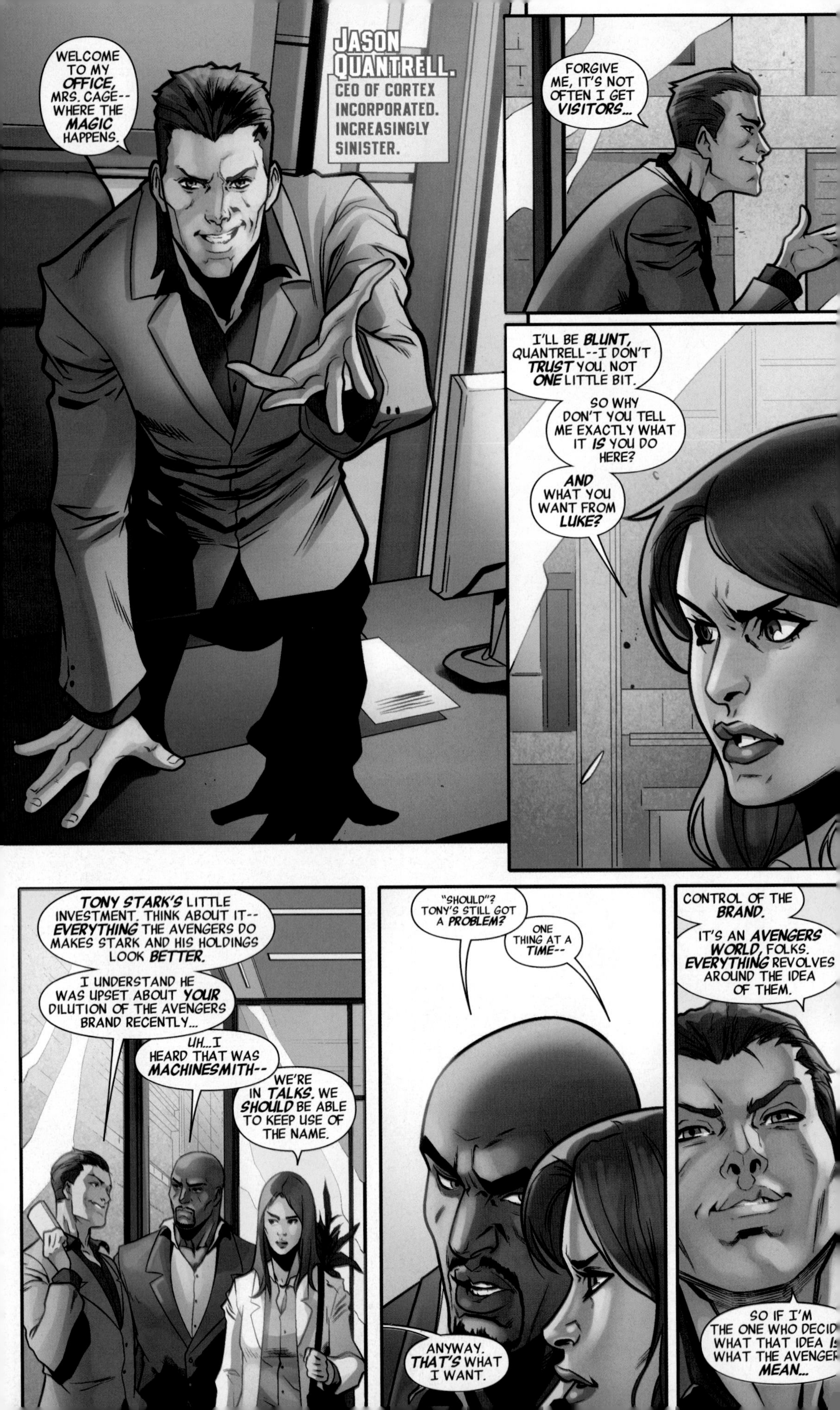
WELCOME TO MY OFFICE, MRS. CAGE-- WHERE THE MAGIC HAPPENS.
JASON QUANTRELL.
CEO OF CORTEX INCORPORATED. INCREASINGLY SINISTER.
FORGIVE ME, IT'S NOT OFTEN I GET VISITORS...
I'LL BE BLUNT, QUANTRELL--I DON'T TRUST YOU. NOT ONE LITTLE BIT.
SO WHY DON'T YOU TELL ME EXACTLY WHAT IT IS YOU DO HERE?
AND WHAT YOU WANT FROM LUKE?
TONY STARK'S LITTLE INVESTMENT. THINK ABOUT IT-- EVERYTHING THE AVENGERS DO MAKES STARK AND HIS HOLDINGS LOOK BETTER.
I UNDERSTAND HE WAS UPSET ABOUT YOUR DILUTION OF THE AVENGERS BRAND RECENTLY...
UH...I HEARD THAT WAS MACHINESMITH--
WE'RE IN TALKS. WE SHOULD BE ABLE TO KEEP USE OF THE NAME.
"SHOULD"? TONY'S STILL GOT A PROBLEM?
ONE THING AT A TIME--
ANYWAY. THAT'S WHAT I WANT.
CONTROL OF THE BRAND.
IT'S AN AVENGERS WORLD, FOLKS. EVERYTHING REVOLVES AROUND THE IDEA OF THEM.
SO IF I'M THE ONE WHO DECID WHAT THAT IDEA I: WHAT THE AVENGER MEAN...

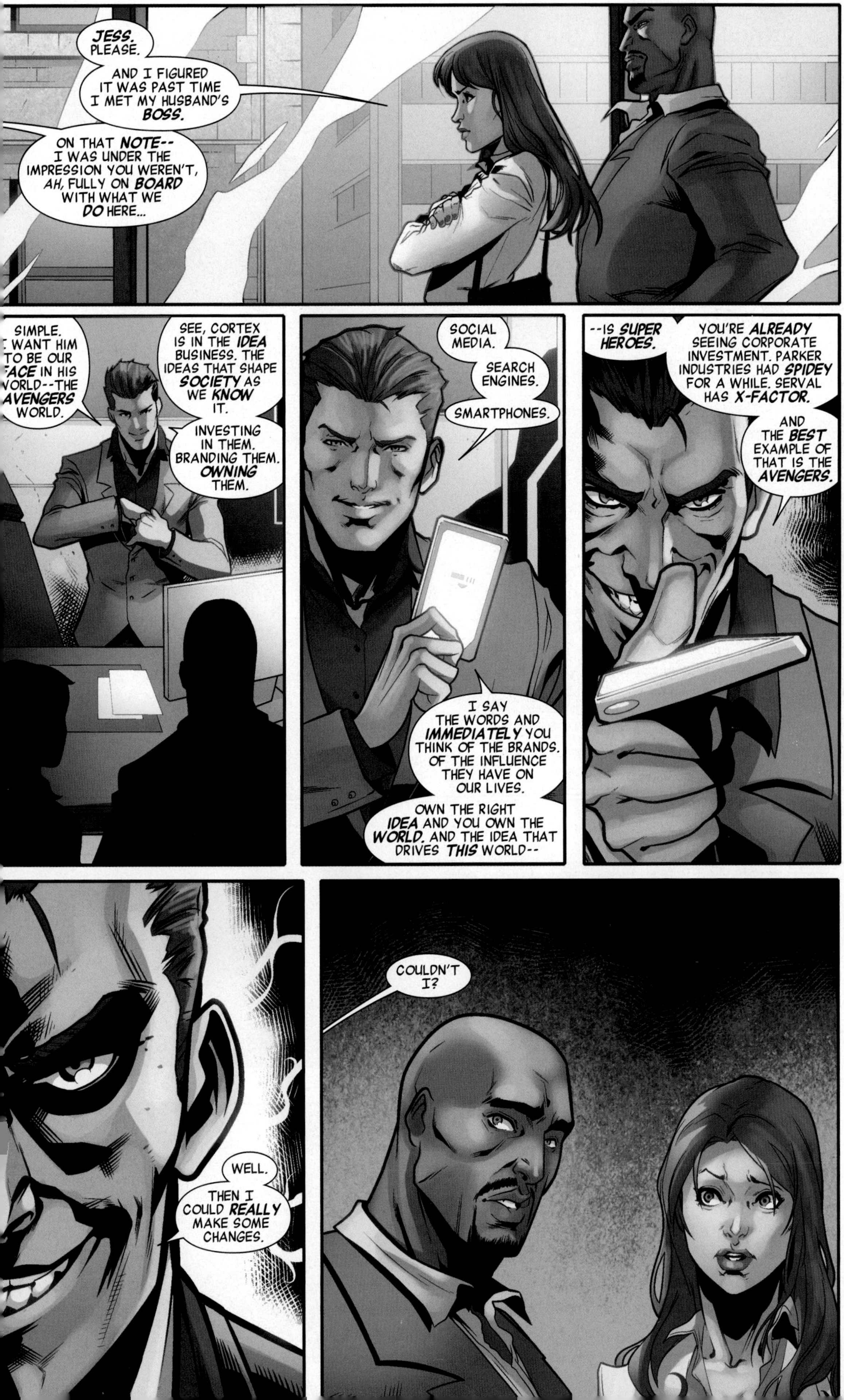
JESS. PLEASE.
AND I FIGURED IT WAS PAST TIME I MET MY HUSBAND'S BOSS.
ON THAT NOTE-- I WAS UNDER THE IMPRESSION YOU WEREN'T, AH, FULLY ON BOARD WITH WHAT WE DO HERE...
SIMPLE. I WANT HIM TO BE OUR FACE IN HIS WORLD--THE AVENGERS WORLD.
SEE, CORTEX IS IN THE IDEA BUSINESS. THE IDEAS THAT SHAPE SOCIETY AS WE KNOW IT.
INVESTING IN THEM. BRANDING THEM. OWNING THEM.
SOCIAL MEDIA.
SEARCH ENGINES.
SMARTPHONES.
I SAY THE WORDS AND IMMEDIATELY YOU THINK OF THE BRANDS. OF THE INFLUENCE THEY HAVE ON OUR LIVES.
OWN THE RIGHT IDEA AND YOU OWN THE WORLD. AND THE IDEA THAT DRIVES THIS WORLD--
--IS SUPER HEROES.
YOU'RE ALREADY SEEING CORPORATE INVESTMENT. PARKER INDUSTRIES HAD SPIDEY FOR A WHILE. SERVAL HAS X-FACTOR.
AND THE BEST EXAMPLE OF THAT IS THE AVENGERS.
WELL.
THEN I COULD REALLY MAKE SOME CHANGES.
COULDN'T I?

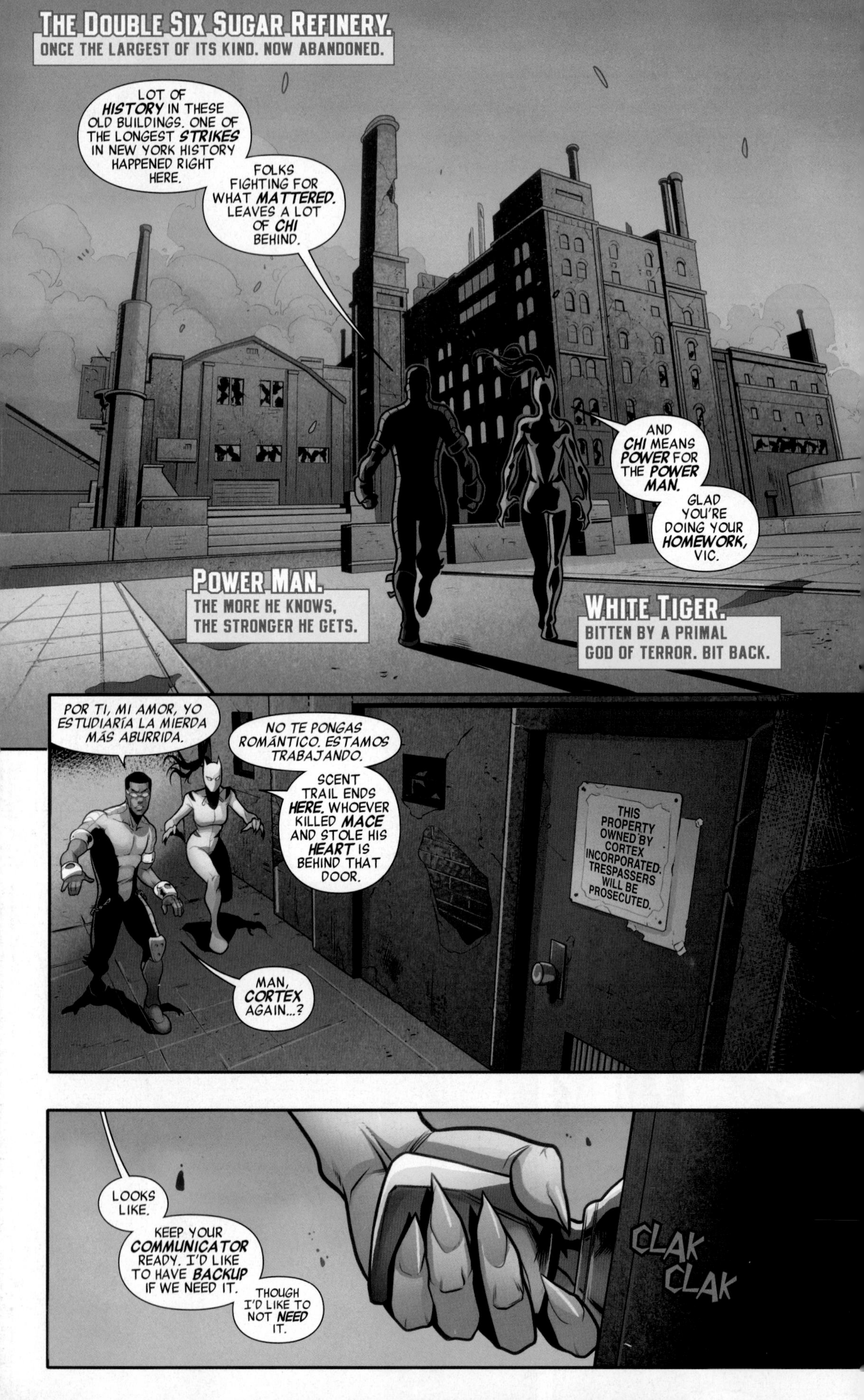

THE DOUBLE SIX SUGAR REFINERY.
ONCE THE LARGEST OF ITS KIND. NOW ABANDONED.
LOT OF HISTORY IN THESE OLD BUILDINGS. ONE OF THE LONGEST STRIKES IN NEW YORK HISTORY HAPPENED RIGHT HERE.
FOLKS FIGHTING FOR WHAT MATTERED. LEAVES A LOT OF CHI BEHIND.
AND CHI MEANS POWER FOR THE POWER MAN.
GLAD YOU'RE DOING YOUR HOMEWORK, VIC.
POWER MAN.
THE MORE HE KNOWS, THE STRONGER HE GETS.
WHITE TIGER.
BITTEN BY A PRIMAL GOD OF TERROR. BIT BACK.
POR TI, MI AMOR, YO ESTUDIARÍA LA MIERDA MÁS ABURRIDA.
NO TE PONGAS ROMÁNTICO. ESTAMOS TRABAJANDO.
SCENT TRAIL ENDS HERE. WHOEVER KILLED MACE AND STOLE HIS HEART IS BEHIND THAT DOOR.
THIS PROPERTY OWNED BY CORTEX INCORPORATED. TRESPASSERS WILL BE PROSECUTED.
MAN, CORTEX AGAIN...?
LOOKS LIKE.
KEEP YOUR COMMUNICATOR READY. I'D LIKE TO HAVE BACKUP IF WE NEED IT.
THOUGH I'D LIKE TO NOT NEED IT.
CLAK CLAK

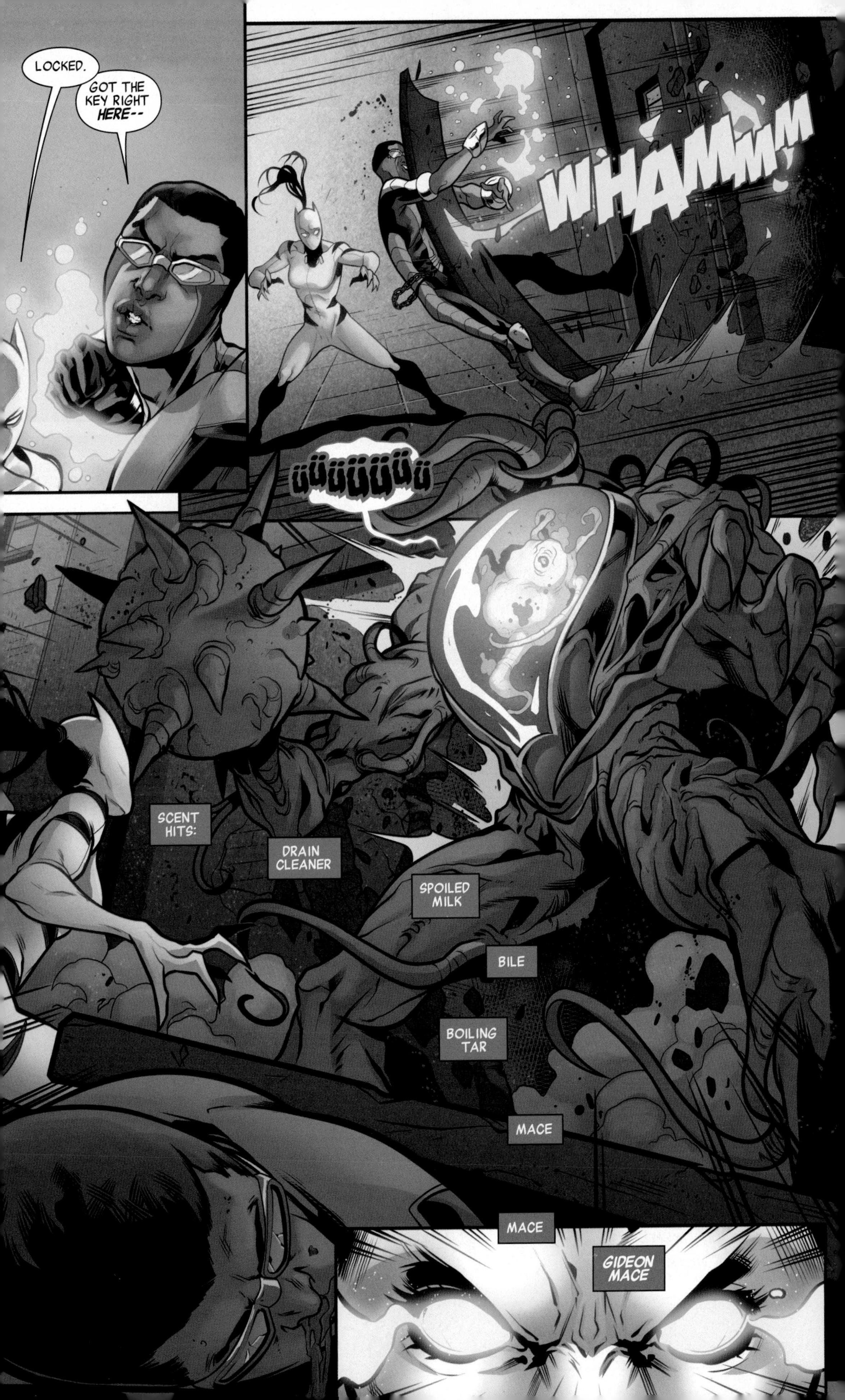
LOCKED.
GOT THE KEY RIGHT HERE--
WHAMMM!
ÜÜÜÜÜÜÜ
SCENT HITS:
DRAIN CLEANER
SPOILED MILK
BILE
BOILING TAR
MACE
MACE
GIDEON MACE

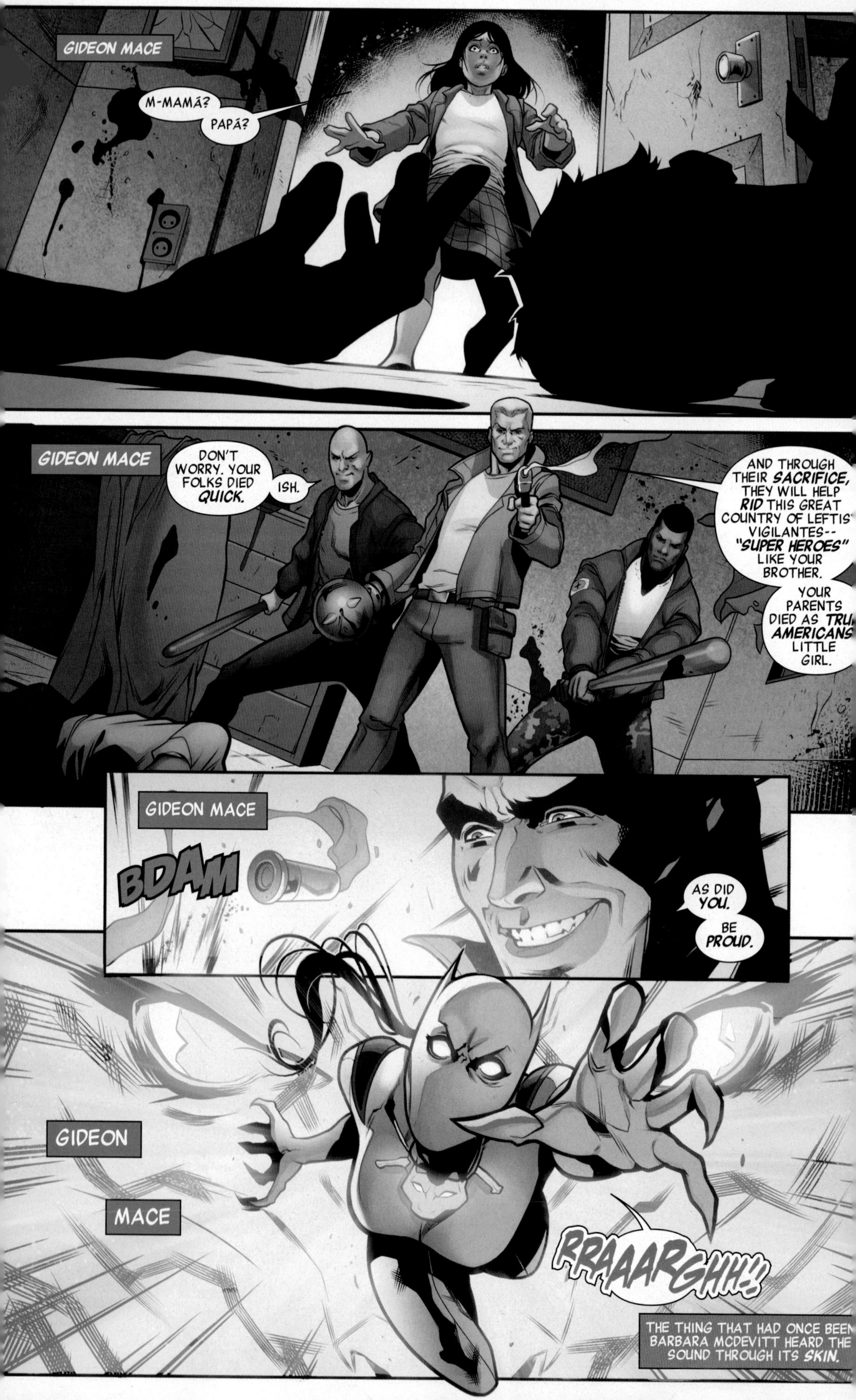
GIDEON MACE
M-MAMÃ?
PAPÃ?
GIDEON MACE
DON'T WORRY. YOUR FOLKS DIED QUICK.
ISH.
AND THROUGH THEIR SACRIFICE, THEY WILL HELP RID THIS GREAT COUNTRY OF LEFTIS
VIGILANTES-- "SUPER HEROES" LIKE YOUR BROTHER.
YOUR PARENTS DIED AS TRU AMERICANS LITTLE GIRL.
GIDEON MACE
BDAM
AS DID YOU.
BE PROUD.
GIDEON
MACE
RRAAARGHH!!
THE THING THAT HAD ONCE BEEN BARBARA MCDEVITT HEARD THE SOUND THROUGH ITS SKIN.

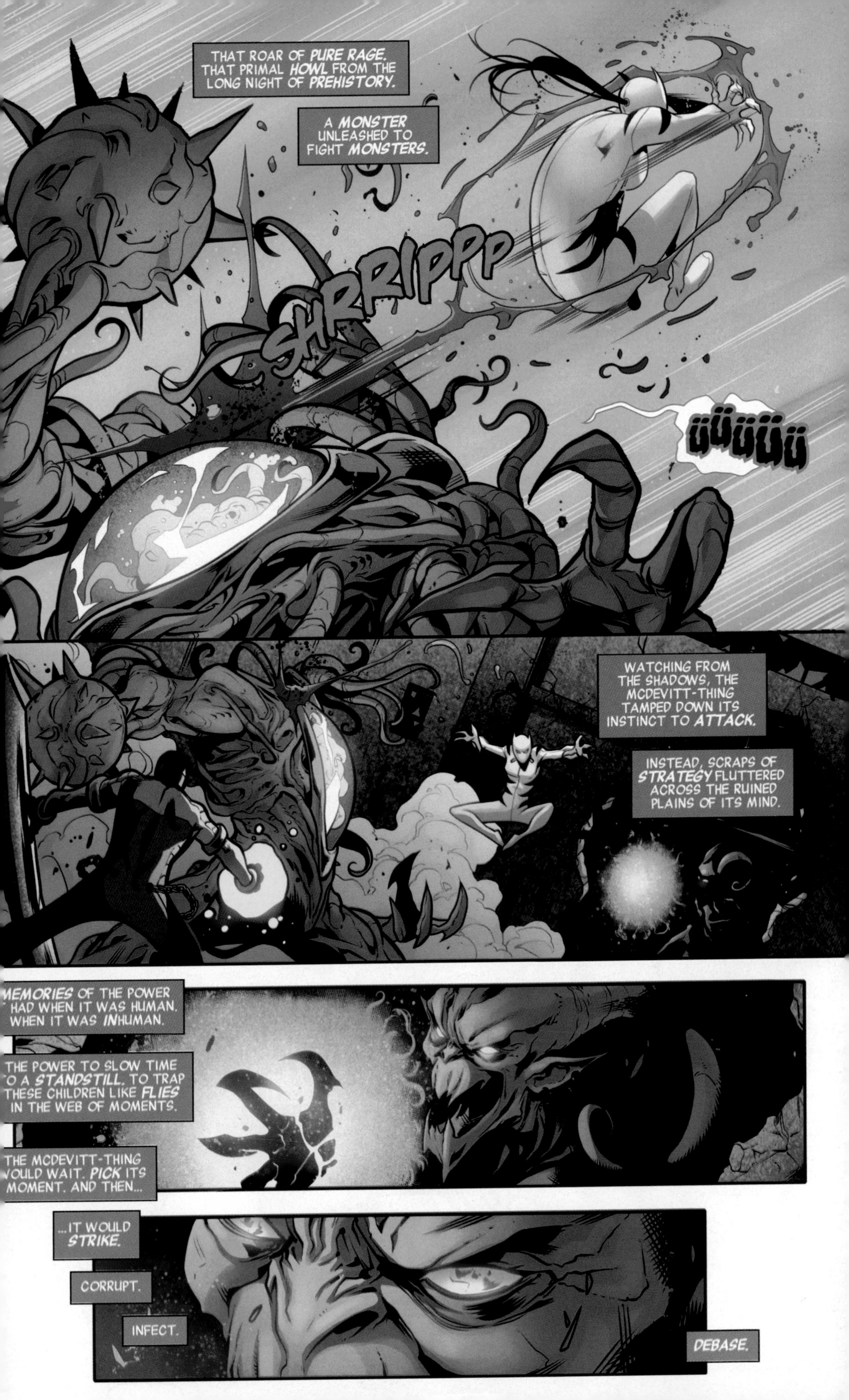
THAT ROAR OF PURE RAGE. THAT PRIMAL HOWL FROM THE LONG NIGHT OF PREHISTORY.
A MONSTER UNLEASHED TO FIGHT MONSTERS.
SHRRIPPP
ÜÜÜÜÜ
WATCHING FROM THE SHADOWS, THE MCDEVITT-THING TAMPED DOWN ITS INSTINCT TO ATTACK.
INSTEAD, SCRAPS OF STRATEGY FLUTTERED ACROSS THE RUINED PLAINS OF ITS MIND.
MEMORIES OF THE POWER HAD WHEN IT WAS HUMAN. WHEN IT WAS INHUMAN.
THE POWER TO SLOW TIME TO A STANDSTILL, TO TRAP THESE CHILDREN LIKE FLIES IN THE WEB OF MOMENTS.
THE MCDEVITT-THING WOULD WAIT. PICK ITS MOMENT. AND THEN...
...IT WOULD STRIKE.
CORRUPT.
INFECT.
DEBASE.

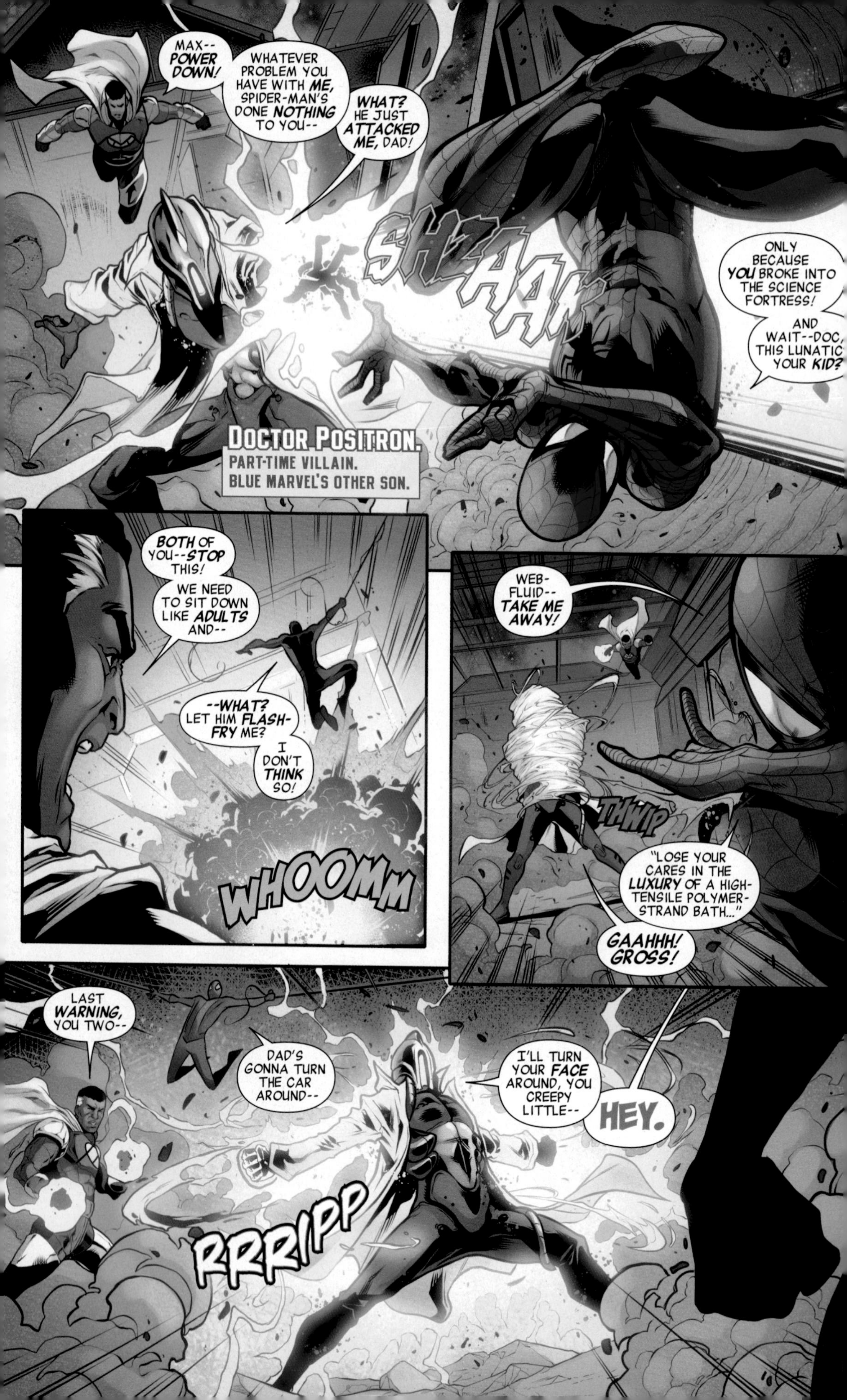
MAX--POWER DOWN!
WHATEVER PROBLEM YOU HAVE WITH ME, SPIDER-MAN'S DONE NOTHING TO YOU--
WHAT? HE JUST ATTACKED ME, DAD!
SHAAAK
ONLY BECAUSE YOU BROKE INTO THE SCIENCE FORTRESS!
AND WAIT--DOC, THIS LUNATIC YOUR KID?
DOCTOR POSITRON.
PART-TIME VILLAIN.
BLUE MARVEL'S OTHER SON.
BOTH OF YOU--STOP THIS!
WE NEED TO SIT DOWN LIKE ADULTS AND--
--WHAT? LET HIM FLASH-FRY ME?
I DON'T THINK SO!
WHOOMM
WEB-FLUID--TAKE ME AWAY!
THWIP
"LOSE YOUR CARES IN THE LUXURY OF A HIGH-TENSILE POLYMER-STRAND BATH..."
GAAHHH! GROSS!
LAST WARNING, YOU TWO--
DAD'S GONNA TURN THE CAR AROUND--
I'LL TURN YOUR FACE AROUND, YOU CREEPY LITTLE--
HEY.
RRRIPP

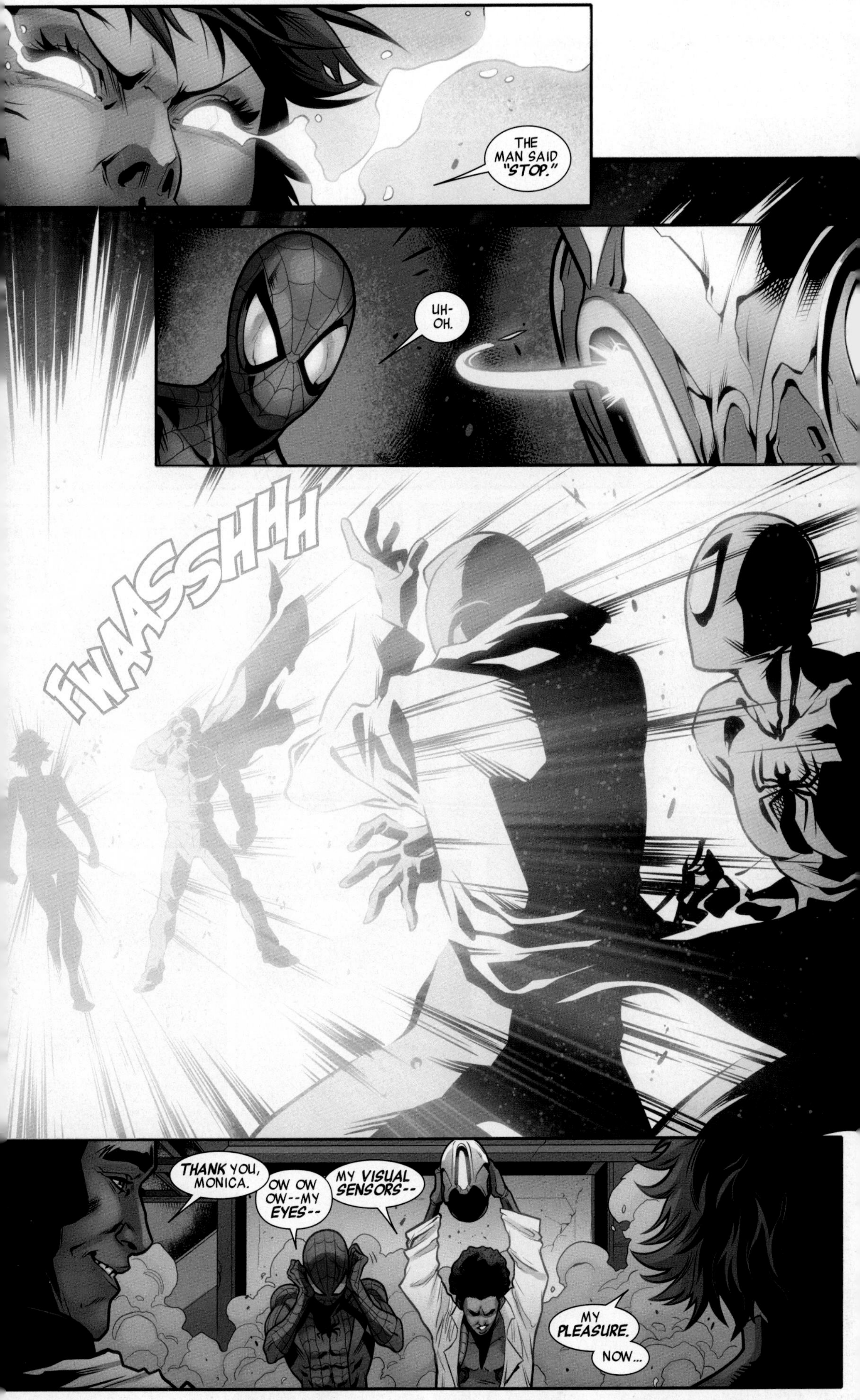
THE MAN SAID "STOP."
UH-OH.
FWASSHHH
THANK YOU, MONICA.
OW OW OW--MY EYES--
MY VISUAL SENSORS--
MY PLEASURE.
NOW...

"...I THINK SOMEONE MENTIONED TALKING LIKE *ADULTS?*"

...THERE I AM, HEADING *PEACEFULLY* ON MY WEBBY WAY, WHEN *BLUE MARVEL JR* HERE BURSTS OUT OF THE PORTAL DRESSED LIKE A *SPACE ALIEN--*

SO I HACKED INTO DAD'S *PORTAL SYSTEM.* SO *WHAT?* IT'S THE QUICKEST WAY HERE.

MAYBE CALL *AHEAD* NEXT TIME?

SO DAD CAN CALL THE *COPS?*

I'D *NEVER* DO THAT, MAX.

CERTAINLY NOT FOR *YOUR* "CRIMES"-- DEFRAUDING *TERRORISTS* TO SAVE YOUR *BROTHER.*

RIGHT. THE BROTHER YOU LOST IN YOUR PRECIOU "*NEUTRAL ZONE.*"

WELL, I FOUND H AGAIN.

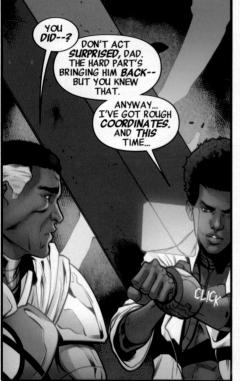

YOU *DID--?*

DON'T ACT *SURPRISED,* DAD. THE HARD PART'S BRINGING HIM *BACK--* BUT YOU KNEW THAT.

ANYWAY... I'VE GOT ROUGH *COORDINATES.* AND *THIS* TIME...

CLICK

...I'VE GOT *SOUND.*

...BEYOND...

...WARN EVERYONE... WARN THE WORLD...FROM BEYOND...

...THEY ARE *FROM* BEYOND...

SO. WHAT DO YOU THINK *THAT* MEANS?

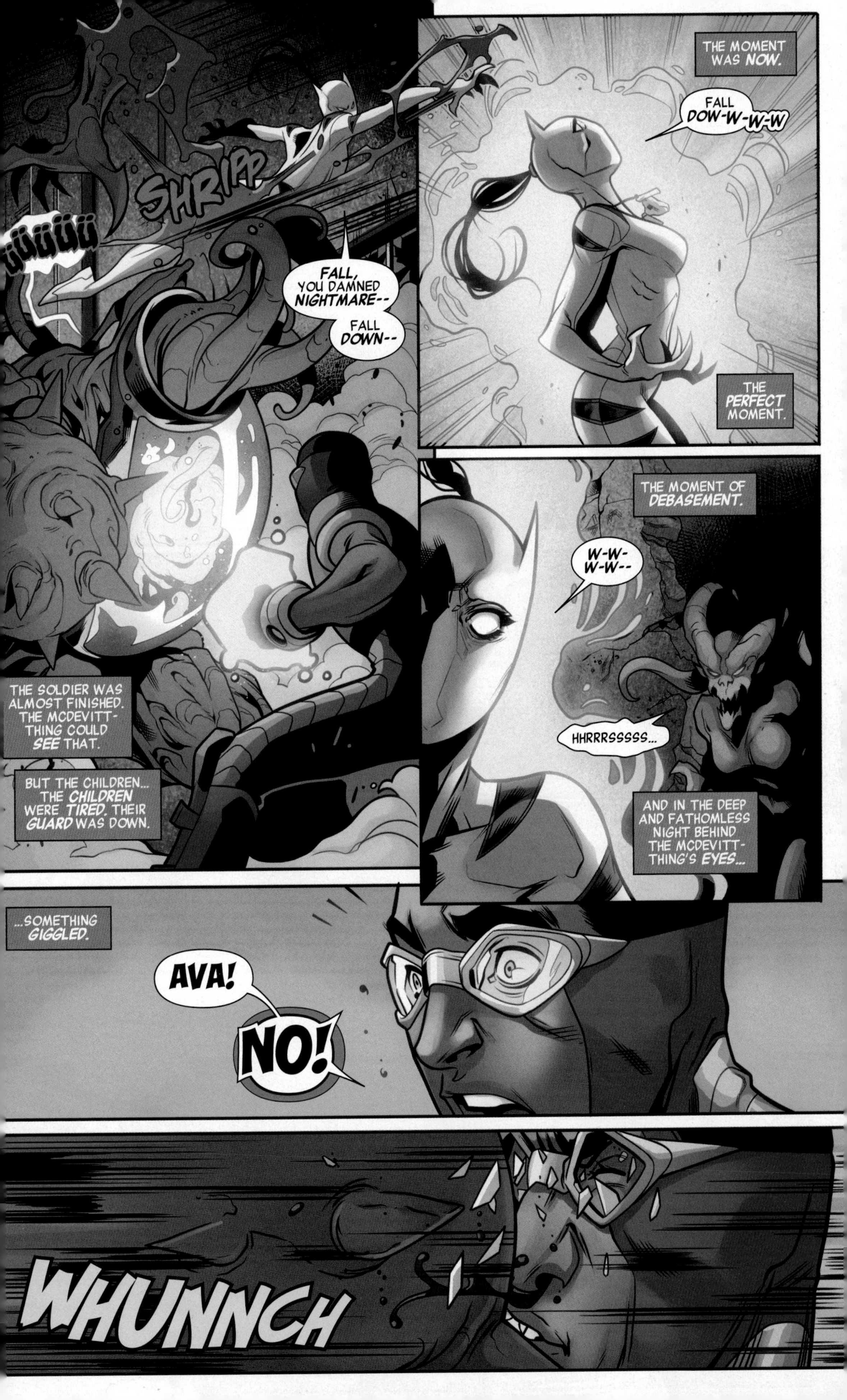

THE MOMENT WAS NOW.
FALL DOW-W-W-W
SHRIPP
ÜÜÜÜÜ
FALL, YOU DAMNED NIGHTMARE--
FALL DOWN--
THE PERFECT MOMENT.
THE MOMENT OF DEBASEMENT.
W-W-W-W--
THE SOLDIER WAS ALMOST FINISHED. THE MCDEVITT-THING COULD SEE THAT.
BUT THE CHILDREN... THE CHILDREN WERE TIRED. THEIR GUARD WAS DOWN.
HHRRRSSSSS...
AND IN THE DEEP AND FATHOMLESS NIGHT BEHIND THE MCDEVITT-THING'S EYES...
...SOMETHING GIGGLED.
AVA!
NO!
WHUNNCH

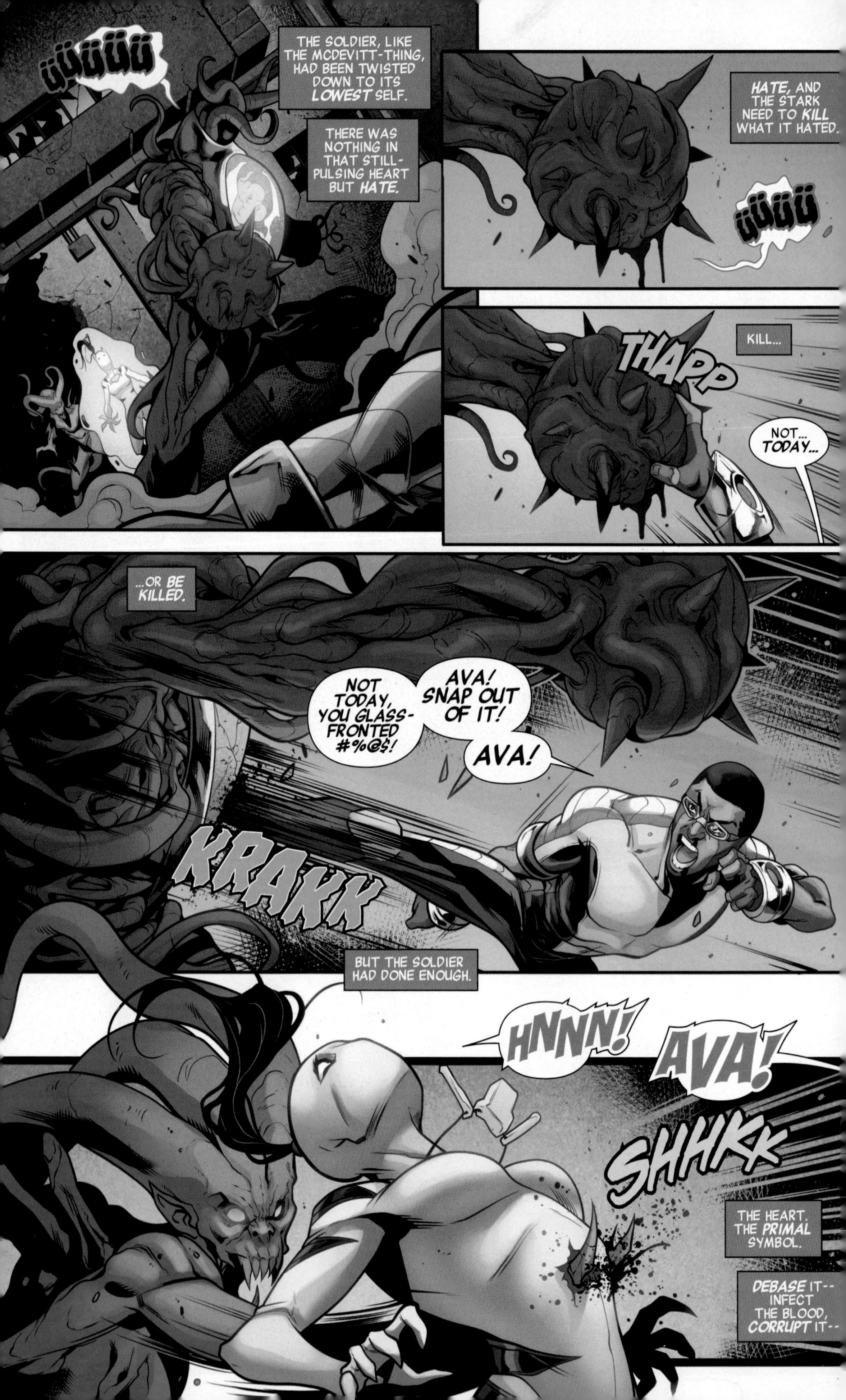
ÜÜÜÜÜ
THE SOLDIER, LIKE THE MCDEVITT-THING, HAD BEEN TWISTED DOWN TO ITS LOWEST SELF.
THERE WAS NOTHING IN THAT STILL-PULSING HEART BUT HATE.
HATE, AND THE STARK NEED TO KILL WHAT IT HATED.
ÜÜÜÜ
KILL...
THAPP
NOT... TODAY...
...OR BE KILLED.
NOT TODAY, YOU GLASS-FRONTED #%@$!
AVA! SNAP OUT OF IT!
AVA!
KRAKK
BUT THE SOLDIER HAD DONE ENOUGH.
HNNN!
AVA!
SHHKK
THE HEART. THE PRIMAL SYMBOL.
DEBASE IT-- INFECT THE BLOOD, CORRUPT IT--

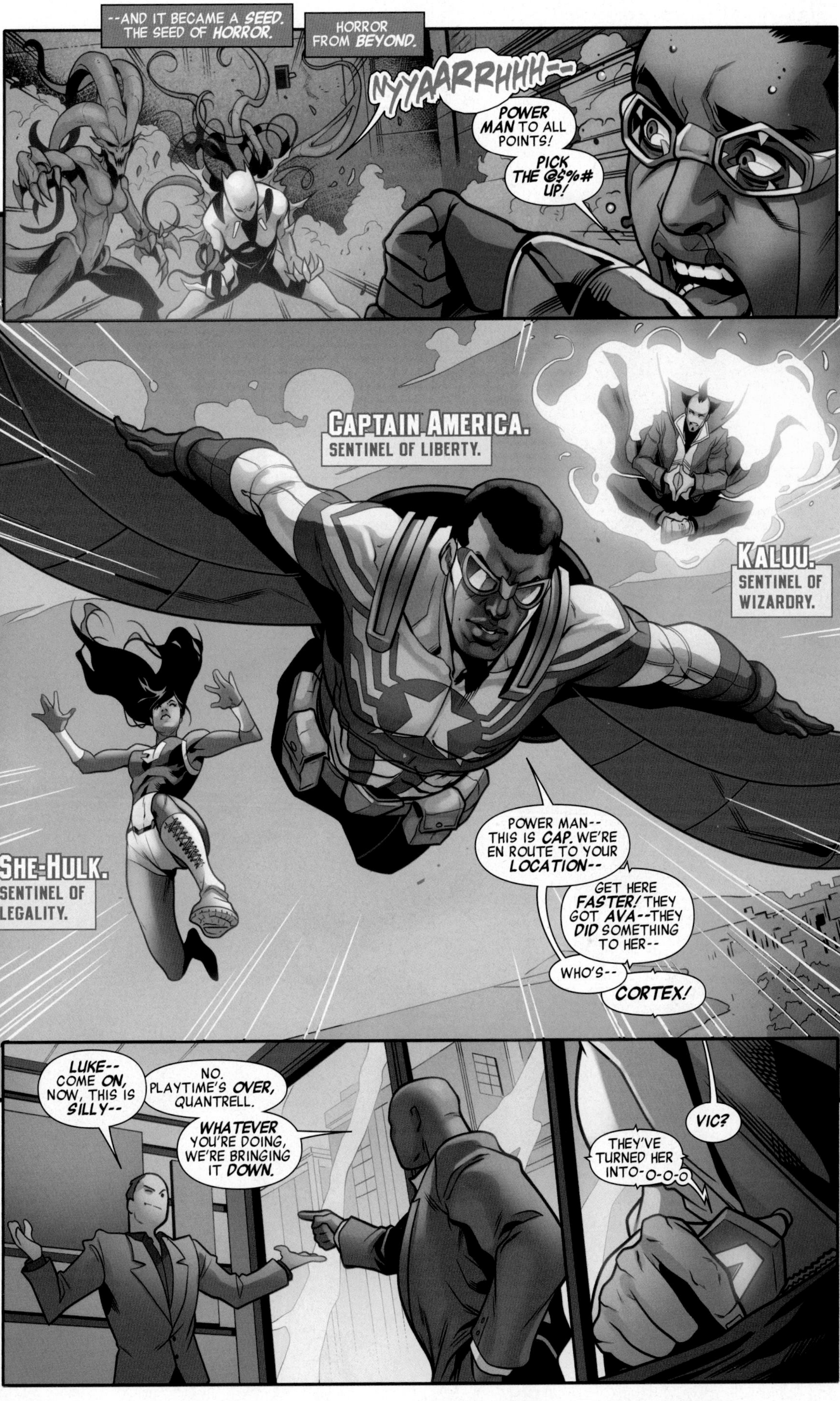

--AND IT BECAME A SEED. THE SEED OF HORROR.
HORROR FROM BEYOND.
NYYAARRHHH--
POWER MAN TO ALL POINTS!
PICK THE @$%# UP!
CAPTAIN AMERICA.
SENTINEL OF LIBERTY.
KALUU.
SENTINEL OF WIZARDRY.
SHE-HULK.
SENTINEL OF LEGALITY.
POWER MAN-- THIS IS CAP. WE'RE EN ROUTE TO YOUR LOCATION--
GET HERE FASTER! THEY GOT AVA--THEY DID SOMETHING TO HER--
WHO'S--
CORTEX!
LUKE-- COME ON, NOW, THIS IS SILLY--
NO. PLAYTIME'S OVER, QUANTRELL.
WHATEVER YOU'RE DOING, WE'RE BRINGING IT DOWN.
VIC?
THEY'VE TURNED HER INTO-O-O-O

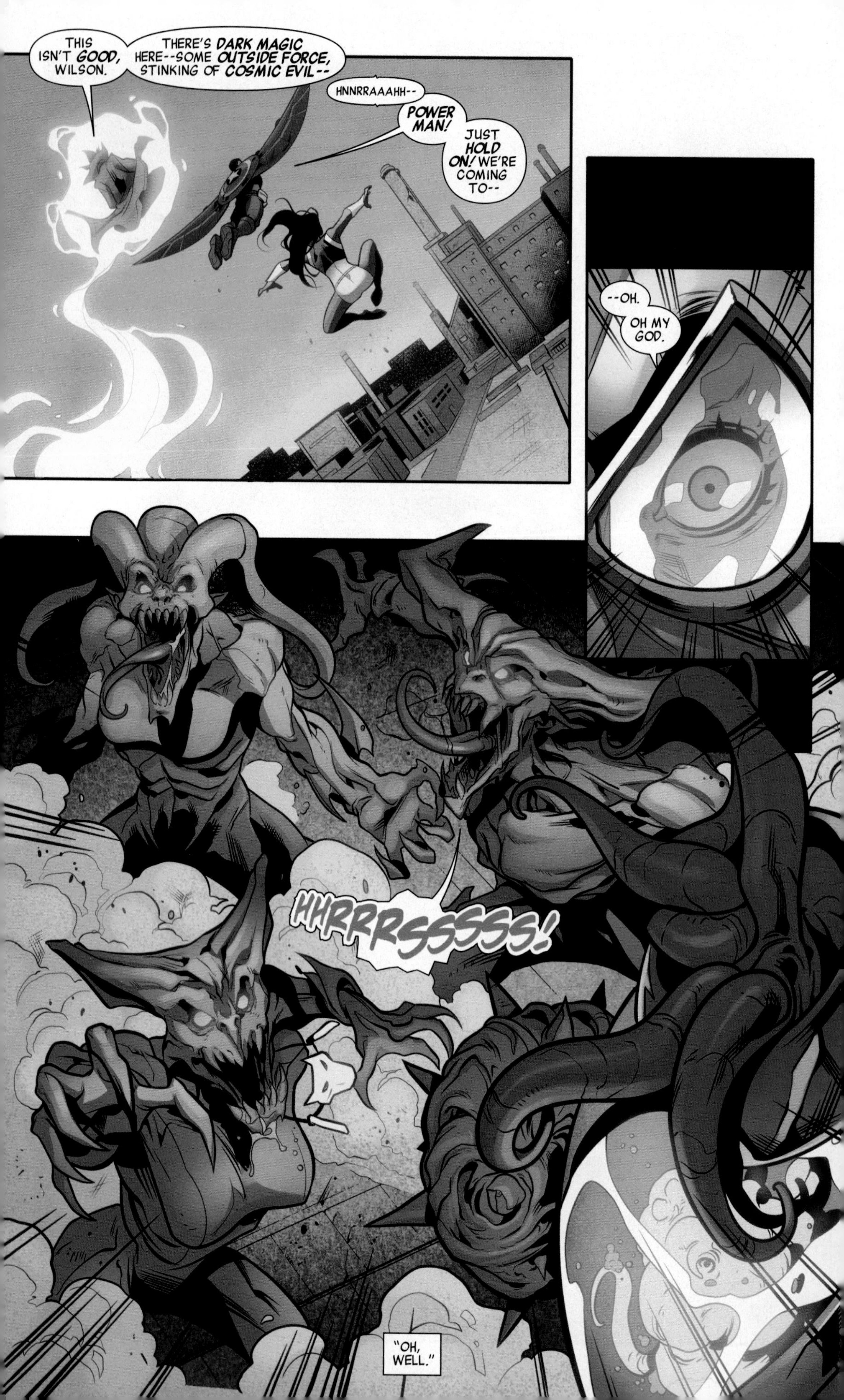
THIS ISN'T GOOD, WILSON.
THERE'S DARK MAGIC HERE--SOME OUTSIDE FORCE, STINKING OF COSMIC EVIL--
HNNRRAAAHH--
POWER MAN!
JUST HOLD ON! WE'RE COMING TO--
--OH.
OH MY GOD.
HHRRRSSSSS!
"OH, WELL."

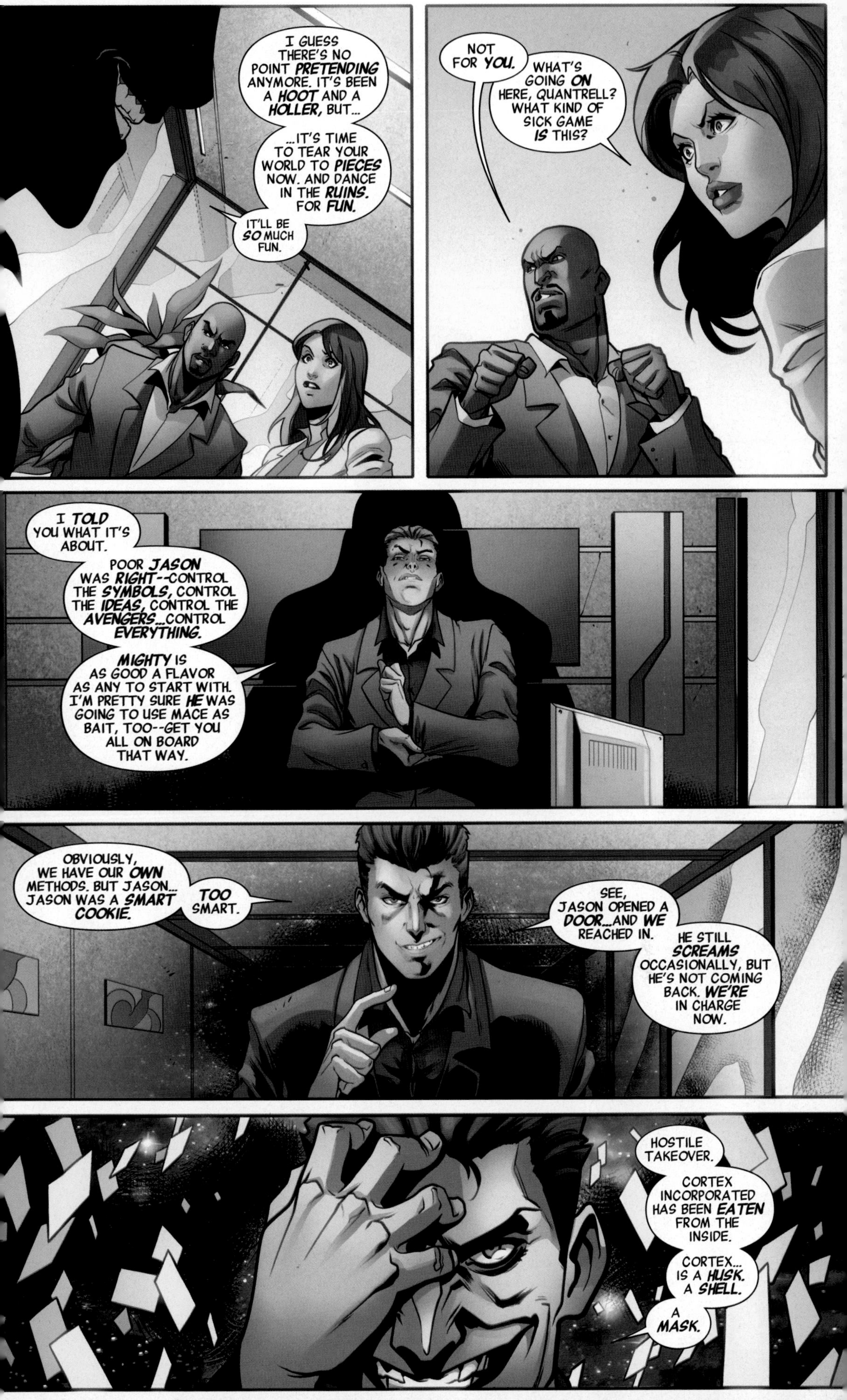
I GUESS THERE'S NO POINT PRETENDING ANYMORE. IT'S BEEN A HOOT AND A HOLLER, BUT...
...IT'S TIME TO TEAR YOUR WORLD TO PIECES NOW. AND DANCE IN THE RUINS. FOR FUN.
IT'LL BE SO MUCH FUN.
NOT FOR YOU.
WHAT'S GOING ON HERE, QUANTRELL? WHAT KIND OF SICK GAME IS THIS?
I TOLD YOU WHAT IT'S ABOUT.
POOR JASON WAS RIGHT--CONTROL THE SYMBOLS, CONTROL THE IDEAS, CONTROL THE AVENGERS...CONTROL EVERYTHING.
MIGHTY IS AS GOOD A FLAVOR AS ANY TO START WITH. I'M PRETTY SURE HE WAS GOING TO USE MACE AS BAIT, TOO--GET YOU ALL ON BOARD THAT WAY.
OBVIOUSLY, WE HAVE OUR OWN METHODS. BUT JASON... JASON WAS A SMART COOKIE.
TOO SMART.
SEE, JASON OPENED A DOOR...AND WE REACHED IN.
HE STILL SCREAMS OCCASIONALLY, BUT HE'S NOT COMING BACK. WE'RE IN CHARGE NOW.
HOSTILE TAKEOVER.
CORTEX INCORPORATED HAS BEEN EATEN FROM THE INSIDE.
CORTEX... IS A HUSK. A SHELL.
A MASK.

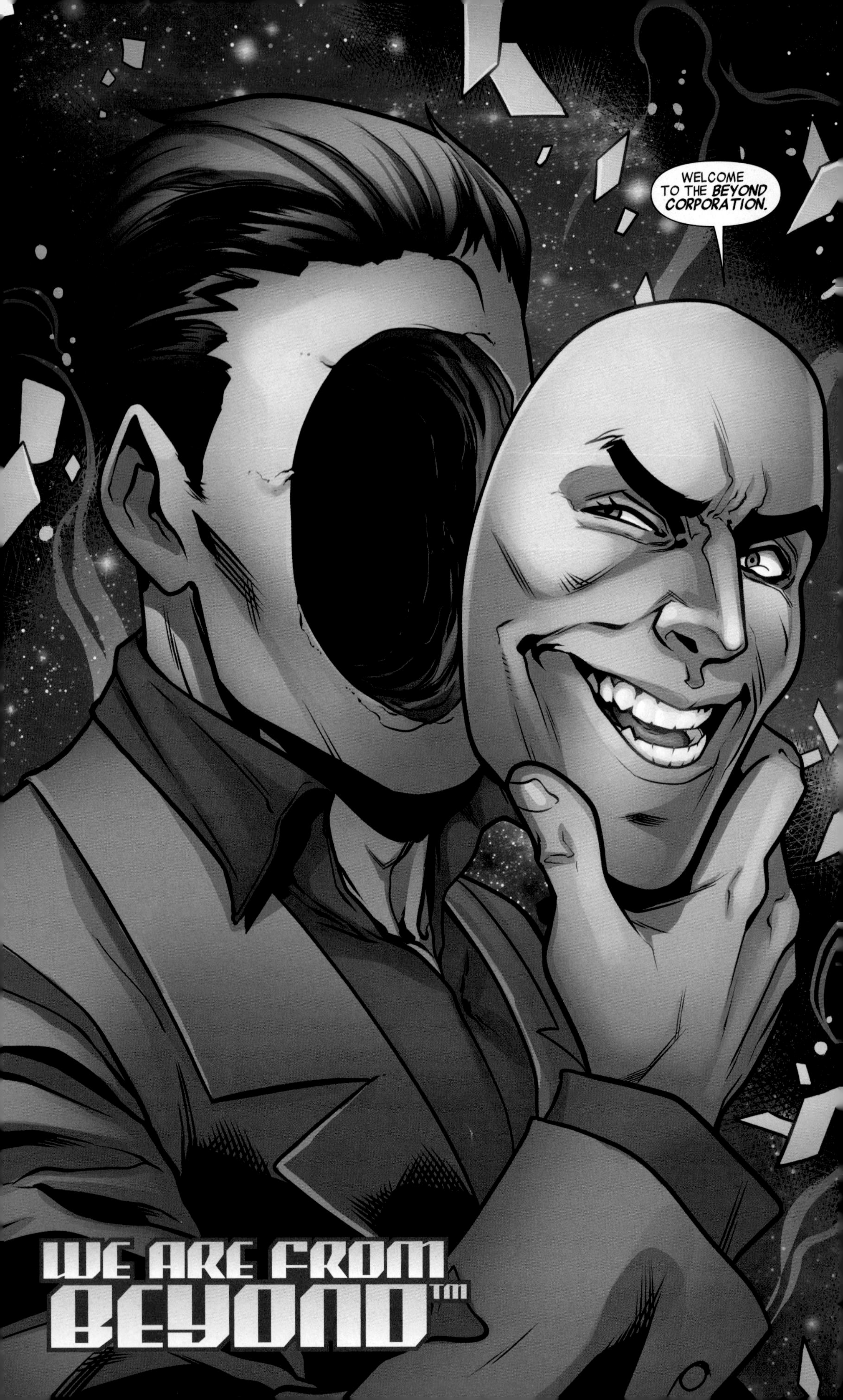
WELCOME TO THE BEYOND CORPORATION.
WE ARE FROM BEYOND™

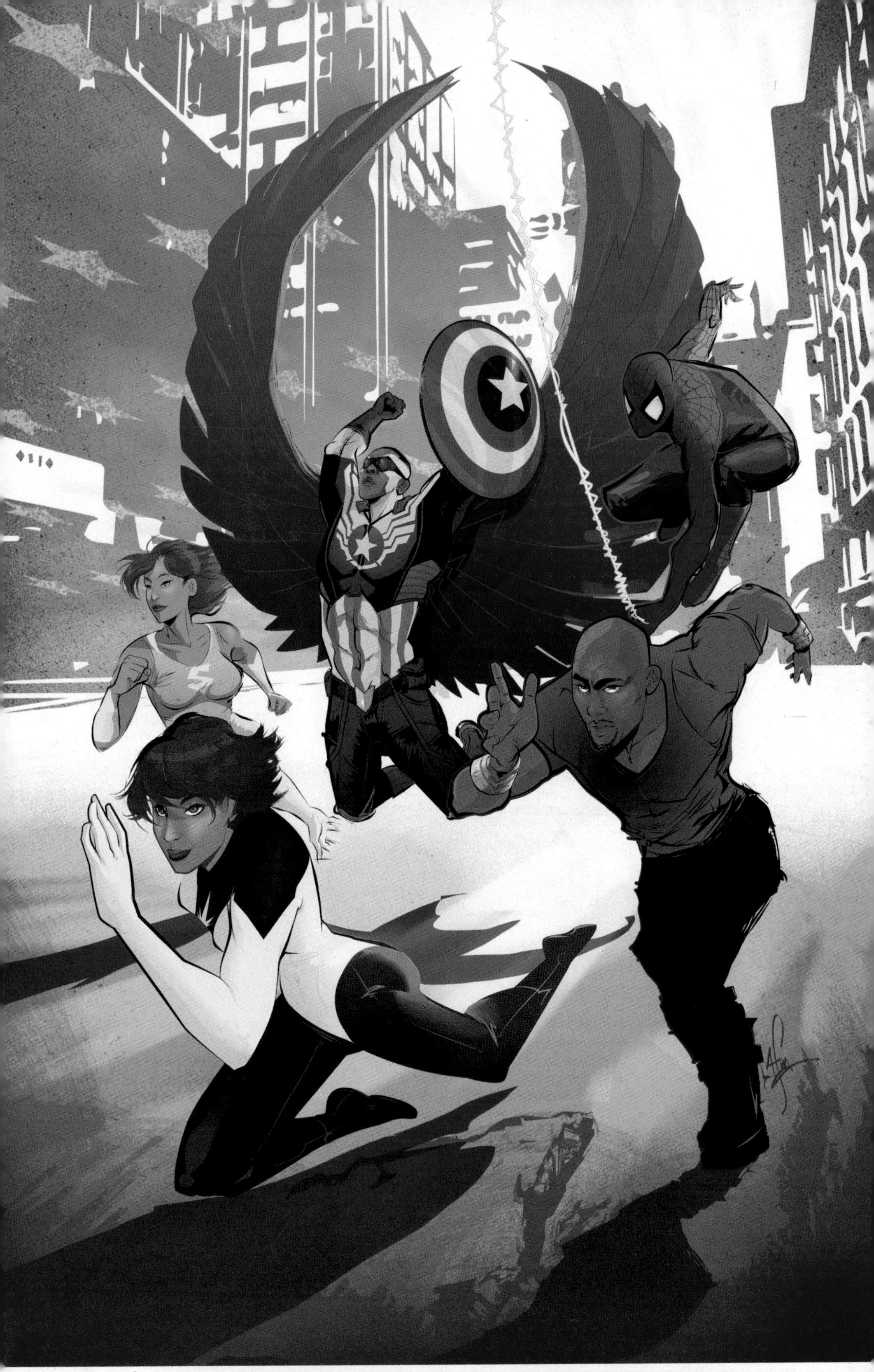

#3 VARIANT BY AFUA RICHARDSON

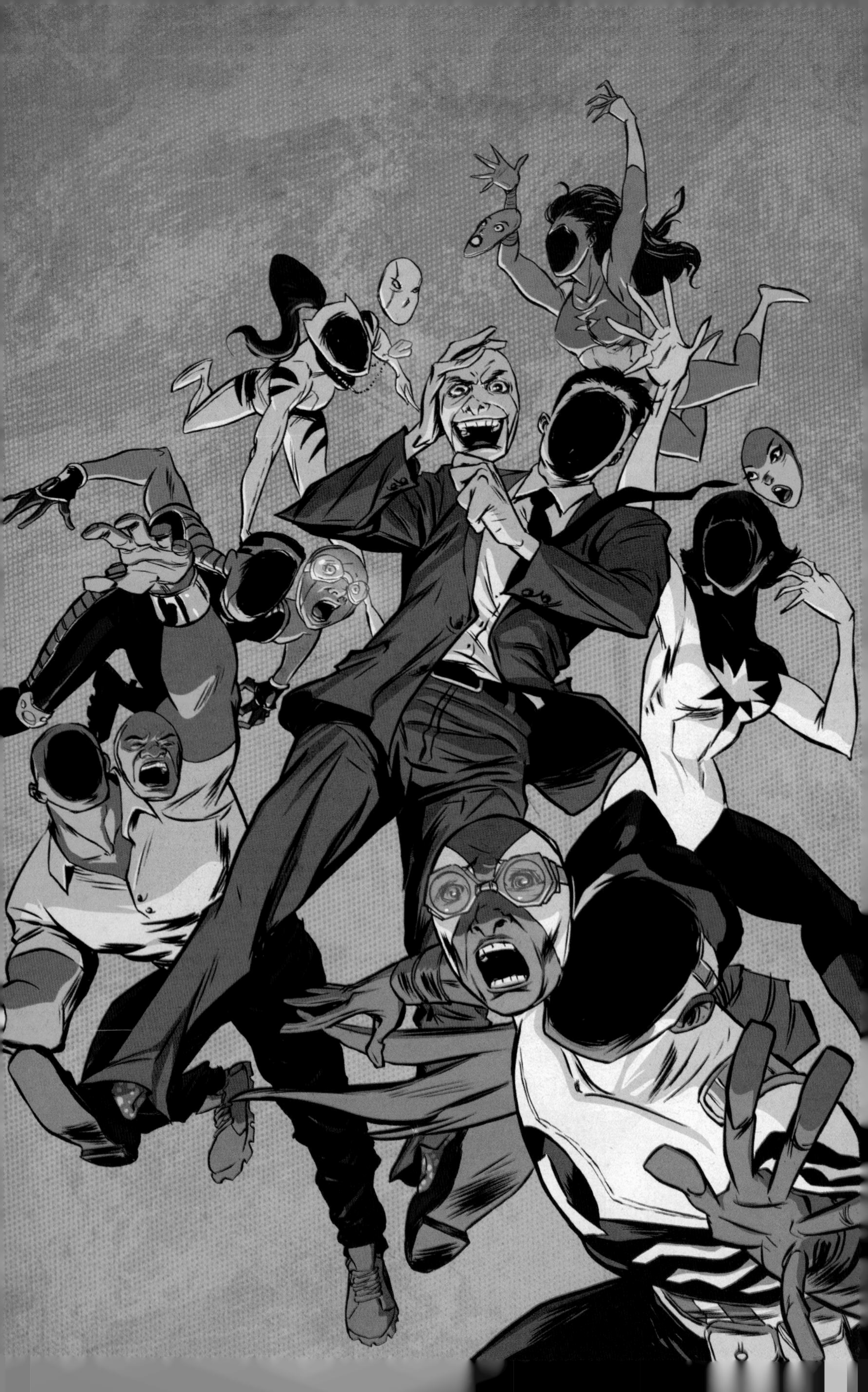

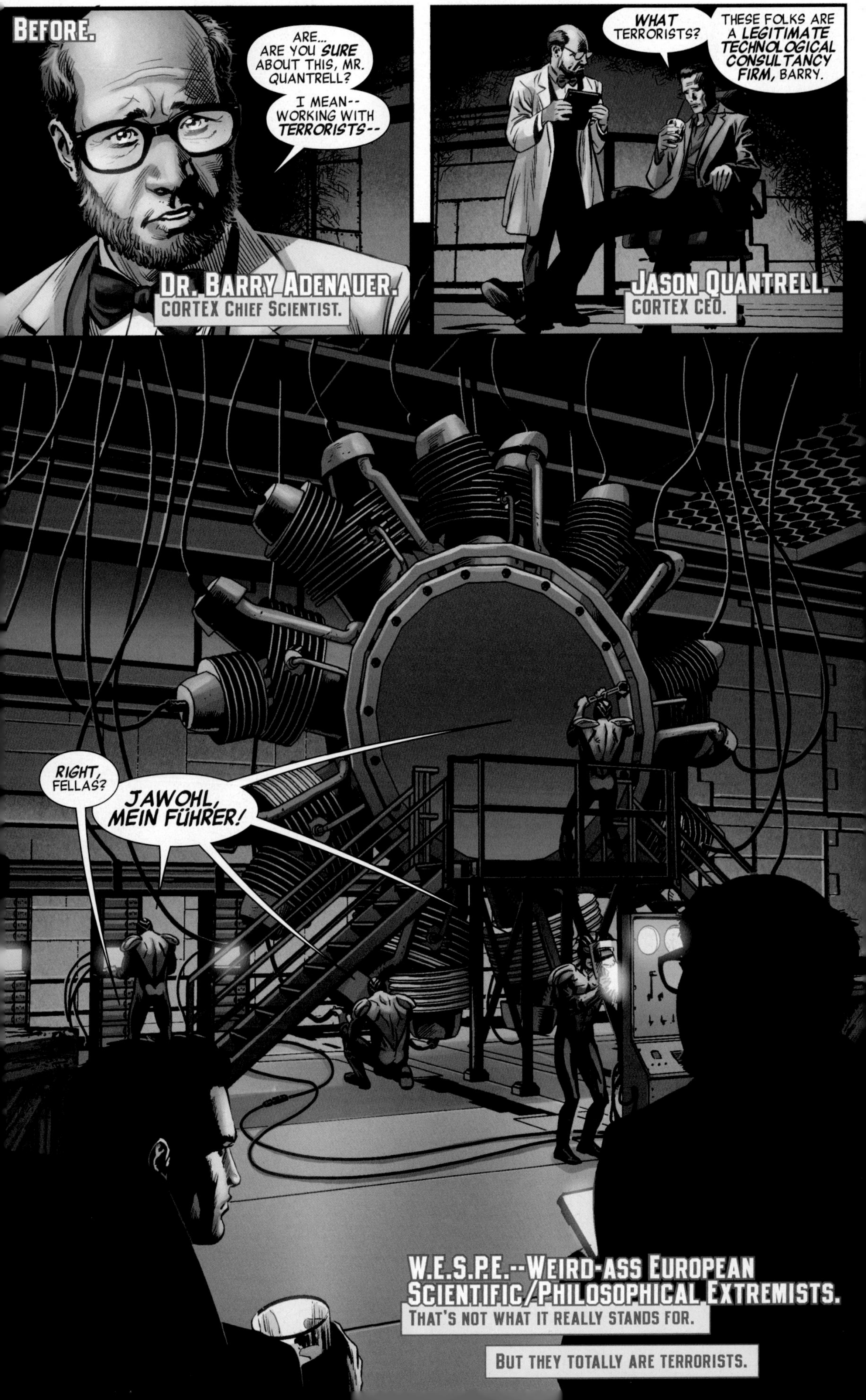

BEFORE.
ARE... ARE YOU SURE ABOUT THIS, MR. QUANTRELL?
I MEAN-- WORKING WITH TERRORISTS--
DR. BARRY ADENAUER.
CORTEX CHIEF SCIENTIST.
WHAT TERRORISTS?
THESE FOLKS ARE A LEGITIMATE TECHNOLOGICAL CONSULTANCY FIRM, BARRY.
JASON QUANTRELL.
CORTEX CEO.
RIGHT, FELLAS?
JAWOHL, MEIN FÜHRER!
W.E.S.P.E.--WEIRD-ASS EUROPEAN SCIENTIFIC/PHILOSOPHICAL EXTREMISTS.
THAT'S NOT WHAT IT REALLY STANDS FOR.
BUT THEY TOTALLY ARE TERRORISTS.

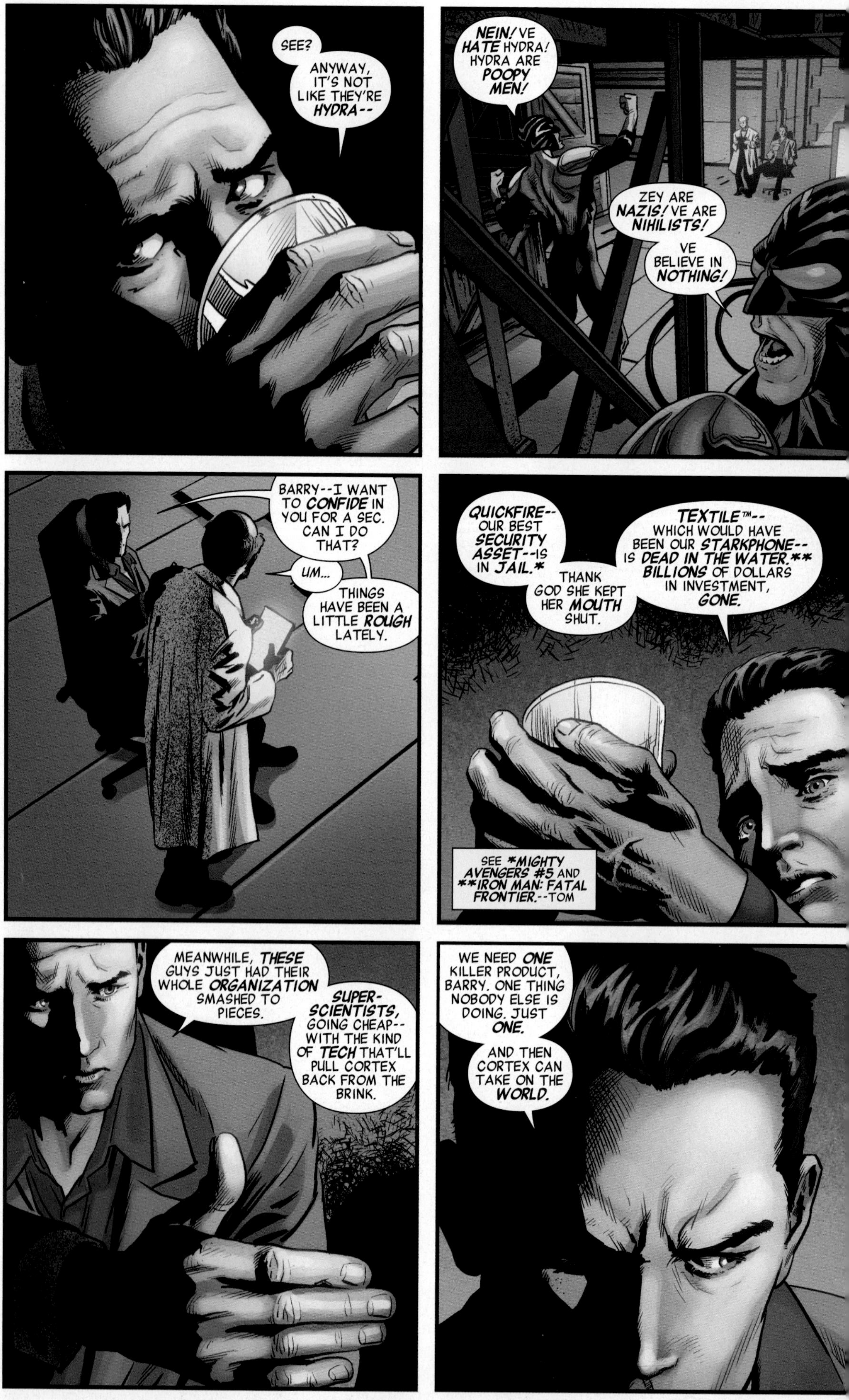

SEE?
ANYWAY, IT'S NOT LIKE THEY'RE HYDRA--
NEIN! VE HATE HYDRA! HYDRA ARE POOPY MEN!
ZEY ARE NAZIS! VE ARE NIHILISTS!
VE BELIEVE IN NOTHING!
BARRY--I WANT TO CONFIDE IN YOU FOR A SEC. CAN I DO THAT?
UM...
THINGS HAVE BEEN A LITTLE ROUGH LATELY.
QUICKFIRE-- OUR BEST SECURITY ASSET--IS IN JAIL.*
THANK GOD SHE KEPT HER MOUTH SHUT.
TEXTILE™-- WHICH WOULD HAVE BEEN OUR STARKPHONE-- IS DEAD IN THE WATER.** BILLIONS OF DOLLARS IN INVESTMENT, GONE.
SEE *MIGHTY AVENGERS #5 AND **IRON MAN: FATAL FRONTIER.--TOM
MEANWHILE, THESE GUYS JUST HAD THEIR WHOLE ORGANIZATION SMASHED TO PIECES.
SUPER-SCIENTISTS, GOING CHEAP-- WITH THE KIND OF TECH THAT'LL PULL CORTEX BACK FROM THE BRINK.
WE NEED ONE KILLER PRODUCT, BARRY. ONE THING NOBODY ELSE IS DOING. JUST ONE.
AND THEN CORTEX CAN TAKE ON THE WORLD.

I, UH, I HEARD *ADAM BRASHEAR* WAS WORKING ON PORTAL TECH--

DO NOT MENTION THAT NAME!

IXNAY ON THE ASHEAR-BRAY. THEY'RE *TOUCHY.*

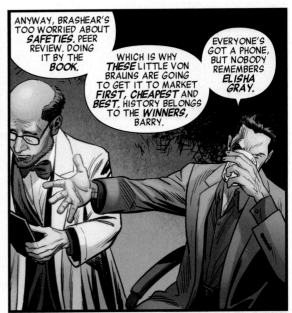

ANYWAY, BRASHEAR'S TOO WORRIED ABOUT *SAFETIES.* PEER REVIEW. DOING IT BY THE *BOOK.*

WHICH IS WHY *THESE* LITTLE VON BRAUNS ARE GOING TO GET IT TO MARKET *FIRST, CHEAPEST* AND *BEST.* HISTORY BELONGS TO THE *WINNERS,* BARRY.

EVERYONE'S GOT A PHONE, BUT NOBODY REMEMBERS *ELISHA GRAY.*

HOW'S IT *COMING,* GENTS?

JA, JA. THE GATEWAY IS *READY,* HERR QUANTRELL.

VE HAFF DONE *SO MUCH* MIT YOUR INVESTMENT, MEIN HERR. *DOKTOR SKORPION* VOULD BE SO *HEPPY* NOW.

ZE GATE VILL OPEN *WIDE.* AND REACH *FAR.*

HEH. WELL, ACROSS THE ROOM IS *FINE*--

ACROSS THE ROOM? SUCH *SMALL* VISION!

YOU MUST LEARN TO *BELIEVE,* MEIN HERR!

BELIEVE IN *NOTHING!*

FOR NOW NOTHING COMES!

NOTHI--

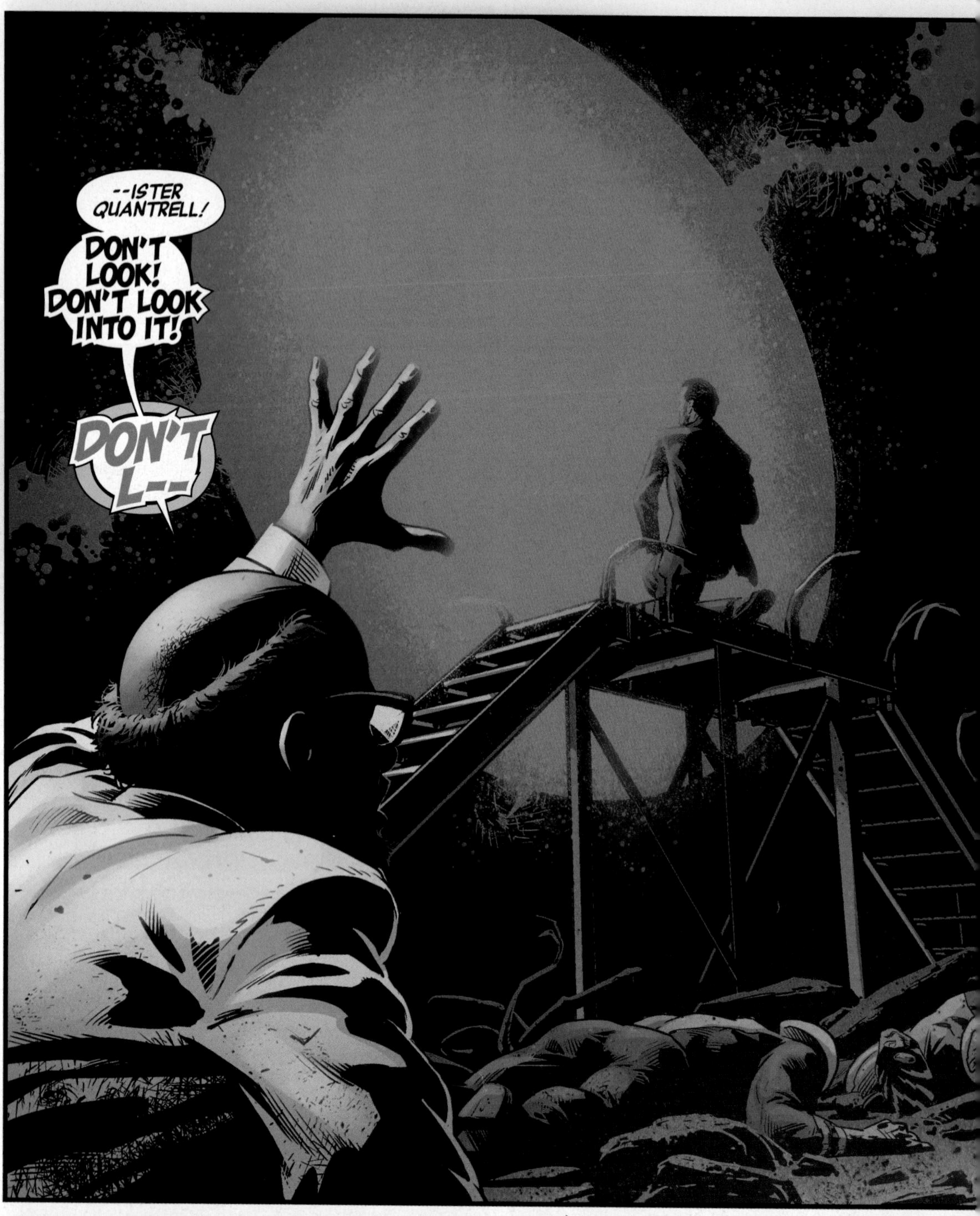
--ISTER QUANTRELL!
DON'T LOOK! DON'T LOOK INTO IT!
DON'T L--

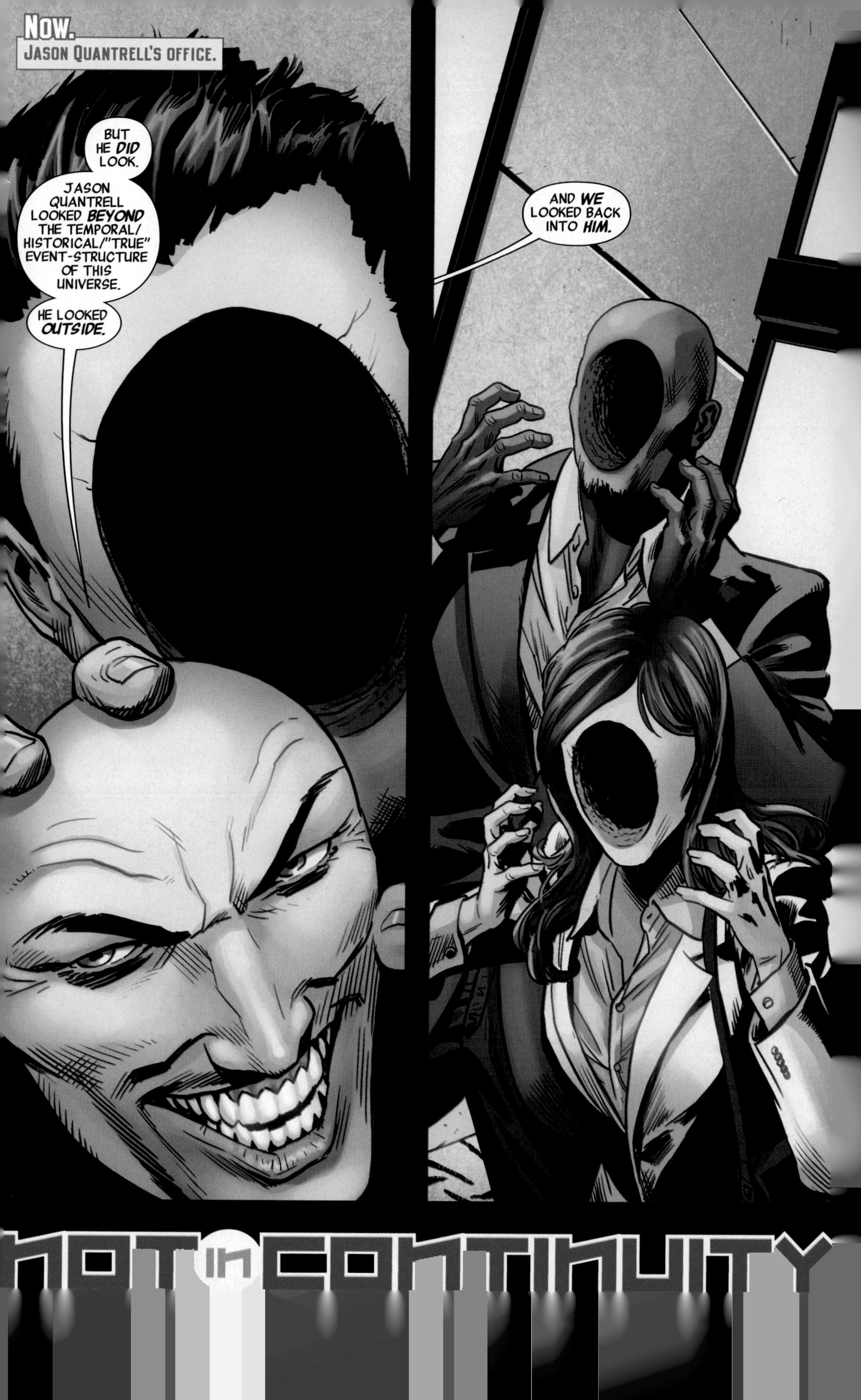

NOW.
JASON QUANTRELL'S OFFICE.
BUT HE DID LOOK.
JASON QUANTRELL LOOKED BEYOND THE TEMPORAL/ HISTORICAL/"TRUE" EVENT-STRUCTURE OF THIS UNIVERSE.
HE LOOKED OUTSIDE.
AND WE LOOKED BACK INTO HIM.
NOT IN CONTINUITY

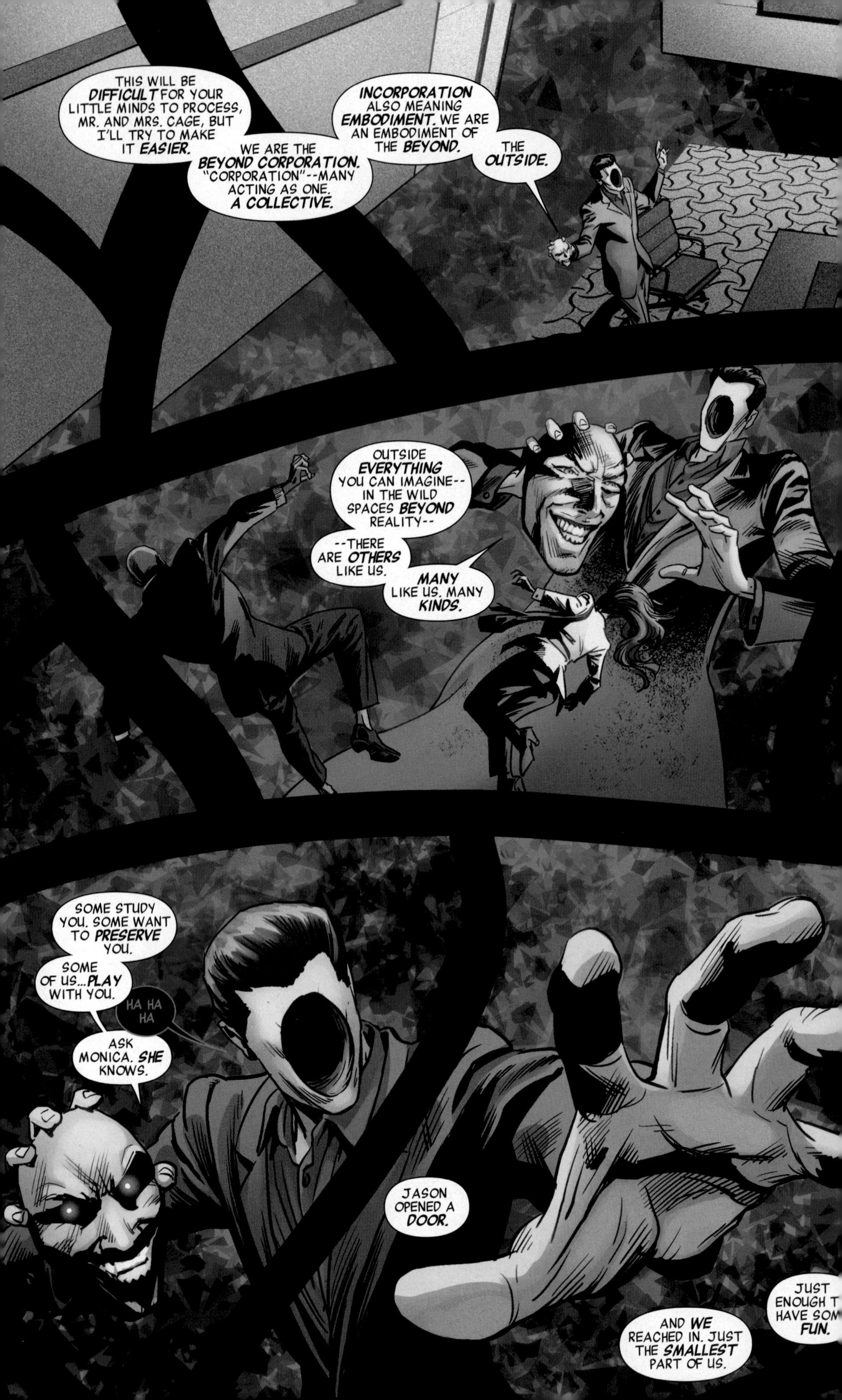
THIS WILL BE DIFFICULT FOR YOUR LITTLE MINDS TO PROCESS, MR. AND MRS. CAGE, BUT I'LL TRY TO MAKE IT EASIER.
WE ARE THE BEYOND CORPORATION. "CORPORATION"--MANY ACTING AS ONE. A COLLECTIVE.
INCORPORATION ALSO MEANING EMBODIMENT. WE ARE AN EMBODIMENT OF THE BEYOND.
THE OUTSIDE.
OUTSIDE EVERYTHING YOU CAN IMAGINE-- IN THE WILD SPACES BEYOND REALITY--
--THERE ARE OTHERS LIKE US.
MANY LIKE US. MANY KINDS.
SOME STUDY YOU. SOME WANT TO PRESERVE YOU.
SOME OF US...PLAY WITH YOU.
HA HA HA
ASK MONICA. SHE KNOWS.
JASON OPENED A DOOR.
AND WE REACHED IN. JUST THE SMALLEST PART OF US.
JUST ENOUGH T HAVE SOM FUN.

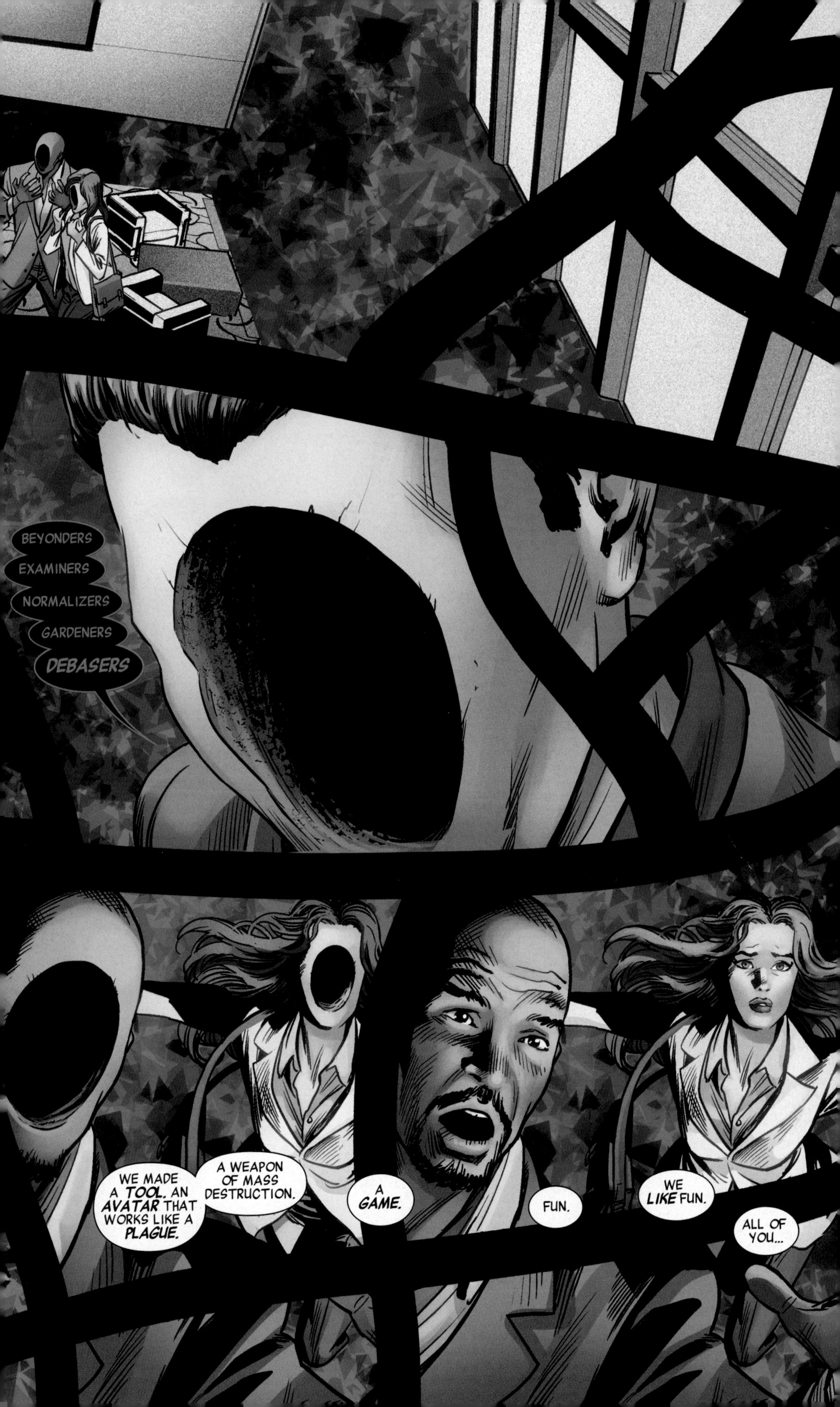

BEYONDERS
EXAMINERS
NORMALIZERS
GARDENERS
DEBASERS
WE MADE A TOOL. AN AVATAR THAT WORKS LIKE A PLAGUE.
A WEAPON OF MASS DESTRUCTION.
A GAME.
FUN.
WE LIKE FUN.
ALL OF YOU...

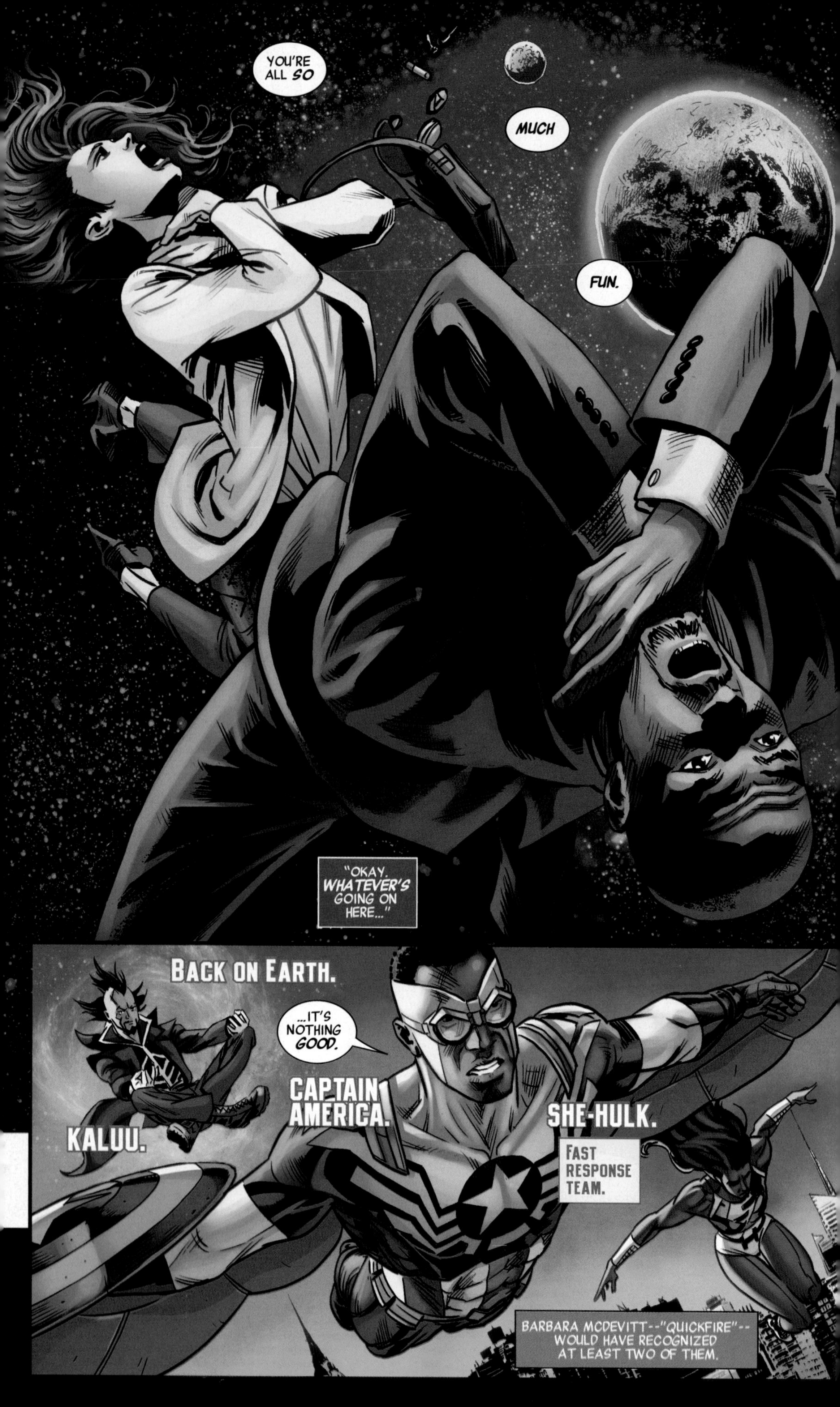
YOU'RE ALL SO
MUCH
FUN.
"OKAY. WHATEVER'S GOING ON HERE..."
BACK ON EARTH.
...IT'S NOTHING GOOD.
CAPTAIN AMERICA.
SHE-HULK.
KALUU.
FAST RESPONSE TEAM.
BARBARA MCDEVITT--"QUICKFIRE"--WOULD HAVE RECOGNIZED AT LEAST TWO OF THEM.

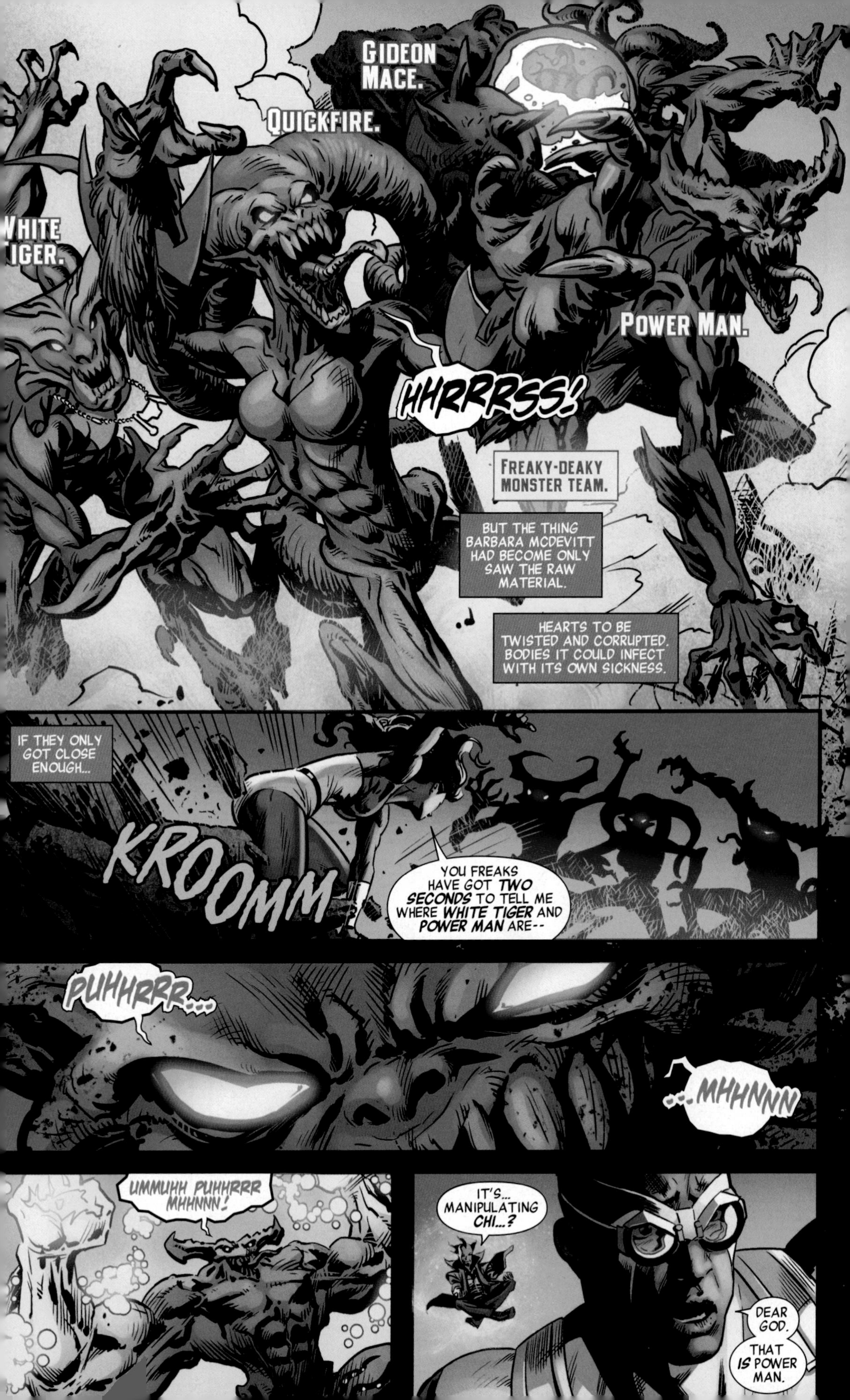
GIDEON MACE.
QUICKFIRE.
WHITE TIGER.
POWER MAN.
HHRRRSS!
FREAKY-DEAKY MONSTER TEAM.
BUT THE THING BARBARA MCDEVITT HAD BECOME ONLY SAW THE RAW MATERIAL.
HEARTS TO BE TWISTED AND CORRUPTED. BODIES IT COULD INFECT WITH ITS OWN SICKNESS.
IF THEY ONLY GOT CLOSE ENOUGH...
KROOMM!
YOU FREAKS HAVE GOT TWO SECONDS TO TELL ME WHERE WHITE TIGER AND POWER MAN ARE--
PUHHRRR...
...MHHNNN
UMMUHH PUHHRRR MHHNNN!
IT'S... MANIPULATING CHI...?
DEAR GOD.
THAT IS POWER MAN.

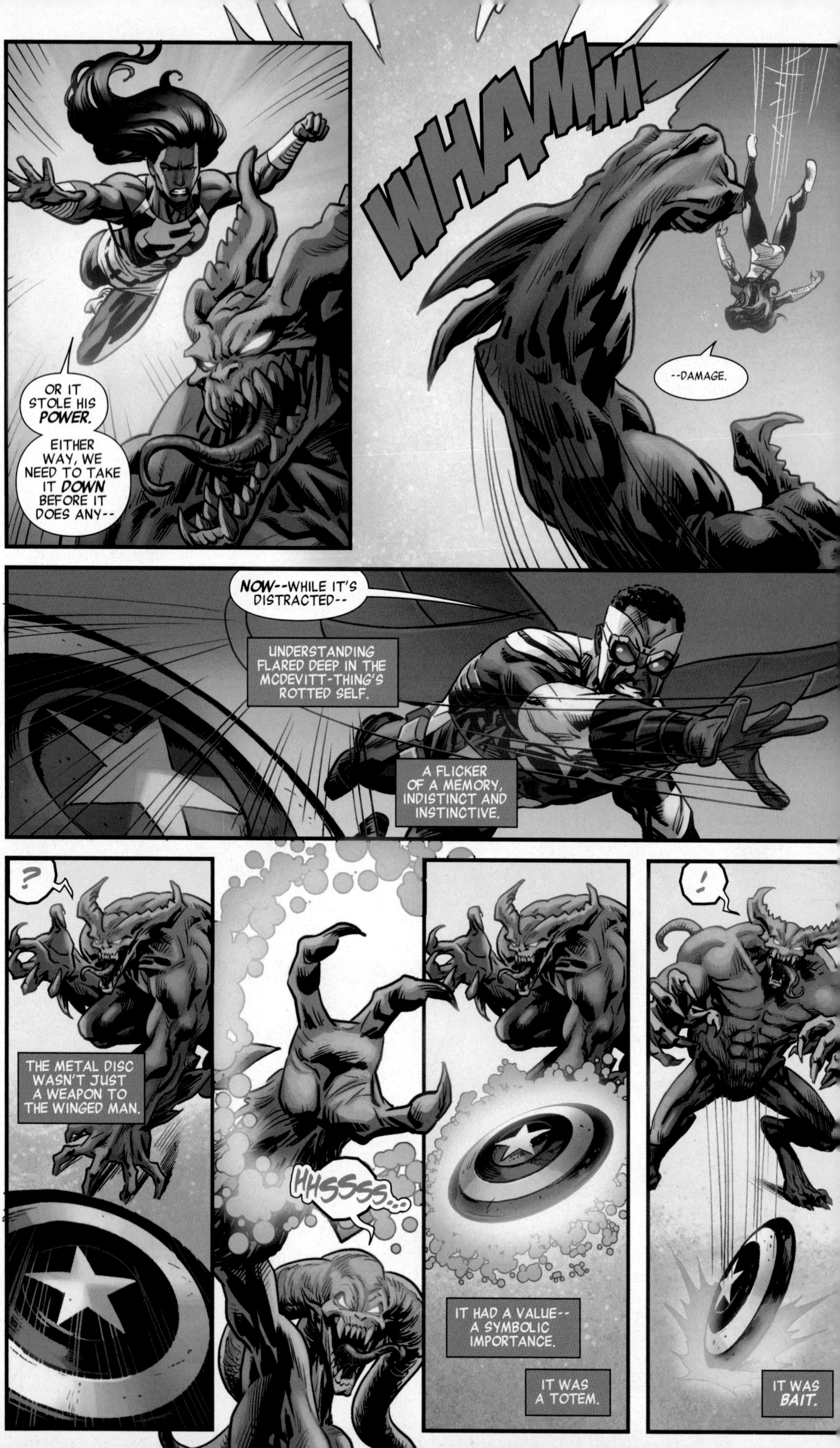

OR IT STOLE HIS POWER.
EITHER WAY, WE NEED TO TAKE IT DOWN BEFORE IT DOES ANY--
WHAMMM
--DAMAGE.
NOW--WHILE IT'S DISTRACTED--
UNDERSTANDING FLARED DEEP IN THE MCDEVITT-THING'S ROTTED SELF.
A FLICKER OF A MEMORY, INDISTINCT AND INSTINCTIVE.
?
THE METAL DISC WASN'T JUST A WEAPON TO THE WINGED MAN.
HHSSSS...
IT HAD A VALUE--A SYMBOLIC IMPORTANCE.
IT WAS A TOTEM.
!
IT WAS BAIT.

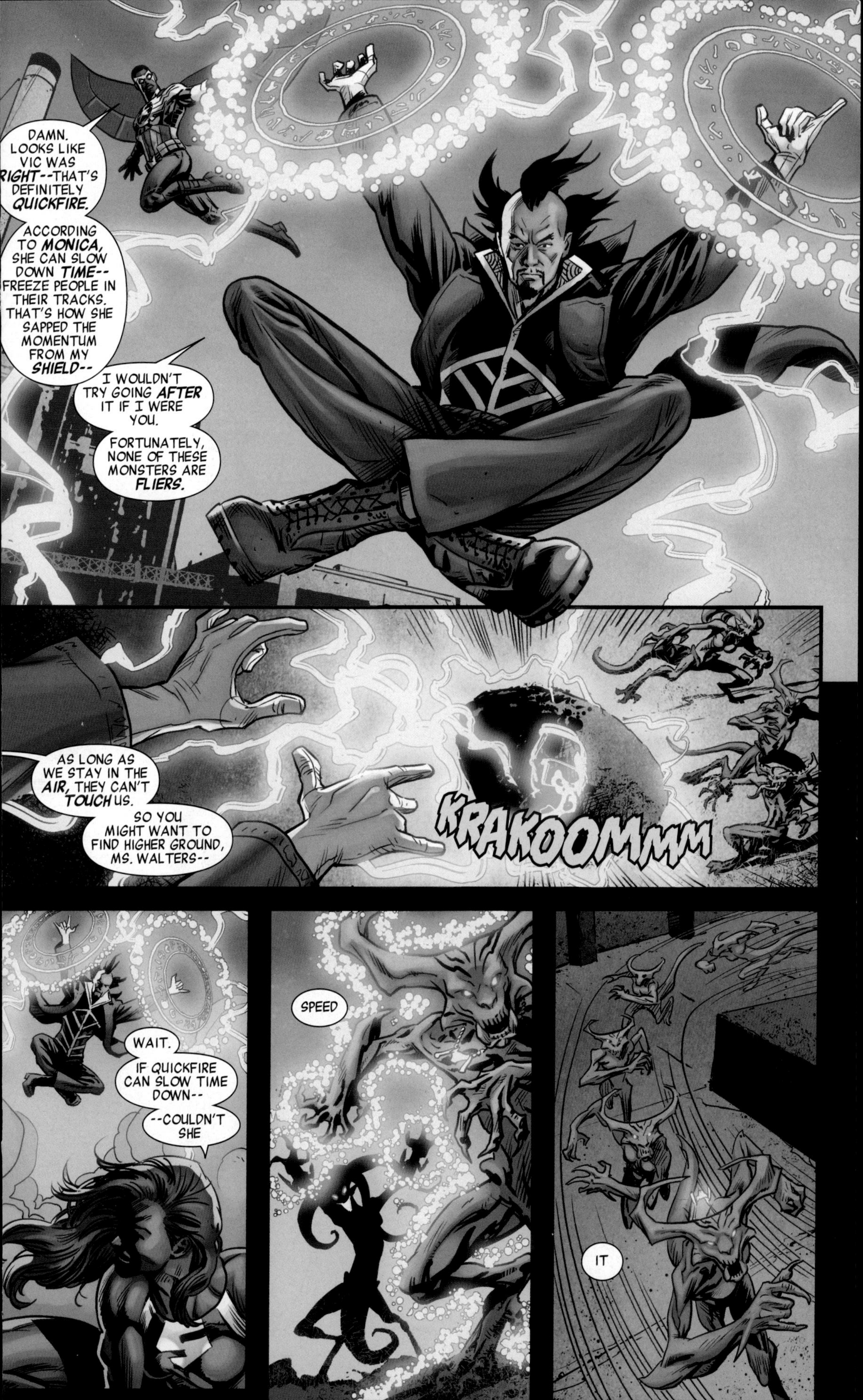
DAMN. LOOKS LIKE VIC WAS RIGHT--THAT'S DEFINITELY QUICKFIRE.
ACCORDING TO MONICA, SHE CAN SLOW DOWN TIME--FREEZE PEOPLE IN THEIR TRACKS. THAT'S HOW SHE SAPPED THE MOMENTUM FROM MY SHIELD--
I WOULDN'T TRY GOING AFTER IT IF I WERE YOU.
FORTUNATELY, NONE OF THESE MONSTERS ARE FLIERS.
AS LONG AS WE STAY IN THE AIR, THEY CAN'T TOUCH US.
SO YOU MIGHT WANT TO FIND HIGHER GROUND, MS. WALTERS--
KRAKOOMMMM
WAIT.
IF QUICKFIRE CAN SLOW TIME DOWN--
--COULDN'T SHE
SPEED
IT

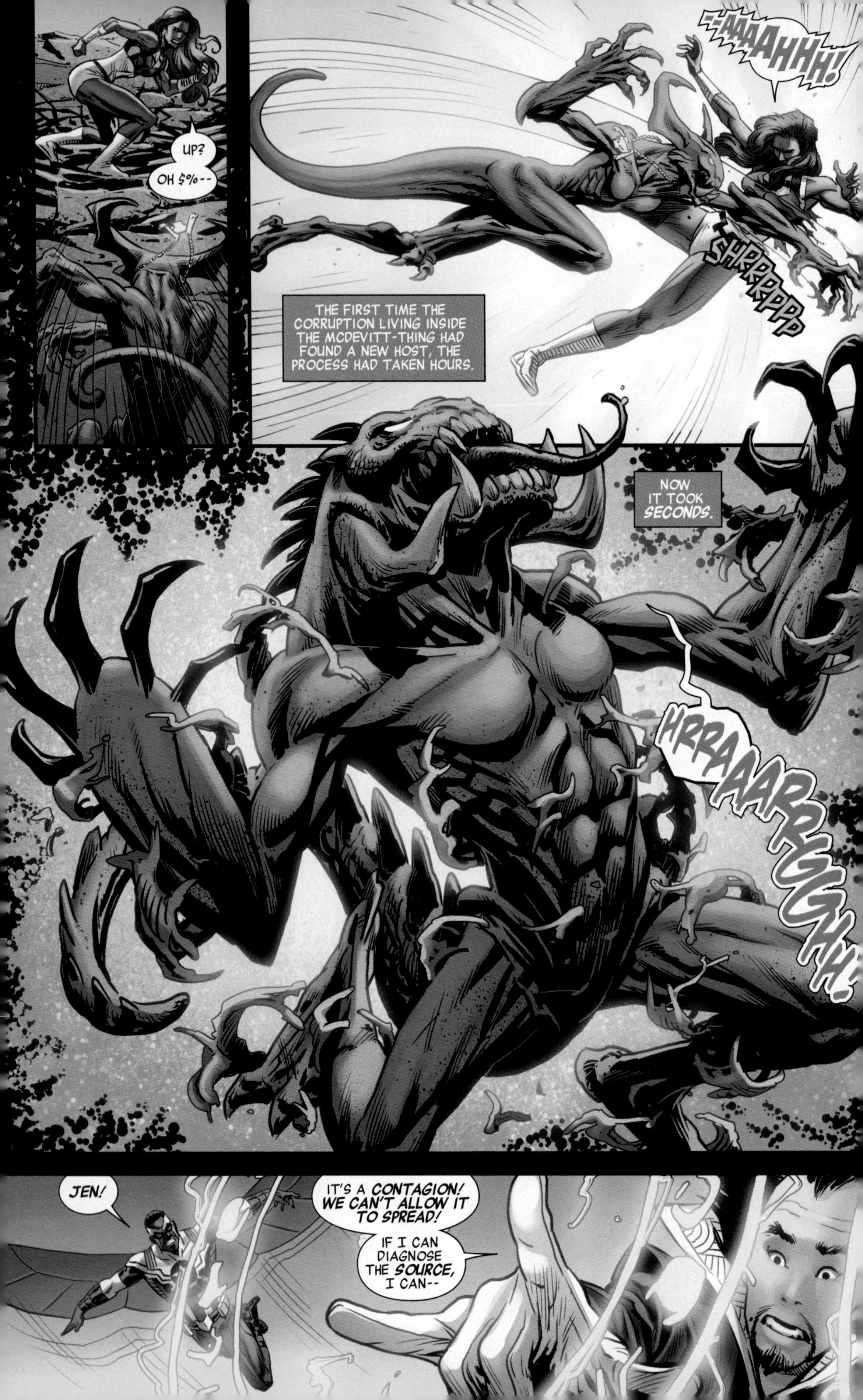
UP?
OH $%--
-AAAAHHH!
SHRRPPP
THE FIRST TIME THE CORRUPTION LIVING INSIDE THE MCDEVITT-THING HAD FOUND A NEW HOST, THE PROCESS HAD TAKEN HOURS.
NOW IT TOOK SECONDS.
HRRAAARRGGHH!
JEN!
IT'S A CONTAGION! WE CAN'T ALLOW IT TO SPREAD!
IF I CAN DIAGNOSE THE SOURCE, I CAN--

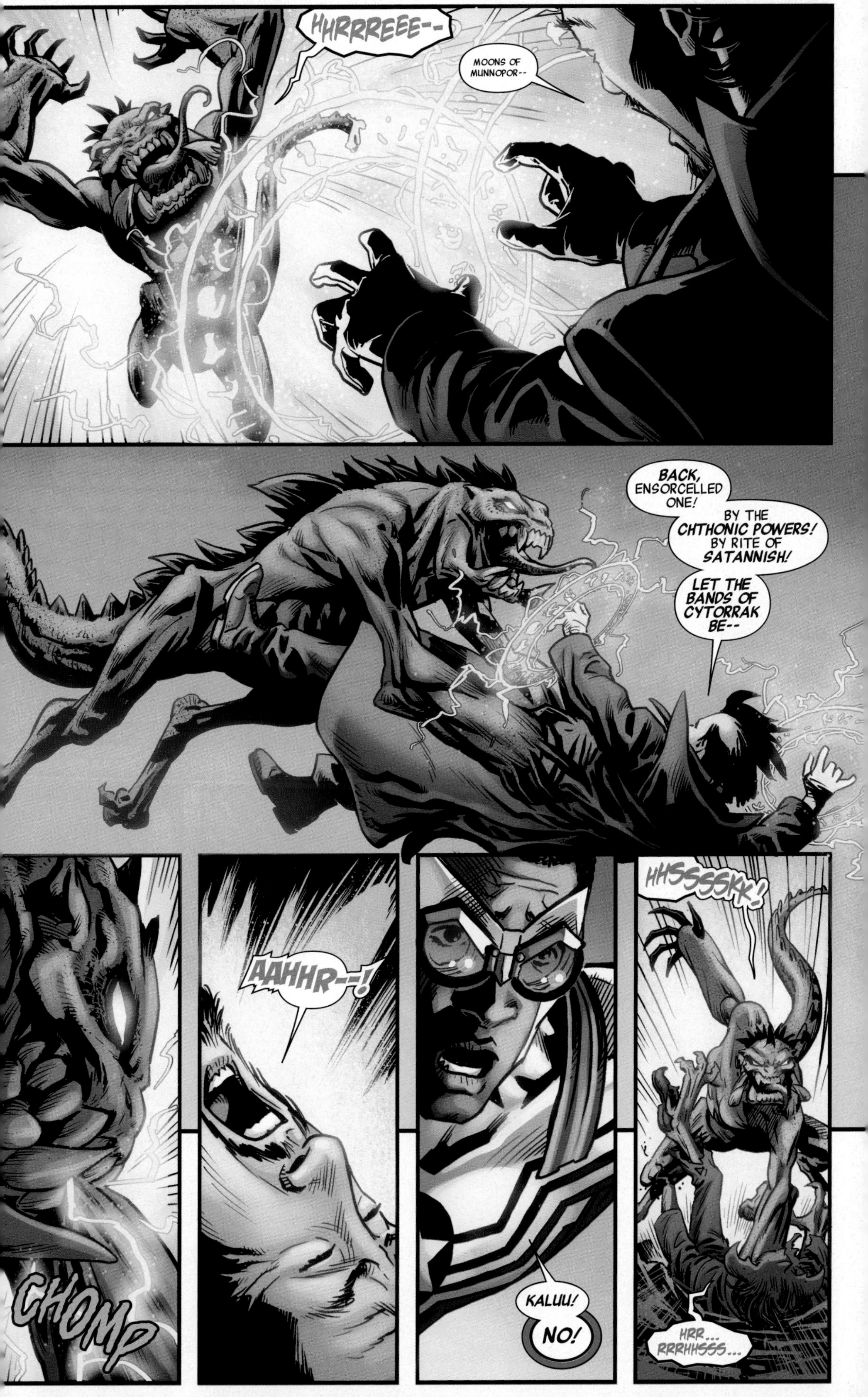
HHRRREEE--
MOONS OF MUNNOPOR--
BACK, ENSORCELLED ONE!
BY THE CHTHONIC POWERS! BY RITE OF SATANNISH!
LET THE BANDS OF CYTORRAK BE--
CHOMP
AAHHR--!
KALUU!
NO!
HHSSSSKK!
HRR... RRRHHSSS...

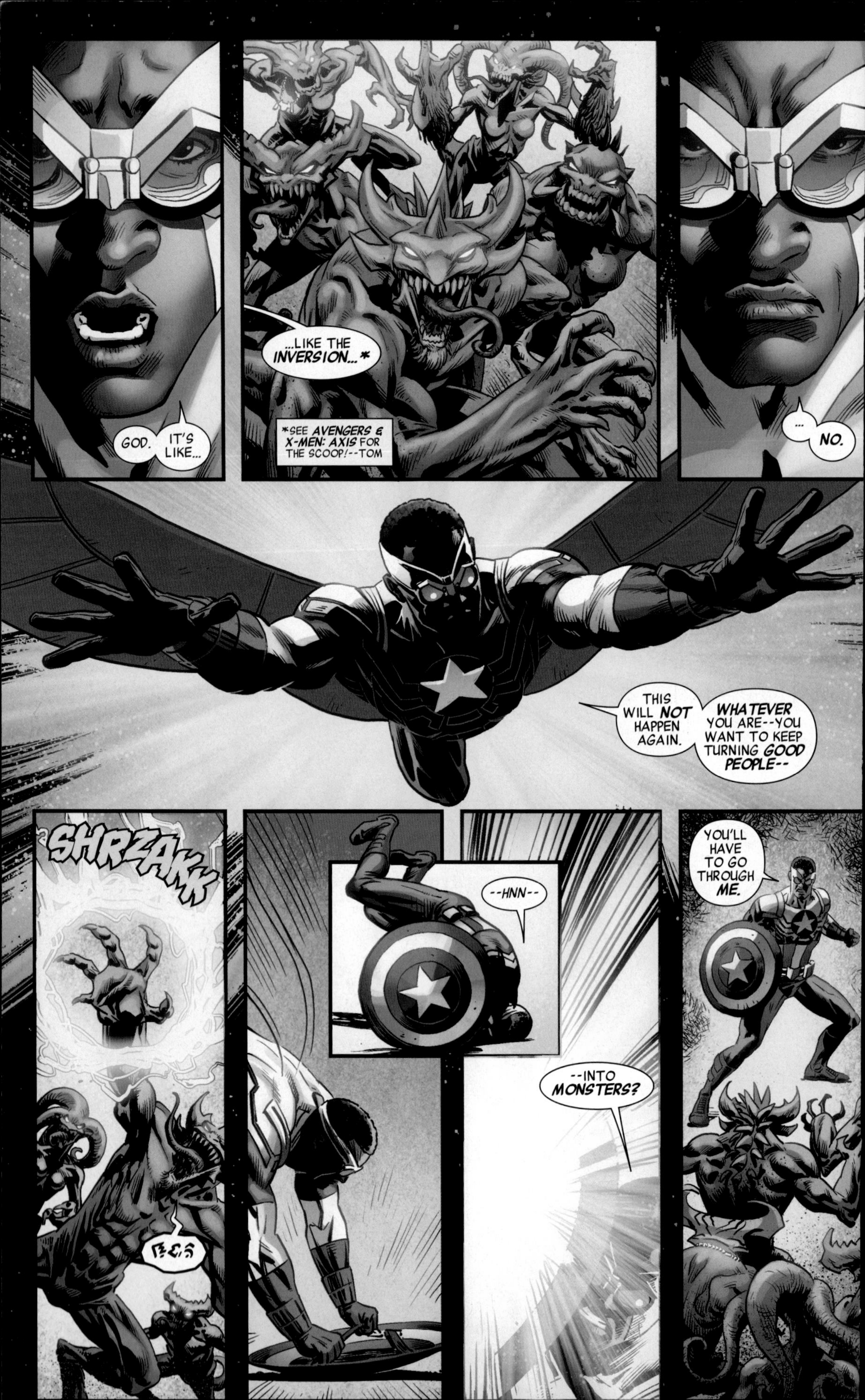
GOD.
IT'S LIKE...
...LIKE THE INVERSION...*
*SEE AVENGERS & X-MEN: AXIS FOR THE SCOOP!--TOM
...
NO.
THIS WILL NOT HAPPEN AGAIN.
WHATEVER YOU ARE--YOU WANT TO KEEP TURNING GOOD PEOPLE--
SHRZAKK
--HNN--
--INTO MONSTERS?
YOU'LL HAVE TO GO THROUGH ME.

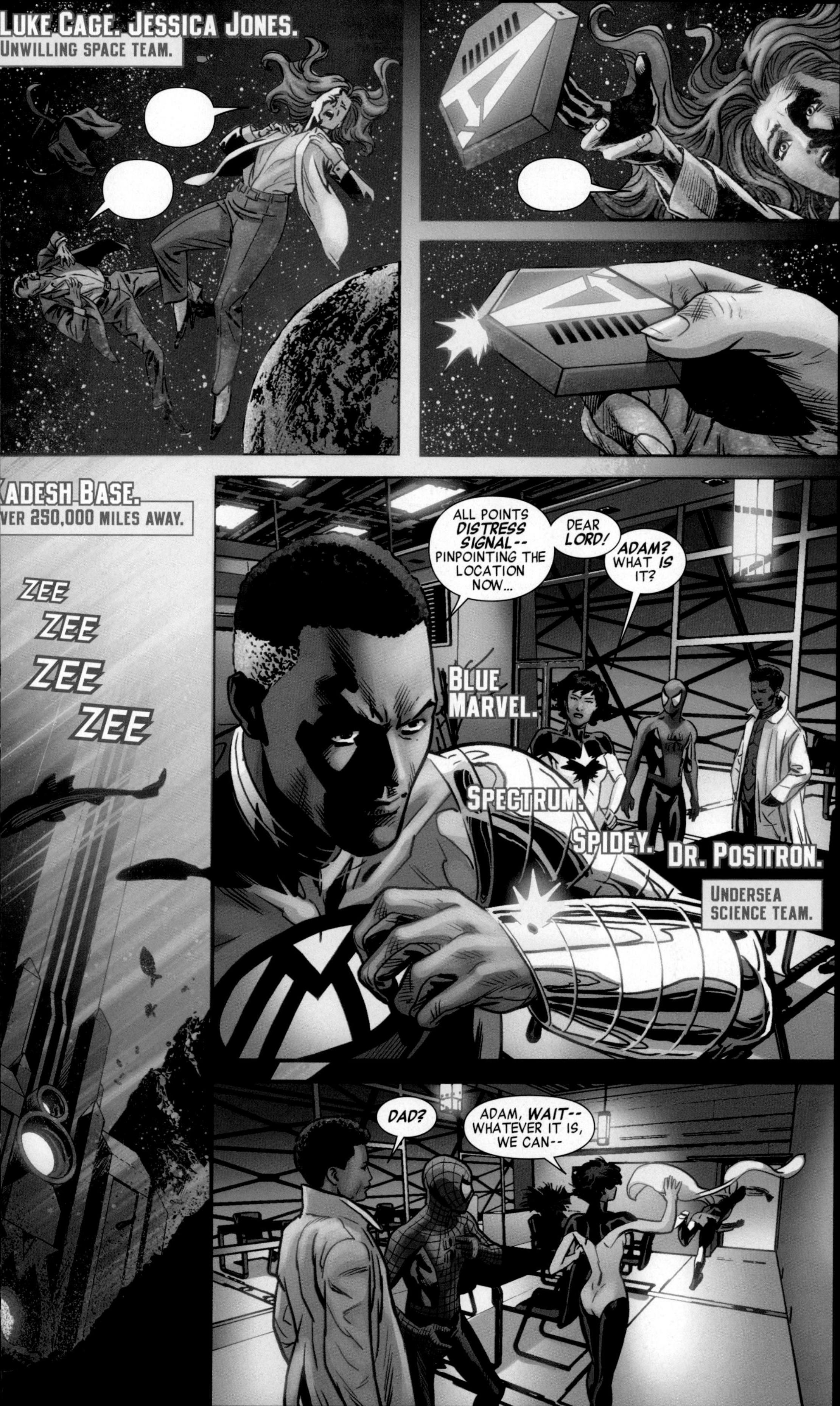
LUKE CAGE. JESSICA JONES.
UNWILLING SPACE TEAM.
KADESH BASE.
VER 250,000 MILES AWAY.
ZEE
ZEE
ZEE
ZEE
ALL POINTS DISTRESS SIGNAL-- PINPOINTING THE LOCATION NOW...
DEAR LORD!
ADAM? WHAT IS IT?
BLUE MARVEL.
SPECTRUM.
SPIDEY.
DR. POSITRON.
UNDERSEA SCIENCE TEAM.
DAD?
ADAM, WAIT-- WHATEVER IT IS, WE CAN--

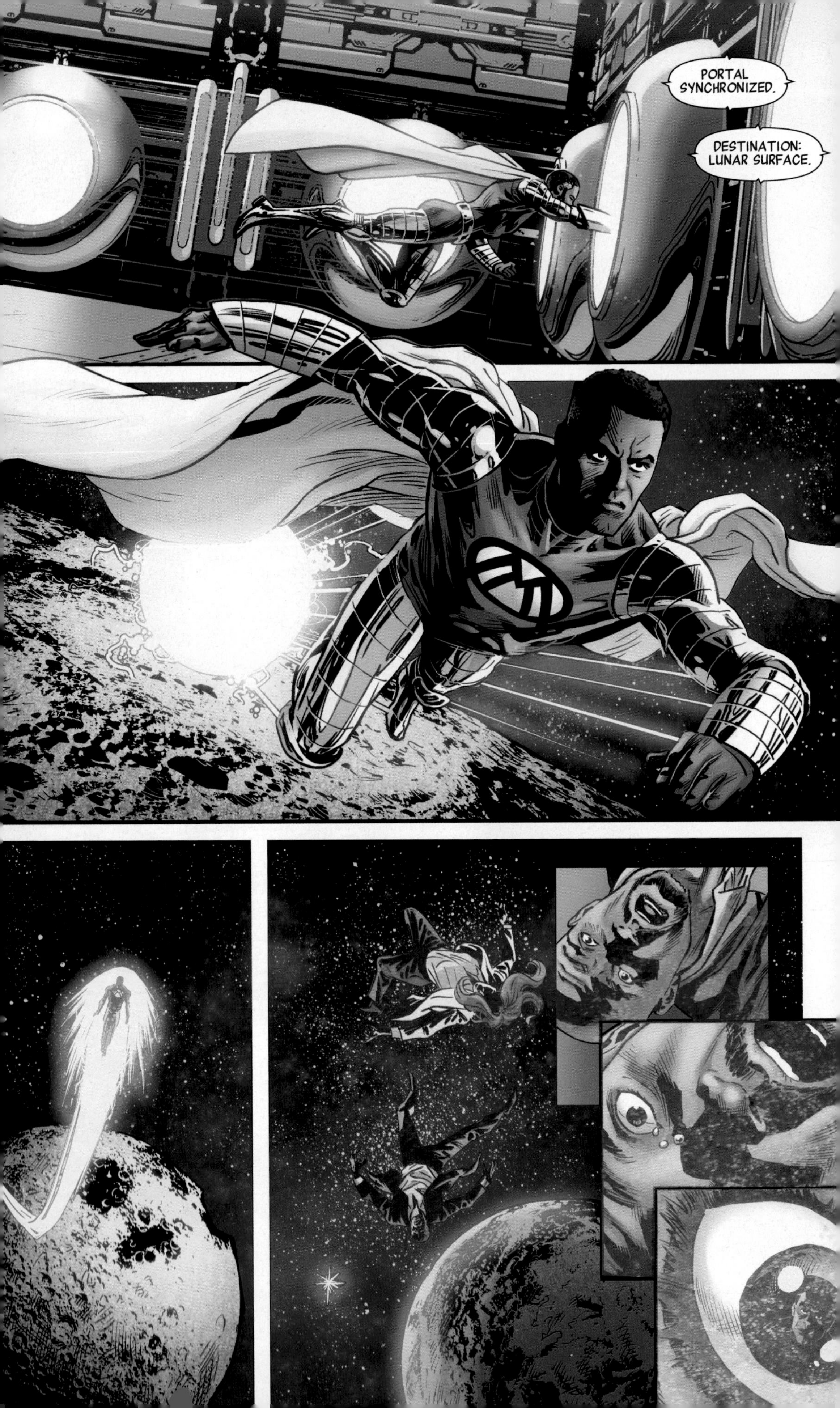
PORTAL SYNCHRONIZED.
DESTINATION: LUNAR SURFACE.

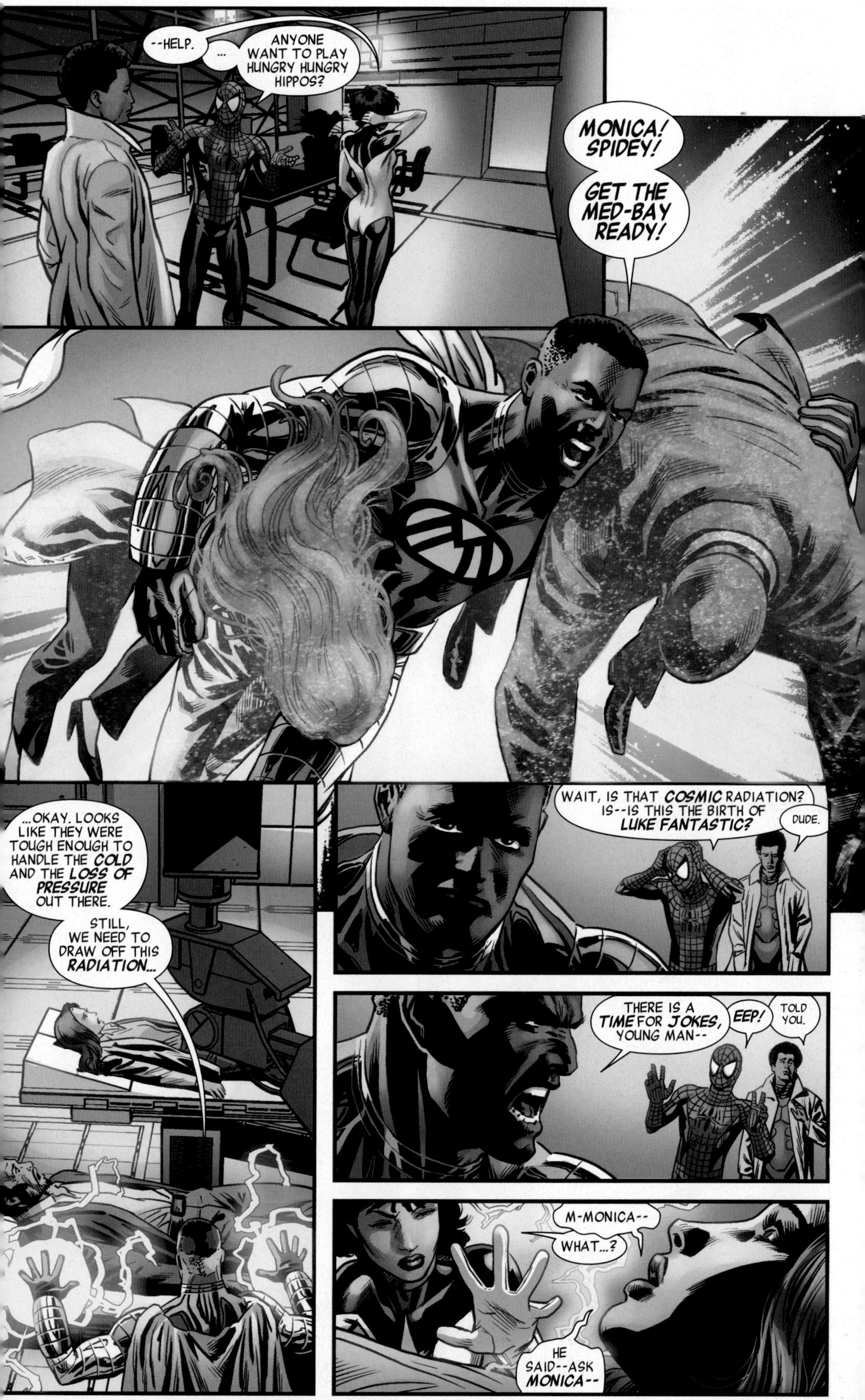
--HELP.
...
ANYONE WANT TO PLAY HUNGRY HUNGRY HIPPOS?
MONICA! SPIDEY!
GET THE MED-BAY READY!
...OKAY. LOOKS LIKE THEY WERE TOUGH ENOUGH TO HANDLE THE COLD AND THE LOSS OF PRESSURE OUT THERE.
STILL, WE NEED TO DRAW OFF THIS RADIATION...
WAIT, IS THAT COSMIC RADIATION? IS--IS THIS THE BIRTH OF LUKE FANTASTIC?
DUDE.
THERE IS A TIME FOR JOKES, YOUNG MAN--
EEP!
TOLD YOU.
M-MONICA--
WHAT...?
HE SAID--ASK MONICA--

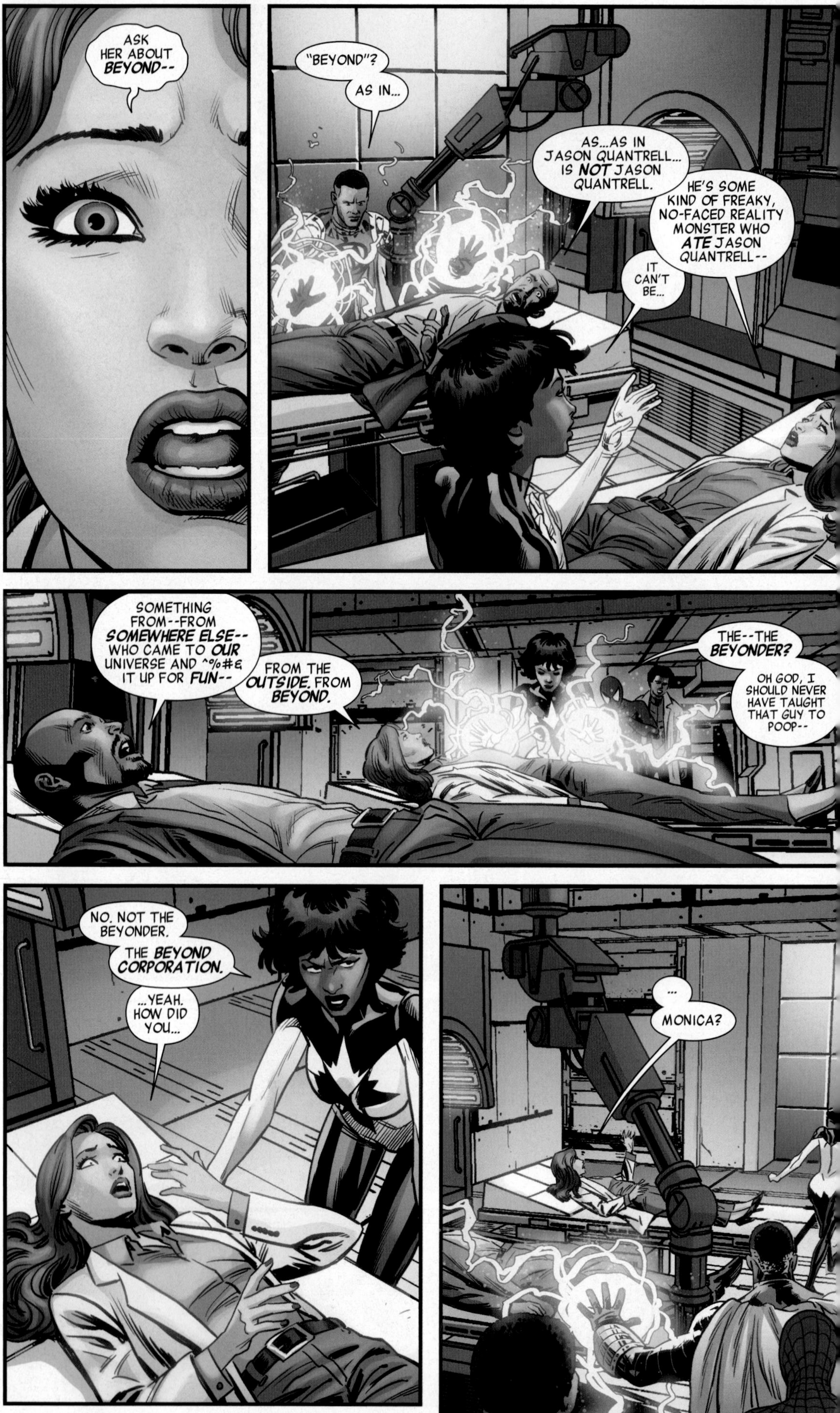

ASK HER ABOUT BEYOND--
"BEYOND"?
AS IN...
AS...AS IN JASON QUANTRELL... IS NOT JASON QUANTRELL.
HE'S SOME KIND OF FREAKY, NO-FACED REALITY MONSTER WHO ATE JASON QUANTRELL--
IT CAN'T BE...
SOMETHING FROM--FROM SOMEWHERE ELSE-- WHO CAME TO OUR UNIVERSE AND ^%#€ IT UP FOR FUN--
FROM THE OUTSIDE. FROM BEYOND.
THE--THE BEYONDER?
OH GOD, I SHOULD NEVER HAVE TAUGHT THAT GUY TO POOP--
NO. NOT THE BEYONDER.
THE BEYOND CORPORATION.
...YEAH. HOW DID YOU...
...
MONICA?

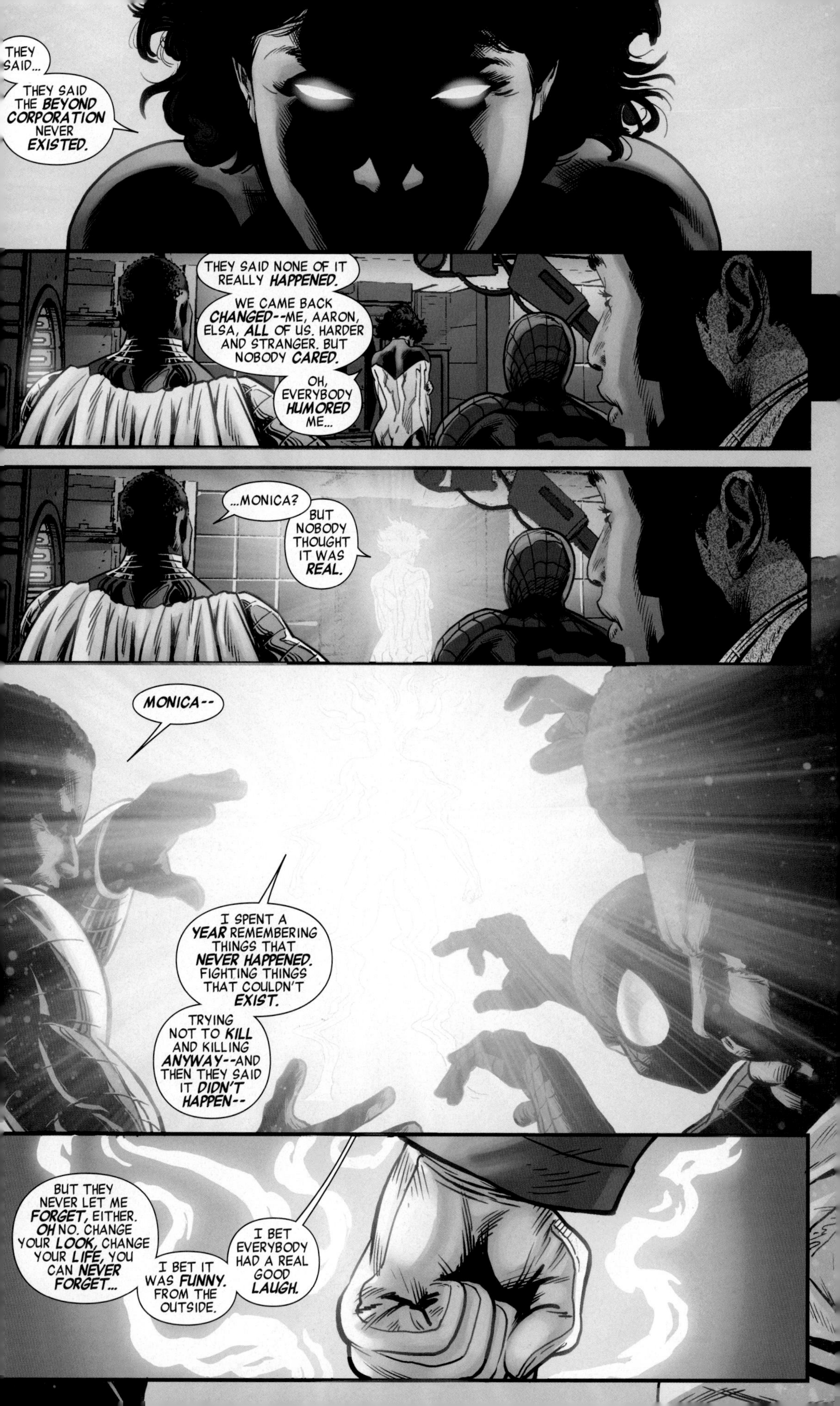

THEY SAID...
THEY SAID THE BEYOND CORPORATION NEVER EXISTED.
THEY SAID NONE OF IT REALLY HAPPENED.
WE CAME BACK CHANGED--ME, AARON, ELSA, ALL OF US. HARDER AND STRANGER. BUT NOBODY CARED.
OH, EVERYBODY HUMORED ME...
...MONICA?
BUT NOBODY THOUGHT IT WAS REAL.
MONICA--
I SPENT A YEAR REMEMBERING THINGS THAT NEVER HAPPENED. FIGHTING THINGS THAT COULDN'T EXIST.
TRYING NOT TO KILL AND KILLING ANYWAY--AND THEN THEY SAID IT DIDN'T HAPPEN--
BUT THEY NEVER LET ME FORGET, EITHER. OH NO. CHANGE YOUR LOOK, CHANGE YOUR LIFE, YOU CAN NEVER FORGET...
I BET IT WAS FUNNY. FROM THE OUTSIDE.
I BET EVERYBODY HAD A REAL GOOD LAUGH.

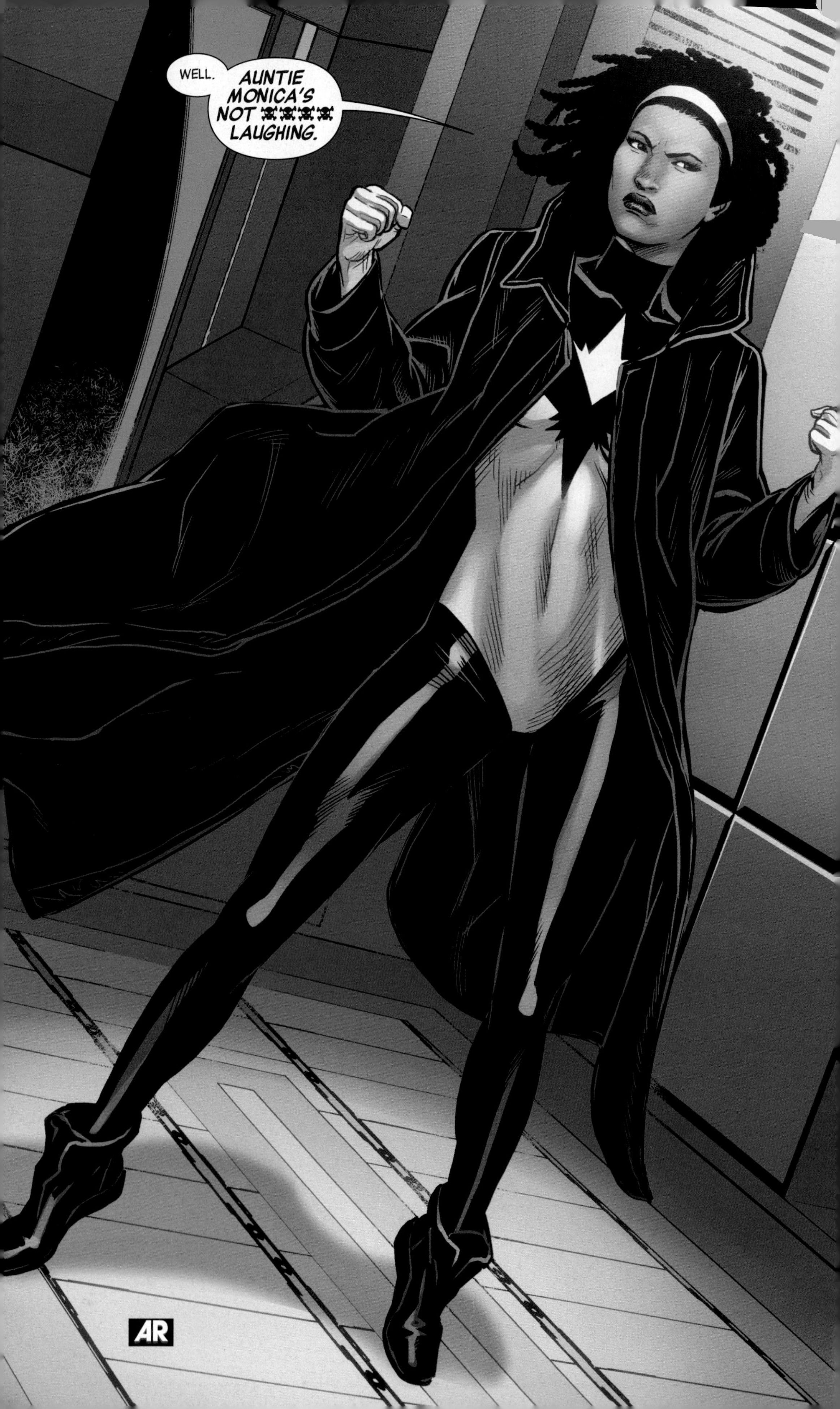
WELL.
AUNTIE MONICA'S NOT ☠☠☠☠ LAUGHING.
AR

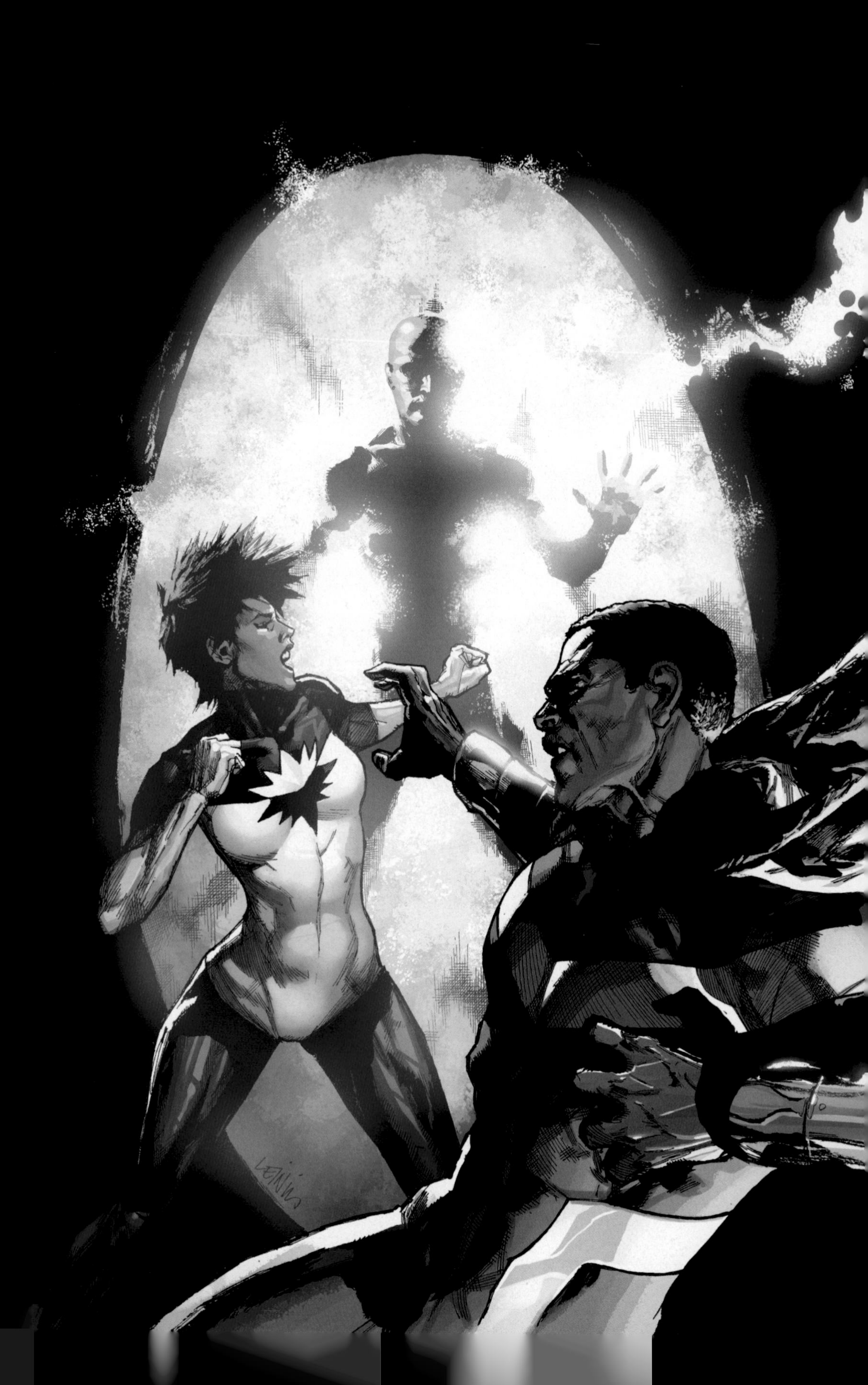

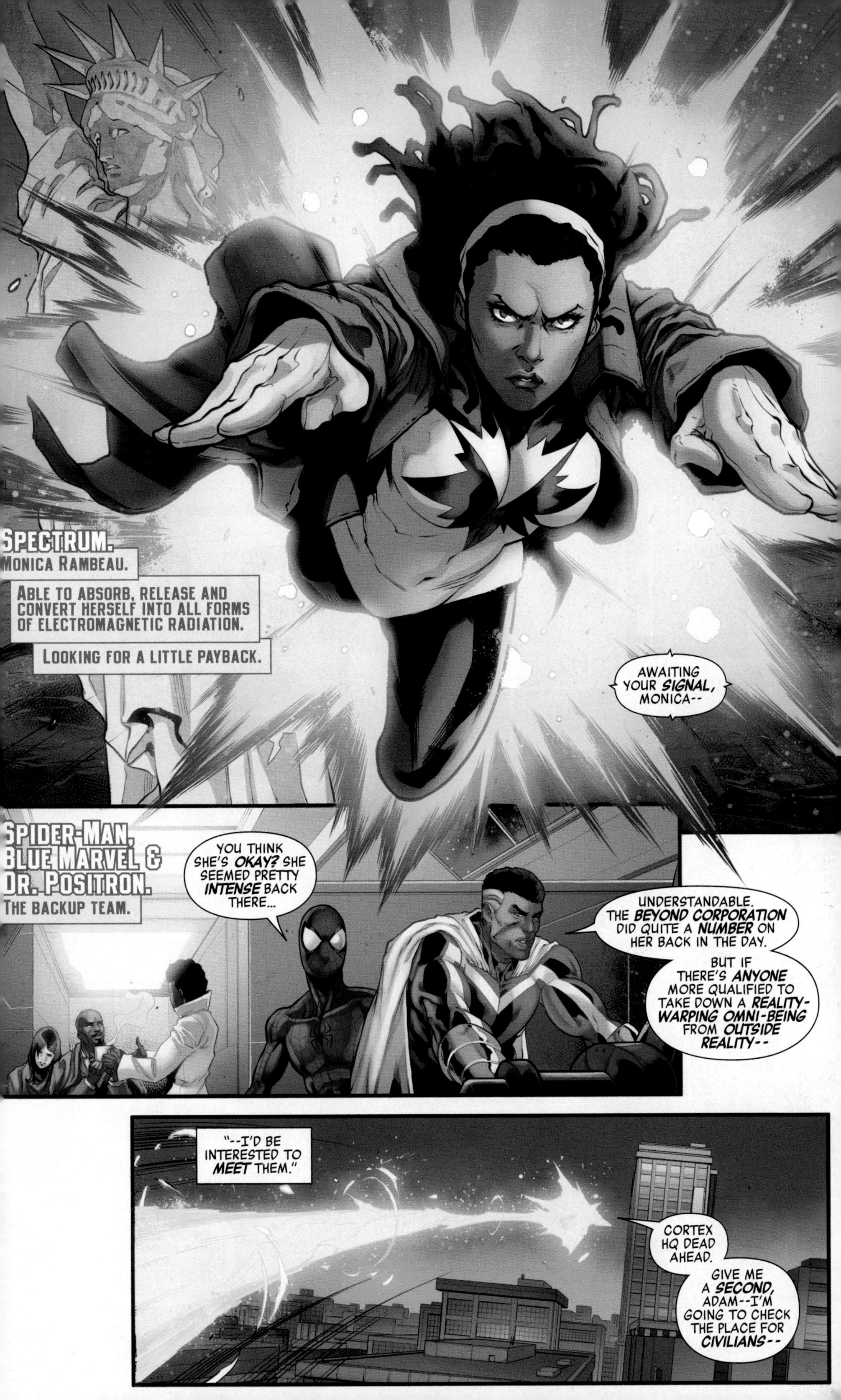

SPECTRUM.
MONICA RAMBEAU.
ABLE TO ABSORB, RELEASE AND CONVERT HERSELF INTO ALL FORMS OF ELECTROMAGNETIC RADIATION.
LOOKING FOR A LITTLE PAYBACK.
AWAITING YOUR SIGNAL, MONICA--
SPIDER-MAN, BLUE MARVEL & DR. POSITRON.
THE BACKUP TEAM.
YOU THINK SHE'S OKAY? SHE SEEMED PRETTY INTENSE BACK THERE...
UNDERSTANDABLE. THE BEYOND CORPORATION DID QUITE A NUMBER ON HER BACK IN THE DAY.
BUT IF THERE'S ANYONE MORE QUALIFIED TO TAKE DOWN A REALITY-WARPING OMNI-BEING FROM OUTSIDE REALITY--
"--I'D BE INTERESTED TO MEET THEM."
CORTEX HQ DEAD AHEAD.
GIVE ME A SECOND, ADAM--I'M GOING TO CHECK THE PLACE FOR CIVILIANS--

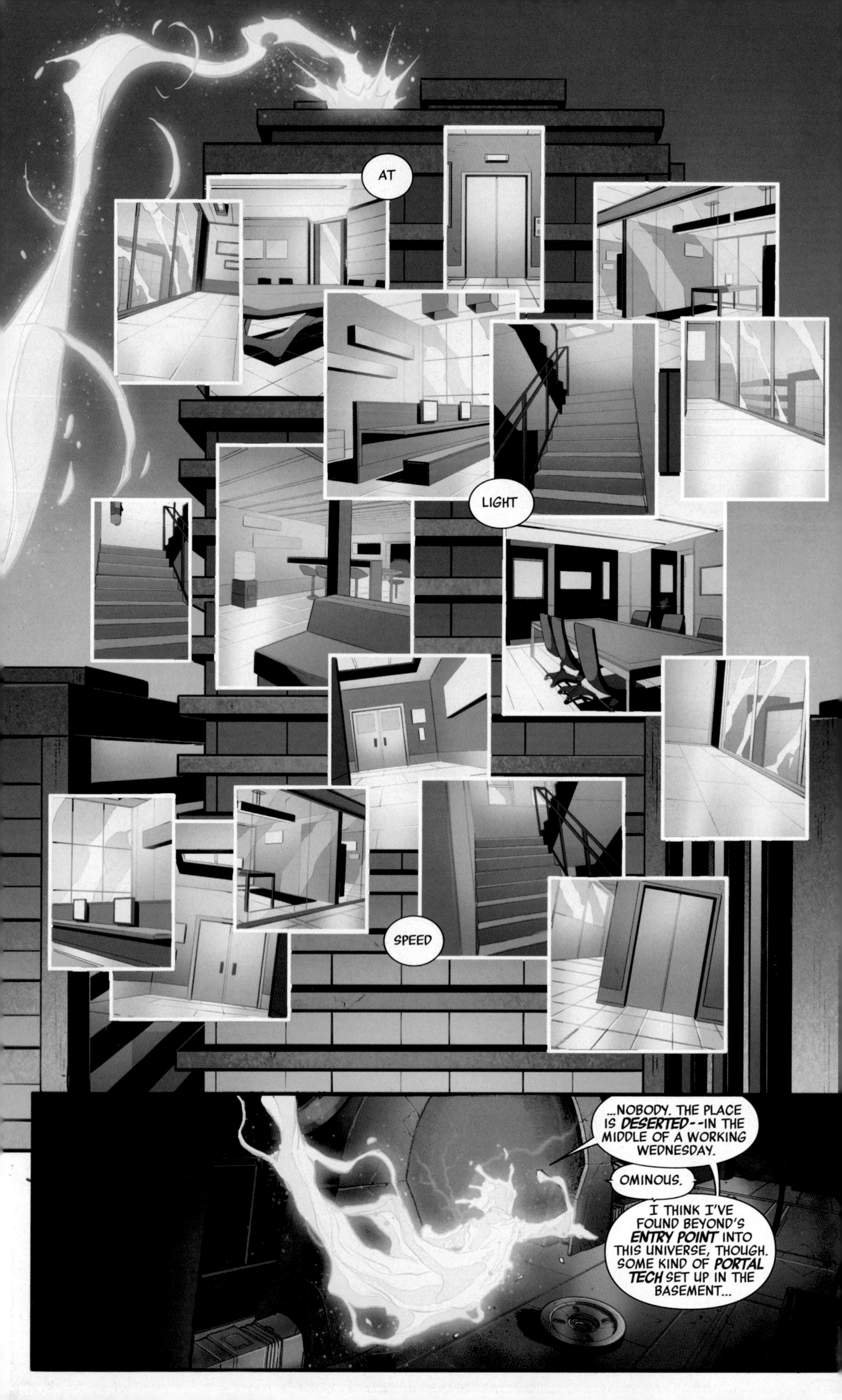
AT
LIGHT
SPEED
...NOBODY. THE PLACE IS DESERTED--IN THE MIDDLE OF A WORKING WEDNESDAY.
OMINOUS.
I THINK I'VE FOUND BEYOND'S ENTRY POINT INTO THIS UNIVERSE, THOUGH. SOME KIND OF PORTAL TECH SET UP IN THE BASEMENT...

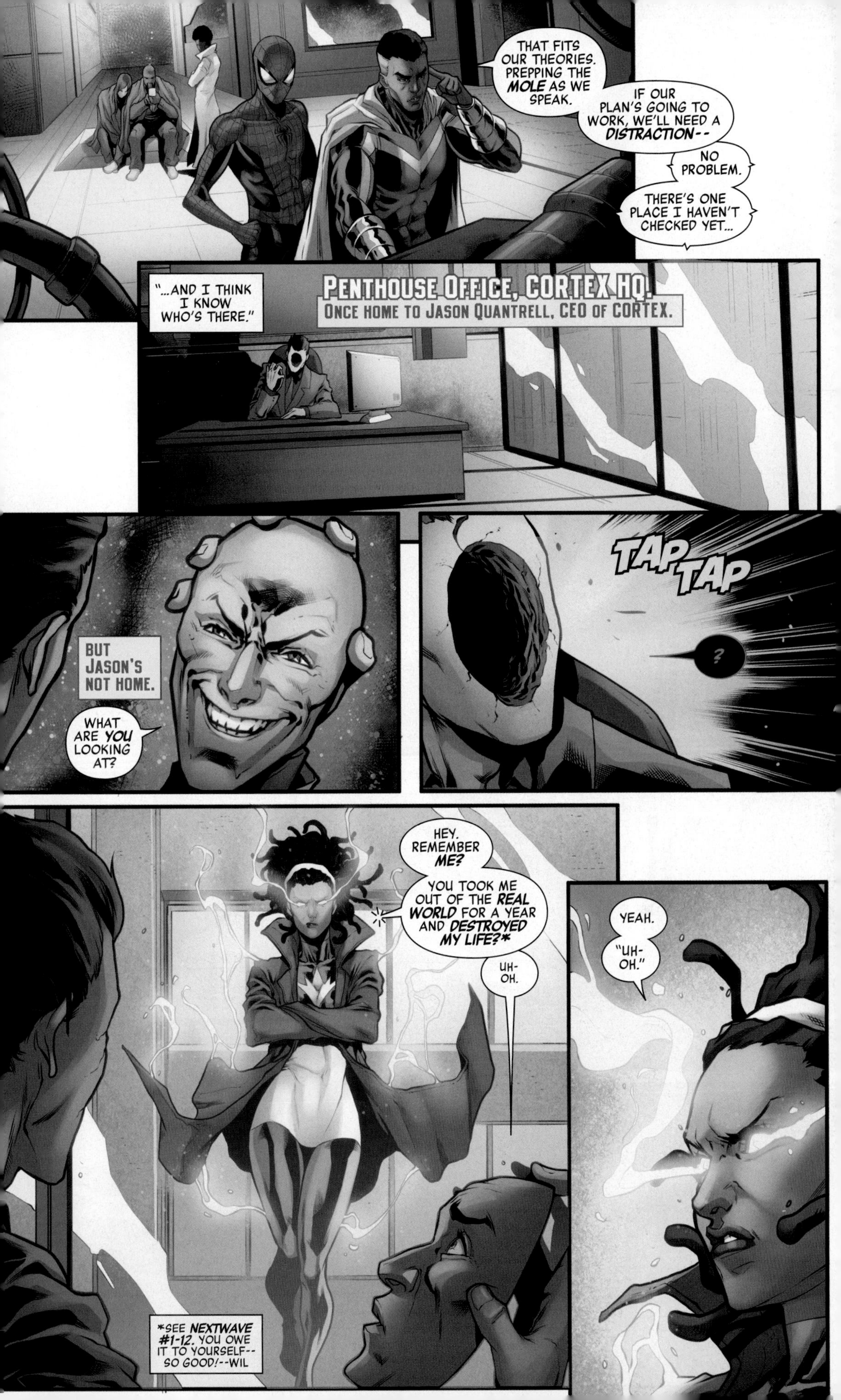

THAT FITS OUR THEORIES. PREPPING THE MOLE AS WE SPEAK.
IF OUR PLAN'S GOING TO WORK, WE'LL NEED A DISTRACTION--
NO PROBLEM.
THERE'S ONE PLACE I HAVEN'T CHECKED YET...
"...AND I THINK I KNOW WHO'S THERE."
PENTHOUSE OFFICE, CORTEX HQ.
ONCE HOME TO JASON QUANTRELL, CEO OF CORTEX.
BUT JASON'S NOT HOME.
WHAT ARE YOU LOOKING AT?
TAP TAP
?
HEY. REMEMBER ME?
YOU TOOK ME OUT OF THE REAL WORLD FOR A YEAR AND DESTROYED MY LIFE?*
UH-OH.
YEAH.
"UH-OH."
*SEE NEXTWAVE #1-12. YOU OWE IT TO YOURSELF--SO GOOD!--WIL

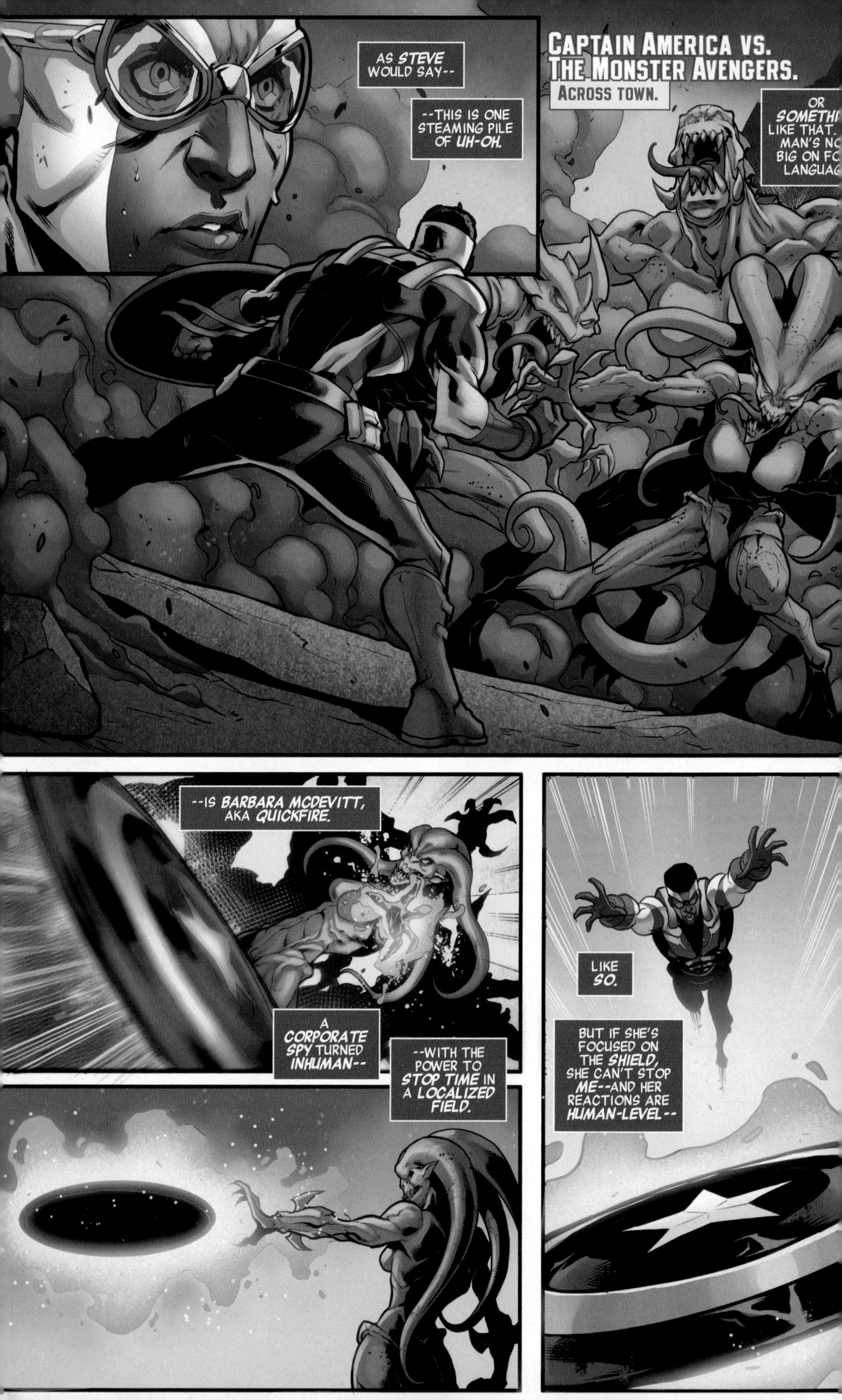

AS STEVE WOULD SAY--
--THIS IS ONE STEAMING PILE OF UH-OH.
CAPTAIN AMERICA VS. THE MONSTER AVENGERS.
ACROSS TOWN.
--IS BARBARA MCDEVITT, AKA QUICKFIRE.
A CORPORATE SPY TURNED INHUMAN--
--WITH THE POWER TO STOP TIME IN A LOCALIZED FIELD.
LIKE SO.
BUT IF SHE'S FOCUSED ON THE SHIELD, SHE CAN'T STOP ME--AND HER REACTIONS ARE HUMAN-LEVEL--

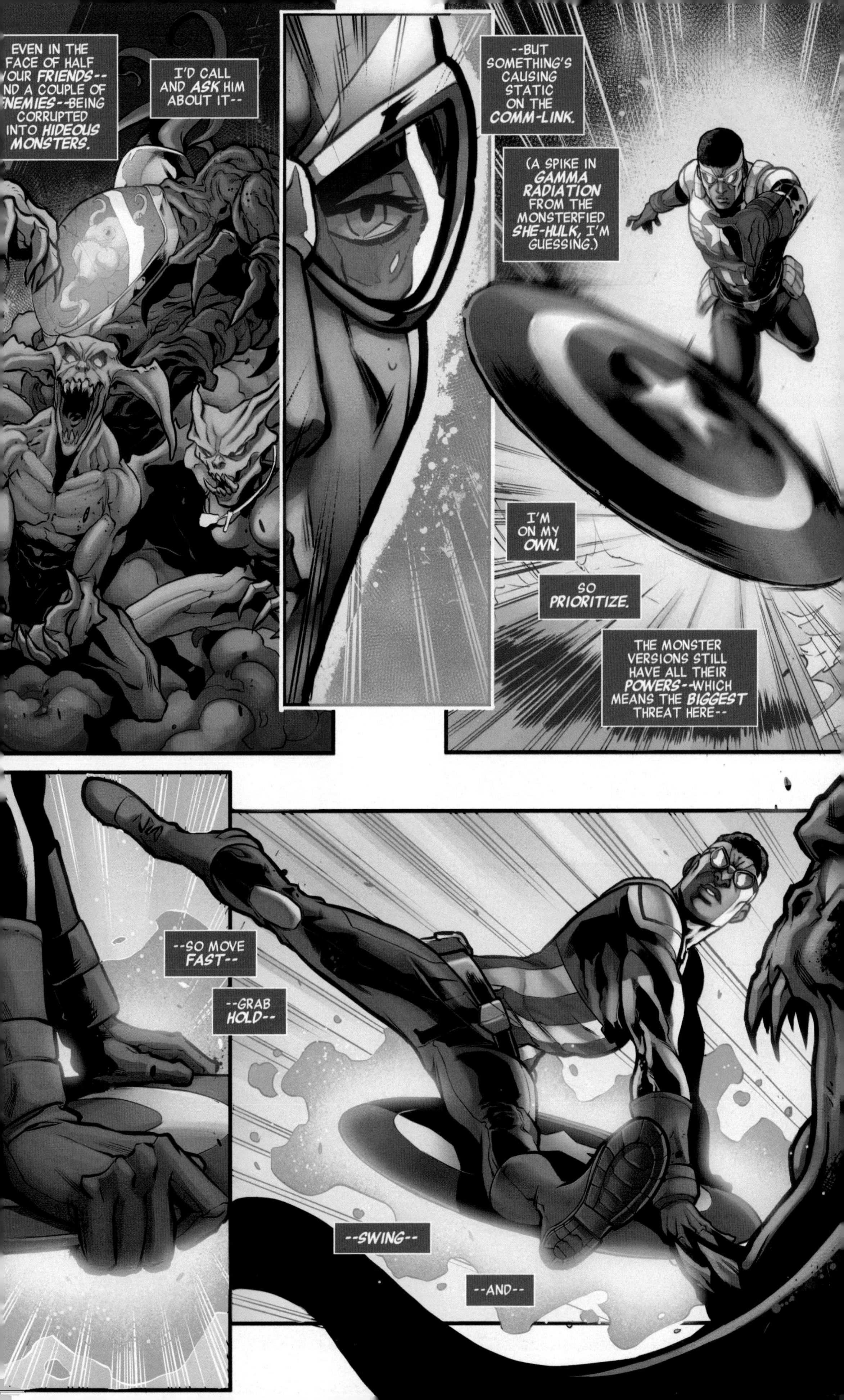
EVEN IN THE FACE OF HALF YOUR FRIENDS-- AND A COUPLE OF ENEMIES--BEING CORRUPTED INTO HIDEOUS MONSTERS.
I'D CALL AND ASK HIM ABOUT IT--
--BUT SOMETHING'S CAUSING STATIC ON THE COMM-LINK.
(A SPIKE IN GAMMA RADIATION FROM THE MONSTERFIED SHE-HULK, I'M GUESSING.)
I'M ON MY OWN.
SO PRIORITIZE.
THE MONSTER VERSIONS STILL HAVE ALL THEIR POWERS--WHICH MEANS THE BIGGEST THREAT HERE--
--SO MOVE FAST--
--GRAB HOLD--
--SWING--
--AND--

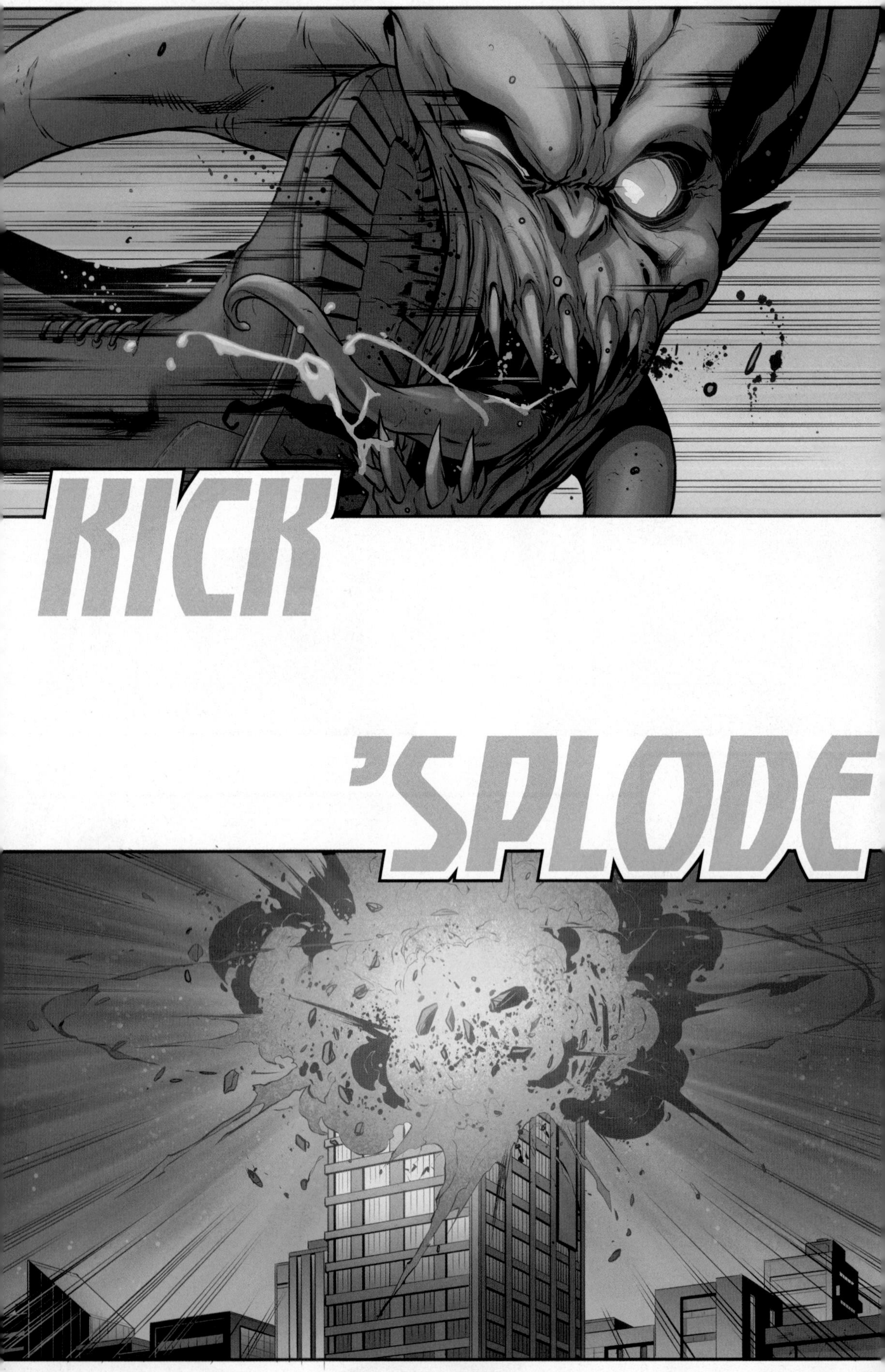
KICK
'SPLODE

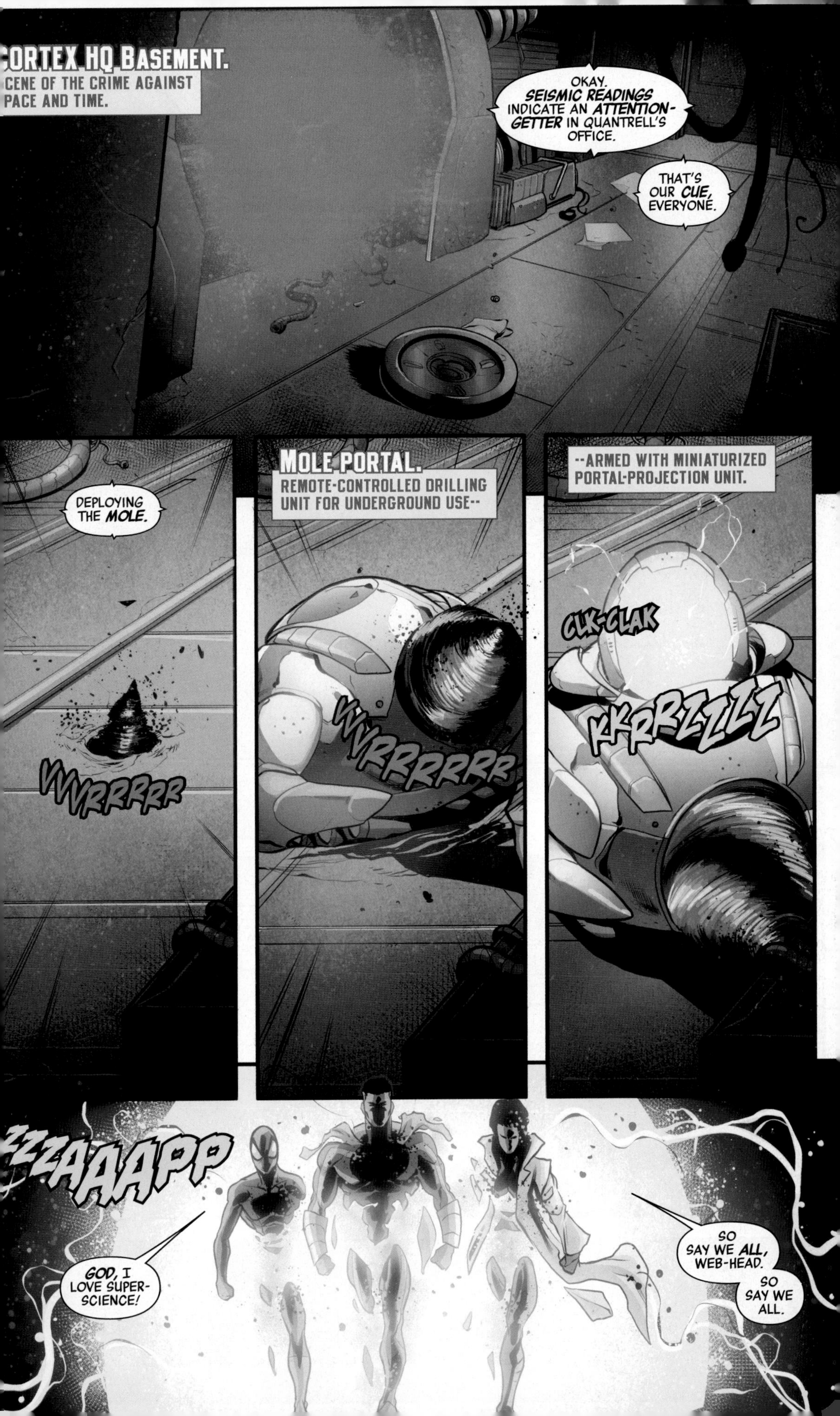
CORTEX HQ BASEMENT.
SCENE OF THE CRIME AGAINST SPACE AND TIME.
OKAY. SEISMIC READINGS INDICATE AN ATTENTION-GETTER IN QUANTRELL'S OFFICE.
THAT'S OUR CUE, EVERYONE.
DEPLOYING THE MOLE.
VVVRRRRR
MOLE PORTAL.
REMOTE-CONTROLLED DRILLING UNIT FOR UNDERGROUND USE--
VVVRRRRRRR
--ARMED WITH MINIATURIZED PORTAL-PROJECTION UNIT.
CLK-CLAK
KKRRZZZZ
ZZZAAAPP
GOD, I LOVE SUPER-SCIENCE!
SO SAY WE ALL, WEB-HEAD.
SO SAY WE ALL.

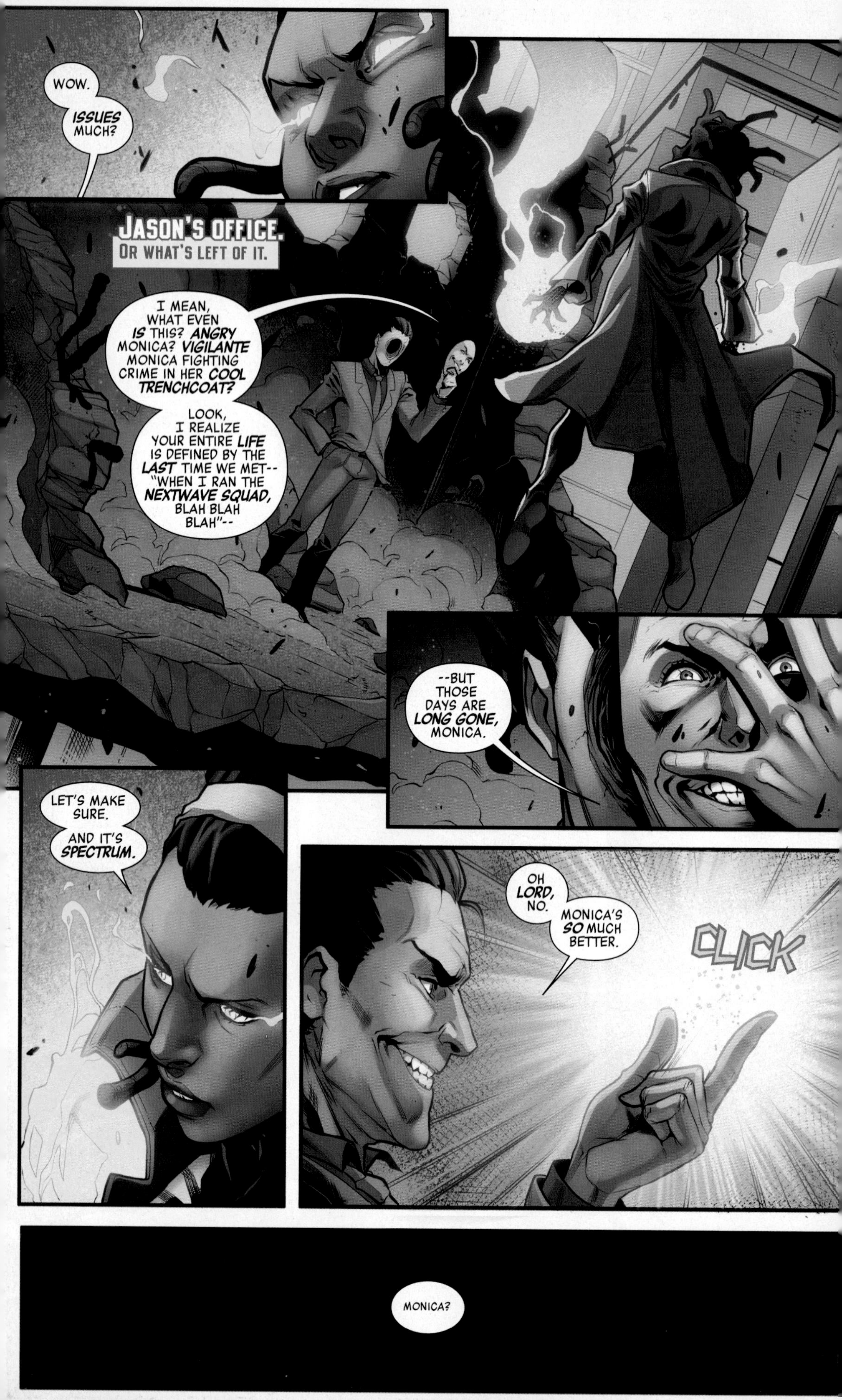

WOW.
ISSUES MUCH?
JASON'S OFFICE.
OR WHAT'S LEFT OF IT.
I MEAN, WHAT EVEN IS THIS? ANGRY MONICA? VIGILANTE MONICA FIGHTING CRIME IN HER COOL TRENCHCOAT?
LOOK, I REALIZE YOUR ENTIRE LIFE IS DEFINED BY THE LAST TIME WE MET-- "WHEN I RAN THE NEXTWAVE SQUAD, BLAH BLAH BLAH"--
--BUT THOSE DAYS ARE LONG GONE, MONICA.
LET'S MAKE SURE.
AND IT'S SPECTRUM.
OH LORD, NO.
MONICA'S SO MUCH BETTER.
CLICK
MONICA?

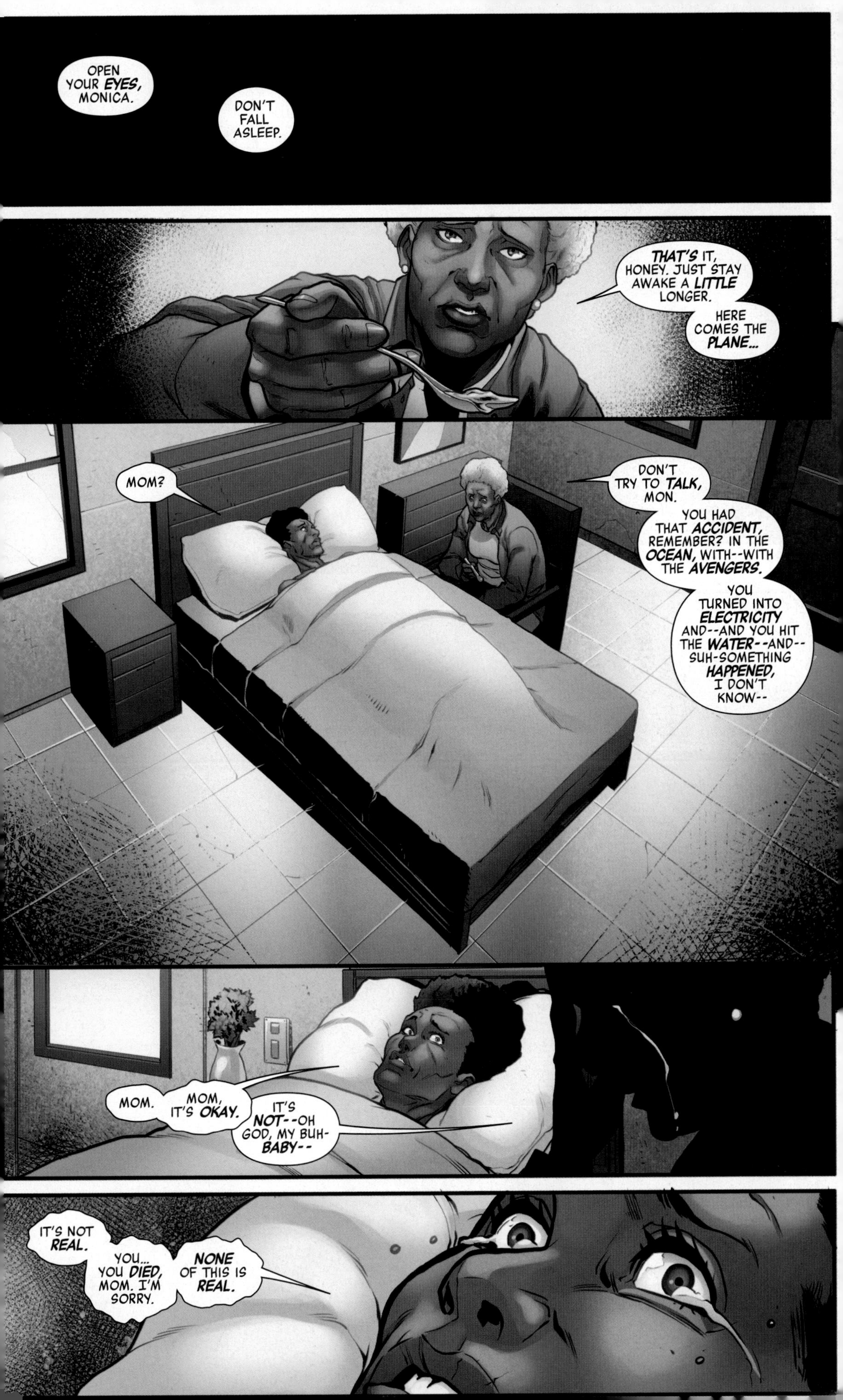
OPEN YOUR EYES, MONICA.
DON'T FALL ASLEEP.
THAT'S IT, HONEY. JUST STAY AWAKE A LITTLE LONGER.
HERE COMES THE PLANE...
MOM?
DON'T TRY TO TALK, MON.
YOU HAD THAT ACCIDENT, REMEMBER? IN THE OCEAN, WITH--WITH THE AVENGERS.
YOU TURNED INTO ELECTRICITY AND--AND YOU HIT THE WATER--AND--SUH-SOMETHING HAPPENED, I DON'T KNOW--
MOM.
MOM, IT'S OKAY.
IT'S NOT--OH GOD, MY BUH-BABY--
IT'S NOT REAL.
YOU... YOU DIED, MOM. I'M SORRY.
NONE OF THIS IS REAL.

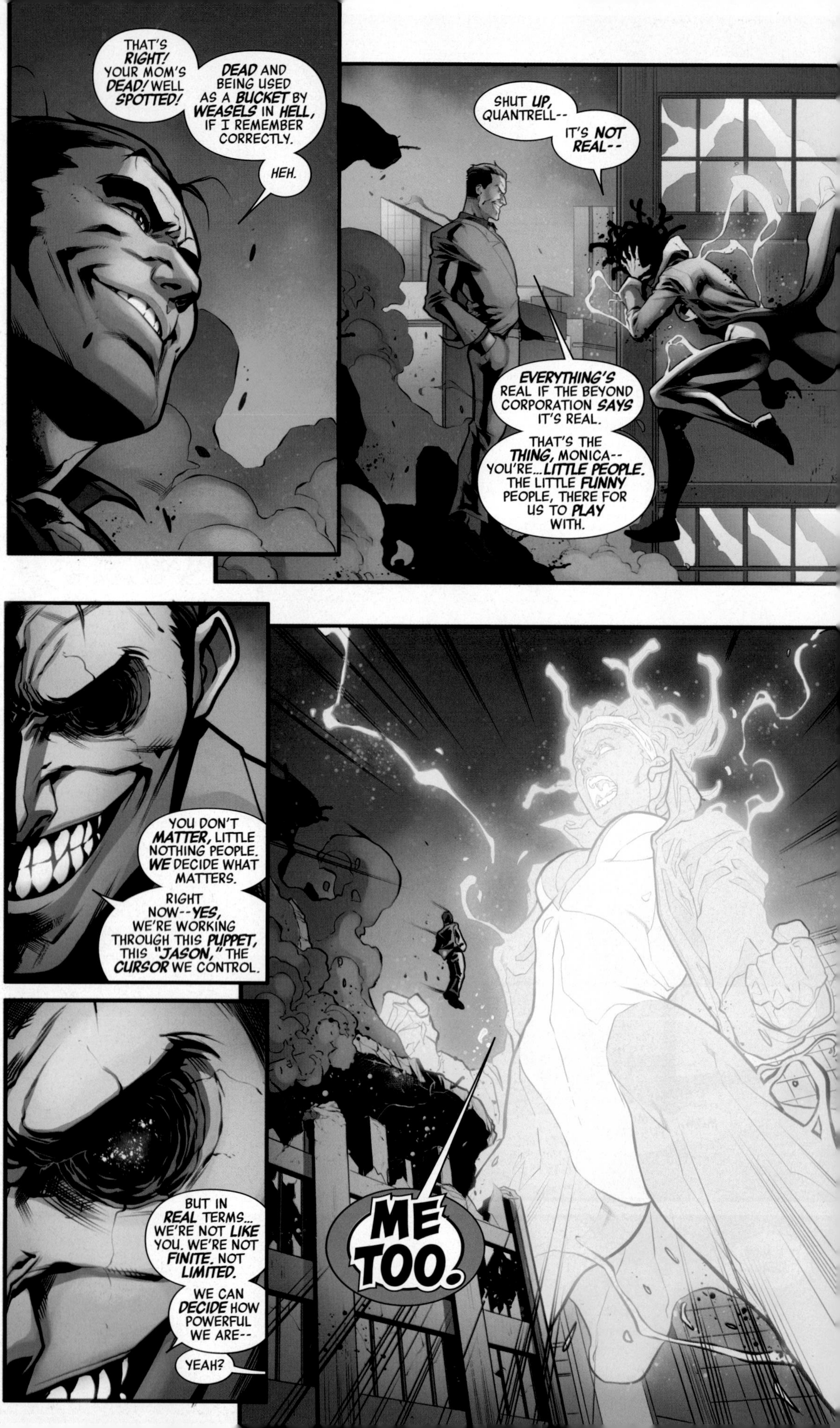

THAT'S RIGHT! YOUR MOM'S DEAD! WELL SPOTTED!
DEAD AND BEING USED AS A BUCKET BY WEASELS IN HELL, IF I REMEMBER CORRECTLY.
HEH.
SHUT UP, QUANTRELL--
IT'S NOT REAL--
EVERYTHING'S REAL IF THE BEYOND CORPORATION SAYS IT'S REAL.
THAT'S THE THING, MONICA-- YOU'RE...LITTLE PEOPLE. THE LITTLE FUNNY PEOPLE, THERE FOR US TO PLAY WITH.
YOU DON'T MATTER, LITTLE NOTHING PEOPLE. WE DECIDE WHAT MATTERS.
RIGHT NOW--YES, WE'RE WORKING THROUGH THIS PUPPET, THIS "JASON," THE CURSOR WE CONTROL.
BUT IN REAL TERMS... WE'RE NOT LIKE YOU. WE'RE NOT FINITE. NOT LIMITED.
WE CAN DECIDE HOW POWERFUL WE ARE--
YEAH?
ME TOO.

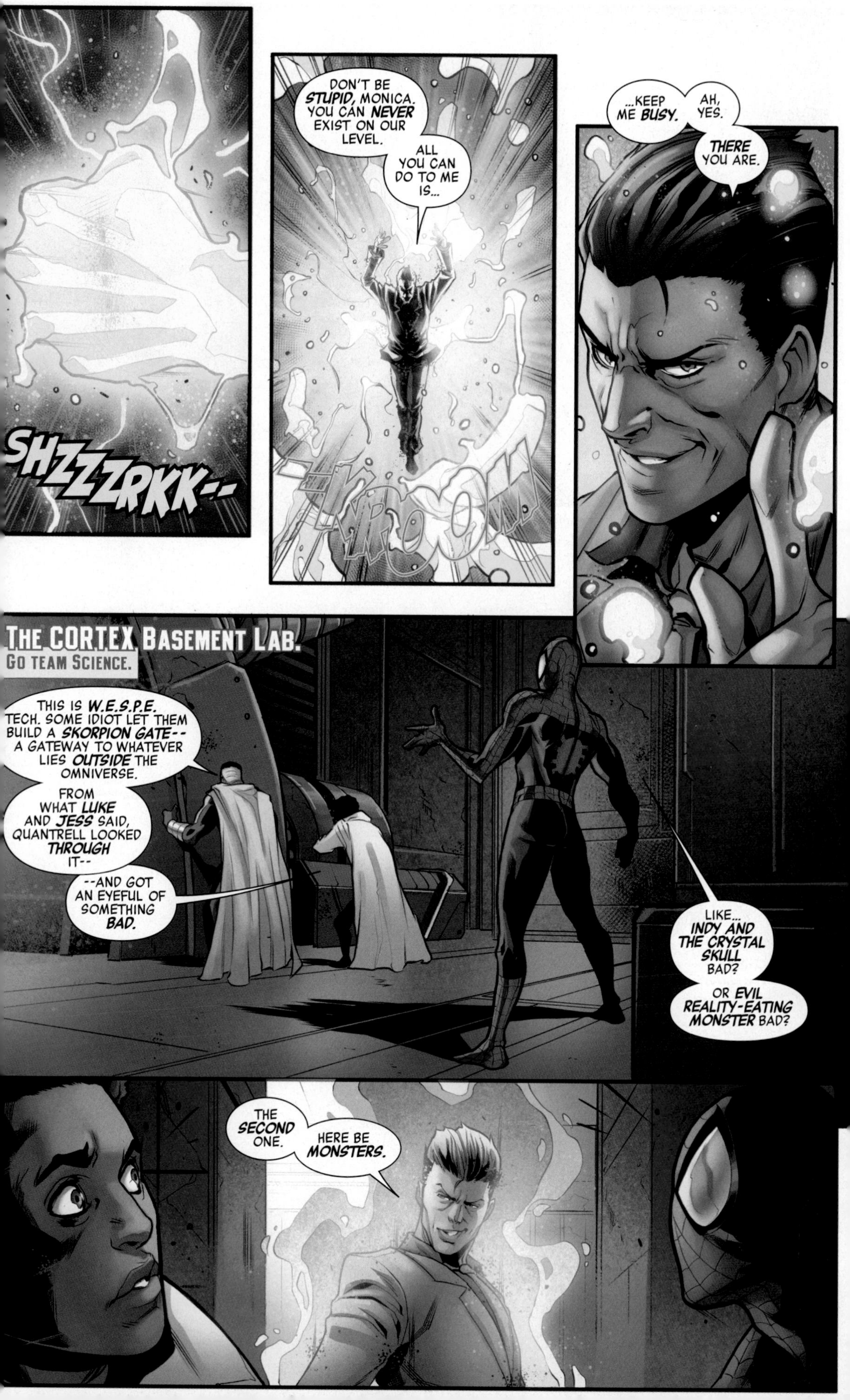

SHZZZRKK--
DON'T BE STUPID, MONICA. YOU CAN NEVER EXIST ON OUR LEVEL.
ALL YOU CAN DO TO ME IS...
-KROOOM
...KEEP ME BUSY.
AH, YES.
THERE YOU ARE.
THE CORTEX BASEMENT LAB.
GO TEAM SCIENCE.
THIS IS W.E.S.P.E. TECH. SOME IDIOT LET THEM BUILD A SKORPION GATE-- A GATEWAY TO WHATEVER LIES OUTSIDE THE OMNIVERSE.
FROM WHAT LUKE AND JESS SAID, QUANTRELL LOOKED THROUGH IT--
--AND GOT AN EYEFUL OF SOMETHING BAD.
LIKE... INDY AND THE CRYSTAL SKULL BAD?
OR EVIL REALITY-EATING MONSTER BAD?
THE SECOND ONE.
HERE BE MONSTERS.

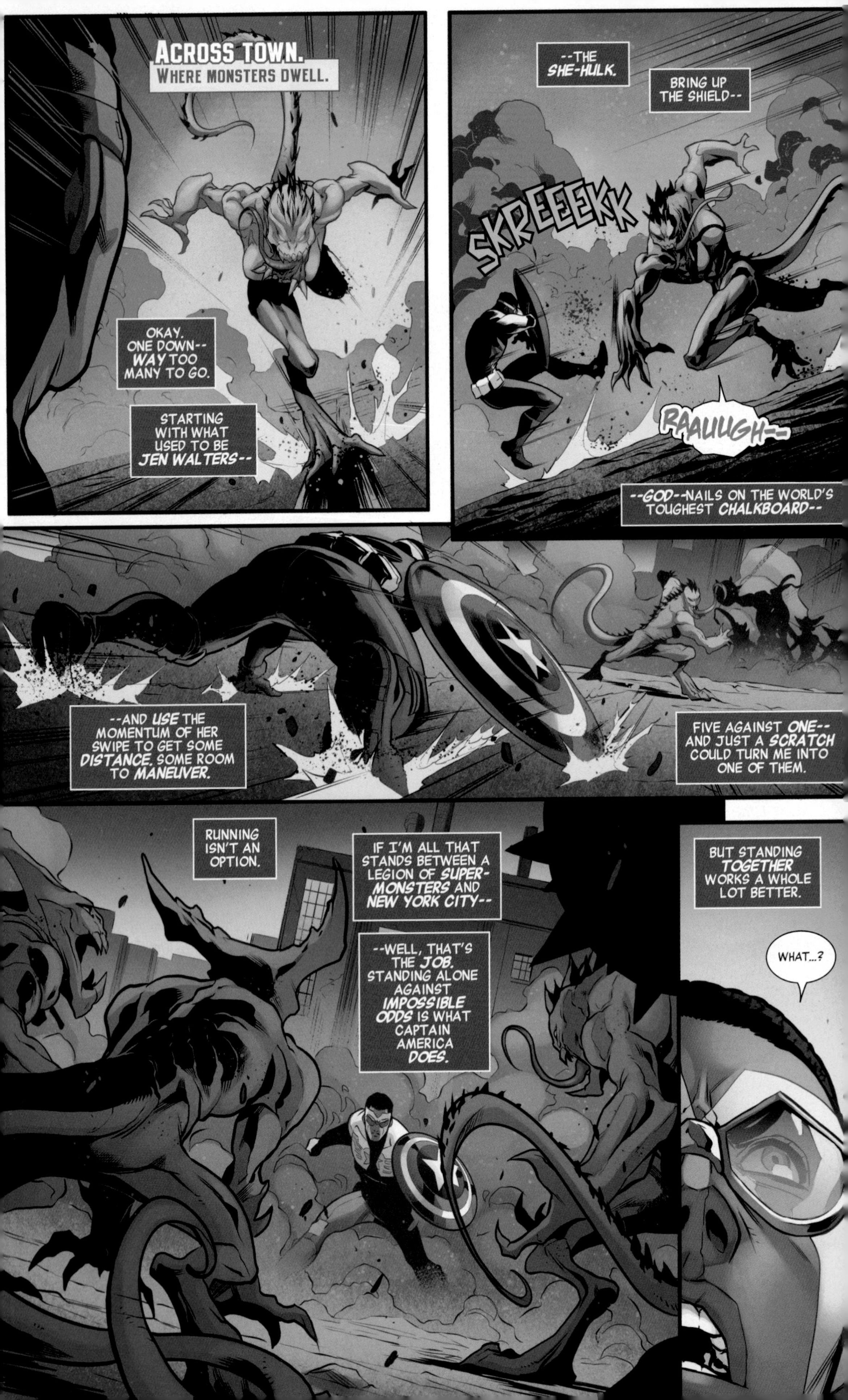

ACROSS TOWN.
WHERE MONSTERS DWELL.
OKAY. ONE DOWN-- WAY TOO MANY TO GO.
STARTING WITH WHAT USED TO BE JEN WALTERS--
--THE SHE-HULK.
BRING UP THE SHIELD--
SKREEEKK
RAAUUGH--
--GOD--NAILS ON THE WORLD'S TOUGHEST CHALKBOARD--
--AND USE THE MOMENTUM OF HER SWIPE TO GET SOME DISTANCE. SOME ROOM TO MANEUVER.
FIVE AGAINST ONE-- AND JUST A SCRATCH COULD TURN ME INTO ONE OF THEM.
RUNNING ISN'T AN OPTION.
IF I'M ALL THAT STANDS BETWEEN A LEGION OF SUPER-MONSTERS AND NEW YORK CITY--
--WELL, THAT'S THE JOB. STANDING ALONE AGAINST IMPOSSIBLE ODDS IS WHAT CAPTAIN AMERICA DOES.
BUT STANDING TOGETHER WORKS A WHOLE LOT BETTER.
WHAT...?

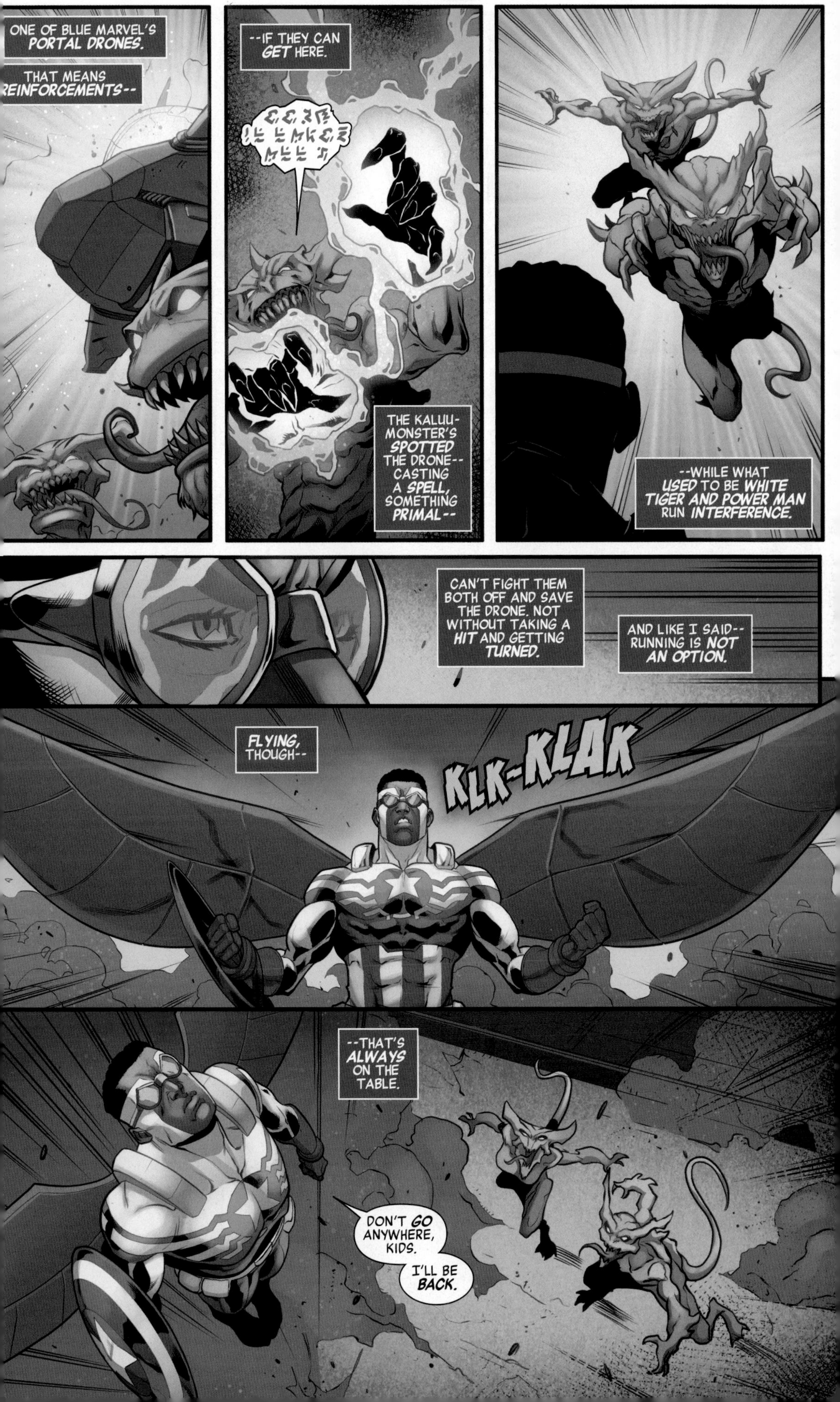
ONE OF BLUE MARVEL'S PORTAL DRONES.
THAT MEANS REINFORCEMENTS--
--IF THEY CAN GET HERE.
THE KALUU-MONSTER'S SPOTTED THE DRONE--CASTING A SPELL, SOMETHING PRIMAL--
--WHILE WHAT USED TO BE WHITE TIGER AND POWER MAN RUN INTERFERENCE.
CAN'T FIGHT THEM BOTH OFF AND SAVE THE DRONE. NOT WITHOUT TAKING A HIT AND GETTING TURNED.
AND LIKE I SAID--RUNNING IS NOT AN OPTION.
FLYING, THOUGH--
KLK-KLAK
--THAT'S ALWAYS ON THE TABLE.
DON'T GO ANYWHERE, KIDS.
I'LL BE BACK.

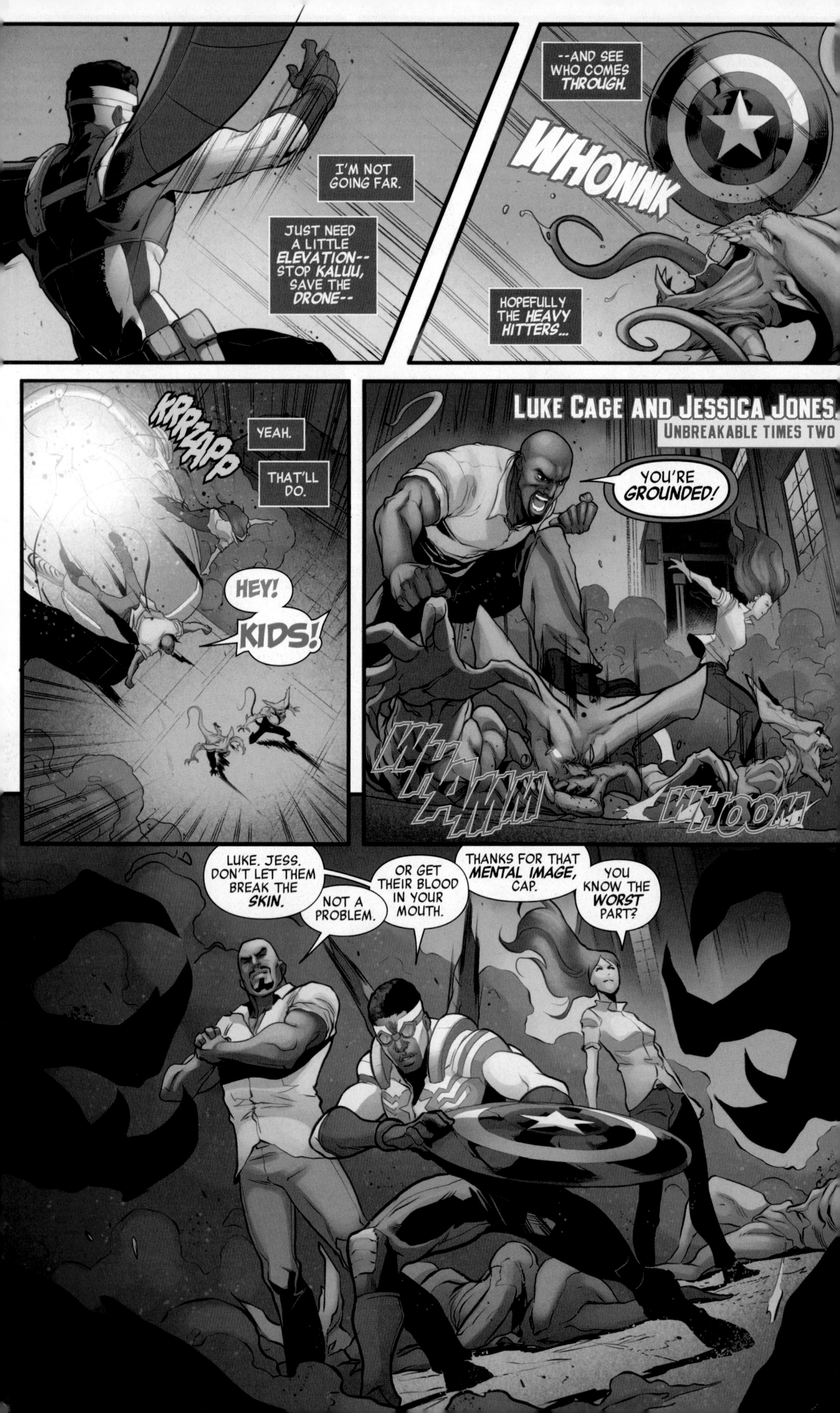
I'M NOT GOING FAR.
JUST NEED A LITTLE ELEVATION-- STOP KALUU, SAVE THE DRONE--
--AND SEE WHO COMES THROUGH.
WHONNK
HOPEFULLY THE HEAVY HITTERS...
KRRZAPP
YEAH.
THAT'LL DO.
HEY! KIDS!
LUKE CAGE AND JESSICA JONES.
UNBREAKABLE TIMES TWO
YOU'RE GROUNDED!
WHAMM
WHOOOM
LUKE. JESS. DON'T LET THEM BREAK THE SKIN.
NOT A PROBLEM.
OR GET THEIR BLOOD IN YOUR MOUTH.
THANKS FOR THAT MENTAL IMAGE, CAP.
YOU KNOW THE WORST PART?

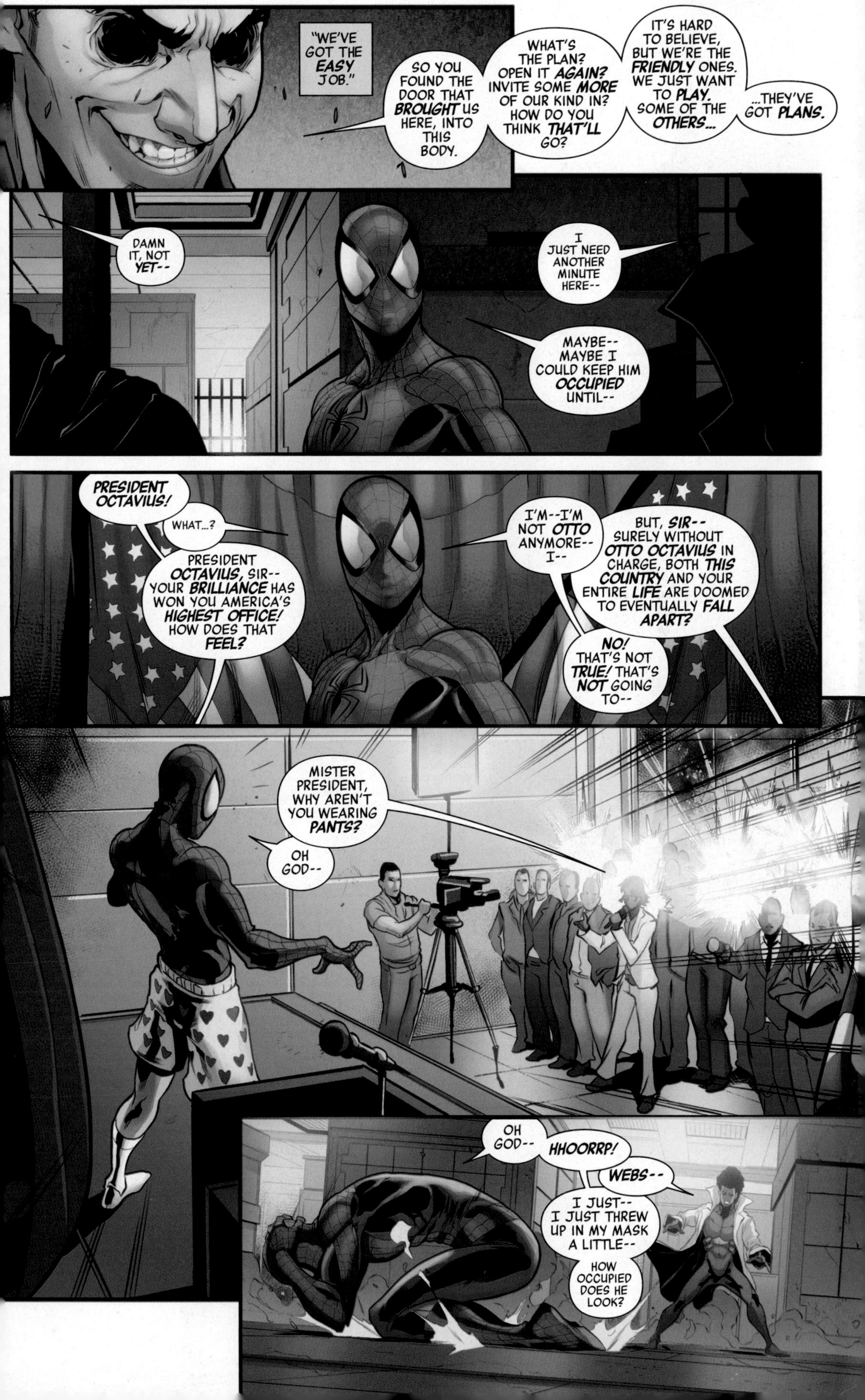
"WE'VE GOT THE EASY JOB."
SO YOU FOUND THE DOOR THAT BROUGHT US HERE, INTO THIS BODY.
WHAT'S THE PLAN? OPEN IT AGAIN? INVITE SOME MORE OF OUR KIND IN? HOW DO YOU THINK THAT'LL GO?
IT'S HARD TO BELIEVE, BUT WE'RE THE FRIENDLY ONES. WE JUST WANT TO PLAY. SOME OF THE OTHERS...
...THEY'VE GOT PLANS.
DAMN IT, NOT YET--
I JUST NEED ANOTHER MINUTE HERE--
MAYBE-- MAYBE I COULD KEEP HIM OCCUPIED UNTIL--
PRESIDENT OCTAVIUS!
WHAT...?
PRESIDENT OCTAVIUS, SIR-- YOUR BRILLIANCE HAS WON YOU AMERICA'S HIGHEST OFFICE! HOW DOES THAT FEEL?
I'M--I'M NOT OTTO ANYMORE-- I--
BUT, SIR-- SURELY WITHOUT OTTO OCTAVIUS IN CHARGE, BOTH THIS COUNTRY AND YOUR ENTIRE LIFE ARE DOOMED TO EVENTUALLY FALL APART?
NO! THAT'S NOT TRUE! THAT'S NOT GOING TO--
MISTER PRESIDENT, WHY AREN'T YOU WEARING PANTS?
OH GOD--
OH GOD--
HHOORRP!
WEBS--
I JUST-- I JUST THREW UP IN MY MASK A LITTLE--
HOW OCCUPIED DOES HE LOOK?

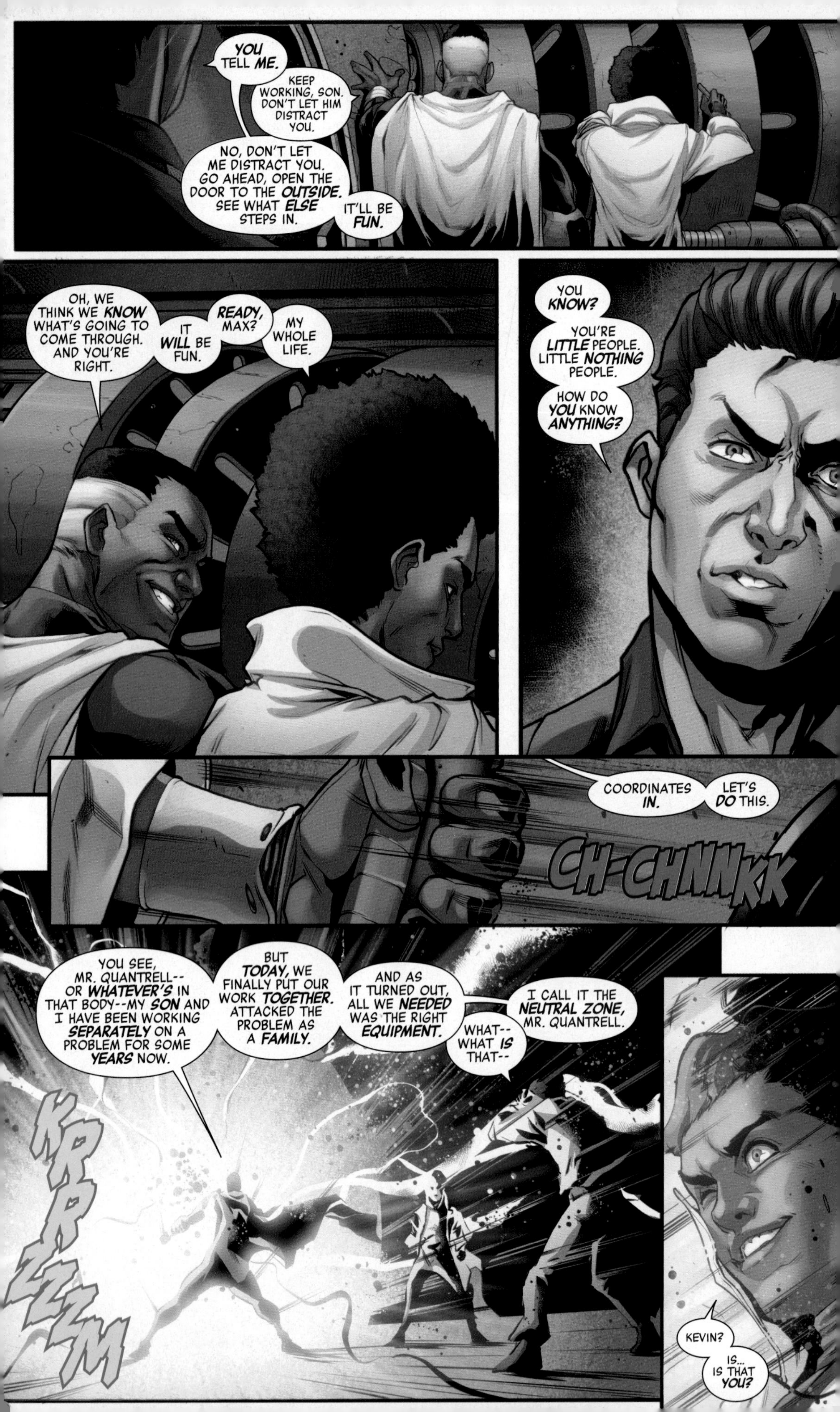
YOU TELL ME.
KEEP WORKING, SON. DON'T LET HIM DISTRACT YOU.
NO, DON'T LET ME DISTRACT YOU. GO AHEAD, OPEN THE DOOR TO THE OUTSIDE. SEE WHAT ELSE STEPS IN.
IT'LL BE FUN.
OH, WE THINK WE KNOW WHAT'S GOING TO COME THROUGH. AND YOU'RE RIGHT.
IT WILL BE FUN.
READY, MAX?
MY WHOLE LIFE.
YOU KNOW?
YOU'RE LITTLE PEOPLE. LITTLE NOTHING PEOPLE.
HOW DO YOU KNOW ANYTHING?
COORDINATES IN.
LET'S DO THIS.
CH-CHNNKK
YOU SEE, MR. QUANTRELL-- OR WHATEVER'S IN THAT BODY--MY SON AND I HAVE BEEN WORKING SEPARATELY ON A PROBLEM FOR SOME YEARS NOW.
BUT TODAY, WE FINALLY PUT OUR WORK TOGETHER. ATTACKED THE PROBLEM AS A FAMILY.
AND AS IT TURNED OUT, ALL WE NEEDED WAS THE RIGHT EQUIPMENT.
I CALL IT THE NEUTRAL ZONE, MR. QUANTRELL.
WHAT-- WHAT IS THAT--
KRRZZZM
KEVIN?
IS... IS THAT YOU?

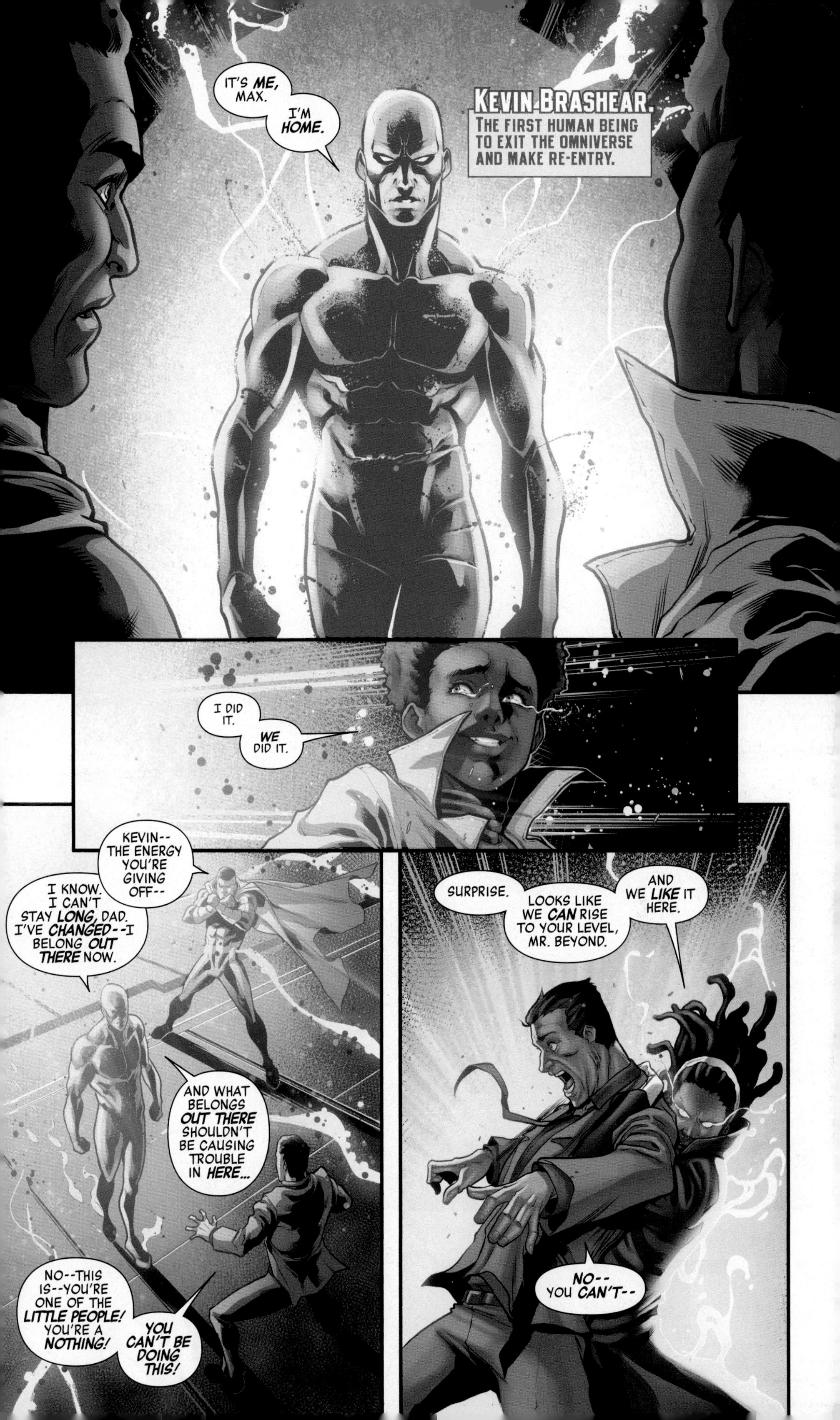
IT'S ME, MAX. I'M HOME.
KEVIN BRASHEAR.
THE FIRST HUMAN BEING TO EXIT THE OMNIVERSE AND MAKE RE-ENTRY.
I DID IT. WE DID IT.
KEVIN-- THE ENERGY YOU'RE GIVING OFF--
I KNOW. I CAN'T STAY LONG, DAD. I'VE CHANGED--I BELONG OUT THERE NOW.
AND WHAT BELONGS OUT THERE SHOULDN'T BE CAUSING TROUBLE IN HERE...
NO--THIS IS--YOU'RE ONE OF THE LITTLE PEOPLE! YOU'RE A NOTHING!
YOU CAN'T BE DOING THIS!
SURPRISE.
LOOKS LIKE WE CAN RISE TO YOUR LEVEL, MR. BEYOND.
AND WE LIKE IT HERE.
NO-- YOU CAN'T--

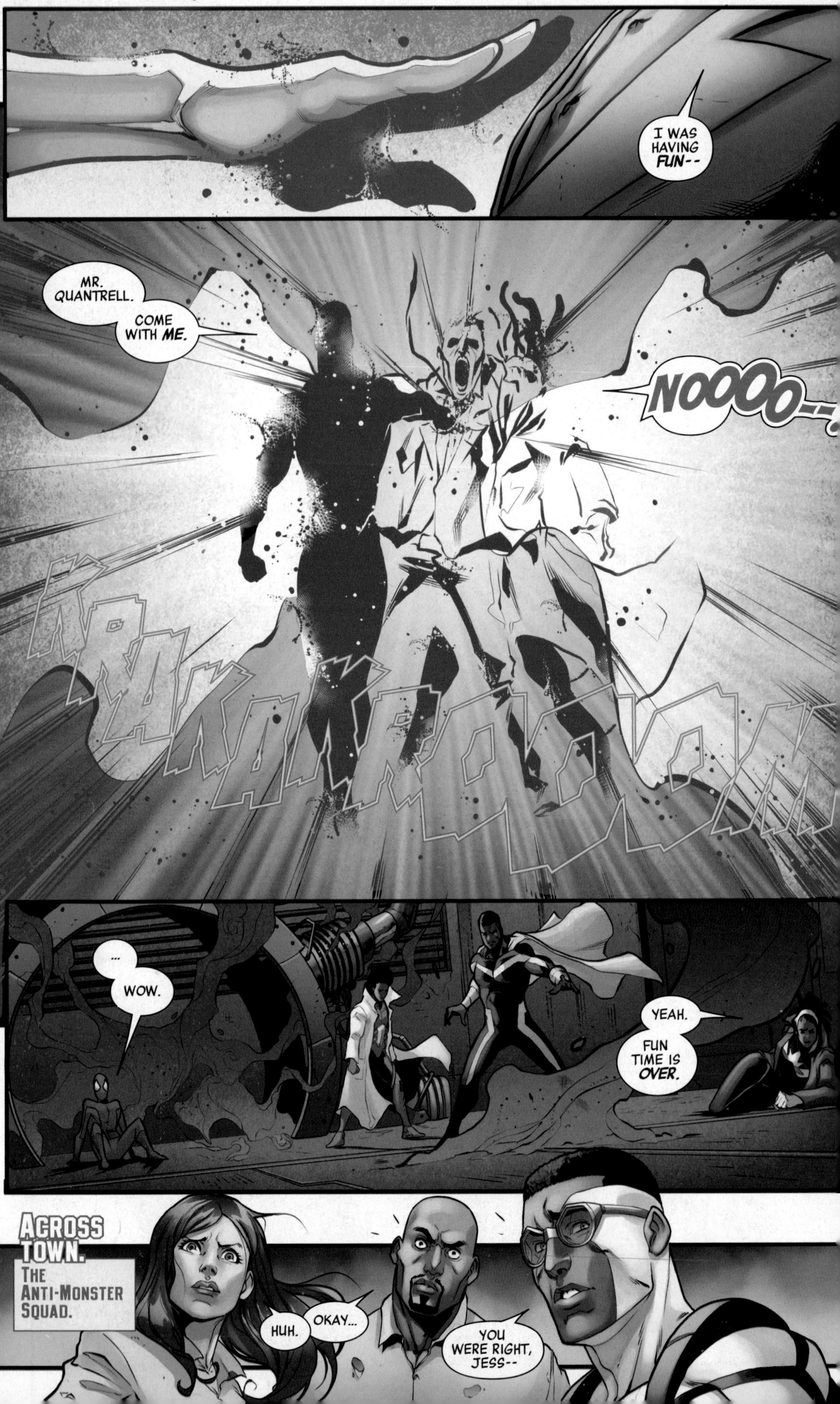

I WAS HAVING FUN--
MR. QUANTRELL.
COME WITH ME.
NOOOO--!
...
WOW.
YEAH.
FUN TIME IS OVER.
ACROSS TOWN.
THE ANTI-MONSTER SQUAD.
HUH.
OKAY...
YOU WERE RIGHT, JESS--

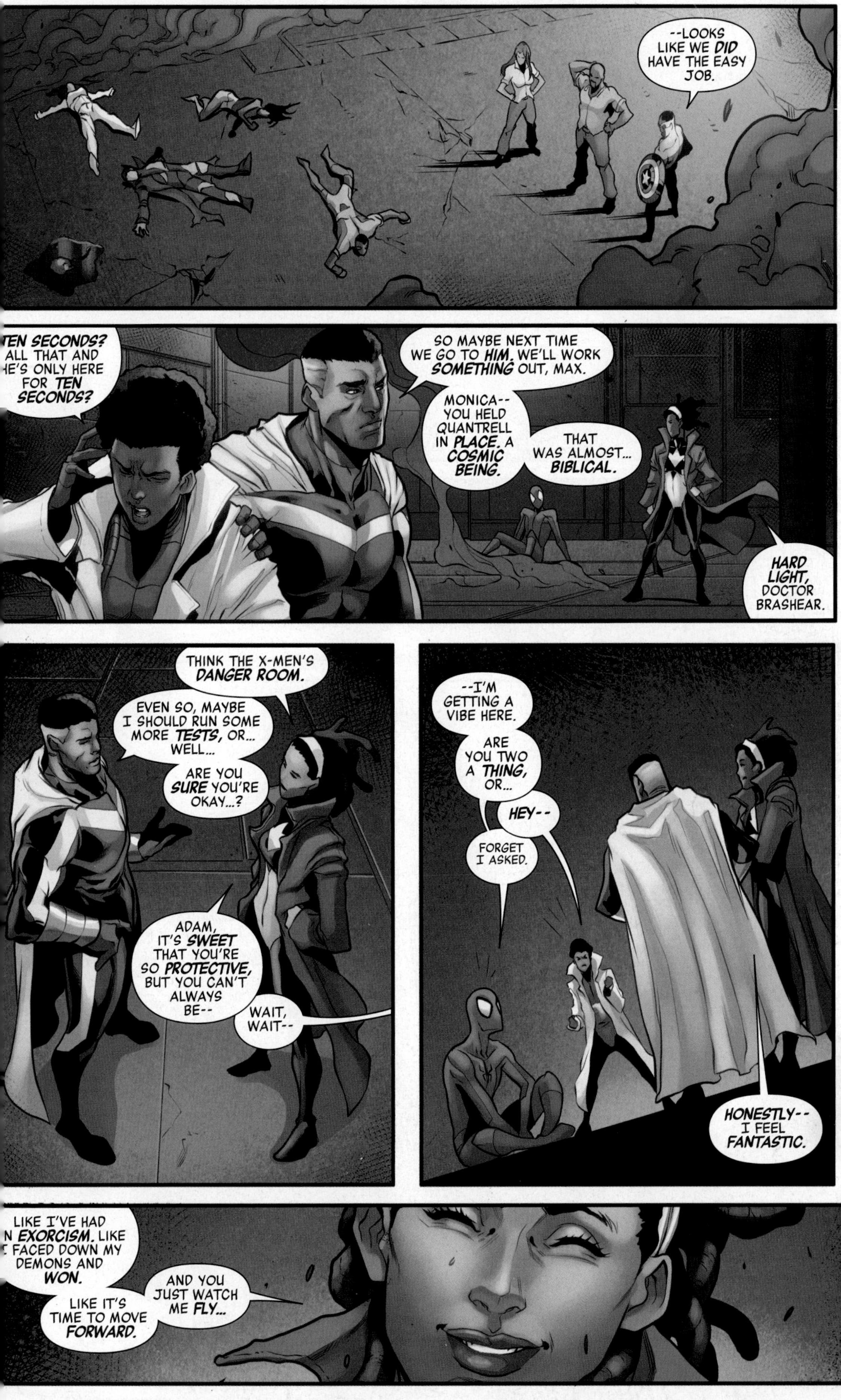
--LOOKS LIKE WE DID HAVE THE EASY JOB.
TEN SECONDS? ALL THAT AND HE'S ONLY HERE FOR TEN SECONDS?
SO MAYBE NEXT TIME WE GO TO HIM, WE'LL WORK SOMETHING OUT, MAX.
MONICA-- YOU HELD QUANTRELL IN PLACE. A COSMIC BEING.
THAT WAS ALMOST... BIBLICAL.
HARD LIGHT, DOCTOR BRASHEAR.
THINK THE X-MEN'S DANGER ROOM.
EVEN SO, MAYBE I SHOULD RUN SOME MORE TESTS, OR... WELL...
ARE YOU SURE YOU'RE OKAY...?
ADAM, IT'S SWEET THAT YOU'RE SO PROTECTIVE, BUT YOU CAN'T ALWAYS BE--
WAIT, WAIT--
--I'M GETTING A VIBE HERE.
ARE YOU TWO A THING, OR...
HEY--
FORGET I ASKED.
HONESTLY-- I FEEL FANTASTIC.
LIKE I'VE HAD N EXORCISM. LIKE FACED DOWN MY DEMONS AND WON.
LIKE IT'S TIME TO MOVE FORWARD.
AND YOU JUST WATCH ME FLY...

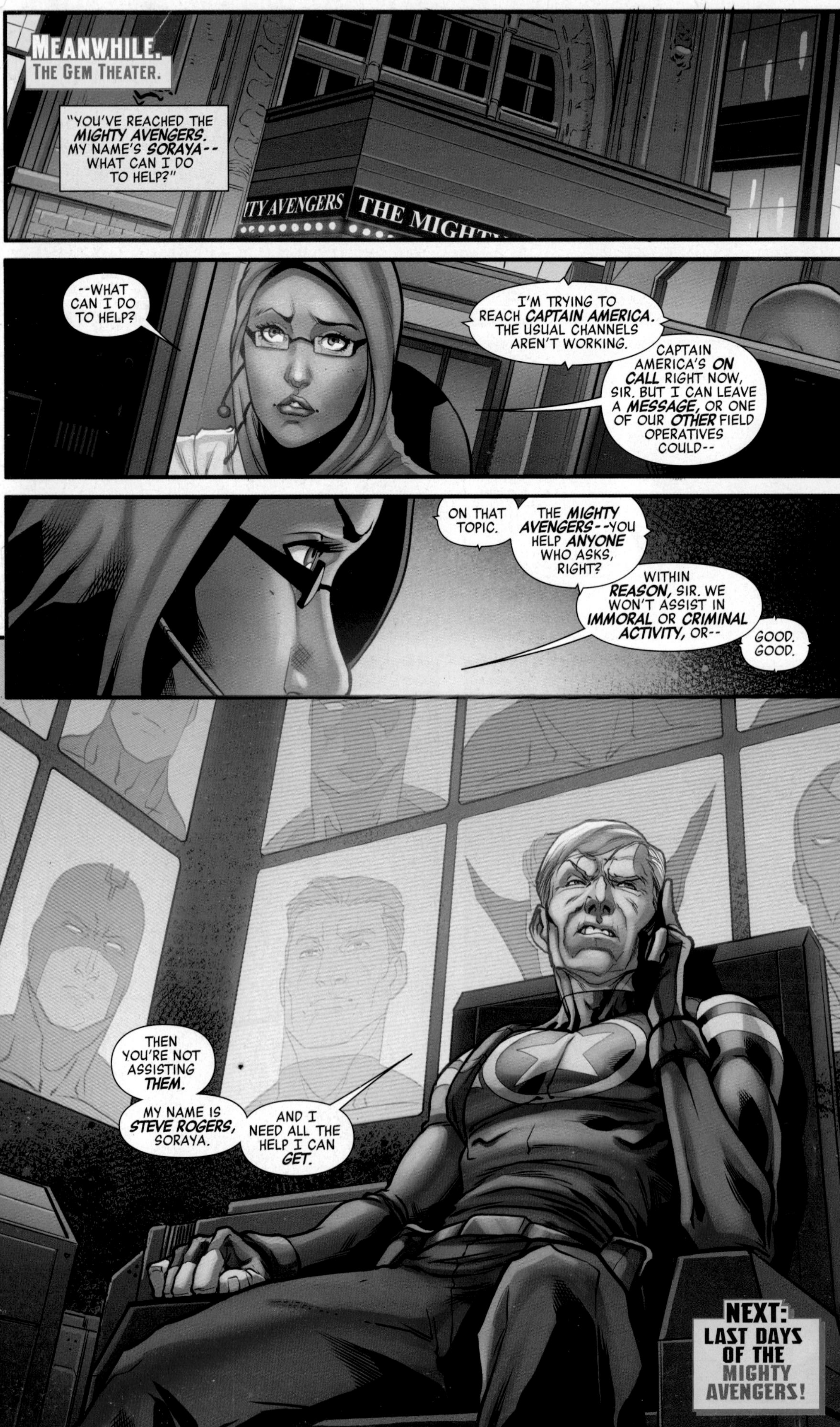
MEANWHILE.
THE GEM THEATER.
"YOU'VE REACHED THE MIGHTY AVENGERS. MY NAME'S SORAYA-- WHAT CAN I DO TO HELP?"
ITY AVENGERS
THE MIGHT
--WHAT CAN I DO TO HELP?
I'M TRYING TO REACH CAPTAIN AMERICA. THE USUAL CHANNELS AREN'T WORKING.
CAPTAIN AMERICA'S ON CALL RIGHT NOW, SIR. BUT I CAN LEAVE A MESSAGE, OR ONE OF OUR OTHER FIELD OPERATIVES COULD--
ON THAT TOPIC.
THE MIGHTY AVENGERS--YOU HELP ANYONE WHO ASKS, RIGHT?
WITHIN REASON, SIR. WE WON'T ASSIST IN IMMORAL OR CRIMINAL ACTIVITY, OR--
GOOD. GOOD.
THEN YOU'RE NOT ASSISTING THEM.
MY NAME IS STEVE ROGERS, SORAYA.
AND I NEED ALL THE HELP I CAN GET.
NEXT: LAST DAYS OF THE MIGHTY AVENGERS!